British Romantic Poets

About Shiv K. Kumar

SHIV K. KUMAR was born and educated in India, and received his Ph.D. in English at Cambridge. He is the author of *Bergson and the Stream of Consciousness Novel* (N.Y.U. Press) and has edited several other collections of essays and verse. He has published papers in American, British, and Continental journals and has lectured on the British Romantic Poets for over sixteen years, both in India and abroad. Dr. Kumar is Professor and Chairman, Department of English, Osmania University, Hyderabad, India.

British Romantic Poets

RECENT REVALUATIONS

Edited by SHIV K. KUMAR

New York • New York University Press
London • University of London Press Limited
1966

© 1966 BY NEW YORK UNIVERSITY
LIBRARY OF CONGRESS CATALOG CARD NUMBER: 66–22219
MANUFACTURED IN THE UNITED STATES OF AMERICA

PREFACE

Since the publication of F. R. Leavis' polemical essay on Shelley, the controversy over the status of Shelley and of Romantic poetry in general has produced, besides much lively debate, some of the best critical writing of our time. If the so-called New Critics have arraigned the Romantic poets for their sloppiness and woolly idealism, the new apologists for the Romantics have vigorously defended them, often discovering in the process those very qualities they miss in contemporary poetry. During recent years, such a vast corpus of critical opinion has accumulated around the subject that it has become increasingly difficult to view in correct perspective these poets belonging to what is certainly one of the most exciting periods in English literary history. However, it is hoped that the selections in this volume will reflect not only present trends in criticism of the Romantic poets but also various other approaches possible to this fascinating subject. General estimates of the poets have been kept down to a minimum to permit the inclusion of more detailed analyses of individual poets. Altogether, these reappraisals, by distinguished British and American critics, should provide a fairly representative sample of current critical practice and achievement.

Two of the essays have not appeared in print so far, while some others were specially revised for this volume. A select bibliography includes both authoritative studies of poets and critical essays on the poems discussed in the book.

I am grateful to Professor Oscar Cargill for his help and encouragement; to Mr. T. G. Vaidyanathan, my friend and colleague, I am thankful for his invaluable editorial assistance.

SHIV K. KUMAR

New York City

v

Part One   Romanticism

Morse Peckham

1 · Toward a Theory of Romanticism

CAN WE HOPE for a theory of romanticism? The answer, I believe, is Yes. But before proceeding further, I must make quite clear what it is that I propose to discuss.

First, although the word "romanticism" refers to any number of things, it has two primary referents: (1) a general and permanent characteristic of mind, art, and personality, found in all periods and in all cultures; (2) a specific historical movement in art and ideas which occurred in Europe and America in the late eighteenth and early nineteenth centuries. I am concerned only with the second of these two meanings. There may be a connection between the two, but I doubt it, and at any rate whatever I have to say refers only to historical romanticism.

Second, in this historical sense "romanticism" as a revolution in art and ideas is often considered to be only an expression of a general redirection of European life which included also a political revolution, an industrial revolution, and perhaps several others. There may be a connection between the revolution in ideas and the arts and the more or less contemporary revolutions in other fields of human activities, but for the time being, at any rate, I think it is wise to dissociate the romanticism of ideas and art from these other revolutions. Just as one of our greatest difficulties so far has arisen from assuming an identity between general and historical romanticism, so much of our difficulty in considering the

Reprinted by permission of the author and the Modern Language Association of America from *PMLA*, LXVI (1951), 5–23.

nature of historical romanticism has come from assuming its identity with all of the other more or less contemporary revolutions. Let us first isolate the historical romanticism of ideas and arts before we beg any questions about the nature of history. For example, I think it is at present wiser to consider romanticism as one of the means then available for hindering or helping the early-nineteenth-century movement for political reform than it is to assume that romanticism and the desire for political reform and its partial achievement are the same thing.

With these two distinctions in mind, I repeat, Can we hope for a theory of the historical romanticism of ideas and art? Such a theory must be able to submit successfully to two tests. First, it must show that Wordsworth and Byron, Goethe and Chateaubriand, were all part of a general European literary movement which had its correspondences in the music, the painting, the architecture, the philosophy, the theology, and the science of the eighteenth and early nineteenth centuries. Second, it must be able to get us inside individual works of literature, art, and thought: that is, to tell us not merely that the works are there, to enable us not merely to classify them, but to deliver up to us a key to individual works so that we can penetrate to the principles of their intellectual and aesthetic being. Can we hope for such a theory? *Dare* we hope for such a theory? To this question I answer, "Yes, we can." I feel that we have it almost within our grasp—that one or two steps more and we shall have mastered this highly perplexing literary problem.

Certainly there is no generally accepted theory of romanticism at the present time. Twenty years ago, and for more than twenty years before that, the problem of romanticism was debated passionately, not least because of the redoubtable but utterly misdirected attacks of Babbitt and More. In his *Romanticism and the Modern Ego* (1943), Jacques Barzun has made a good collection of some of the definitions that have been more or less widely used in the past fifty years: a return to the Middle Ages, a love of the exotic, the revolt from Reason, a vindication of the individual, a liberation of the unconscious, a reaction against scientific method, a revival of pantheism, a revival of idealism, a revival of Catholicism, a rejection of artistic conventions, a return to emotionalism,

a return to nature—and so on. The utmost confusion reigns
in the whole field. In the past fifteen or twenty years, most
scholars have done one of two things. Either they have given
up hope for any sense to come out of this tangle and have
stoutly denied that there was such a movement, or, less pes-
simistically, they have continued to use one or more concepts
or ideas—theories which they feel to be unsatisfactory yet
which they continue to employ because there is nothing
better. Most students are convinced that something happened
to literature between the death of Pope and the death of
Coleridge, but not very many are willing, when you question
them sharply, to tell you exactly what happened. The situation is all the more discouraging in that it is generally conceded that romanticism is a central problem in literary history,
and that if we have failed to solve that problem, we can
scarcely hope to solve any general problems in literary history.

Too many scholars, then, will try either to avoid the
term entirely, or failing that strategy—and it always fails—
will isolate some idea or literary effect and will say, "This is
romanticism." Or such a scholar will use the term with the
full knowledge that the reader will recognize the difficulties
involved and will charitably permit him to beg the question.
He will very rarely begin with a theory of romanticism and
seek to place a particular poem or author in relation to that
theory or seek to use the theory in unlocking a baffling and
complex work, or even a simple one for that matter. He
will fit his ideas into whatever notion of romanticism he
may have, usually without specifying what it might be, but
very rarely, at least in public and in print, will he use a
considered theory of romanticism as a starting point for his
investigations. It is a discouraging situation, but my purpose
is to suggest that it is not so discouraging as it appears.

In the last few years there have been signs that some
scholars at least are moving toward a common concept of
romanticism. In 1943 Jacques Barzun spoke of romanticism
as a biological revolution,[1] and in 1949, he defined it as part
of "the great revolution which drew the intellect of Europe
. . . from the expectation and desire of fixity into desire and
expectation of change." [2] Stallknecht, in his fascinating book
on Wordsworth, *Strange Seas of Thought* (1945), spoke of

how romanticism established the sentiment of being in England, and then, reversing his statement, suggested that the sentiment of being established romanticism. In his admirable introduction to his edition of *Sartor Resartus* (1937), C. Frederick Harrold—whose death has deprived us of one of the most valuable of contemporary students of Victorian literature—wrote of Carlyle's ideas about organicism and dynamism. And in his and Templeman's excellent anthology of Victorian prose (1938) there is an appendix "illustrative of nineteenth-century conceptions of growth, development, evolution." But the most recent attempt to tackle the problem, the best yet, though I think not entirely satisfactory, has been René Wellek's two articles, "The Concept of Romanticism," published in 1949 in the first two issues of *Comparative Literature*. There he offered three criteria of romanticism: imagination for the view of poetry, an organic concept of nature for the view of the world, and symbol and myth for poetic style.

Wellek does establish to my mind three things in his article: first, there *was* a European intellectual and artistic movement with certain intellectual and artistic characteristics, a movement properly known as romanticism; second, that the participators in that movement were quite conscious of their historic and revolutionary significance; and third, that the chief reason for the current skepticism in America about a theory of romanticism was the publication in 1924 of Arthur O. Lovejoy's famous article, "On the Discrimination of Romanticisms." [3] In this article Lovejoy pointed out that the term is used in a fearful variety of ways, and that no common concept can include them all. Indeed, the growth of skepticism about any solid conclusions on romanticism does seem to begin—or at least start to become very powerful and eventually dominant—with the publication of that article. Wellek decries what he calls Lovejoy's excessive nominalism and skepticism, and refuses to be satisfied with it. He also puts in the same category of nominalism and skepticism Lovejoy's 1941 article, "The Meaning of Romanticism for the Historian of Ideas." [4] Here Lovejoy offered three criteria of romanticism, or rather the three basic ideas of romanticism, "heterogeneous, logically independent, and sometimes essentially antithetic to one another in their implications." These ideas are organicism, dynamism, and diversitarianism. Now in discussing Lovejoy's

1941 paper Wellek has made, I think, an error. He seems to have confused the nature of the two articles, because, apparently, he has forgotten about the last three chapters of *The Great Chain of Being* (1936).[5]

Lovejoy's great book is a landmark of scholarship and also for scholarship. It is a book on which some of the most useful scholarship of our times has been based, and it is as useful to the teacher who uses it with intelligence as it is to the scholar. Twenty-five years from now, scholars of literature will look back on the publication of *The Great Chain of Being* as a turning point in the development of literary scholarship; for it has been of astonishing value in opening up to our understanding in quite unexpected ways the literature of the sixteenth, seventeenth, and eighteenth centuries. But so far as I know, almost no use has been made of the last three chapters, especially of the last two, in explaining romanticism and romantic works. It is a curious situation; for these chapters contain the foundations for a theory of romanticism which will do everything that such a theory must be able to do—place works and authors in relation to each other and illuminate individual works of art as they ought to be illuminated.

By ignoring (at least in his two papers) *The Great Chain of Being*, Wellek concluded that the same kind of skepticism was present in both Lovejoy's 1924 and 1941 articles. Actually, *The Great Chain of Being* is an answer to Lovejoy's 1924 article. Without emphasizing the fact, Lovejoy *did* in 1933 and 1934, when he delivered the lectures on which the book is based, what in 1924 he said could not be done. To be brief, in 1936 he stated simply that literary romanticism was the manifestation of a change in the way of thinking of European man, that since Plato European man had been thinking according to one system of thought—based on the attempted reconciliation of two profoundly different ideas about the nature of reality, both stemming from Plato—and that in the late eighteenth and early nineteenth centuries occidental thought took an entirely different direction, as did occidental art. Furthermore, he says that the change in the way the mind works was the most profound change in the history of occidental thinking, and by implication it involved a similar profound change in the methods and objects of European art.

I

What I wish to do in the rest of this paper is, first, to
explain what these new ideas of the late eighteenth century
involved, to reconcile Wellek and Lovejoy, and Lovejoy with
himself, and to show the relevance of certain other ideas about
romanticism I have mentioned; and second, to make one addition to the theories of Lovejoy and Wellek, an addition
which I hope goes far toward clearing up an essential problem which Lovejoy scarcely faced and with which Wellek is
unable to come to terms.

It is scarcely necessary here to outline what *The Great
Chain of Being* implied. Yet I should like to reduce the concepts involved to what I think to be their essentials. Briefly, the
shift in European thought was a shift from conceiving the
cosmos as a static mechanism to conceiving it as a dynamic
organism: static—in that all the possibilities of reality were
realized from the beginning of things or were implicit from the
beginning, and that these possibilities were arranged in a complete series, a hierarchy from God down to nothingness—including the literary possibilities from epic to Horatian ode, or lyric;
a mechanism—in that the universe is a perfectly running machine, a watch usually. (A machine is the most common metaphor of this metaphysic.) Almost as important as these concepts
was that of uniformitarianism, implicit both in staticism and in
mechanism, whenever these two are separated, as frequently
happens. That is, everything that change produces was to be
conceived as a part to fit into the already perfectly running
machine; for all things conformed to ideal patterns in the mind
of God or in the nonmaterial ground of phenomena.

If, in short, you conceive of the universe as a perfectly
ordered machine, you will assume that any imperfections you
may notice are really things you do not understand. You will
think of everything in the universe as fitting perfectly into
that machine. You will think that immutable laws govern
the formation of every new part of that machine to ensure
that it fits the machine's requirements. And, although with
delightful inconsistency—as Pope made his *Essay on Man*
the basis of his satires—you will judge the success of any
individual thing according to its ability to fit into the workings of the machine, your inconsistency will be concealed, for
a time, by the influence of either original sin, if you are an

orthodox Christian, or of the corruptions of civilization, if you are a deist or a sentimentalist—not that there is much difference. Your values will be perfection, changelessness, uniformity, rationalism.

Now this mighty static metaphysic which had governed perilously the thoughts of men since the time of Plato, collapsed of its own internal inconsistencies in the late eighteenth century—or collapsed for some people. For most people it still remains the unrealized base for most of their values, intellectual, moral, social, aesthetic, and religious. But to the finer minds of the eighteenth and nineteenth centuries, it was no longer tenable. There are a number of reasons why this should have been so. The principal cause was that all its implications had been worked out; they stood forth in all their naked inconsistency. It became impossible to accept a theodicy based upon it. More and more, thinkers began searching for a new system of explaining the nature of reality and the duties of men.

I shall omit the development of the new idea. The grand outlines have been magnificently sketched by Lovejoy, and the details are steadily being filled in. Rather, I shall present the new idea in its most radical form. Let us begin with the new metaphor. The new metaphor is not a machine; it is an organism. It is a tree, for example; and a tree is a good example, for a study of nineteenth-century literature reveals the continual recurrence of that image. Hence the new thought is organicism. Now the first quality of an organism is that it is not something made, it is something *being* made or growing. We have a philosophy of becoming, not a philosophy of being. Furthermore, the relation of its component parts is not that of the parts of a machine which have been made separately, i.e., separate entities in the mind of the deity, but the relation of leaves to stem to trunk to root to earth. Entities are an organic part of that which produced them. The existence of each part is made possible only by the existence of every other part. Relationships, not entities, are the object of contemplation and study.

Moreover, an organism has the quality of life. It does not develop additively; it grows organically. The universe is alive. It is not something made, a perfect machine; it grows. Therefore change becomes a positive value, not a negative value; change is not man's punishment, it is his opportunity. Anything that continues to grow, or change qualitatively, is not perfect, can, perhaps, never be perfect. Perfection ceases to be a positive value. Imperfection becomes a positive value. Since the universe is changing and growing, there is consequently a positive and radical intrusion of novelty into the world. That is, with the intrusion of each novelty, the fundamental character of the universe itself changes. We have a universe of emergents. If all these things be true, it therefore follows that there are no pre-existent patterns. Every work of art, for instance, creates a new pattern, each one has its own aesthetic law. It may have resemblances even in principle to previous works of art, but fundamentally it is unique. Hence come two derivative ideas. First, diversitarianism, not uniformitarianism, becomes the principle of both creation and criticism. The romantics, for example, have been accused of confusing the genres of poetry. Why shouldn't they? The whole metaphysical foundation of the genres had been abandoned, or for some authors had simply disappeared. The second derivative is the idea of creative originality. True, the idea of originality had existed before, but in a different sense. Now the artist is original because he is the instrument whereby a genuine novelty, an emergent, is introduced into the world, not because he has come with the aid of genius a little closer to previously existent pattern, natural and divine.

In its radical form, dynamic organicism results in the idea that the history of the universe is the history of God creating himself. Evil is at last accounted for, since the history of the universe—God being imperfect to begin with—is the history of God, whether transcendent or immanent, ridding himself, by the evolutionary process, of evil. Of course, from both the old and the new philosophy, God could be omitted. Either can become a materialism.

In a metaphysical nutshell, the older philosophy grounded itself on the principle that nothing can come from nothing. The newer philosophy grounded itself on the principle that something *can* come from nothing, that an excess can come from a deficiency, that nothing succeeds like excess.

II

I have presented these ideas in a radical form to make them as clear as I can and to bring out in the strongest possible colors the contrast between the old and new methods of thought. Now I should like to apply them to Lovejoy and Wellek. Lovejoy stated that the three new ideas of romantic thought and art were organicism, dynamism, and diversitarianism. He says that they are three separate and inconsistent ideas. I agree that they often appear separately, but I am convinced that they are all related to and derived from a basic or root-metaphor, the organic metaphor of the structure of the universe.[6] Strictly speaking, organicism includes dynamism, for an organism must grow or change qualitatively, but I prefer to use the term "dynamic organicism" in order to emphasize the importance of imperfection and change. Diversitarianism, of course, is in these terms a positive value; for the diversity of things and their uniqueness is the proof of the constant intrusion of novelty in the past, the present, and the future.

Turning to Wellek and his three criteria, I have already included one, organicism; the other two are imagination and symbolism. Wellek means the creative imagination, and a little thought will show that the idea of the creative imagination is derived from dynamic organicism. If the universe is constantly in the process of creating itself, the mind of man, his imaginative power, is radically creative. The artist is that man with the power of bringing new artistic concepts into reality, just as the philosopher brings new ideas into reality. And the greatest man is the philosopher-poet who, supremely gifted, simultaneously does both. Furthermore, the artist is the man who creates a symbol of truth. He can think metaphorically, and, if the world is an organic structure, only a statement with the organic complexity of the work of art can create an adequate symbol of it. And is this not the method of symbolism? In allegory, a symbolic unit preserves its meaning when taken from its context. The Cave of Error *is* the Cave of Error. There is a direct one-to-one relationship between any unit in the world of phenomena and any unit in the world of ideas. But in symbolism, a symbolic unit has power only because of its relationships to everything else in the work of art. Ahab has symbolical value because of the whale, and the whale because of Ahab. In symbolism the interrelationships of the symbolic units involved are equated with the interrelationships of a group of concepts. Let a series of 1,

2, 3, 4, etc., stand for a series of ideas in the mind, and a similar series of a, b, c, d, etc., stand for a series of things in the real world or in the world of the concretizing imagination. Now in allegory, if "a" is a symbolic unit, it stands for "1," "b" for "2," and so on. Thus the Dragon in the *Faerie Queene*, Canto i of Book I, stands for Error, whether the Red Cross Knight is there or not, and the Knight, on one level of interpretation, stands for Holiness, whether the Dragon is there or not. But in symbolism, "a" or "b" or "c" has no direct relation to "1" or "2" or "3." Rather, the interrelationships among the first three have symbolic reference to the interrelationships among the second group of three. Moby Dick has symbolic power only because Ahab is hunting him; in fact, he has symbolic power only because almost everything else in the book has symbolic power as well.

The now current, though probably not widely accepted, critical principle that a symbolic system is capable of an indefinite number of equally valid interpretations is itself a romantic idea, in the sense that the work of art has no fixed or static meaning but changes with the observer in a relationship between the two which is both dialectical, or dynamic, and organic.

Thus we may conclude that Wellek's three criteria—organicism, imagination, and symbolism—are all three derivable from the basic metaphor or concept of dynamic organicism.

There is yet another profoundly important idea which I have not so far mentioned, the idea of the unconscious mind, which appears in Wordsworth, in Coleridge, in Carlyle, and indeed all over the nineteenth and twentieth centuries. In 1830 in his magnificent essay, *Characteristics*, Carlyle says that the two big ideas of the century are dynamism and the unconscious mind. The idea of the unconscious mind goes back to Hartley, to Kant, to Leibniz, and is implicit in Locke. Indeed it goes back to any poet who seriously talks about a muse. But it appears only in full force with the appearance of dynamic organicism. Best known to the English romantics in the mechanistic associationism of Hartley, it became a central part of their thought when they made the mind radically creative. Heretofore the divine had communicated with man either directly through revelation or indirectly through the evidence of his perfect universe. But with God creating himself, with an imperfect but growing universe, with the constant intrusion of novelty into the world, how can there be any apprehension of truth? If reason is inadequate—because it is fixed and because historically it has failed—the truth can only be apprehended intuitively, imaginatively, spontaneously, with the whole personality, from the deep sources of the fountains that are within. The unconscious is really a postulate to the creative imagination, and as such continues today without the divine sanction as part of present-day critical theory. It is that part of the mind through which novelty enters into the personality and hence into the world in the form of art and ideas. We today conceive of the unconscious spatially as inside and beneath; the earlier romantics conceived of it as outside and above. We descend into the imagination; they rose into it. The last method, of course, is the method of transcendentalism.

Furthermore, as I shall shortly show, not only was the unconscious taken over from Locke and Kant and Hartley and converted into something radically creative, it also became an integral part of dynamic organicism because a number of the early romantics proved it, as it were, empirically, by their own personal experience. It became to them proof of the validity of the new way of thinking. Hence also romantic subjectivism, the artist watching his powers develop and novelty emerging from his unconscious mind.

What then is romanticism? Whether philosophic, theologic, or aesthetic, it is the revolution in the European mind against thinking in terms of static mechanism and the redirection of the mind to thinking in terms of dynamic organicism. Its values are change, imperfection, growth, diversity, the creative imagination, the unconscious.

III

Perhaps the result of my remarks so far is to make a much larger group of determined skeptics on the subject of romanticism. The proof of the Martini is in the drinking, and in the rest of what I have to say I hope to show not only that a group of literary works can be related in terms of the ideas I have given but also that particular literary works can be genuinely illuminated by these ideas, can be given richer content, can be more readily understood. And in addition I wish also to advance one more concept, the only one indeed to which I lay any claim of originality, for what I have already said is only an attempt to reconcile various ideas about romanticism which seemed to be fairly close together and to develop them into some consistent whole, on the basis of Lovejoy's statement that the coming of romanticism marked a great turn in the direction of European thought. For instance, Barzun's "desire and expectation of change" is an important part of my proposal; Stallknecht's "sentiment of being," i.e., of a living universe, is right at the heart of it; Harrold's ideas of growth are equally central. Nevertheless, the theory is still incomplete.

Dynamic organicism, manifested in literature in its fully developed form with all its main derivative ideas I have called "radical romanticism." To this term I should now like to add "positive romanticism," as a term useful in describing men and ideas and works of art in which dynamic organicism appears, whether it be incomplete or fully developed. But by itself, "positive romanticism" for the purposes of understanding the romantic movement is not only frequently useless; it is often worse than useless. It is often harmful. If some of my readers have been muttering, "What about Byron?" they are quite right in doing so. Positive romanticism cannot explain Byron; positive romanticism is not enough. To it must be added the term "negative romanticism," and to that I now turn.[7]

It may at first seem that I am here denying my basic aim of reducing the multiplicity of theories of romanticism to a single theory, but this is not really so. Negative romanticism is a necessary complement to positive romanticism, not a parallel or alternative to it, with which it must be reconciled. Briefly, negative romanticism is the expression of the attitudes, the feelings, and the ideas of a man who has left static mechanism but has not yet arrived at a reintegration of his thought and art in terms of dynamic organicism. I am here, of course, using a method of analysis which is now so common that one inhales it with the dust of our libraries, the method of analyzing the works of a man in terms of his personal development. Before we study any artist, we begin by establishing his canon and chronology. We *begin*, that is, by *assuming* that there is a development in his art.

I hope I am not being merely tedious in pointing out that this method is in itself a particular application of one of the main ideas derived from dynamic organicism, or positive romanticism—the idea of evolution in the nineteenth-century sense. But to show what I mean by negative romanticism, therefore, and how it fits in with positive romanticism, and to show how the theory works in practice, I shall discuss very briefly three works from the earlier years of the Romantic Movement: *The Ancient Mariner, The Prelude,* and *Sartor Resartus.* Briefly, all three works are about spiritual death, and rebirth, or secular conversion. In its baldest form, such an experience amounts to this: A man moves from a trust in the universe to a period of doubt and despair of any meaning in the universe, and then to a re-affirmation of faith in cosmic meaning and goodness, or at least meaning. The transition from the first stage to the second, we may call spiritual death; that from the second to the third, we may call spiritual rebirth.

Let us first consider *The Prelude.* The subtitle, not Wordsworth's, is *The Growth of a Poet's Mind.* After Wordsworth had started *The Recluse,* he found that in order to explain his ideas he must first explain how he came to have them. This decision is in itself a sign of positive romanticism. If you think in static terms, you will, as Pope did in *The Essay on Man,* present the result of a process of thought and experience. But if you find that you cannot explain your ideas except in terms of the process of how you have arrived at them, your mind is working in a different way, according to the principles of development and growth. The central experience which Wordsworth describes is spiritual death and rebirth. He began by having a complete faith in the principles of the French Revolution as the deistic *philosophes* and constitutionalists explained it. Their basic political principle was that we have only to restore to man his originally pure but now corrupt political organization and social contract, and a perfect society will necessarily result. Wordsworth accepted this as he also accepted the sentimentality, most notably and fully expressed by Shaftesbury, which was the eighteenth-century emotional expression of faith in the perfection and goodness of the universe, a sentimentalism which became more strident and absurd as its basic theodicy became increasingly

less acceptable. Any man who is defending an idea in which
he is emotionally involved, will become more emotional and
passionate in its defense as his opponent shows with increasing clarity that the idea is untenable.

The French Revolution, to Wordsworth, failed. It made
men worse instead of better, and from the creation of political and intellectual freedom it turned to tyranny, slaughter,
and imperialist expansion. He saw that he had been misled
by his emotions into too facile an acceptance. It was then
that he rejected sentimentalism and brought all values before the bar of reason, so that reason might sit in judgment.
But reason also was not enough. The boasted reason of the
enlightenment could neither explain the failure of the French
Revolution nor provide a means of acceptance. Then occurred
his spiritual death. He had invested heavily in emotion and
in reason. Each had betrayed him. He was spiritually bank-
rupt. Where was a means of acceptance? Moving to Race-
down, rejoining Dorothy, coming to know Coleridge, and
going to live near him at Nether Stowey, he reorganized all
his ideas with Coleridge's and Dorothy's intellectual and emotional help, and reaffirmed in new terms his faith in the
goodness and significance of the universe. He stood, he said,
"in Nature's presence a sensitive being, a *creative* soul"; that
is, his creative power was a "power like one of Nature's."
Nature and the creative soul maintain, he believed, an en-
nobling and enkindling interchange of action. The voice of
nature was a living voice. And there are moods when that
living voice can be heard, when "We see into the life of
things," when we feel "a sense sublime / Of something far
more deeply interfused; . . . / A motion and a spirit, that
impels / All thinking things, all objects of all thought, / And
rolls through all things."

The universe is alive, not dead; living and growing, not
a perfect machine; it speaks to us directly through the creative mind and its senses. Its truth cannot be perceived from
the "evidences of nature" but only through the unconscious
and creative mind. And this is the point of the famous description of the ascent of Mt. Snowdon, in the last book of
The Prelude. Climbing through the mist, Wordsworth comes
to the top of the mountain. Around and below him is a sea
of clouds, with the moon shining over all, clear, beautiful,

and bright. But through a gap in the clouds comes the roar of the waters in the valleys around the mountains. Thus in the moon he beheld the emblem of a mind "That feeds upon infinity, that broods / Over the dark abyss, intent to hear / Its voices issuing forth to silent light / In one continuous stream." This is his symbol of the unconscious mind, both of man and the universe, ultimately identical, both striving to become as well as to be. He has by a profound experience proved to himself the existence and the trustworthiness and the power of the unconscious mind, of the life of the universe, of the continuous creative activity of the cosmos.

Let me also add that he also, unfortunately I think, retained within his new attitudes a nostalgia for permanence, an ideal of eternal perfection. Thus early do we have the compromise called Victorian. And this inconsistency was to prove his eventual undoing, to cause his loss of creative power, comparatively speaking, and to effect his return to a kind of revised Toryism, to a concept of an organic society without dynamic power. But that is another story and I cannot go into it here.

Leaving chronological order aside, I turn now to *Sartor Resartus*. The central chapters of Carlyle's work are "The Everlasting No," "The Center of Indifference," and "The Everlasting Yea." They obviously present a pattern of spiritual death and rebirth. Carlyle, speaking of himself under the guise of Professor Teufelsdröckh, tells us how he lost his religious belief. "The loss of his religious faith was the loss of everything." "It is all a grim Desert, this once-fair world of his." "Invisible yet impenetrable walls divided me from all living; was there in the wide world, any true bosom I could press trustfully to mine? No, there was none. . . . It was a strange isolation I then lived in. The universe was all void of Life, of Purpose, of Volition, even of Hostility; it was one huge dead immeasurable Steam-engine, rolling on, in its dead indifference, to grind me limb from limb." "The Universe had pealed its Everlasting No authoritatively through all the recesses of his being." But in the moment of Baphometic fire-baptism he stood up and cried out that he would not accept that answer. This was not yet the moment of rebirth, but it was the first step, the step of defiance and rebellion.

There follows the Center of Indifference, of wandering
grimly across the face of Europe, of observing the absurdities
and cruelty and wickedness of mankind; he is a wanderer, a
pilgrim without any shrine to go to. And then one day, surrounded by a beautiful landscape, in the midst of nature and
the tenderness of the natural piety of human beings, came
a change. "The heavy dreams rolled gradually away, and I
awoke to a new Heaven and a new Earth. . . . What is
nature? Ha! Why do I not name thee GOD? Are not thou
the 'Living Garment of God'? The universe is not dead and
demoniacal, a charnel-house with spectres, but godlike and
my Father's." It is alive. Nature—as he tells us later in the
book, in the chapter called "Organic Filaments"—Nature
"is not completed, but ever completing. . . . Mankind is a
living movement, in progress faster or slower." Here indeed
is a positive romanticism so complete that it is almost a
radical romanticism, though Carlyle, like Wordsworth, retained
an inconsistent static principle in his thought. Like Wordsworth, his nostalgia for a static principle or static ground to
the evolving universe was to prove his undoing, but that again
is another story.

In *The Ancient Mariner* Coleridge tells us of an experience which is the same as that given by Wordsworth and
Carlyle. The mariner, on his journey around the world, or
through life, violates the faith of his fellow-man by shooting
the albatross, the one thing alive in the world of ice and
snow, always symbols of spiritual coldness and death. His
fellow mariners reject him, marking him with the sign of his
own guilt. From the world of ice and snow they come to
the world of fire and heat, again symbols of spiritual death,
alienation, and suffering. The soul of the mariner is won by
Life-in-Death. He alone remains alive while his fellow sailors,
silently and with reproachful eyes, die around him. As Carlyle
put it, "it was strange isolation I lived in then." And Carlyle
also uses the symbols of ice and fire to describe his condition. Isolation, alienation, and guilt possess the soul of the
mariner. He is alone, in a burning and evil universe. "The
very deep did rot," and the slimy and evil watersnakes surround his ship. And as he watches them in the moonlight he
is suddenly taken with their beauty, and "I blessed them unaware." From the depths of the unconscious rose an impulse

of affirmation, of love, of acceptance. The albatross drops
from his neck into the sea. The symbol of guilt and alienation and despair vanishes. The universe comes alive. It rains,
and the rain is the water of life. The wind blows; the breath
of a living universe wafts the ship across the ocean. The air
is filled with voices and the sky is filled with living light.
The spirit of the land of ice and snow comes to his aid. (As
Carlyle put it, even in his most despairful moments there
was within him, unconsciously, a principle of faith and affirmation.) Angels come into the bodies of the dead sailors and
work the ship. The whole universe comes to the mariner's
aid, and he completes his journey.

And thereafter, though he has been forgiven and reac-
cepted into man's life by the act of confession, there comes
an impulse to tell his story, the creative impulse of the poet
rising powerfully from his unconscious mind. Poetry is conceived of as a compulsive but creative act. In a sense Coleridge
is more profound than either Wordsworth or Carlyle. He
knows that for a romantic, once alienated means always alienated. He cannot join the wedding feast. Edwin Markham put
it well:

> He drew a circle that shut me out—
> Heretic, rebel, a thing to flout:
> But Love and I had the wit to win:
> We drew a circle that took him in!

Though a man may create a synthesis that includes the ideas
of his fellow men, to those very men he will always be outside the circle of accepted beliefs, even though he blesses all
things great and small.

At any rate we see here a highly radical positive romanticism. It is the record of a process; it affirms the unconscious
mind and the creative imagination; it affirms the principle
of the living universe; it affirms diversitarianism; and it is a
fully developed symbolism, an organic symbolism in which
the shooting of the albatross is without symbolic power
unless it is thought of in terms of the power and the interrela-
tions of the various symbolic units.

These interpretations, to me at least, demonstrate the
excellence of Lovejoy's three principles of romanticism—organicism, dynamism, and diversitarianism—to get us inside
various works of romantic art and to show us the relationships

that tie them together into a single literary movement. And
again to me, they show that these ideas are not heterogeneous,
independent ideas, but closely associated ideas, all related to
a central concept or world-metaphor.

And now to define negative romanticism. I have, of course,
taken the term from Carlyle's Everlasting No. As various individuals, according to their natures, and their emotional and
intellectual depths, went through the transition from affirming the meaning of the cosmos in terms of static mechanism
to affirming it in terms of dynamic organicism, they went
through a period of doubt, of despair, of religious and social
isolation, of the separation of reason and creative power. It
was a period during which they saw neither beauty nor goodness in the universe, nor any significance, nor any rationality,
nor indeed any order at all, not even an evil order. This is
negative romanticism, the preliminary to positive romanticism,
the period of *Sturm und Drang*. As the nineteenth century
rolled on, the transition became much easier, for the new
ideas were much more widely available. But for the early
romantics the new ideas had to be learned through personal
and painful experience. The typical symbols of negative romanticism are individuals who are filled with guilt, despair,
and cosmic and social alienation. They are often presented,
for instance, as having committed some horrible and unmen-
tionable and unmentioned crime in the past. They are often
outcasts from men and God, and they are almost always
wanderers over the face of the earth. They are Harolds, they
are Manfreds, they are Cains. They are heroes of such poems
as *Alastor*. But when they begin to get a little more insight
into their position, as they are forced to develop historical
consciousness, as they begin to seek the sources for their negation and guilt and alienation, they become Don Juans. That
is, in *Don Juan*, Byron sought objectivity by means of satire,
and set out to trace in his poem the development of those
attitudes that had resulted in himself. As I said earlier, positive romanticism cannot explain Byron, but negative romanticism can. Byron spent his life in the situation of Wordsworth
after the rejection of Godwin and before his move to Race-
down and Nether Stowey, of the mariner alone on the wide,
wide sea, of Teufelsdröckh subject to the Everlasting No and
wandering through the Center of Indifference.

It is the lack of this concept that involves Wellek's second article and much of Barzun's book, for all their admirable insights, in certain difficulties, in such a foredoomed attempt to find in figures who express negative romanticism and figures who express positive romanticism a common and unifying element. Theirs is the same difficulty as that with which Auden gets involved in *The Enchaféd Flood*. It is true that both positive and negative romanticism often cause isolation of the personality, but as Coleridge of these three men alone realized, negative romanticism causes isolation and despair because it offers no cosmic explanations, while positive romanticism offers cosmic explanations which are not shared by the society of which one is a part. To Arnold, "Not a having and a resting, but a growing and a becoming, is the character of perfection as culture conceives it." His ideas isolated him from Barbarians, Philistines, and Populace; they were impressed but they did not follow; for they could not comprehend, so far were his fundamental attitudes separated from theirs. Picasso has in his painting expressed profoundly the results of the freedom that romanticism has given to the creative imagination, but he is detested by most people who have seen his cubist or post-cubist paintings—as well as by a great many who have not. He is at home in the universe, but not in his society.

IV

My proposal is now complete. This theory does, I firmly believe, what such a theory must do. It gets us inside of various works of art, and it shows the relevance of one work of art to another. . . . [However], I wish to make one final suggestion, to issue a warning to anyone who may be taken enough with these ideas to try to employ them.

Although negative and then positive romanticism developed by reaction out of the static-mechanistic-uniformitarian complex, with its cosmic Toryism, its sentimentalism, and its Deism, they were also superimposed upon it. At any point in nineteenth- or twentieth-century culture it is possible to take a cross section and find all three actively at work. The past one hundred and fifty years or so must be conceived as a dramatic struggle, sometimes directly between positive romanticism and static, mechanistic thought, sometimes three-

cornered. It is a struggle between minds and within minds.
It is seen today in the profound disparity between what is
sometimes called high art and popular art; it is expressed in
the typical modern cultural phenomena of the *avant garde*,
which is as modern as Wordsworth and Coleridge. . . . It
appears in the antagonism between our relativistic critics and
our absolutistic critics. It appears in the theological struggle
between the theology of such a man as Charles Raven [8] and
the proponents of the "theology of crisis." A very pure positive romanticism is at the heart of Ruth Benedict's *Patterns
of Culture;* her ideal of a good society is organic, dynamic,
and diversitarian. In short, the history of ideas and the arts
in the nineteenth and twentieth centuries is the history of
the dramatic struggle among three opposing forces: static mechanism, negative romanticism, and positive romanticism. In
this drama, to me the hero is dynamic and diversitarian organicism, and I think Goethe and Beethoven and Coleridge and
the other founders of the still vital romantic tradition—a
tradition often repudiated by those who are at the very heart
of it, and understandably—have still much to say to us, are
not mere intellectual and aesthetic curiosities. Nevertheless,
I am aware that to many scholars and thinkers, positive romanticism is the villain, responsible for all the ills of our
century. The drama may indeed turn out to be a tragedy, but
if it does, it is because static mechanism persists in staying
alive.

Of course the fact that my attitude towards the continuing and future usefulness of positive romanticism may not
after all be justified is not essential to my argument, or even
germane to it. I ask only that my readers take under serious
consideration, and test in their studies, in their reading, and
in their classrooms the theories about romanticism which I
have outlined. I trust that many of them will find these ideas
useful, even though they withhold final assent.

Notes

1. Jacques Barzun, *Romanticism and the Modern Ego* (New York,
1943).
2. "Romanticism: Definition of a Period," *Magazine of Art,* XLII
(November, 1949), 243.
3. PMLA, XXXIX, 229–53; republished in his *Essays in the History
of Ideas* (Baltimore, 1948).

4. *Journal of the History of Ideas*, II, 237–78.

5. Wellek's confusion, or apparent confusion, lies in his implication that the "Romanticisms" Lovejoy discussed in 1924 are the same as the "romantic ideas" which in 1941 he called "heterogeneous, logically independent, and sometimes essentially antithetic to one another in their implications." As I read the 1941 article, I interpret the latter as these three: organicism, dynamism, and diversitarianism. (See Section II of this paper.) These are not the "Romanticisms" of 1924. (See the first paragraph of Wellek's article, "The Concept of 'Romanticism' in Literary History," *Comparative Literature*, I, 1.)

6. I am alarmed at finding myself in disagreement with Lovejoy. Although I think his three ideas are not heterogeneous, but homogeneous, or at least derived from a common root-metaphor, the possibility that they really *are* heterogeneous does not deprive them in the least of their value in understanding romanticism, nor does their possible heterogeneity have any effect on my proposal which follows.

7. Wellek, for instance, says that Byron "does not share the romantic conception of imagination," or does so "only fitfully." He quotes *Childe Harold*, Canto III, written and published in 1816, when Byron was temporarily under Wordsworth's influence through Shelley. Byron's romantic view of nature as an organism with which man is unified organically by the imagination is equally fitful and limited to the period of Shelleyan influence.

8. Raven is both biologist and theologian. See his *Science, Religion, and the Future* (Cambridge, Eng., and New York, 1943).

2 · The Commitment to Metaphor:

Modern Criticism and Romantic Poetry

MODERN POETRY and the most influential modern criticism are indebted to the Romantic tradition in spite of a frequently proclaimed antipathy to Romantic attitudes. In his penetrating study of the continuance of this tradition, Frank Kermode would place T. E. Hulme, W. B. Yeats, Ezra Pound and others fully in it; he says of Hulme's concept of the "intensive manifold,"

> it is accessible only to intuition, belonging to a different order of reality. It is "indescribable but not unknowable." The artist knows it; it is his Image. It is finite; hence the need for precision. Its meaning is the same thing as its form, and the artist is absolved from participation with the discursive powers of the intellect.

> This theory, as Hulme explains it, makes a show of being in opposition to Romantic imprecision . . . but in fact it is fundamentally a new statement of the old defence of poetry against positivism and the universe of death. It is a revised form of the old proclamation that poetry has special access to truth, and is not merely light entertainment for minds tired out by physics.[1]

This is acutely perceived, but if it is incorrect to see modern criticism simply as a reaction against Romanticism, it is equally an oversimplification to treat Hulme's attacks on humanism, romanticism and imprecision as of little significance. What seems rather to be displayed by Hulme and

to have persisted in the work of later critics is a confusion of
attitudes which are in many ways contradictory. This may be
brought out sufficiently by reference to remarks by two important modern critics.

In his essays on *Tradition and the Individual Talent*
(1917) and *The Function of Criticism* (1923), T. S. Eliot
said that the critic works to correct taste by setting a new
poet "for contrast and comparison among the dead." He attacked "interpretation" as illegitimate, without defining exactly what this word meant to him, and argued that no poet
has his complete meaning alone, but only in relation to the
"simultaneous order" composed by all literature. In general,
the attitude outlined in these essays is an objective one,
corresponding to what Mr. Eliot called classicism, the need
for men to give allegiance to something, an unquestioned
spiritual authority, outside themselves. For immediate purposes,
the classical outlook may be described in terms of an assumption that there is an order which provides a frame of reference for evaluating all things. In general terms, this order may
be represented in myths, in religions, in a social order, in the
great chain of being; art partaking of such an order finds its
subject-matter in the possibilities or failures of life in the
context of the order, and as it has a common frame of reference, it tends to make use of common forms and observe
classical rules. The function of criticism in relation to such
art is of an objective kind, in that works of art may be judged
in terms of one another and in relation to the common frame
of reference; they compose a simultaneous order.

W. K. Wimsatt, Jr., in his *The Verbal Icon* (1954),
observes how Mr. Eliot praised an objective attitude in criticism, described fact-finding as a valuable activity, and attacked as corrupters of taste "those who supply opinion or
fancy," but points out that much of Mr. Eliot's own criticism
consists of exhortations, opinions and judgments of a personal kind. There is a discrepancy between his theory and his
practice, and in his practice he seems to fall into what Mr.
Wimsatt calls the "affective fallacy," reporting his feelings in
an impressionistic way, describing what a poem does rather
than what it is. Mr. Wimsatt also complains of criticism
which falls into the "intentional fallacy," or commences from
the author's intentions, and defines the critic's function thus:

The function of the objective critic is by approximate descriptions of poems, or multiple restatements of their meaning, to aid other readers to come to an intuitive and full realization of poems themselves, and hence to know good poems and distinguish them from bad ones.[2]

This is an interesting definition because the word "objective" seems to be at odds with what the critic is supposed to do. It would seem that he is to regard the poem as unique, existing in and for itself, as autotelic, a line of thought which can be traced back to Romantic theories of art as organic; he is to analyze a poem's meaning by practical criticism, and to judge it presumably in terms of complexity and integration. Except for its special emphasis on meaning, this mode of criticism is in fact a subjective one, and stems from a Romantic outlook. By this is meant the assumption that there is no general order, that in an anarchic society in which men are isolated from one another, a principle of order must be sought within the self. It is in this sense that Romantic poetry is subjective, in that the poet creates his own order; there are no formal rules for him to work by, and he is likely to be praised for originality. The criticism appropriate for such poetry is subjective, the kind of criticism that Mr. Eliot objected to so strongly and practiced, as Mr. Wimsatt noticed, so consistently, and the kind of criticism defined by Mr. Wimsatt as "objective."

In the senses of the terms outlined above, it might be said that in spite of his advocation of a classical attitude, Mr. Eliot writes criticism which belongs to the Romantic tradition; and that Mr. Wimsatt, for all that he accepts fully the Romantic view that "A poem should not mean but be," and proposes a subjective reading of each poem as a contained whole, wishes to claim a classical or objective character for such criticism. The combination of opposed attitudes represented in these critics is very common in modern criticism, which, like criticism at any period, is closely linked to what poets are trying to do, to the evaluation and defense of contemporary poetry. This may be seen in the attempts that have been made in the last forty years to describe new poetry in Mr. Eliot's terms as a modification of an already established order of the past, to exercise a classical function and place modern poetry in relation to a supposedly objective order. This has involved much rewriting of literary history. As Frank Kermode has brilliantly shown in his examination of T. S. Eliot's concept of a "dissociation of sensibility" taking place in the seventeenth century, and its counterparts in the views of other critics like T. E. Hulme and W. B. Yeats, this has consisted of a search for a

> golden age when the prevalent mode of knowing was not positivist and anti-imaginative; when the Image, the intuited, creative reality was habitually respected; when art was not permanently on the defensive against mechanical and systematic modes of inquiry. Since the order of reality postulated as the proper study of the poet tends, in one way or another, to be granted supernatural attributes, the ideal epoch is usually a religious one.[3]

In particular, there has been a widespread upgrading of early seventeenth-century poetry, including Jacobean tragedy, and a devaluation of Milton and of much Romantic and nineteenth-century poetry.

Both the combination of Romantic and classical attitudes in modern criticism, and the tendency to depreciate or disregard the poetry of the nineteenth century, and incidentally long poems in general, point to important differences between the poetry of the present age and Romantic poetry. Our world is still the world of the Romantics insofar as it seems anarchic, as the poet needs to impose an order on the chaos of existence; but it differs from theirs in significant respects, for instance in the growth of an urban way of life[4] in which the breakdown of ties, the isolation of the individual in the crowd, has become notorious; in the decay of faith in the face of material and scientific advances which appear to have taken control of man's destiny; in a shift from optimism about man's possible greatness to despair of his ever achieving a harmonious world. The predominant note of Romantic poetry is its assertion, its vision of a universe or a society resolved into concord, of "the one life within us and abroad," of

> The feeling of life endless, the great thought
> By which we live, Infinity and God,
> *(The Prelude*, XIII, 183–84)

or of man as "Sceptreless, free, uncircumscribed . . . the King Over himself; just, gentle, wise." The predominant note of modern poetry is its sense of conflict or tension; the poets no

longer offer general solutions, only local and particular ones, and
the universal vision has given way to images of disintegration
or local and personal resolutions of conflicts, the sense that "I
can connect Nothing with nothing," the image of "That
dolphin-torn, that gong-tormented sea," the defiance of joy
to set against despair,

> Some moralist or mythological poet
> Compares the soul to a solitary swan;
> I am satisfied with that,
> Satisfied if a troubled mirror show it,
> Before that brief gleam of its life be gone,
> An image of its state;
> The wings half spread for flight,
> The breast thrust out in pride
> Whether to play, or to ride
> Those winds that clamour of approaching night.
>   (W. B. Yeats,
>   *Nineteen Hundred and Nineteen*)

The cross-breeding of Romantic and classical attitudes in
criticism is connected with this change in poetry from a vision of universal order to a reflection of disintegration or
images of local order. The mirroring of disintegration in, for
instance, T. S. Eliot's *The Waste Land*, is given shape and
strength in terms of the order and magnificence of past ages
and literatures of the past; and the local images of order in,
for instance, the poetry of W. B. Yeats, are given validity
in the context of Byzantium, Urbino or Coole Park. Modern
poets tend to look for a historical period which seems to
reflect the qualities they value,[5] in order to establish their
local images and personal resolutions of oppositions as being
of general significance, to create for them the context of a
larger frame of reference. The transcendental vision of the
Romantic poet, which makes use of "the kind of symbol
which is rooted in our universal natural experience," gives
place to a limited vision disturbed by an overriding sense of
disorder, which tends to employ personal images that have to
be "validated by the manipulation of the artist in a special
context." [6] One result of this change is that modern criticism
gives special attention to the study of poetic imagery in the
narrow sense of metaphor and simile, that, as Mr. Wimsatt
says, "The theorist of poetry tends more and more today to
make metaphor the irreducible element of his definition of

poetry." [7] The transcendental vision has diminished into the image, into metaphor.

II

The growth of interest in poetic imagery can be related to the development of organic theories of art in the nineteenth century. The notion of the unconscious mind became useful to account for poetry valued as being unpremeditated, the spontaneous overflow of powerful feelings, so that Carlyle could assert, "unconsciousness is the sign of creation." [8] Poetry came to be regarded as nonpropositional, as expressing feeling and being independent of truth, and hence as having an intrinsic value as an end in itself. In this way critics were able to combat the seeming encroachment of science upon all aspects of life and the world, what some felt to be a circumscribing of the imagination, by distinguishing between scientific truth and poetic truth. The finest poetry was identified with the most impassioned language, and the lyric or short poem took on a special character as "more eminently and peculiarly poetry than any other." [9]

Such views underlie the modern concern with poetic imagery. The work of the unconscious mind has come to be associated particularly with metaphor and simile, and the assumption is often made that there is some kind of border line in poetry between "conscious" reference and "unconscious" image, the latter being the more valuable. The most impassioned language and the most imaginative language are thought to coalesce in metaphor, which is regarded as the supreme mode of expression, the true essence of poetry; and a commonplace nineteenth-century distinction between poetry as expressing feeling and prose as conveying information, rephrased now in the assertion that poetry employs the connotations (associations) of words as well as the denotations, prose only the denotations (the literal senses), is extended to embrace imagery: "The imagery of poetry is in the main complex and suggestive; the imagery of prose single and explicit." [10] A regard for metaphor as the essence of poetry encouraged the analysis of poetic imagery for its own sake, and often in isolation from its context, so that the poem tends to disappear as the image takes its place. Some critics make a further distinction in value between the terms of the image,

considering the vehicle (subject matter) [11] as of special importance as welling up from the poet's unconscious mind, in contrast to the tenor (object matter or reference) which is ignored
as having merely, as it were, a prose character.

These are some ways in which the present interest in
imagery may be seen as allied to the organic theories of poetry
which developed with the Romantic movement; but at the
same time this interest reflects a kind of poetry and a kind of
criticism which differ greatly from Romantic poetry and Romantic criticism, and are in large measure hostile to them.
The differences are most clearly seen in the criticism which
has been influenced by the ideas of T. S. Eliot, T. E. Hulme
and I. A. Richards. The last named developed a psychological
theory of the value of poetry, which, like nineteenth-century
critics, he claimed was independent of scientific truth, and he
argued that critical study should be devoted to the evaluation
of a poem as an end in itself:

> Every poem . . . is a strictly limited piece of experience, a
> piece which breaks up more or less easily if alien elements
> intrude. We must keep the poem undisturbed by these or we
> fail to read it and have some other experience instead. For
> these reasons we establish a severance; we draw a boundary
> between the poem and what is not the poem in our experi-
> ence.[12]

Good poetry became "inclusive" poetry, which offered an
experience in its entirety, complex and full of contradictions,
and this was contrasted with "exclusive" poetry, which omitted
unpleasant or discordant impulses. The Romantic resolution
of all things into a general harmony was thus altered and re-
duced to a resolution of the contradictions within a "strictly
limited piece of experience"; and the best poems, which are
self-sustaining, are those which reconcile oppositions in this
limited sense, and emerge into irony or paradox.

The poem then becomes a "pattern of resolved stresses," [13]
built out of conflict. The "affective fallacy" and the "intentional fallacy" are denounced because "The outcome of either
fallacy . . . is that the poem itself, as an object of specifically
critical judgment, tends to disappear." [14] The greatness of a
poet "depends upon the extent of the area of experience which
he can master poetically," and "inclusiveness" is the mark of
the good poet, who

proves his vision by submitting it to the fires of irony, . . . wishes to indicate that his vision has been earned, that it can survive reference to the complexities and contradictions of experience.[15]

Three terms in particular have come into use as measures for analyzing and judging poems, all arising from the idea that a good poem must "work by contradiction and qualification" in order to display the conflicting elements which, it is assumed, are characteristic of experience: the only solution for the poet, it has been claimed, is paradox, and the language of poetry has been identified with "The Language of Paradox." [16] This first term, paradox, suggesting a strict opposition of meanings, has perhaps seemed to many critics too rigid a schematization to be applied to poetry, and the word "tension" has been used to indicate something of the same idea, that in good poetry there must be a tension between opposing themes. It has been given a special sense in relation to the philosophical terms "extension" and "intension": "the meaning of poetry is its 'tension,' the full organized body of the extension and intension that we can find in it," that is, of the literal and figurative significances.[17] The third term, irony, is related to the other two, inasmuch as the poetry of paradox, of tension, is "able to fuse the irrelevant and discordant, has come to terms with itself, and is invulnerable to irony"; hence irony becomes a "principle of structure" in good poetry.[18]

The development and application of these terms has been fortified also by the reaction against humanism and romanticism, the demand for a poetry "all dry and hard," finite and precise, stimulated by T. E. Hulme.[19] The poetry of T. S. Eliot was acclaimed as the first to employ techniques "adequate to the ways of feeling or modes of thought of adult sensitive moderns," to break away from a sterile Victorian tradition which saw "the actual world as alien, recalcitrant and unpoetical." [20] The new poetry and the new criticism were related to seventeenth-century poetry, and other literature has come to be measured against these as representing "the consciousness of the age." [21] Three of the criteria used in judging poetry in this way are especially significant. One is the treatment of all poetry as if it were contemporary poetry, which can be detached from its context in time and studied without reference to its historical meanings. Another is the demand for complexity, for the inclusion of the "extraneous and distracting elements which might seem to contradict what the poet wishes to communicate"; [22] this kind of complexity, consisting in the balance and tension between conflicting elements held in suspension in the unity of the poem and emerging in irony and paradox, is characteristic of metaphysical and much modern poetry, and is perhaps only possible in a relatively short poem. A third criterion is the demand that each line of a poem be able to bear the severest scrutiny, that each line reflect the qualities of "inclusive" poetry.

The long poem does not fulfill this kind of demand ("The apology of a long poem should be: 'I am really a long *short poem*'" [23]), and is not amenable to the methods of analysis which have developed in association with the new critical standards, methods which seek to identify closely the possibilities of meaning in each line of "inclusive" poetry, as these range from a simple ambiguity to a full contradiction of opposed meanings. The most vivid and characteristic means by which the tension of opposed meanings is sustained within the line or short poem is metaphor, and consequently metaphor takes chief place in the study of poetry, "the metaphysicals and the modernists stand opposed to the neoclassic and Romantic poets on the issue of metaphor." [24]

What the critic looks for in a poem is a structure of meanings contained largely in its metaphor, and forming an autonomous whole to be evaluated in and for itself. Although such a view stems from a Romantic theory of poetry, for instance in its claim that poetry is autotelic, an end in itself, it represents an outlook that is generally hostile or indifferent to Romantic and Victorian poetry. It parades the old idea, deriving from Mallarmé and the earlier conception of a poem as a spontaneous product of feeling, that a poem should not mean but be, but twists this into a new significance by then asserting that a poem can only be through its meaning.[25] It uses formulae derived from Coleridge, seeing the poem also as a product of imagination, but it modifies the character of the imagination so that it merges into intelligence.[26] It has substituted for the Romantic idea of a poem as revealing eternal verities, the concept of a complex of limited meanings; a poet is more likely to be castigated for being unintelligent than for lacking imagination, to be disapproved for failing to exploit the full resources of words than for having nothing urgent to say. The Romantic commitment to a vision has given way to a narrower, more intellectual poetry, in which the only commitment is a commitment to metaphor: "One can sum up modern poetic technique by calling it the rediscovery of metaphor and the full commitment to metaphor." [27]

The technique of much modern criticism could be summed up in the same terms. Some of the critics who share this outlook like to think that the language of Romantic and Victorian poetry is shown to be inadequate by its failure to measure up to their criticism; but it seems better to suppose that their criticism is unsuitable for this kind of poetry, that what is called carelessness, a lack of intelligence, or a failure to represent the conflicting elements of experience, may be "more often the highly adroit and skilful writing of a kind of poetry which they do not understand because they do not like that kind of poetry." [28]

Notes

1. Frank Kermode, *Romantic Image* (London, 1957), p. 129.
2. W. K. Wimsatt, *The Verbal Icon* (Lexington, Ky., 1954), p. 83. I am deliberately abstracting from a subtle and complicated discussion by W. K. Wimsatt, but I hope, not unfairly. Several of his penetrating essays are concerned with the nature and limitations of modern criticism, but while he clearly recognizes that Romantic poetry works in a different way from metaphysical and modern poetry, and has a different structure, he tries to accommodate it within the terms of modern criticism: metaphor, wit, complexity, etc.
3. *Romantic Image*, p. 143.
4. Wordsworth could hardly have foreseen the overwhelming urbanization of modern life when he complained at the beginning of the century of the "increasing accumulation of men in cities," which he saw as one of a number of forces then combining to blunt "the discriminating powers of the mind" (*Preface to Lyrical Ballads*, 1800); but the process had commenced then.
5. See Frank Kermode, *Romantic Image*, p. 145.
6. These phrases are borrowed from Robert Penn Warren, *The Rime of the Ancient Mariner* (New York, 1946), p. 75.
7. *The Verbal Icon*, p. 128.
8. *Characteristics* (1831), cited in M. H. Abrams, *The Mirror and the Lamp* (New York, 1953), p. 217; this contains an excellent full account of the development of the ideas touched on here.
9. Cited from *Early Essays by John Stuart Mill*, ed. J. W. M. Gibbs (1897), p. 208; also in Abrams, *The Mirror and the Lamp*, p. 98.
10. J. Middleton Murry, "Metaphor," in *Shakespeare Criticism, 1919–1935*, ed. Ann Bradby (London, 1936), p. 234.

11. I. A. Richards in *The Philosophy of Rhetoric* (New York, 1936) called the term imported to illustrate or modify the underlying idea in an image the "vehicle" (which is the same as the "subject-matter" of Caroline Spurgeon, *Shakespeare's Imagery and What It Tells Us,* 1935, and the "minor term" of H. W. Wells, *Poetic Imagery,* New York, 1924); the other term becomes the "tenor" (or "object-matter," though Miss Spurgeon did not use this word, or "major term"). These terms have also been called "content" and "reference" by Owen Barfield, *Poetic Diction* (London, 1928).

12. I. A. Richards, *The Principles of Literary Criticism* (London, 1924), p. 78.

13. Cleanth Brooks, *The Well Wrought Urn* (New York, 1947), p. 186.

14. *The Verbal Icon,* p. 21.

15. Robert Penn Warren, "Pure and Impure Poetry," *Kenyon Review,* V (1943), 250, 252.

16. *The Well Wrought Urn,* Chapter I; the quotation is on p. 9.

17. Allen Tate, "Tension in Poetry" (1938), in *On the Limits of Poetry, Selected Essays: 1928–1948* (New York, 1948), p. 83.

18. Cleanth Brooks, "Irony as a Principle of Structure," in *Literary Opinion in America,* ed. Morton D. Zabel (Revised Edition, New York, 1951), p. 732.

19. T. E. Hulme, *Speculations* (London, 1924), p. 126.

20. F. R. Leavis, *New Bearings in English Poetry* (London, 1932), pp. 25, 15.

21. F. R. Leavis writing in *Scrutiny,* II (1932), 134–35.

22. *The Well Wrought Urn,* p. 46.

23. Laura Riding and Robert Graves, *A Survey of Modernist Poetry* (London, 1927), p. 57.

24. Cleanth Brooks, *Modern Poetry and the Tradition* (Chapel Hill, 1939), p. 22.

25. *The Verbal Icon,* p. 4.

26. So for instance F. R. Leavis says of Milton that his "defect of intelligence is a defect of imagination," *Revaluation* (London, 1949), p. 58.

27. Cleanth Brooks, "Irony as a Principle of Structure," p. 729.

28. F. A. Pottle, "The Case of Shelley," *PMLA,* LXVII (1952), 589–608.

Part Two   *Wordsworth*

Douglas Bush

3 · Wordsworth: *A Minority Report*

WORDSWORTH IDENTIFIED HIMSELF, and has always been identified by his readers, with a special message concerning nature's relation to man and man's relation to nature. While his mature experience was a natural sequel to that of his childhood and youth, it was not simply a spontaneous growth; it was a strong and conscious revolt against the scientific view of the world and man. To such temperaments as Wordsworth and Coleridge, it seemed that both the outer and the inner world had been thoroughly mechanized by scientists and psychologists; the physical universe and the soul of man were alike governed by mechanical laws and subject to rationalistic analysis. Wordsworth and Coleridge saw the universe and man as enveloped and interpenetrated by mystery and by the all-comprehendng unity of spirit:

> Our destiny, our being's heart and home,
> Is with infinitude, and only there.

And one might add the still more familiar lines of "Tintern Abbey":

> And I have felt
> A presence that disturbs me with the joy
> Of elevated thoughts; a sense sublime
> Of something far more deeply interfused,
> Whose dwelling is the light of setting suns,
> And the round ocean and the living air,

Reprinted from *Wordsworth: Centenary Studies* edited by Gilbert T. Dunklin, by permission of the author and Princeton University Press. Copyright 1951 by Princeton University Press.

And the blue sky, and in the mind of man:
A motion and a spirit, that impels
All thinking things, all objects of all thought,
And rolls through all things.

Such opposed doctrines were not of course essentially new. In the seventeenth century the mechanistic thought of Descartes and Hobbes had aroused the Cambridge Platonists to assert the active reality and unity of spirit. And by the end of the eighteenth century Newtonian science, which at first had been welcomed by poets, and sensationalist psychology, which at first was welcomed by Coleridge and Wordsworth, had come to seem like mechanistic strait jackets imposed upon the universe and the human soul. In the century or more since Wordsworth and Coleridge died, science has gone infinitely farther than they could have anticipated in mechanizing civilization and the heart of man, and a good deal of modern poetry has carried on a new "romantic revolt" against the claims and the desiccating effects of scientific rationalism. All this being so, it might be supposed that Wordsworth would be the inspiration and tutelary genius of the modern movement, whereas it is clear that he is not, that he has meant very little to most modern poets. And what of the common reader, who nowadays is more conscious than ever before of the antagonism between science and any kind of religious or semireligious idealism? He would be glad to have Wordsworth as a great ally, but does he turn to Wordsworth's faith in the spiritual power of nature and the deep illumination and joy that it offers to man? I do not think he does.

No one has ever revered Wordsworth more than Arnold (who, it has been said, had a tendency to regard himself as Wordsworth's widow), and no one wrote more earnestly of the poet's "healing power":

He too upon a wintry clime
Had fallen—on this iron time
Of doubts, disputes, distractions, fears.
He found us when the age had bound
Our souls in its benumbing round;
He spoke, and loos'd our heart in tears.
He laid us as we lay at birth
On the cool flowery lap of earth;
Smiles broke from us and we had ease.
The hills were round us, and the breeze
Went o'er the sun-lit fields again:

> Our foreheads felt the wind and rain.
> Our youth return'd: for there was shed
> On spirits that had long been dead,
> Spirits dried up and closely-furl'd,
> The freshness of the early world.[1]

These lines, written in April 1850, express what Arnold felt that he and his age owed to Wordsworth. Almost thirty years later, in the essay that prefaced his anthology, Arnold delivered the verdict that Wordsworth was, and would remain, the greatest English poet after Shakespeare and Milton, and that he was superior to all modern continental poets, because the ample body of his poems, especially the many good short ones, were "superior in power, in interest, in the qualities which give enduring freshness, to that which any one of the others has left." But we may think that Arnold the semi-official critic was farther removed from his own deepest experience and convictions, and from ours, than Arnold the poet had been. Arnold's poetry in general is a troubled testimony that Wordsworth's healing power was not enough. Empedocles, the despairing representative of the restless and ruthless modern intellect, looked back with longing, as Arnold looked back to Wordsworth, upon that time when

> we receiv'd the shock of mighty thoughts
> On simple minds with a pure natural joy,

but he could only think of it as gone forever. Empedocles, or Arnold, saw no hope of man's regaining the capacity for simple, natural feeling that belonged to the youth of the race and the youth of the individual. Even the memorial tribute I quoted is a tacit admission that the poet of nature did not meet but withdrew from the problems of the modern mind. And, not to cite further evidence, Arnold made the plain statement with which we began, that

> Wordsworth's eyes avert their ken
> From half of human fate.

In other words, the poet's trust in nature, his trust in feeling, his hopefulness and joy, grew out of a temperament and out of circumstances which slighted the darker and grimmer elements in life, the miseries that flesh and mind are heir to, the high proportion of unhappiness in human existence.

    If in the middle of the nineteenth century the

priest to us all
Of the wonder and bloom of the world

could no longer relieve the spiritual distresses of the modern
mind (not to mention other kinds of trouble), what can be
said in the middle of the twentieth, when the world and man
have gone so much farther into the sandy desert that Arnold
so clearly saw, when science has become the dominant religion,
when naturalistic and positivistic philosophy has made the
general mind distrustful of everything except the empirical
fact? Even if we grant that Wordsworth's rejection of rigor-
ously mechanistic thought was essentially right (though it took
science a long time to reorientate itself), it might still be said
that his peculiar faith in nature evaded rather than transcended
scientific rationalism. It could not and did not survive among
his immediate poetic disciples, or indeed for himself.

At this point it might be well to anticipate one possible
objection by recalling the famous passage on science in the
Preface to the second edition of *Lyrical Ballads*:

> Poetry is the first and last of all knowledge—it is as immortal
> as the heart of man. If the labours of Men of science should
> ever create any material revolution, direct or indirect, in our
> condition, and in the impressions which we habitually receive,
> the Poet will sleep then no more than at present; he will be
> ready to follow the steps of the Man of science, not only in
> those general indirect effects, but he will be at his side, carry-
> ing sensation into the midst of the objects of the science itself.
> The remotest discoveries of the Chemist, the Botanist, or
> Mineralogist, will be as proper objects of the Poet's art as any
> upon which it can be employed, if the time should ever come
> when these things shall be familiar to us, and the relations
> under which they are contemplated by the followers of these
> respective sciences shall be manifestly and palpably material
> to us as enjoying and suffering beings. If the time should ever
> come when what is now called science, thus familiarised to
> men, shall be ready to put on, as it were, a form of flesh and
> blood, the Poet will lend his divine spirit to aid the trans-
> figuration, and will welcome the Being thus produced, as a dear
> and genuine inmate of the household of man.

Wordsworth's prophecy sounds brave and reassuring, but
it was to prove no more accurate than prophecies generally do.[2]
His conception of nature, the main basis of his faith and his
poetry, was hardly compatible with biology and the struggle
for existence. Moreover, he could not foresee what a multiplied

menace even machinery and gadgets were to become—the change, to go no further, from the surrey with the fringe on top to the sound of horns and motors in the spring. Wordsworth did see the rapacious commercialism and the spiritual debasement that accompanied the Industrial Revolution, but he could not foresee that science was to alter the whole tempo and quality of human life and thought and feeling, that it was to change not only the face but the soul of civilization and even threaten its survival. In a word, he dreamed of the humanizing of what was to grow more and more inhuman. That is not, certainly, a charge against Wordsworth himself and in his own time, but it does have some bearing on Wordsworth today. Since he, so to speak, offered a reply and an antidote to science, it is surely permissible to consider if the antidote was adequate. I do not of course mean to imply that a poet may not hold a belief or idea unless it is sanctioned by science, which operates on another level and has often been dogmatically wrong anyhow, but only that there are some hard facts which imaginative intuition cannot override or ignore.

In answer to these various large questions, many things might be said: that Arnold was only a single disconsolate voice, not an oracle for his own age or ours; that Wordsworth was not a primitivistic escapist and did not avert his eyes from human suffering, but fully recognized the common lot; that he remains a light and a stay for a multitude of modern readers; that, even if he does not, the fault is much less in him than in the temper of an especially troubled age; that science and positivistic thought, however dominant and arrogant, have not extinguished and cannot extinguish the life of the spirit, the human affections, the admiration, hope, and love by which we live; and that in any case the power of great poetry does not depend on the validity of the beliefs and ideas expressed by the poet (who is not a philosopher), but on the total experience we receive from reading him.

Most of these questions and answers are endlessly debatable, and I can only offer some highly debatable comments. Whether or not Wordsworth is actively cherished by a large number of modern readers I do not know, since one cannot sit down at the telephone and inquire, "Have you a book? What poet are you now reading?" So that question must be passed by. In regard to the validity and importance of a poet's philoso-

phy, some readers and critics would deplore any emphasis on
what a poet believes and says, and would insist that Wordsworth
is entitled to the diplomatic immunity we freely grant to other
and older poets who are still alive for us—the Greeks and
Romans, Dante and the Christian poets of the English Renaissance from Chaucer to Milton. Well, granted that poetry is
an aesthetic experience, it seems to me that unless it ministers,
in more than aesthetic ways, to what used to be called our
souls, there is not much reason for its being read or written.
And I do not think that we common readers are able, even if
we wish, to maintain an equal degree of receptivity, or an
equally willing suspension of disbelief, toward all kinds of
creeds; our knowledge and experience and individual temperaments make some congenial and some not. When we read the
Greeks and Romans we may be conscious of being in a pagan
and alien world, but we are also conscious of universal human
values and, in some poets, of a view of life that is religious by
any standard. As for the Christian poets, from Dante to Milton, we may or may not share the chief articles of their religious
creed, but—to put the matter in its lowest terms—that creed
is at least in our bones. It has the traditional dignity and authority of the greatest of historic religions, and—what is more
important—it remains the highest inspiration and criterion of
our own religious and ethical gropings because its recognition
of what is evil and what is good, of the conflict between the
natural and the supranatural, between pride and humility, remains, even for many nonbelievers, the most penetrating revelation or insight that man has attained concerning his own
nature. But I think that some basic beliefs of Wordsworth,
whether we call them pantheism or primitivism, a private myth
or autointoxication, or whether we use more laudatory names,
are more alien to us, less realistic and less satisfying, than those
of the pagan or the Christian poets.

In Wordsworth's gospel of nature and man the dualism of
both classical and Christian ethics was pretty much dissolved.
That fact might validate it for our naturalistic age, but naturalistic thinkers would probably boggle at Wordsworth's faith
in the instinctive goodness of man and the inspiring goodness
of nature. That Wordsworth's optimistic and humanitarian
faith in man has a foundation of doubtful solidity and breadth
I think is true. If recent poets and writers in general have been

too much inclined to despair, Wordsworth can be charged with a partial view of the opposite kind. In saying that—not that it is a novel opinion—one may of course be an unwitting victim of the partial view characteristic of our melancholy time. But a similar conclusion might emerge from a comparison of Wordsworth with those poets who have most nearly arrived at a comprehensive view of human nature and experience. It would be unfair to Wordsworth, as it would be to most poets, to appeal to the greatest Greeks, or to Lucretius and Virgil, or to Dante and Shakespeare; but no one could object to a comparison with Spenser and Milton or the lesser Chapman and Greville, and I would submit that these and other classical-Christian poets of the Renaissance—whatever their varying poetic power—share a larger, more central, more realistic, and more permanently valid comprehension of the facts of human nature and human life. Wordsworth, like the other romantic poets, stood more or less outside Christianity and had to find a religion for himself; also, he inherited the sentimentalism of the eighteenth century. Though he gave it his own elevated complications and refinements, there was not much room in that doctrine for the sobering conception of man as fallen. If anyone asks, in astonishment, "Why should there be?" it might be said that a conviction of sin is likely to be more conducive to spiritual health than impulses from a vernal wood. One of the chief penalties that attend Wordsworth's kind of thought and feeling—as we see also in Emerson and others—is the loss or attenuation of the sense of evil, the tragic sense. What Wordsworth mourned in "Tintern Abbey" and "Intimations of Immortality" was, to be sure, the loss of what he had lived by, but that was the capacity for sensuous and emotional response to nature.

I am not forgetting that he wrote, with moving power and beauty, of

> the heavy and the weary weight
> Of all this unintelligible world,

though I cannot remember many great poems in which these words find a substantial "objective correlative." I am not forgetting, either, the painful reality of the struggles through which Wordsworth arrived at his belief in nature's beneficent ministry to man. I am only asking if we, who are more concerned with his poetry than his biography, can find there, not merely solace, but a realistic and sustaining consciousness of what we may call the human predicament, or, if you like, original sin. "Intimations of Immortality," beautiful as it is, records a very individual kind of depression and a very individual solution. The loss that Wordsworth felt so intensely is not one that many people can share, nor is the positive gain in which he rejoiced—since our primal sympathy with man is rarely a compensation for our failing responsiveness to nature. And the passage on the six-year-old child as "Mighty Prophet! Seer blest!" is so unreal a fantasy that it may almost vitiate the whole. When we think of Henry Vaughan's "The Retreat," we must—even if we say Vaughan's Christian faith was no more "authentic" than Wordsworth's pseudoplatonism—we must admit that Vaughan's celebration of childish innocence, his grief for sin, and his longing for the pure light of heaven have a more than private validity. If these few remarks are distressingly flat-footed and blind, I can only say that I am not unaware of several recent, sympathetic, and admirable expositions of the ode, Mr. Trilling's among them.[3] And I might add that I would not go nearly so far as Mr. Fairchild in his formidable arraignment of the romantic poets.[4]

As Wordsworth's mythical or mystical view of nature was largely the creation of his own mind, so in a considerable degree his view of man was a mental abstraction or idealization rather imposed upon than drawn from flesh-and-blood humanity. He has a fair amount of poetry or verse about deserted mothers and their offspring, but that theme is not quite a major segment of normal experience. Nor is Wordsworth's abstract vision of life greatly broadened or deepened in other "objective" poems from "Guilt and Sorrow" to "Michael"; with all its beauty and pathos "Michael" is a simple pastoral. How often, we might ask, does Wordsworth make us feel "the fierce dispute Betwixt damnation and impassion'd clay?" To quote Keats is to recall the famous letter in which he said, among other things, that Milton's "Philosophy, human and divine, may be tolerably understood by one not much advanced in years," and that Wordsworth had penetrated more deeply into the human heart.[5] The latter opinion may be true, but Keats shows no sign of having understood *Paradise Lost* apart from its aesthetic qualities, and Milton's central consciousness of the war between good and evil in the world and in the soul of man seems to me to leave Wordsworth nowhere—unless we take in *The Excursion*, and most people do not regard it as an active part of the canon. In short, the ethical Wordsworth tends to see man with the somewhat blurred or farsighted eyes of the mystical Wordsworth. The world of reflection and intuition in which he lives does not except at moments coalesce with our world. To our questionings about man in the universe, man in society, or even man in solitude, Wordsworth does not give much help toward an answer, or toward a realization of the problems.

It may be said, with indignation, that we have no right to expect such help from a poet. But as long as poets speak, and use words that have a meaning, I think we may ask what they mean and where their meaning stands in our scale of values— always remembering, as I hope I am, that we are not judges interpreting a fixed constitution, but that we read poetry because it purifies and enriches our values. It is obvious that Wordsworth's insights came rather from observation of his conscious and unconscious self than from observation of people, that a very high proportion of his writing was a record of his own inner history, his own feelings. He did not, like Chaucer or Shakespeare or Milton, lead the life of a man among men; he was for the most part a brooding recluse, wholly devoted to poetry. And it does not appear that he was actually very intimate with the kind of rural folk he sometimes wrote about, or a very close observer of nature. He was an intensely subjective and introspective poet who had received an illumination that he had to express; but, as I have said, it was a very individual and peculiar illumination, which few can share except in its elementary phases, and which, for Wordsworth himself, excluded large areas of life. He thought of his main theme as "man, the heart of man, and human life," and doubtless many readers would warmly endorse that claim; and some would say, in the up-to-date language of psychology, that the poet created authentic myths and dealt with important states of mind. It seems to me that his main theme of contemplation was not so much man and nature but himself contemplating man and nature. That was not an unimportant subject, but has it a breadth and depth and concreteness that we in our altered world can recognize and respond to? Is Wordsworth's

presentation of his experience of reality and man confined in
general too closely to the terms of his personal creed to transcend it, to carry those larger implications that make poetry
universal? Although Wordsworth's personal beliefs may be less
remote from ours than Mr. Eliot's, are we moved by most of
his poetry as we are by "Four Quartets"?

So far we have been concerned with the Wordsworth of
the great decade, who has always been *the* Wordsworth. But
if it is improper to question the ethical value of impulses from
a vernal wood, it would be still worse not to remember that
the poet himself, through much of that decade, was led to increasing questioning of spontaneous impulse and to increasing
acceptance of inward discipline and order, to a new vision of
reality. One early product of such a mood was "Resolution and
Independence." Two years later came the very explicit "Ode
to Duty," in which, with a nostalgic tribute to those whose
spontaneous love and joy are an unerring light, Wordsworth
recognizes his need of a stronger control than blind trust in
feeling. And then, in the "Character of the Happy Warrior"
and "Elegiac Stanzas," his embracing of the law of reason and
conscience was emotionally strengthened by grief for the death
of his brother—"A deep distress hath humanised my soul."
The word "humanised" seems to imply an admission that there
had been something inhuman in his detached serenity, and
that the religion of nature was no very sure support against the
real sorrows of mankind. We cannot pursue Wordsworth's
ethical development through further poems, including *The
Excursion,* and can only say that his half-Stoic, half-Christian
appeal to self-discipline was the transitional stage between his
earlier trust in pure feeling and his later more or less orthodox
Christianity. But there is again the fact that "the poetry of
Wordsworth" means, with a few exceptions, the poetry of his
happy faith in nature and man; and some readers, even devout
admirers, so dislike the "Ode to Duty," *Laodamía,* and similar
poems that they would say Wordsworth had only put off the
old man to put on the old woman. Whatever his poetical fate,
it does not seem necessary to conclude, for poets in general,
that the attainment of moral wisdom means the end of poetry.
As regards Wordsworth himself, the poetry of his great decade
might have been greater if more of it had been born of conflict
between the ideals of "unchartered freedom" and order. As it

was, much of the poetry we have cherished was the outpouring of a too simple harmony of soul.

If Wordsworth is not an active force in our time (and the mainly negative evidence suggests that he is not), we have looked at some of the possible reasons, especially what may be thought the nebulous quality of his mysticism and of his sentimental ethics, and the really very limited range of experience that he explores. Most or all of what I have said may be quite wrongheaded—though I did not fully realize when I began to take stock of my opinions that I was cast for the sour role of devil's advocate or counsel for the prosecution. However, Wordsworth is not likely to be injured, and mine may be a *felix culpa* if it arouses ardent opposition. I shall gladly be a martyr in so good a cause—provided that those who kindle the fire will take oath that the poetry of Wordsworth is one of their most frequent and precious companions. In going further than I expected to in discussing possible barriers between Wordsworth and us, I have not, I may say, given an altogether fair account of even my own reactions and the balance cannot be redressed in a limited space. But I should like to make a beginning.

If we common readers were compiling our own Wordsworth anthology, it would probably be a much smaller selection than Arnold made or than textbooks offer. There are many short poems, such as those addressed to flowers and birds, which make pleasant reading but which I at least could spare. We must have a few of the narrative and reflective poems, and of course "Tintern Abbey" and "Intimations of Immortality." We probably read *The Prelude* more as a document than as a poem, and the choice of passages would have to be left to individual discretion; but one might venture to ask if more than fractions of the work can be called great poetry. *The Excursion* —which, I may remark, I have gone through much oftener than Francis Jeffrey and most modern readers—yields a few fine bits, such as that on the Greek religion of nature and some on reason and discipline. And the shorter poems on this last theme, which were referred to before, I should keep, not without misgivings as to whether Wordsworth's "new light" is always carried alive into the heart by passion.

For the rest, the poetry that seems to me the finest, that speaks to us most directly, is mainly of two kinds. One kind or group comprises some short poems in which nature is sub-ordinated to humanity and in which there is little or no phil-osophizing. Of these "The Solitary Reaper" might stand as a perfect example. Here the slightest of rural incidents, which could have occurred in any country in any age, is not artificially heightened but simply realized, with a power of verbal and rhythmical suggestion that is at once homely and rich, concrete and magical. And to that may be added some other pieces of similar timeless and "commonplace" universality, such as the best of the Lucy poems.

The other group embraces a good many of the sonnets, those on Milton, on British ideals of the past and sins of the present, on Toussaint L'Ouverture, and kindred subjects, and some on various themes, from the sight of London at sunrise to mutability. In the public sonnets Wordsworth speaks, not with the voice of a bird watcher, but in the ringing tones of a man among men, a man whose magnanimous idealism and pro-found anxiety entitle him to deal with nations and great events. Whatever the poet's debt to Milton, this poetry springs from real conflict and has massive strength. In these heroic sonnets, and in others of quieter nobility, Wordsworth is in line with the great poets back through Milton to the ancients. Because he has here a sober consciousness of the facts of human nature and life, he earns the right to celebrate man's unconquerable mind; he does make us feel that we are greater than we know.

Notes

1. *Memorial Verses*, pp. 42–57.
2. Parts of this paragraph are borrowed from *Science and English Poetry*, by Douglas Bush (New York, 1950).
3. *The Liberal Imagination* (New York, 1950), pp. 129–59.
4. *Religious Trends in English Poetry*, Volume III: 1780–1830 (New York, 1949).
5. Letter to John Hamilton Reynolds, May 3, 1818.

Thomas M. Raysor

4 · The Themes of Immortality and Natural Piety in Wordsworth's Immortality Ode

THERE IS a well-known note in A. C. Bradley's *Oxford Lectures on Poetry* (pp. 139–41) which defines Wordsworth's "sense or consciousness of 'immortality'" as "at once a consciousness that he (in some sense of that word) is potentially infinite, and a consciousness that 'he' belongs to, is part of, is the home of, or *is*, an 'active principle' which is eternal, indivisible, and the 'soul of all the worlds.'" Bradley quotes (very incorrectly) three passages from *The Excursion*[1] as evidence that we "remain entirely outside Wordsworth's mind" if we read "immortality" without extending the conception to mean infinity, and quotes again from *The Prelude* a passage to illustrate "the mind's infinity or immortality," as if the concepts are not merely related but synonymous.

No one will argue that Wordsworth was a representative "of that false secondary power / By which we multiply distinctions." The vague outlines of his abstract terms are inevitable in the philosophic poetry of one to whom, as to Coleridge, "the unity of all hath been revealed." And everyone who reads Wordsworth will probably agree that his conception of immortality was one thing in childhood, another in poetic maturity (when he seems to think of the finite soul as at least a sharer in infinity), and still another as he gradually becomes increasingly orthodox in religion, with much wavering within these broad outlines of his development, as with other men. But Bradley embarrasses the reader when he says that he "pur-

Reprinted by permission of the author and the Modern Language association of America from *PMLA*, LXIX (1954), 861–75.

posely" uses "vague alternative terms" for a definition of immortality which seems to offer the part as an alternative for
the whole. Wordsworth often thinks of the mind as a part
of, a sharer in, infinity, and therefore immortal, as Bradley's
quotations show; but to think of the mind as infinity is to
think of it as God, not as the human mind.[2] And the particular passages which Bradley cites do not by any means
support an identification of immortality and infinity in Wordsworth's poetry, however closely they may be related. Such study
of the Concordance as I have made supplies no better evidence, though I should be grateful to anyone who would
undertake a complete analysis of such concepts in Wordsworth's cloudy and baffling metaphysical idealism. Even when
he uses loose spatial figures of speech for temporal concepts,
as in the Immortality Ode, the relation of the immortal soul
to the infinity of which it is a part is not wholly that of a
wave to the ocean, because the soul has its finite, individual
self-consciousness through life on earth, though even on earth
it has also, at the same time, its relation to the infinite. And I
feel that some evidence, and rather full evidence, should be
offered before one assumes that Wordsworth at any time gave
up completely the concept of a finite personal soul after death,
or accepted the idea of the annihilation of personal identity
and self-consciousness by absorption into the infinite. Perhaps
he ought to have done so, if he had followed his thought to the
end, but Wordsworth was far from being a systematic idealist
philosopher. He was a poet who used philosophical or religious
concepts only as they formed part of his intuitive experience.

Bradley himself does not attempt to make the obvious application of his thesis to the Immortality Ode, but his great
influence has caused others to do so in ways which seem to me
to distort Wordsworth's intention and adapt his thought to
that of the later British idealism of Bosanquet and F. H.
Bradley, or even to the naturalism of our own time. Beatty remarks, for instance, that "The 'immortality' in this poem is
not the theological term which signifies endlessness of life, but
the infiniteness of the human consciousness," [3] as if for Wordsworth the immortal soul is itself infinity rather than a partaker
of the infinity from which it comes. And, for very different
reasons, Trilling says that "In only a limited sense is the Ode
a poem about Immortality." [4] He thinks instead that it is a

poem about "growing up," and he develops in a naturalistic Freudian frame of reference an interpretation of the poem which is related to Beatty's analysis of Wordsworth's progress from childhood through youth to maturity. He regards the experiences of Wordsworth's childhood not as intimations of immortality, or as intimations of infinity, but as psychological illusions which the poet outgrows, like the religious intuitions of Freud's poet-friend—the "oceanic sense" of the infinite— which Freud felt that he could explain away.

These opinions are errors, I think, but they are not easy to refute from evidence in the text of the poem. They may perhaps be suggested by a legitimate objection to the convenient shortened title of the poem, which I myself have used in referring to it as the Immortality Ode. Surely, one may say, the theme of immortality is not directly treated. But the visionary gleam, the glory and the dream of childhood, which once rested upon nature but does so no more, is an intimation of the child's nearness to God, who is our home, whose glory makes possible the celestial light in which every common sight is clothed. Thus it is an *intimation* of immortality, like "those obstinate questionings / Of sense and outward things" of Wordsworth's trances of metaphysical idealism in childhood. If nearly all of the poem is given to *intimations* of immortality from recollections of early childhood rather than to immortality itself, which is mentioned only briefly, still immortality is the end to which these intimations lead and is the ultimate meaning of the whole poem. The title is not the consequence of confusion in the mind of Wordsworth, but an attempt to clear up confusion in the mind of others, after Wordsworth and his friends had read the early reviews. Henry Crabb Robinson takes credit for it, saying that the Ode "had no title till I urged the necessity of it, to guide the reader to a perception of its drift." [5]

The brief direct references to the theme of immortality are more specific, I think, than Beatty's comment would suggest. When Wordsworth apostrophizes the child, "over whom thy Immortality / Broods like the Day," I should say that he certainly means immortality rather than infinity, because it is exactly at this point in early versions of the Ode that Wordsworth speaks of the child as one

> To whom the grave
> Is but a lonely bed without the sense or sight

Of day or the warm light,
A place of thought where we in waiting lie.[6]

Though this image was withdrawn after Coleridge stigmatized
it as "frightful" and "horrid" in *Biographia Literaria*, it is invaluable as evidence that for the moment at least Wordsworth
was thinking of an individual immortality which even took the
form of resurrection of the body. And later, when he is comforted in maturity by glimpses of "that immortal sea / Which
brought us hither," I should say that the symbol of the sea is
the symbol of infinity as life without end, of which the soul of
the child is a part.[7] The part is not identical with the whole.
It may indeed be merged with the whole without individual
identity, both before and after life on earth, but if so, one is
drawing conclusions from a figure of speech which is used
again later in the beginning of the first essay *Upon Epitaphs*,
with no such implications. In the essay *Upon Epitaphs* the figure is varied so that the ocean of infinity is both the origin and
destination of the individual stream, and one thinks for a
moment "That even the weariest river / Winds somewhere
safe to sea," in Wordsworth's essay as in Swinburne's "Garden
of Proserpine." But Swinburne immediately draws the conclusion that the soul is swallowed up by the sea and gains "Only
the sleep eternal / In an eternal night." This does not seem to
be the end of the soul either in Wordsworth's poem or his
essay. And in the poem the grand but terrible implications of
Wordsworth's figure of speech are balanced, or I should think,
even nullified by the image of death as sleep in the grave.

These are the only lines of the poem in which Wordsworth uses the word "immortal" or "immortality"; yet surely
when he finds consolation and strength "In the soothing
thoughts that spring / Out of human suffering," these thoughts
are explained by the following line as "the faith that looks
through death," and no one doubts that this is the hope of immortality. In this particular context, after what has just been
said, I suppose that even the added consolation in the next line
of "years that bring the philosophic mind" means not merely
Stoic fortitude, but rather the discipline of Christian resigna-
tion based on the hope of immortality. So in the "Elegiac
Stanzas," Wordsworth welcomes "fortitude and patient cheer,"
which are a paraphrase of "the philosophic mind," and then
passes on at once to the reason, in the theme of immortality—

"Not without hope we suffer and we mourn." Wordsworth's "philosophic mind" is that of the Christian philosopher who perceives through reflection what the child perceived intuitively, that is, the immortality of the soul.

II

Though the argument from the text must end here, the argument from Wordsworth's comments on his poem presents so much and so familiar evidence that one is ashamed to repeat it, and wonders why that should be necessary. One must suppose that the evidence is discounted because it does not seem to be sufficiently supported by the text, or perhaps because it is later than the poem, and possibly warped by Wordsworth's increasing orthodoxy in middle life and old age. I have argued that the text does support the title; and I should argue also that though Wordsworth speaks again of the subject only somewhat later, after his brother's death, or even late in life, he refers his conviction of immortality to early childhood, as in the note on the Ode which he dictated to Miss Fenwick: "Nothing was more difficult for me in childhood than to admit the notion of death as a state applicable to my own being." And he refers to the rhetorical question of the first stanza of "We Are Seven." "A simple child. . . . What should it know of death?" He immediately guards against the possibility that his childish conviction should be explained away as rising merely from feelings of "animal vivacity," as indeed his own phrase (or rather, Coleridge's) would suggest. No, his difficulty with the conception of death came "from a sense of the indomitableness of the spirit within me"; and he goes on to speak of his childish brooding over stories of the translation of Enoch and Elijah to heaven without suffering death. Even in his evasive apology for the heresy of pre-existence in the Ode he recurs to "our instincts of immortality," and finally speaks of "this Poem on the 'Immortality of the soul.'" In all these repeated references to the theme, Wordsworth not only makes clear how much weight and value he gives to it, but describes the convictions of childhood as faith in the permanence of self-conscious individual identity. No annihilation of the individual consciousness, merged in infinity, is compatible with the emphasis of the Fenwick note and though the note was dictated in the orthodoxy of old age and refers

chiefly to childhood, it refers to childhood in its bearing on
the meaning of the great Ode.

In like manner, his letter of December 1814 to Mrs. Clarkson says that "This poem rests entirely upon two recollections of childhood; one that of a splendour in the objects of
sense which is passed away; and the other an indisposition
to bend to the law of death, as applying to our own particular case. A reader who has not a vivid recollection of these
feelings having existed in his mind in childhood cannot understand that poem." [8] It is interesting to observe that here
he does not mention pre-existence as a possible explanation
of the early splendor of the senses or as an argument for
immortality, and that he says nothing of another recollection
of childhood, the trances of idealism which he explained not
only to Miss Fenwick but to R. P. Graves and Bonamy Price.[9]
Perhaps these striking omissions may indicate the relative importance in Wordsworth's mind of the various themes. But
if this is so, the emphasis upon the childish conviction of
immortality, which is clear in the Fenwick note and the letter
to Mrs. Clarkson, is not equally clear in the poem, at least
after the deletion of the passage which refers to the grave
as "A place of thought where we in waiting lie."

It is certainly quite clear in "We Are Seven"; and the
reference to "We Are Seven" in the Fenwick note to the
Ode justifies Dowden and later editors in calling attention to
the passage in the first essay *Upon Epitaphs* in which Wordsworth unmistakably refers to "We Are Seven" in affirming
the conviction of immortality in childhood. "If we look back
upon the days of childhood, we shall find that the time is
not in remembrance when, with respect to our own individual
Being, the mind was without this assurance [that some part
of our nature is imperishable]. . . . Forlorn, and cut off from
communication with the best part of his nature, must that
man be, who should derive the sense of immortality, as it
exists in the mind of a child, from the same unthinking gaiety
or liveliness of animal spirits with which the lamb in the
meadow, or any other irrational creature is endowed; who
should ascribe it, in short, to blank ignorance in the child;
to an inability arising from the imperfect state of his faculties
to come, in any point of his being, into contact with a notion
of death; or to an unreflecting acquiescence in what has been
instilled into him." [10]

The editors refer to the passage just quoted in illustration of the Immortality Ode instead of "We Are Seven," to which it evidently alludes, apparently because it refers to "We Are Seven" in almost exactly the same way as the Fenwick note on the Ode. Even without the similarity to the Fenwick note the passage would be worth quoting as an illustration of Wordsworth's childish convictions, which are certainly among the "intimations" of immortality in the Ode. And one might add that the passage from the essay *Upon Epitaphs* has a peculiar appropriateness from the relation of the Ode to Wordsworth's classification of his poems. After the "Poems Referring to the Period of Old Age" come the "Epitaphs and Elegiac Pieces," and after them, the Ode. So one passes from the poetry of old age to the poetry of death and finally to the poetry of life after death, as in Tennyson's poems one comes at the end to "Crossing the Bar."

III

Let us suppose then that both the text of the poem and Wordsworth's comments upon it indicate that Wordsworth was right when he named the poem by its full title, "Intimations of Immortality from Recollections of Early Childhood." This is certainly the subject of the poem as a whole, I think, and I submit that other interpretations of its meaning are errors. Yet they are sometimes merely errors of emphasis, since a poem of such intellectual amplitude carries with it a complex of various experiences capable of independent development, such as the visionary splendor of the senses in childhood, the presumption of pre-existence, the childish trances of idealism, and the Christian fortitude of sober maturity. These are all intimations of immortality except the last, and even Wordsworth's stoicism is something more than naturalistic human fortitude, since it is based on hopes of the life of the soul after death. But there is still another major theme which everyone thinks of at once because it appears both in the epigraph of three lines at the beginning of the poem and in the concluding stanza, thus receiving from Wordsworth himself an emphasis which may easily become overemphasis in his interpreters. This is not immortality or even an intimation of immortality, but the "natural piety," as Wordsworth calls it in the epigraph, which reverently cherishes and hopes to preserve in maturity the childish ecstasy in the presence of

nature. It is essentially the same as "the primal sympathy /
Which having been must ever be," of the Ode, and is the
continuation in maturity of

> those first-born affinities that fit
> Our new-born existence to existing things

in Wordsworth's description of childhood in *The Prelude*
(1, 555–56).

But to recognize the return at the end of the poem to
this theme is by no means to say that natural piety tends in
any way to subordinate the childish intimations of immortality of all the earlier stanzas; or that it is a repetition at the
end of the Ode of the development from childhood to maturity which Wordsworth describes in the Tintern Abbey
poem; or that it is a growing up beyond the illusions of childish visions to a mature conception of human tragedy. Such
views of the last stanza in the Ode seem to me to introduce
the idea of spiritual progress instead of the idea of permanence in the midst of change, which is fundamental in "natural piety," and therefore in the Ode.

To argue the point one must look closely at both the
epigraph and the concluding stanza, and the epigraph must
be considered not only as it appears at the beginning of the
Ode, but also in its original position as the last three lines
of the little poem which Dorothy Wordsworth called "The
Rainbow":

> My heart leaps up when I behold
>   A rainbow in the sky:
> So was it when my life began;
> So is it now I am a man;
> So be it when I shall grow old,
>   Or let me die!
> The child is father of the Man;
> And I could wish my days to be
> Bound each to each by natural piety.

When one rereads the little poem as a whole, one sees
immediately the difference in mood from the great Ode, though
we know that the Ode was begun only one day later. "The
Rainbow" may hint at fears for the future, but it is much
more confident in tone than the elegiac Ode and admits no
such loss of the glory of childhood as Wordsworth recognizes
in the Ode. Presumably this is the reason for using only the

last three lines to introduce the Ode. But the necessary omission of the preceding lines has partly obscured his meaning. They are indispensable as a clear statement of "the primal sympathy / Which having been must ever be," that is, of the childish delight in nature which must be preserved by "natural piety." Without them the three lines used for the epigraph have no specific reference to nature and merely affirm the deeper continuity of human personality. And the earlier lines of the little poem are useful for another and more important reason, because they show that Wordsworth felt no such mature superiority to childhood as that which he expressed in the Tintern Abbey poem. The continuity of human personality which is to be preserved by natural piety is not a development to higher forms of experience.

As the theme is stated in the epigraph to the Ode it is not immediately supported, since in the first four stanzas Wordsworth's days are clearly not "Bound each to each by natural piety." Instead "there hath past away a glory from the earth," and Wordsworth grieves over the loss of the visionary splendor of the senses which he has once possessed. But this splendor is the light which we bring with us from our life with God and slowly fades as we become more and more remote from childhood. Only the child is "Haunted for ever by the eternal mind" of which it is still a part and lives in the consciousness of its immortality. Nevertheless "nature yet remembers" in maturity the childish trances of perception in which the life of the mind is the only reality, in which outward things fall away and seem to vanish into immateriality:

> Those shadowy recollections . . .
> Are yet a master-light of all our seeing.[11]

By their light we can see even in maturity, and "Our Souls have sight of that immortal sea" of eternal life.

Then the poem turns back to the splendid visions which have been lost, and from this point one must look more closely at details of the thought. The discarded variant readings of the MSS help repeatedly to keep clear the course of thought. "What though it be past the hour / Of splendour in the grass, of glory in the flower" [12] is the reading of MS "M," emphasizing more than the final text the decline of sensibility in maturity. "We will grieve not," Wordsworth says firmly, and finds consolation where he can. He remembers first the "primal sympathy" which must still exist, even if it has lost its glory. The glory suggests the ineradicable kinship of the soul with the life of God, and the hope of immortality. He finds strength

> In the soothing thoughts that spring
> Out of human suffering;
> In the faith that looks through death.

And finally this support of hope encourages the soul in the fortitude of religious reflection.

He goes on then in the last stanza with the natural piety which preserves the primal sympathy in maturity, rather than with the hope of immortality. But it must be remembered that the primal sympathy is itself one of the intimations of immortality and therefore suggests immortality even in this last stanza.

Though less splendid, the love of nature is more habitual, and Wordsworth considered for a moment whether he might even say "higher": "I only have relinquished one delight / To acknowledge under you [under Nature] a higher sway." But in the final version of the poem he abandoned the comparison, and thus perhaps consciously refused to disparage the glory of childhood as a lower level of experience, as Beatty's interpretation of the poem would demand. He does, however, assert rashly and perhaps inconsistently that he loves the brooks "Even more"; and insists, though now less confidently, that the dawn "Is lovely yet."

Then comes a curious turn of thought, almost without transition in the final text. The course of thought should lead from dawn to sunset as illustrations of the *habitual* sway of nature, but the symbolic sadness of sunset diverts Wordsworth to a quite different theme, through a transition which appears only in the manuscripts: [Dawn]

> Is lovely yet;
> Nor (Not) unaccompanied with blithe desire
> Though many a serious pleasure it inspire.

No one would wish to restore this rather awkward passage, yet the disappearance of the "serious pleasure" of dawn, which is too vaguely mentioned to be identified,[13] furnishes the transition to the "sober" coloring of sunset darkening into night and therefore to its symbolism of "man's **mortality.**" The theme of natural piety which preserves the past in the present by the "habitual" sway of nature is now entirely dropped for the symbol of sunset:

> The Clouds that gather round the setting sun
> Do take a sober colouring from an eye
> That hath kept watch o'er man's mortality.

So the poem returns to the theme of fortitude again, and I should suggest also to the theme of immortality, for the reference to "mortality" is surely not contradictory of Wordsworth's thought. It is the mortality of the flesh, which inevitably implies, in this poem, immortality of the soul: to speak of mortality here is also to speak of immortality.

Commentators do not seem to agree with each other on the exact meaning of the next line: "Another race hath been, and other palms are won." What are the two races, and what are the distinct palms of victory in each? I should say that the reference to sunset indicates that another race has been run on earth, like the race of the sun from dawn to sunset, with its palms of victory in sad human experience and sympathy, following the first race of life in heaven as part of God's life, with its rewards of blessedness, a blessedness retained on the earth only by the child. Probably, I think, one should add to rewards of victory in earthly life the hope of immortality, considering what has been said of sunset and the mortality of the flesh, but the humanitarian tenderness of sad experience is more clearly indicated by the succeeding lines:

> Thanks to the human heart by which we live,
> Thanks to its tenderness, its joys, and fears,
> To me the meanest flower that blows can give
> Thoughts that do often lie too deep for tears.

IV

These are the thoughts that take one back again to the epigraph, to a love of nature in maturity which is bound to the love of nature in childhood by natural piety. Here at the end is the one passage in the Ode in which one can return to the great Tintern Abbey poem for a legitimate parallel and commentary. The "human heart by which we live," with "its tenderness, its joys, and fears" in the Ode corresponds to "The

still, sad music of humanity" of the poem written near Tintern
Abbey, for which Coleridge gives the most pertinent interpretation. Coleridge's comment says that "as the poet hath himself well described in his lines 'on re-visiting the Wye,' manly
reflection and human associations had given both variety, and
an additional interest to natural objects, which in the passion
and appetite of the first love they had seemed to him neither
to need or permit." [14] In "thoughtless youth," the "passion"
and "appetite" for nature "had no need of a remoter charm /
By thought supplied," Wordsworth tells us in the poem. These
unthinking, somewhat irresponsible joys in sensation and emotion in youth are not at all equal in glory to the "celestial
light" which Wordsworth remembers in the Ode, but they
share the same fate and disappear in manhood. And part of
the consolation for the loss of such "aching joys" is like part
of the consolation in the Ode for loss of the glory of childhood. "The still, sad music of humanity" which the mature
man can hear suggests the humanitarian thoughtfulness of
pity, which has power "To chasten and subdue" all irresponsible ecstasy, and leads to a sense of a spiritual presence in
nature as well as in man. If there is such a spiritual harmony
in the mind of man and in nature, then the sadness of human life is "still," not ultimately "harsh" or "grating," though
Wordsworth is not yet ready in the Tintern Abbey poem to
suggest a healing Christian Providence or the consolation of
return of the soul to its life in the life of God, as in the Ode.
If this is the course of mature thought in the Tintern Abbey
poem, it is easy to see that what Coleridge calls "manly reflection" gives additional interest to nature through "human
associations," chiefly through the symbolism in nature of life
and death, and the suggestion of infinity.

It is here that we return to the great Ode. The striking
peculiarity of Coleridge's comment on "The still, sad music
of humanity" is that he supposes Wordsworth to value the
tenderness of human sympathy not so much for itself (as in
the "Elegiac Stanzas Suggested by a Picture of Peele Castle
in a Storm") as because of the richness of human associations
which it gives to the love of nature. In the Ode this different
love of nature in maturity is far from being "Abundant recom-
pense" for what has been lost, as in the Tintern Abbey poem,
and is indeed profoundly elegiac in tone; but at least one

can say that there is gain as well as loss. The gain can be
set against the loss and binds the poet's days and years each
to each throughout life. The gain in mature human tenderness is not a substitute which takes the place of the love of
nature, whether inferior or superior; it is a means to continue
the love of nature in a different form.

This conclusion is to my mind the most difficult part of
the poem, partly because I cannot accept the thought from
parallels in my own experience. Neither this theme nor the
theme of intimations of immortality means to me as much
as other themes in the poem which suggest the typical romantic, idealistic metaphysics, and I suspect that the same
difficulty causes others also to overemphasize what I regard
as lesser elements of the thought. But there are anticipations
and even verbal echoes of the conclusion of the Ode elsewhere in Wordsworth's poetry which are so suggestive as to
furnish the strongest evidence of the poet's intention.

One of these, which De Selincourt says is "an 'overflow'
from 'Nutting' and was written in the summer of 1798," [15]
tells us that the man who feels the wholesome teaching of
nature will bless "His teacher, that *even meanest objects* [16]
. . . insensibly will cleave / To his affections," and he will
cherish nature as "A temple, made for reverence and love."
Such habitual tenderness cannot fail in the end to soften his
heart for human beings as well as for nature.[17] And so it is
in another passage, much better known because it comes from
one of the noblest speeches of the philosopher Pedlar of *The
Excursion,* who admonishes the Solitary to discipline his melancholy through the love of nature. From "The joy of that
pure principle of love" he will learn later to "seek for objects
of a kindred love / In fellow-natures," that is, in other human
beings like himself:

> And further; by contemplating these Forms
> In the relations which they bear to man, . . .
> Trust me, that for the instructed, time will come
> When they will meet no object but may teach
> Some acceptable lesson to their minds
> Of human suffering, or of human joy.[18]

The remote verbal parallel to the "meanest flower that
blows" ("no object but may teach / Some acceptable lesson")
is in itself almost unrecognizable without the general parallel

of thought to the discarded passage from "Nutting" which
I have already quoted. And the general line of thought in
both passages is "the love of nature leading to the love of
man," as in *The Prelude*, not the love of man enriching the
love of nature, as in the conclusion to the Ode and in Coleridge's comment on "the still, sad music of humanity." But
this striking reversal of direction is scarcely a real change. Has
not the theme always been the interaction of the love of nature and the love of man, each reinforcing the other? If the
love of nature teaches the love of man, does not Wordsworth
love nature more for that teaching? He is able now to see the
glories of nature under the sign of human experience.

Some such interaction of human affections seems to be
suggested by an obscure passage in the reply to "Mathetes"
in *The Friend* of 1809–1810, in which Wordsworth gives an
instance of "nature teaching seriously and sweetly through the
affections, melting the heart." It is a memory from childhood
of the dying glow of an extinguished candle, which seems to
the child a symbol of human mortality, like the sunset of the
great Ode. Later in life, in maturity, "the image of the dying
taper may be recalled and contemplated, though with no sadness in the nerves, no disposition to tears, no unconquerable
sighs, yet with a melancholy in the soul, a sinking inward
into ourselves from thought to thought, a steady remonstrance,
and a high resolve." [19]

This strange conclusion, which gives such exaggerated
weight to a very inadequate symbol of death, seems to me
to be one of the most suggestive parallels in Wordsworth to
the "Thoughts that do often lie too deep for tears," and this
taper is perhaps the same taper which appears in a rejected
passage of *The Prelude*, apparently written in 1804, at a time
when the Ode was in Wordsworth's mind. Wordsworth speaks
there of the power of nature "to nourish in the heart / Its
tender sympathies" . . . "*The commonest* images of nature—
all, / No doubt, are with this object charg'd,—a path, / A
taper burning through the gloom of night." [20] But the taper
in *The Friend*, unlike that in *The Prelude* MS, softens the
heart by its symbolism of death, by a specifically *human* association which is not necessary at all to the general softening
and harmonizing influence of natural images elsewhere in
Wordsworth's poetry. It comes nearer, then, to the thought

of the Ode, since now love of man leads back to the love of nature, enriched by the association of human sympathies.

The natural piety of the concluding stanza seems then to reassert the love of nature of childhood, lacking the glory and the gleam to be sure, but acquiring in their place inestimably rich human associations for every natural object. The deep attachment to nature of the mature man is a consolation for the loss of the ecstasy of childhood. But it is attained through associations of nature with sad human experience, and that sadness itself requires consolations of the sort which Wordsworth finds in *The Excursion*. These are more fully developed in the fourth book of the poem than anywhere else, but the nearest of the parallels to the Immortality Ode is in a very late addition to the story of the Ruined Cottage in Book I. The Wanderer finds consolation in Christian faith for the grief which the story of Margaret gives his friend. Margaret herself had

> learned, with soul
> Fixed on the Cross, that consolation springs,
> From sources *deeper far than deepest pain* . . .
>   (I, 936–38; my italics)

The phrase is a specifically Christian echo of the thoughts that do often lie "too deep for tears," and could scarcely have been written by the poet without raising the memory of his own Ode. In both the Ode and *The Excursion*, the mind sinks through pain to a level of thought deeper than pain; but in 1845, when the passage quoted from *The Excursion* appears first in print, the deeper level is that of Christian faith and hope. In the Ode it might possibly be the same, since it is after all the Immortality Ode. But I hesitate to argue the point, as I have before, for in this context of the last stanza, nothing more is directly suggested than the softening of the heart to sympathy by the love both of nature and of man. And even in *The Excursion*, the Christian consolation is a late addition. In the 1798 MS version of this part of *The Excursion* and even in the printed text until 1845 [21] Wordsworth sought for consolations in nature, but only in the impersonal, impassive beauty which makes one forget personal grief and even individual personality.

In all of these vague parallels which seem to me to illustrate the characteristic quality of Wordsworth's thought in the end of the last stanza, I have turned away from the theme of immortality in the Immortality Ode, as I think Wordsworth himself turned away. But does the parallel with "the still, sad music of humanity" in the Tintern Abbey poem mean that the great Ode follows a comparable course of thought, as Beatty thinks; or that it is a poem about "growing up," of maturing beyond childish illusions as Trilling thinks? I find it difficult to accept either view. Childhood in the Ode is not disparaged as a time of "the coarser pleasures of my boyish days / And their glad animal movements." It is not even regarded as a period of divine illusions, but rather of celestial insight into reality. The human tenderness of maturity is not an advance beyond childish visions but a consolation for the loss of the glory in nature, which in some sort compensates for that loss by a different love of nature— a love of nature which is deepened by human associations. Perhaps also it is deepened by the hopes of immortality which are suggested by the human fear of death and by the whole preceding thought of the poem, the intimations of immortality. In that case the "Thoughts that do often lie too deep for tears" are the whole poem. They are the meditative pathos which Wordsworth distinguished from ordinary human pathos in the "Essay Supplementary to Preface" in 1815: "a sadness which has its seat in the depths of reason, to which the mind cannot sink gently of itself—but to which it must descend by treading the steps of thought." [22]

Notes

1. *Excursion* IV, 738–39, I, 227–28, IV, 1189. The last of these is simply misquoted, since the line reads "Far-stretching views into eternity," not "far-stretching views of immortality," as Bradley says. The second also is misquoted: "All things among the mountains breathed immortality" should read "All things, responsive to the writing, there / Breathed immortality"; and "the writing" is the Bible, "the volume that displays / The mystery, the life which cannot die," as Wordsworth describes it just before (224–25). The lines immediately following the quotation associate immortality with infinity, with a remote verbal parallel ("the least of things / Seemed infinite") to the conclusion of the Ode. The first quotation is correct, but the succeeding passage (745–62) clearly shows that Wordsworth means "immortality," in spite of Bradley's doubts.
2. Wordsworth continually seems to approach and then to draw back from some such conclusion, like Coleridge, but I can think of only one explicit statement of a view like that of Bradley. In this passage Wordsworth speaks of "the one interior life"

—In which all beings live with god, themselves
Are god, Existing in the mighty whole,
As indistinguishable as the cloudless East
At noon is from the cloudless West, when all
The hemisphere is one cerulean blue.

But this striking passage is from an early MS which was never used either for *The Prelude* or *The Excursion* and never printed at all until it appeared in the notes of the De Selincourt edition of *The Prelude* (1926), pp. 512–13. It was certainly not rejected because of its inferiority as poetry. Coleridge suspected that the line in the Ode "Haunted for ever by the Eternal mind" might conceal some such view and pointed out that even Spinoza or Behmen or the ancient pantheists would not "confound the *part, as* a part, with the whole, *as* the whole." Lessing, he says, could not admit "the *possibility* of personality except in a finite Intellect." *Biographia Literaria* (Oxford, 1907), II, 112–13.

3. Wordsworth, *Representative Poems*, ed. Arthur Beatty (New York, 1937), p. 661.

4. Lionel Trilling, *The Liberal Imagination* (New York, 1951), p. 132. The essay on Wordsworth's Ode in this volume is, after Garrod's, the fullest and most ambitious of all treatments of Wordsworth's great poem, but in this article I question some of its views as attempting to adapt Wordsworth to a twentieth-century type of naturalism.

5. *Correspondence of Henry Crabb Robinson with the Wordsworth Circle* (Oxford, 1927), II, 838–39.

6. I suspect that this conclusive passage has been neglected merely because of the figure of speech, which Coleridge questioned in *Biographia Literaria* (Ch. xxii). He not only questioned "the propriety of making a 'master *brood* o'er a slave,' or the *day* brood *at all*," but he also criticized, rather unfairly, the whole apostrophe, including the four lines on the grave, which Wordsworth later omitted in deference to his criticism. In the Fenwick note on the Ode and in the first essay *Upon Epitaphs* Wordsworth answered Coleridge by his comment on "We Are Seven." The child is not unconscious of the "omnipresent Spirit," as Coleridge argued; and the child's belief in immortality does "differ from that of his father and mother, or any other adult and instructed person."

7. I accept most of the interpretation of N. P. Stallknecht in *Strange Seas of Thought* (Durham, N.C., 1945), p. 269, in which the close association of "immortality" and "infinity" is recognized, without the strange identification of the two concepts, as in Bradley's note. This little essay is, I think, of the highest value, but I should argue that it might well be extended by references to different conceptions of immortality at different ages, and specifically in childhood.

8. *Letters of William and Dorothy Wordsworth: The Middle Years*, ed. De Selincourt (Oxford, 1937), II, 619. Cf. Wordsworth's comment to Christopher Wordsworth on his childhood as represented in the Ode: "At that time I could not believe that I should lie down quietly in the grave, and that my body would moulder into dust." Christopher Wordsworth, *Memoirs of William Wordsworth* (1851), II, 476.

9. For very interesting similar experiences in Wordsworth's poetry, see *The Prelude* II, 348–52, and the beautiful little fragment from the Alfoxden notebook printed by De Selincourt and Darbishire, Wordsworth's *Poetical Works* (Oxford, 1940–1949), V, 341 (Appendix B, II, IV). All references to Wordsworth's poetry in this article are to the De Selincourt

and Darbishire edition of the *Poetical Works*, or to the De Selincourt parallel-text edition of *The Prelude* (Oxford, 1926).

The intuition of pre-existence in the Ode does not fall within the limits of this article, but I believe I should refer to the treatment of the subject in *The Mind of a Poet* by R. D. Havens, pp. 79, 306, and to *The Prelude* I, 553–58 (with the important rejected version in De Selincourt's notes, p. 508), and v, 507–22 (a brief version of the Ode).

10. *Poetical Works*, v, 445–46.

11. Here follows in MS "L" (*Poetical Works*, IV, 283) a passage of two lines which shows that "those first affections, / Those shadowy recollections" are the same as "those obstinate questionings / Of sense and outward things, / Fallings from us, vanishings." Trilling suggests that "those first affections" may refer to the description of infancy in *The Prelude*, II, 232–65. But against this one may argue that in the rejected passage "Those first affections"

> Throw off from us, or mitigate, the spell
> Of that strong frame of sense in which we dwell.

They are, therefore, obstinate questionings of sense, not affections of infancy. N. P. Stallknecht discusses the thought of this passage most interestingly in *Strange Seas of Thought*, Appendix to Ch. v, but I should suggest that the "master light of all our seeing" is a repudiation of the concrete universe of which Stallknecht speaks. That universe dissolves and is absorbed into the mind. The experience is then an intimation of immortality, I think, but scarcely to be called "this sense of immortality" (Stallknecht, p. 270).

12. *Poetical Works*, IV, 284. Since all textual variants of the Ode are cited from the De Selincourt and Darbishire edition of the *Poetical Works*, no further specific references need be given.

13. The symbolism of sunset suggests that dawn also is symbolic, symbolic of "recollections of early childhood," and probably even "intimations of immortality from recollections of early childhood."

14. *Biographia Literaria*, ed. Shawcross (Oxford, 1907), I, 58.

15. *Prelude* (1926), p. 592.

16. My italics.

17. *Prelude*, p. 594.

18. *Excursion* IV, 1207–38. This is a passage written some years before the Ode, in early 1798. For the early text, see De Selincourt and Darbishire, v, 400–401.

19. Wordsworth's *Literary Criticism*, ed. Nowell C. Smith, pp. 68–70. Or see the *Friend* of 1818, Second Section, Introduction.

20. *Prelude*, p. 559. My italics.

21. *Poetical Works*, v, 403, 39 (textual notes).

22. *Poetical Works*, II, 428.

Edwin Morgan

5·A Prelude to *The Prelude*

IN HIS LETTER of May 1st, 1805, to Sir George Beaumont announcing the completion of *The Prelude* Wordsworth wrote of the work: "Here, at least, I hoped that to a certain degree I should be sure of succeeding, as I had nothing to do but describe what I had felt and thought." This, as he realized, was a most unusual way of proceeding in any long and important poem; the apparent baring and simplifying of poetic activity implied in the mere description of things previously felt and thought does in fact bristle with hazards and difficulties. What Wordsworth was to do was to take poetry one step further back into the creative chaos, or to make poetry out of material one step nearer the original mass of all his experience. His task was not to describe the growth of a poet's mind, but to make poetry, using as material his recollection of the growth of a poet's mind. "Il n'est pas une recherche du temps passé, mais une oeuvre d'art dont la matière-prétexte est ma vie d'autrefois," as Jean Genet says of his *Journal du Voleur*. However important it may have seemed to him intellectually to be setting down this record, as something significant in itself, it is obvious from the completed work that *The Prelude* came alive under his hands and in the end gave him and us a new kind of poetic utterance in addition to the unprecedented material.

I have called Wordsworth's method a seeming simplification, as compared with the methods the great poets have

Reprinted by permission of the author and the editor from *Essays in Criticism*, Vol. 5, No. 4 (October 1955), pp. 341–53.

normally followed, because at first sight his proposed activity
looks like a concession to weakness: he is not going to exert
himself till his imagination "bodies forth the forms of things
unknown" but simply to tell his readers what he has been
feeling and thinking, and how it has come about, for the
past twenty years. We recall, in support of this initial suspicion, how other great poets begin, as it were, where Wordsworth leaves off. They take for granted, as something superfluous
to discuss, the fact that their minds have known a steady,
enriching, and interesting growth in power and sympathy, and
they lose little breath or time in reminiscence over the incidents which have made them what they are, because they
know that all these incidents have become a part of their
whole consciousness and must of themselves issue out and
rise up in the creative action of writing, causing and forming
their similes and metaphors, and giving their style the stamp
of the past man plunged in the wax of the present. The
material of each individual poet's experience is accepted merely
as the rich ground from which new and hitherto unexperi-
enced forms will arise; it shapes these forms, even in the dramatic poet, but it is the new forms themselves which are of
the first importance to him, not the scattered experiences lying
behind and through them. . . .

This is the attitude characteristic of great poetry; behind
the imagery, staring at us like a lion from a cage, in the
poet's experience, a huge but dimly felt bulk of strength
seen in reserve. The impact of the physical world, through
great poetry, has a tendency to come not directly but as a
component of larger forms whose total effects use it and make
it subservient as imagery. Clearly then, to describe, as Wordsworth said, what he had felt and thought was something very
different from the usual exercise of the imagination in the
best poetry. It was, as I have suggested, a conscious reaching
back to the material, normally left lying in the subconscious
memory, from which poetry takes the basic and (one might
say) primordial elements of its life; and the newness of Wordsworth's attempt lay in his determination to make of that itself a body of poetry, by which the past, with all its feeling
as it then existed, was to be brought into sharp and vivid
recollection. Now since the imagination is one faculty, and
can hardly exercise itself in two disparate activities, Words-

worth was taking an unusual and considerable risk. "I desire
to press in my arms the loveliness which has not yet come
into the world," wrote Stephen Dedalus. Creation normally
concentrates its desire upon some future object still indistinct
in its form, in the making of which countless fragments of
unconsidered experience will be fused, the new whole having
undistinguishable parts, whereas in what Wordsworth proposed creation was to take place at a more primitive level,
with experiences being separated one from another and dis-
tinctly contemplated by a mind intent least of all on combining or embellishing or enriching them. Wordsworth was not
perhaps aware when he began, though his boldness was to be
justified, that his starting point would have been a paradox
for his great predecessors in poetry: he was to *imagine* his
recollections. But imagination is a taking fire of the dead
wood of ordinary thought and feeling, and whatever is described under that light, whether it is new or old, becomes
new in the quality of vitality which informs it and allows it
to enter and illuminate living minds. In most great poetry, in
drama and epic, the poet imagines a series of actions in which
he is not usually himself concerned, and the quality of his
mind is known at second hand through the power of his
statements and imagery; in *The Prelude* the personality of
the poet is everything, and yet the imagination has aroused
itself, sometimes to the highest degree and in sustained
stretches, over happenings and thoughts which in another poet
might furnish the single metaphor of one line. There is little
poetry that would conform to Wordsworth's definition of
"emotion recollected in tranquillity" taken in the strict sense
he intended, but that was the phrase for his own practice,
and it is of great interest to study this "recollection" as a
source of imaginative power, and so of poetry. What is important to discover is the relation of *The Prelude's* theme to
its manifesting of the imaginative power.

   Wordsworth describes the main events of his life, as a
child, at school, at Cambridge, in the Alps, in London, and
in France, in considerable detail and with some reflection on
them; the narrative is sometimes interrupted, but on the
whole preserves its character as a personal history. Within
this framework the central theme, as it emerges nakedly and
purely from the events, is set forth with unmistakable clarity:

the benign influence exerted by nature on the growing faculties of the whole man, the peculiar and perfect adaptation of
nature to man, as of things made to interact, and the emer-
gence of the complemental beauty of man's mind above but
not severed from the beauty of nature. These aspects of the
theme follow the course of the history. At the beginning,
when the poet is a child, what is emphasized is the influence
of natural forms in shaping his imagination and vision; at the
end he has reached a point where the mind and character
have developed a beauty in their own right, strengthened by
human intercourse and sympathy but sustained still and always at the deeper wells of feeling in the presence of natural
objects.

Such was the ultimate concern of the poet. Many events
had to be related, however, and many sequences of thought
followed out, for sincerity and completeness, which were certainly a part of his story but which tended to stultify his
inspiration. These were usually scenes of human bustle and
confusion, like the second-rate description of London streets
in Book VII, and incursions into contemporary history and
political and intellectual comment, as in Books IX–XI. For
the first of these he was personally unsuited (as Lamb's letters
amusingly remind us). His feelings were engaged by the hubbub
of the city crowds and he was not able to write other than me-
chanically and dutifully about what he calls the "perpetual whirl
of trivial objects." These things, not trivial in themselves, and
indeed the center of a huge mass of that very human life
he was investigating, were trivial, disturbing, exasperating, and
meaningless to Wordsworth; simplicity and the sense of order
were wanting, and when they were absent he could not be
at ease. Of the other less-than-successful part, dealing with
"residence in France," it is to be said that much of the material, reflections on theories and public events, was intracta-
ble, and behind the writing of the narrative part of these
books we can often sense a deadening of impulse which seems
to come from his knowledge that he is now to describe not
advances and acquisitions but losses and retreats, the loss of
his simple faith and a retreat from nature, and in such description he was cutting himself off from the two main sources
of his strength. He had placed the books in a commanding
position, and he gave the French matter very extended treat-

ment, yet it appears in his life and can be used in the poem
only as an incident which fortifies the deeper theme existing
before it and victoriously returning after it. It had the great
intellectual importance of being a testing-time for that strength
Wordsworth indicated himself as possessing, his lack (as he
says) of "trepidation for the end of things," but feelings so
troubling to that strength were probably looked back on with
positive distaste and certainly without the necessary fire of
mind. The inadequacy of such determined, labored, and even
pompous writing as we often find in these books shows the
main difficulty of the recollectional method. The imagination
works only sympathetically; it is like the horse you take to
the well but cannot force to drink; and when it is used to
describe things past, its enthusiasm will not spring up unless
what is being described has a lasting and present reality to
the poet's feelings. The result for the reader is boredom, when
the author, forgetting for a time that he must be communica-
tively lively even when recollectionally serious, buries himself
in his photograph album and draws the dead leaves over his
head. In prose, this boredom lurks in the most masterly and
evocative reminiscential writers, such as Proust and Gide; we
cannot be surprised to find it in the blank verse of a serious-
minded poet. Wordsworth had felt and thought deeply about
the French Revolution, but this had sunk down into his mind
and had failed in the end to change the characteristics which
existed before it began, though it gave them perhaps a profounder meaning; and it is those permanent characteristics, as
I must now indicate, that Wordsworth had to learn how to
tap and to use, if his verse was to be raised above the merely
discursive level.

In the first book we find him exploring his theme in a
variety of incidents, and indeed laying down the pattern he
was later to elaborate again and again. There is simple description of the mere physical delight of activity in the open
air, in the skating episode, where pure word-painting of scene
and action in a self-contained form reaches high art; there
is description of an episode simple in itself but illustrative
of the sense of mystery in nature which was important to
Wordsworth, in "A Night-piece" where he speaks of snaring
woodcock in the hills and hearing the strange breathing and
footsteps behind him; and there is the more detailed relation

of an incident which is a powerful incentive to description
but had also a greater significance as showing the early workings of conscience and terror, in the story of the stolen boat.
This last example shows the beginnings of what is going to
be Wordsworth's method: he has some point of his mental
development to make clear, he wants to give it imaginative
utterance, he looks back not along the line of his thoughts
but into the actions he has been engaged in, he finds an incident where he himself in conjunction with nature in some
form was visited or refreshed by the idea in question, and
then the scene he has chosen is described from the viewpoint
of its significance, and becomes alive in the act of writing
because this interlocking of scene and thought is his permanent possession. It is the recollection of emotion, but the
emotion is unabstractable from circumstance; it is the poetry
of time and place, the "faces and places, with the self which,
as it could, loved them" of "Little Gidding." In this first
book Wordsworth gives us his own version of what has just
been said, as if in a careless summing-up of his art: he is
speaking of composition itself, of the memorial process, and
he praises

> those lovely forms
> And sweet sensations that throw back our life,
> And almost make remotest infancy
> A visible scene, on which the sun is shining.

With this should be compared some lines at the very end of
the poem, where he says of the inception of his work:

> Anon I rose
> As if on wings, and saw beneath me stretched
> Vast prospect of the world which I had been
> And was; and hence this Song . . .

Nothing could be clearer than this identification, in which
his childhood, and then his entire life, are seen as sunlit vistas
of physical landscape. The one beauty on which his imagination fed was the beauty of nature, and whatever else he
knew to be beautiful, whatever he had to lay before his imagination for working up into poetry, had to be related to natural
objects and seen by the light that shone on them. His subject was the growth of his mind, an abstract and intangible
one for any poet, yet for Wordsworth there was scarcely a
difficulty in that problem which was not solved, apart from

the few "dead" patches already referred to, since at the most important stages of his progress he unerringly directed his imagination towards concrete and living scenes, and in the blaze of feeling which enwrapped his recollection of these he was instantly warmed to an appreciation of his subject adequate for poetry. So it is that for all purposes the inward theme emerges clearly as the influence of nature on human feelings, because for Wordsworth all feelings of worth go back to the early promptings of nature, and even those sympathies which are awakened with a new interest in men themselves are found to have come originally from his first association with such men as work continually close to nature.

(In this connection one is reminded of a strangely and improbably similar forerunner. It is curious to observe how Lucretius, grappling with the intangibles of the *De Rerum Natura*, turns his great and passionate mind towards the same poetic solutions. "The nature of things" becomes "things in nature"; and automaton is given breath; the atoms and their laws grow visible in earth and sky and sea. Compare, for method, *De Rerum Natura*, Book V, 1183 ff, where he describes men's primitive superstitious fear in the face of snow and hail, comets and constellations, thunder and lightning, and strengthened by these physical references bursts out with the lyrical and majestic

O genus infelix humanum . . . !

with *The Prelude*, Book XII, 225 ff, where Wordsworth describes the "visionary dreariness" of the moor, the gibbet, the pool, and the solitary woman walking into the wind, and the full feeling again works itself up to the surface suddenly in his cry

Oh! mystery of man . . . !

In both, there is a rare lyricism of the abstract, reached through the living forms of nature.)

In the presentation of Wordsworth's theme, the more important steps may be noted.

First comes his dedication to poetry in Book IV. The recounting of this great moment of his life, which it was evidently his duty to make an occasion of excellent verse, is initiated with a characteristic care. Just before it, he reminds the reader of his method by evolving an elaborate simile de-

scribing how his recollectional activity "incumbent o'er the
surface of past time" has been like that of a gazer from a
boat into the depths of the water he passes through; it is
a fine example of the suggestive power of a concrete description exactly denoting events which take place at a different
level, in this case within the creating mind. Then comes the
story of the midnight dance, the journey back through the
fields at dawn, and the poet's sense of his destiny and meaning on this earth. What is most remarkable in this passage
is that scarcely any words are required to state the theme of
it in intellectual terms: it is a triumph of symbolic natural
description. After we leave the clamor and gaiety of the dance
behind and move on into the outstandingly evocative forms
of the breaking day, and feel the joy of it, and the sense of
refreshment and reawakening and preparation most aptly completed by the last picture of the laborers going out into the
fields to begin their work, the reason for the whole description becomes so apparent that we know it is Wordsworth
himself who seems just such a laborer meditating his work in
such a dawn, and he needs only a few lines more to confirm
for us the knowledge, in more abstract terms, of his dedication to the labor of verse.

My second example is from Book VI, at the point before the travellers enter the Simplon Pass. Here, the subject
is the tremendous hunger of the imagination, unsatisfied except that it is itself a satisfaction to the soul, after that body
of an invisible world which it surmises from the glimpses
and flashes it has seen through the glory of natural objects:

> With hope it is, hope that can never die,
> Effort, and expectation, and desire,
> And something evermore about to be.

Again, the great passage is led up to and made immediate
and actual by natural description. The traveler, eagerly setting
out after a rest to conquer a new Alpine peak, has in fact
taken the wrong path and must now descend; the Alps have
been crossed, and there is no more climbing to be done; but
his mind feeds on the imagined heights he must leave, and
is loath to accept the fact that its longing cannot be satisfied, while at the same time recognizing that its desire is a
sign of its greatness, that "the passions of men . . . do im-
measurably transcend their objects" (*The Convention of*

Cintra). The whole incident, written in simple narrative style, yet becomes a symbol of considerable strength, because of this correspondence with the intellectual theme which is seen only after the reader has absorbed the influence of nature.

At a third point, in Book VIII, Wordsworth is concerned to relate some of the origins of his interest in his fellow-creatures and the grandeur he feels them to possess. As always, he works from the particular to the general, from one man to many; and from one occupation of man, and from one moment of that man's occupation when everything about it and him seemed to be significant. He describes a shepherd as seen by him at three different times: on the hills looming with his sheep through mist, walking in sudden sunset light, and at a great distance standing at the edge of the horizon. From these appearances, where a man moved into the poet's consciousness clothed with something of nature rather than human rags, even though it was only illusions of light, his imagination was stimulated at an early age to see men as creatures of dignity and power and beauty, which later became an appreciation of the mind:

> hence [he says] the human form
> To me became an index of delight,
> Of grace and honour, power and worthiness.

The mist and the sunset light, and the distance, are in fact the mysteriousness, the radiance, and the remotely-fetched greatness present in Wordsworth's own imagination as he looks on man.

Fourthly, I take the account of the death of Robespierre in Book X, and the release of some of Wordsworth's anxiousness and wretchedness over the failure of the Revolution to be what it set out to be. As before, the mental liberation, here related in the scant words "Robespierre is dead!" is almost imperceptibly won out of the physical; it needed only those words to round off the joy that was already filling his heart from another source. This source, the natural scene of the river estuary, the sun, and the clouded mountain-tops, has a peculiar aptness in the manner of its description. Any such atmosphere, glorious in itself, might have been depicted to show something of a general happiness, but Wordsworth makes it significant by suggesting in the occasion the very thought he is to reveal. This thought is the glad an-

nouncement, from a band of travelers on the beach, of the
death of the French tyrant; and in the preceding description,
where the peaks and clouds are met

> In consistory, like a diadem
> Or crown of burning seraphs as they sit
> In the empyrean,

we see as it were the grand type of such an announcement,
as if the consistory in the clouds had come together as the
fountain and authorization of the news, as if those seraphs
were speaking to the imagination what the human travelers
were next to speak to the intelligence. The echo of the
Satanic consistory at the beginning of *Paradise Regained*, from
which Wordsworth's usage very possibly arose, strengthens the
sense of an assembly of spirits met to give forth some important utterance.

For a fifth example, there is the passage at the end of
Book XII dealing with the death of Wordsworth's father.
What the poet wants to emphasize is the power past incidents have over the mind when they recombine with present
thoughts, rising up like admonitions, not changed in substance from what they were but given poignance by the passage of experience; and what in fact this emphasis amounts
to, though nowhere stated, is an account of the combining
power of past and present feelings in the making of poetry.
The point he has to set out is that natural incidents, events
taking place fully in the outdoor world of nature or closely
associated with that world, are impressed on the memory according to the human feeling of joy or fear or mystery surrounding them, and what seems at the time to be a power
these scenes themselves possess is afterwards known to have
been a reflection of the mind contemplating them by its
"auxiliar light." Again he makes everything grow out of the
concrete setting, and this time there are two stages of emer-
gence from it. First he describes, in simple narrative with
no comment, the desolate wild misty day on the crag where
he is waiting impatiently for a sight of the horses that are
to take him home. Then he tells how, after his father's
death, that scene returned vividly to his mind, with all its
imagery become symbols of bleakness, of loneliness, and of
a more than physical cold. Lastly he recalls more recent visitations of that imagery, mingling suddenly with his ordinary

thoughts for no reason apparent to the intelligence, but effecting in them a grave displacement and disturbance, various according as the emotion in which they first arose is agreeable or harsh to his present feeling. From these hints the reader must take what he can. Wordsworth is probing, in an almost Lucretian fashion, some of the seminal "hiding-places of man's power":

> *sic alid ex alic per te tute ipse videre*
> *talibus in rebus poteris caecasque latebras*
> *insinuare omnis et verum protrahere inde.*
> (I, 407–409)

A sixth and final point is taken from the last book, from the incident of the night on Snowdon. As this is the last great example of the process, so it is also the best; in it Wordsworth now fully explores the potentialities of his chosen method. In the most awesome of all his pictures he builds up the vast prospect of mountain-tops, clouds, moon, and stars, seen like another sea stretching out from Snowdon into the Atlantic main, while from below he hears the roaring of torrents mounting up into the calm. Then with neither hedging nor pause, but rather with a full consciousness of adequacy, he plunges into the correspondence, one of the most audacious images in our poetry and perhaps the surest measure of his own mind. The mountain, with all the forms of clouds and waters surrounding and washing it, in his symbol of "a majestic intellect" raised far above (but still a part of) the plain of ordinary feeling; the clouds and mists which stream out from its summit into the unbounded spaces above the Atlantic are the thoughts sent out by imagination over the bottomless depths of knowledge; and the sound of the torrents underneath is heard as the glad thoughts or poems of the thinker or imaginer issue from the profound unseen wells and springs of his nature. Just as the mountain appeared to lean up and out into space, so it becomes

> the emblem of a mind
> That feeds upon infinity.

And as the image here was particularly large and grand, so the verse which follows it is ample and sustained; and we have in fact not simply the majesty of the mountain, and from that the imagined majesty of the intellect, but finally an example of such majesty as that intellect in action can create. Thus we are first made to feel the power of the circumstantial situation; then we are introduced to the analogy describing the symbol; and in the end we have an application in poetry of the body of what has been said.

In all these examples we can watch Wordsworth coming gradually to a realization of where and how his theme and his power were to be fused. He had to find out, from many kinds of description, from discursive reasoning, and from the analogies of tales and incidents, that anything he was to re-create through recollection must spring from the ground of the natural world, whether in itself a human emotion, an intellectual idea, or an article of faith; and he had to learn, up to the concluding book of *The Prelude,* how to infuse into his natural descriptions that absolute suggestive correspondence which makes them reveal and underscore the theme itself. He had to overcome the abstractness of his subject not by writing of abstractions in thick concrete imagery, as Shakespeare did, but by giving clear brilliant pictures separated from the intellectual content while imaginatively evoking it as something about to be told, this being necessitated by the recollectional method contemplating actual incidents in singleness.

The resulting work, although it is a poem, is a poem of a very peculiar kind. It is rightly named "The Prelude," because it is the prelude to an unwritten poem; but in the business of preparing for that poem it has drained off so much life from the imaginary work still gestating in Wordsworth's mind that we have another case of the child being father of the man—even a child unborn. *The Prelude* is not, therefore, completely unified in either intention or method. It is a record of the past; a creation of poetry out of the interaction of past and present; and a trial flight for imagined poetry of the future. Wordsworth's great victory came from his realization that these three processes had to find, and could find, a common meeting-ground.

6·The Tragic Flaw
in Wordsworth's Philosophy

MUCH CAN BE SAID in defense of the "Ode to Duty," even by a Wordsworth enthusiast whose center of gravity lies deep in *The Prelude*, especially if he reads the "Ode" in the version published in 1807, which, alone of all the editions of the poem, contains as its sixth stanza the following lines:

> Yet none the less would I throughout
> Still act according to the voice
> Of my own wish; and feel past doubt
> That my submissiveness was choice:
> Not seeking in the school of pride
> For "precepts over dignified,"
> Denial and restraint I prize
> No farther than they breed a second Will more wise.

Here duty and enlightened inclination seem capable of reconciliation in the life of the morally successful man. The rigor of a categorical imperative and the "confidence of reason" which such a formula is said to supply are seen as preliminary or probationary supports of the comparatively immature moral agent. At least the above stanza suggests such doctrine. Thus Wordsworth seems to have hesitated between a philosophy of complete stoicism and a reformed version of the humanism of *The Prelude*. As late as 1809, the date of the pamphlet on the *Convention of Cintra*, there remains some trace of the earlier philosophy. The people are in many cases, we are told, greater than their leaders who,

being immersed in political competition, quite fail to understand and often betray them. Wordsworth speaks enthusias-
tically of the foundations of popular virtue, "the instincts of
natural and social man, the deeper emotions, the simpler
feelings, *the spacious range of the disinterested imagination,*
the pride in country for country's sake, when to serve has
not been a formal profession . . ." (italics mine).

But, we may comment, if leaders are not to be trusted, the
people in their homely wisdom ought not to follow them. The
moral is clear. Since the people cannot lead themselves, there
should be no change in social and political life. And Wordsworth was soon to recognize this conclusion, implicit in the
development of his thought. The Cintra pamphlet presents a
truncated form of the philosophy of *The Prelude.* Popular virtue is recognized and similarly explained in both writings; but
in the later work there is obvious a suspicion concerning the
very possibility of great, radical leadership. This is symptomatic
of Wordsworth's development, as he passes from *The Prelude*
to *The Excursion,* where reactionary politics begin to be
clearly manifest. This retreat is inevitable; for unless some individuals are recognized as possessing the right and the strength
to consider themselves as prophetic reformers, distinct from
the multitude, no philosophy of revolution or even of progress
is possible. Nothing could emphasize the development of this
later attitude more sharply than Wordsworth's appreciation
of Burke inserted in *The Prelude,* according to De Selincourt,
not before 1820. Here Wordsworth praises the philosopher who

> Declares the vital power of social ties
> Endeared by Custom; and with high disdain,
> Exploding upstart Theory, insists
> Upon the allegiance to which men are born . . .[1]

In the last book of *The Excursion,* some few years previously, Wordsworth had insisted that "The primal duties shine
aloft—like stars" and that knowledge of right and wrong based
upon reason, imagination, and conscience are vouchsafed alike
to all. But in praising Burke, a few years later, he was willing
to emphasize Custom as the great teacher.

The triumph of the democratic fallacy, with its pernicious
leveling of great minds and small, leads to an inevitable and
ironic conclusion. It finally destroys faith in democracy. If we
are to identify ourselves with "the Kind" and accept the virtues

of endurance, we will come to accept the traditional supports of the humble and gather stoically beneath the orthodox and conservative strongholds of church and state. With these great fortresses of security we shall not care to tamper. In fact, there seems something indecent in any attempt to recast the scheme of things. Of such development in Wordsworth's thinking we are all only too well aware. The extreme illiberalism which resulted in his political thought is too well known to require much comment. His opposition to reform, expressed with timid and suspicious querulousness, is almost identical with the attitude of an aristocratic arch-conservative, although the fear of change which is its usual aspect has an ultimate origin quite distinct from any aristocratic sentiment. This fear of change led Wordsworth to oppose universal education and the freedom of the press, and this latter as early as 1814, within ten years of the completion of the first draft of *The Prelude*. But Wordsworth's intellectual progress from "Elegiac Stanzas" was an inevitable one. Once doubt the value of the intellectual and spiritual independence of the individual, and the rest follows.

The vacillations of Wordsworth's thought while he passes from *The Prelude* to *The Excursion* [may be described] as a wavering between the philosophies of "I *want*" and of "I *must*," between the ideal of self-realization and the ideal of self-transcending duty. In this his thought is clearly less balanced than that of Dante or even of Goethe, if we consider the latter's thought as expressed in such a poem as his "Vermächtniss." It is this vacillation that reveals the tragic flaw in Wordsworth's philosophy. The moral insight so brilliantly presented in *The Prelude* is very shortly marred and finally, in the later poems, wholly obscured by Wordsworth's failure to perceive that these two approaches to morality can be rendered mutually consistent. Wordsworth faces a fatal disjunction: either we are to develop ourselves, our insights and our sympathies and proceed according to a romantic version of Augustine's formula, *Ama et fac quod vis*, or we are to submit ourselves wholly to the discipline of an established principle of duty. There can be no alternative or middle course. This becomes clear when we consider Wordsworth's final deletion of the important sixth stanza of the 1807 "Ode to Duty."

We have only to compare the moral tone of *Laodamía*

with that of the "Ode to Duty" to recognize how significant a turning point the repudiation of this stanza marks. After all, in the "Ode" duty is presented, as also in the letter to "Mathetes," as an attractive and beautiful ideal in harmony still with Wordsworth's natural religion. The ideal of *Laodamía* is heroic but forbidding, almost dour; the gods frown more readily than the flowers laugh.

In the 1807 "Ode," respect for temporarily unpleasant duty may through our appreciation of its full significance be transmuted into a "second will" free from the earlier tensions. This is in no very important respect inconsistent with the doctrine of *The Prelude*, where Wordsworth admits that in ethical development we must "complete the man . . . made imperfect in himself." [2]

Had Wordsworth proceeded in this way and expanded the important ideas involved, the philosophy of *The Prelude* might well have been richly supplemented. But here Wordsworth failed. Imagination and spontaneous enjoyment are discounted in favour of stoic endurance such as appears in the *White Doe*. And I very much fear that this evaluation is founded largely upon the feeling that in accepting dutiful endurance as the prime virtue, we are identifying ourselves with "the Kind." Thus the democratic fallacy seems to triumph.

Wordsworth's failure to integrate the philosophy of *The Prelude* with a theory of duty constitutes a real loss to our modern culture. It is one of our fundamental weaknesses that we habitually see life as divided between play and real enjoyment on the one hand and important work and duty on the other. What we want to do and what we ought to do stand apart even in theory. This is perhaps inevitable in an irreligious and commercial civilization. But against this error Wordsworth's teaching might well have proven to be a great force had he overcome his own confusion, for he at least faced our problem and in his happier periods held a key to its solution.

But let us here in fairness to Wordsworth admit that the democratic fallacy, confused and perverse as it is, rests upon one sentiment among others, which is clearly an honorable one. This is an intense dislike of making an exception of oneself. It is from this underlying motive, which in the minds of rationalist philosophers may be interpreted as a respect for strict logical consistency in practical life, that the real power of Kant's categorical imperative derives. Consider Walt Whitman's famous resolve to accept nothing that all men might not enjoy on the same terms. This may be a sound foundation for equalitarian ethical doctrine, but of course it should be read as requiring equal opportunity rather than any limitation of achievement to the common level.

Wordsworth's later attitude toward religion is worth attention. We may grant that the need of a spiritual security to be drawn from sources external to the self initiates a sound approach to religion. But Wordsworth becomes too eager to accomplish his pilgrimage, too dogmatically certain of what is to be learned from humility. He will take no chances, so strong is his philosophy of self-defense, in religion any more than in politics. The "wise passiveness" of his earlier philosophy, the willingness to follow where his richly expanding experience might lead him is now quite vanished. His religion lacks plasticity and what Professor A. E. Taylor has called the element of surprise.

Compare the fourth "Evening Voluntary" (1834) with any poem which expresses a genuinely active religion, say Blake's "A Sunflower" or Herbert's "The Pulley":

> But who *is* innocent? By grace divine,
> Not otherwise, O Nature! we are thine,
> Through good and evil thine, in just degree
> Of rational and manly sympathy.
> To all that Earth from pensive hearts is stealing,
> And Heaven is now to gladdened eyes revealing,
> Add every charm the Universe can show
> Through every change its aspects undergo—
> Care may be respited, but not repealed;
> No perfect cure grows on the bounded field.
> Vain is the pleasure, a false calm the peace,
> If He, through whom alone our conflicts cease,
> Our virtuous hopes without relapse advance,
> Come not to speed the Soul's deliverance;
> To the distempered Intellect refuse
> His gracious help, or give what we abuse.[3]

What mechanical piety this is! As mechanical as the verse. But we must look for little else. For the Wordsworth of this period faith is no longer seeking understanding. It repudiates the very sources from which understanding once sprang. All is fixed and unquestionable. Doubt and intellectual independence have no real function, not even that of leading us toward

profounder insight. Nor does the poet listen with "wise passiveness" for the old Eolian visitations.[4] Neither reason nor inspiration is needed now.

But such considerations only convince us how much the
English-speaking world has lost by the tragic failure of Wordsworth's philosophy.

Notes

1. 1850, Bk. VII, ll. 527 ff.
2. Bk. XIII, l. 202.
3. "Evening Voluntary," IV, ll. 16–31.
4. We have only to recall Wordsworth's growing emphasis on craftsmanship and the "art" of poetry—his comments on which, as his letters
show, could grow pedantic—to recognize that he quite "outgrew" the
philosophy of poetry and of life expressed in the lyrics of 1798. See
especially the letter to Sir William M. Gorman, April 16, 1834.

Part Three   Coleridge

L. G. Salingar

7·Coleridge: Poet and Philosopher

COLERIDGE WAS A POET and philosopher by calling and, largely by circumstance, a journalist, preacher, lecturer, and playwright. His main work was to transform the mechanistic psychology of the eighteenth century and to initiate a reaction against it. He revived the older tradition of Platonism and introduced to England the new idealism of Germany. He set out to explore the unconscious workings of the mind—"the *terra incognita* of our nature"—for poetry. He completed the revolution of taste which has enthroned Shakespeare as a genius no less remarkable for his judgment than his inventiveness. More than any other of the English Romantics, he brought about the revolution in literary thought that consists in regarding the imagination as the sovereign creative power, expressing the growth of a whole personality. Besides all this, he wrote and talked incessantly about politics and religion, biology and language and education. And, in addition, his career was a chain of unfinishable Utopian projects, from his scheme with Southey in 1794 for Pantisocracy (which was to provide a model for social regeneration in the founding of a communal farm beside the Susquehanna) to the all-embracing prose epic or "Logosophia" he was compiling at the end of his life, which was to ensure the reconciliation of religion and philosophy. All the published prose of the second half of his life, including *Biographia Literaria* (1817), consists of frag-

Reprinted from *The Pelican Guide to English Literature*, Vol. 5, edited by Boris Ford, by permission of Penguin Books Ltd. Copyright 1957 by Penguin Books Ltd.

ments and digressions wrenched from him by the occasion, but
intended as preparatives for this vast undertaking, which
Coleridge thought of as his counterpart to Wordsworth's
Prelude.

It is hardly surprising, then, that Coleridge—aided here
by his self-comparison to Hamlet and his reputation as a victim of opium—should have earned the name of a subtle but
aimless and irreclaimable dreamer. "There is no subject on
which he has not touched," said Hazlitt, "none on which he
has rested"; and René Wellek today calls him a random eclectic. Nevertheless, a contrary and probably more adequate
impression of Coleridge is the sense of his intellectual determination. "He was most wonderful," said Wordsworth, the
best placed of authorities, "in the power he possessed of
throwing out in profusion grand central truths from which
might be evolved the most comprehensive systems." And
Keats criticized Coleridge precisely for lacking the "Negative
Capability" of suspending judgment in the midst of mysteries
and doubts; "he was incapable of remaining content with half-
knowledge."

The central truths that Coleridge was after were always
to be drawn from "facts of mind," whether under the guise
of perfectionistic enlightenment or of disenchanted self-
knowledge. Through all his shifts of topic and doctrine his
attention was fixed on the "increase of consciousness," the
causes favoring or hindering it, and its effects. For Coleridge,
as Keats and Wordsworth imply, the increase of consciousness
should never willingly stop short of the whole. His ideal poet,
as he is described in his main statement in *Biographia* (Ch.
XIV), is not a dreamer at all, but a man of rounded character:
"The poet, described in *ideal* perfection, brings the whole soul
of man into activity, with the subordination of its faculties to
each other, according to their relative worth and dignity." Nor
was wholeness of mind possible, in Coleridge's view, for a self-
contained individual; on the contrary, it entailed the individual's perception, his consenting recognition, of the "absolute
oneness" of the whole universe: "The dim intellect," he wrote
in 1803, "sees an absolute oneness, the perfectly clear intellect
knowingly perceives it. Distinction and plurality lie in the betwixt." Again: "*All* is an endless fleeting abstraction; *the
whole* is a reality." Although Coleridge never proclaimed the

poet as such to be a healer, a prophet, or an unacknowledged legislator, he came very near to doing so; and clearly a doctrine requiring the intuition of wholeness entrusts or saddles the poetic imagination with a heavy metaphysical burden.

The burden was not altogether of Coleridge's seeking. Dr. Johnson (who died while Coleridge was a schoolboy) had always rejoiced "to concur with the common reader" in applauding a poet's expression of generally accepted truths. But for Coleridge there was no "common reader"; only, in London and the new manufacturing districts, a huge miscellaneous "reading public," uninformed but exacting, pressing for excitement and receptive to revelation. And in a lifetime of public upheavals—an "age of anxiety," in Coleridge's phrase—there could be no sentiments that found an echo in every bosom unless, as Wordsworth contended, the poet could first put them there. There were strong social motives, then, in Coleridge's insistence on wholeness. Strong personal motives, too; for Coleridge lacked the local roots and local pieties, besides the strength of temperament, that helped Wordsworth to recover from the stresses of the 1790s. He was an orphan who got on badly with his elder brothers, a keenly affectionate but often sick and frustrated man, who was constantly haunted by self-pity or remorse, by his yearning for family happiness and his impulse to run away. In a sense, the *"ideal* perfection" of the poet in *Biographia* is Coleridge's ideal for himself in his struggle for self-mastery.

The prevailing attitude of Coleridge's formative years—not without fluctuations—was an emotional pantheism. He declared later that pantheism had only appealed to his head; but in 1802 he wrote that "strong feeling and an active intellect conjoined" will at first lead a philosopher almost inevitably to Spinoza, and as late as 1826 he noted that he required a deliberate effort to resist his old pantheistic "habit of feeling." [1] In the 1790s a nature-worship like Wordsworth's appealed to his heart as well as his head. It seconded his political creed, which might be described as a compound of Milton, Godwin, and Rousseau; it supported him emotionally after 1798, when his hopes in the French Revolution broke down; and it held together his favorite themes of speculation. He was both a student of "facts of mind" in the Neoplatonic mystics and a disciple of the enlightenment descended from Locke and

Hartley, believing with them that the contents of the mind are formed from sense-impressions combined by association, and even maintaining "the corporeality of *thought*—namely that it is motion." Coleridge's pantheism gave house-room to these unlikely partners. For his associationism (or "necessitarianism") meant for Coleridge the Pantisocrat that evil was the product of civilization and private property; while his Neoplatonic faith was a faith that "fraternized" by revealing that all men were "Parts and proportions of one wonderous whole." His first ambitious poem, "Religious Musings" (1794–1796), is a phil-anthropic hymn wherein he nominates Hartley and Newton to the Elect, together with Milton and the Unitarian Priestley. And Coleridge's pantheism was ultimately to lead him to his central problem as a critic. In a letter to Sotheby of 10 Septem-ber 1802, after asserting that "a Poet's *Heart & Intellect* should be *combined, intimately* combined & *unified*, with the great appearances in Nature," Coleridge claims that Greek religious poetry at best exhibits Fancy, for to the Greeks "all natural Objects were *dead*"; whereas the Psalms show Imagination, for "in the Hebrew Poets each Thing has a Life of its own, & yet they are all one Life." This argument contains Coleridge's first reference to his distinction between imagination and fancy; he brings it forward as "a most compleat answer to those, who state the Jehovah of the Jews, as a personal & national God."

From 1801 to 1803, however, Coleridge was engaged on an intensive rethinking of his philosophy, which was at the same time a prolonged effort to recover the "self-impelling, self-directing Principle" in his personal life.[2] His new outlook, though yet to undergo many, and sometimes bewildering, changes of detail, was in essentials a reversal of the old. In 1803, with the renewal of the Napoleonic War, Coleridge emerged as a nationalist and a disciple of Burke, holding that government must be founded on property and inequality. At the same time, he returned to Anglican orthodoxy—or, rather, to a prolonged reinterpretation of Protestantism in the light of Plato and of Kant. By the end of 1803, similarly, he was repudi-ating Wordsworth's nature worship and rejecting Hartley's theory of the mind, or severely limiting its application, mainly because he had now come to locate the source of moral evil in submission to the senses, in "the streamy nature of the associa-tive faculty," especially with people like himself, "who are most reverie-ish and streamy." His cardinal doctrine now was the freedom and initiative of the moral will—the divine spark in each of us, "the 'I' of every rational Being," the ultimate source alike of religious faith and of genuine perception. And the moral or rational will is now outside the chain of natural causes and effects altogether; it is apparently the same as the "primary Imagination" of a famous and oracular passage in *Biographia*, namely "a repetition in the finite mind of the eternal act of creation in the infinite I AM" (Ch. XIII). While he was preparing *Biographia*, Coleridge wrote to Wordsworth that the aims of *The Prelude* should have been to refute the school of Locke, to show how man's senses are evolved from his mind or spirit and to show how the doctrine of redemption rescues mankind "from this enmity with Nature." The corner-stone of "Logosophia" was to be the idea that "Life begins in detachment from Nature and ends in unition with God."

Coleridge still seeks the Whole as urgently as before. But the Bible now is emphatically not a pantheist document. It still reveals, as Coleridge writes in *The Statesman's Manual* (1816), that "every agent" (if not "each Thing") has "a life of its own, and yet all are one life." But now, "the elements of necessity and free-will are reconciled in the higher power of an omnipresent Providence, that predestinates the whole in the moral freedom of the integral parts." And, since now God is not in Nature but omnipresent outside it, the poet's sense of wholeness cannot be a single decisive revelation (as the letter of 1802 to Sotheby implies), but must be a progressive development or a perpetual re-creation. In the passage in *Biographia* defining the act of perception, or "primary Imagination," as a form of the creative will, Coleridge goes on to define the poetic (or "secondary") imagination as one of its derivatives. As everywhere in Coleridge's critical writings, the poetic imagination imposes unity on its material; but here, on very different terms from those of the letter of 1802:

> The secondary Imagination . . . dissolves, diffuses, dissipates, in order to recreate; or where this process is rendered impossible, yet still at all events it struggles to idealize and to unify. It is essentially *vital*, even as all objects (*as* objects) are essentially fixed and dead.

Although the intention of this passage and of *Biographia* as a whole is to bring out a contrast between Fancy and Imagination, it is noticeable that Imagination now stands where the Greek Fancy had stood in 1802; for the Greeks, "all natural Objects were *dead*."

Evidently, then, Coleridge held two different theories about poetic creation. According to the first, it springs from self-identification with Nature; for the second, it is a product of the autonomous will. Both theories involve the cooperation of the poet's whole personality. But the main problem before the first is to account for Mind in the process; that of the second, to account for Nature.

Many of Coleridge's favorite images in his poems and notebooks, are related closely to his interests in Hartley and in the mystics. They are images of illumination—moonlight suffusing the sky, or the Neoplatonic symbol of the sun dispersing mists of ignorance and superstition.[3] Or they are images of natural motion-studies of waterfalls ("the continual *change* of the *Matter*, the perpetual *Sameness* of the *Form*"), studies of a ship's foam, of clouds or the leaves of a tree in the wind, of the flight of insects or of birds. He delights in noting how individuals or particles of matter seem to combine in spontaneous motion; or how the mind itself appears to move in sympathy (or empathy) during the act of observation:

> One travels along the lines of a mountain.
> Years ago I wanted to make Wordsworth sensible
> of this . . .

And in "The Eolian Harp" (1795) Coleridge presses the wind-harp into service as a symbol both of spontaneous inspiration and of the life-force as a whole:

> What if all of animated nature
> Be but organic harps diversely framed,
> That tremble into thought, as o'er them sweeps
> Plastic and vast, one intellectual breeze,
> At once the Soul of each, and God of all?

Here he struggles to reconcile associationism with the concept of a "plastic," "organic" World-Soul that he may have borrowed from the Cambridge Platonists of Milton's day. For the moment he recoils from such "idle flitting phantasies," "shapings of the unregenerate mind"; but the appeal of an ecstatic communion with nature was too strong to be repelled. For example, in "France: An Ode" (or "The Recantation," 1798), he turns away from men to the elements to find true Liberty ("The guide of homeless winds, and playmate of the waves"). And as Liberty means the sensation of projecting his spirit into nature, "Possessing all things with intensest love," so, in "The Nightingale: A Conversation Poem" (addressed, a few weeks later, to William and Dorothy Wordsworth), happiness means "surrendering his whole spirit," to "the influxes/Of shapes and sounds and shifting elements." A letter to Thomas Wedgwood early in 1803 relates how, as he climbs a mountain, away from men and animals, he feels a conviction of universal life rush in on him in "a wild activity, of thoughts, imaginations, feelings, and impulses of motion," so that his spirit "courses, drives, and eddies, like a Leaf in Autumn." There is a striking antici-pation of Shelley in this account of inspiration.

The trouble with most of this spontaneous, "involuntary" inspiration in Coleridge is that he wants it to teach a doctrine and has clearly come by it in obedience to a doctrine. The strongest influences behind his poetry are Milton and the semi-Miltonic tradition of sublimity and pathos represented by Gray and Collins; and many of his poems, either in Miltonic blank verse or the form of odes, are philosophical declamations, somewhat like the contemporary prophetic writings of Blake, descended, like them, from the strains of Gray's "Bard," with its echoes of Milton, Pindar, and the Bible, and its background of mountain torrents and primitive liberty. What Coleridge aimed at was "that impetuosity of transition, and that precipi-tation of fancy and feeling, which are the *essential* excellencies of the sublimer Ode" (1796); and this tradition of bardic sub-limity was very much in his thoughts when he wrote his letter about imagination to Sotheby in 1802. But impetuosity to order is difficult to sustain.

Coleridge was more at home in his personal verse, which begins with sentimental "effusions" and continues with "con-versation poems" like "The Eolian Harp" and 'The Nightin-gale," and finally with the long series of miscellaneous lyrics springing from his love for Sara Hutchinson, Wordsworth's sister-in-law. In the blank-verse "conversation poems" written during the productive months that led on to Lyrical Ballads (1798)—and especially in the fine "Frost at Midnight"—Coleridge finds a distinctive manner of his own. They are sensitive descriptive pieces within the framework of a verse-letter of domestic monologue. They owe something to "the divine Chit chat of Cowper" and something, no doubt, to Wordsworth's friendship and his theory of plain speech. But Coleridge's landscape is no longer that of Cowper or of Bowles, with their "perpetual trick of *moralizing* every thing"; nor is it Wordsworth's landscape, with its haunting presences and solitary encounters. It is intimate, tender, and animated. His conversation poems have the same qualities of keen, extemporized analysis and affectionate communication as the best of his letters. Nevertheless, Coleridge could not remain satisfied with intimacy in poetry unless he could infuse it with the sublime.

Coleridge could only reach his goal of unselfconscious communion with nature, therefore, by evading (or repressing) the demands of his rational will—or else by finding a new synthesis of mind and feelings altogether. The triumph of "Kubla Khan" and *The Ancient Mariner* represents the first of these alternatives. In the autumn of 1797, when he was about to begin work on *The Ancient Mariner* and—it seems likely— had just composed "Kubla Khan," Coleridge wrote to Thelwall that he could often wish to sleep or die, or "like the Indian Vishnu, to float about along an infinite ocean cradled in the flower of the Lotos, & wake once in a million years for a few minutes." [4] The complete transmutation of the bardic ode in "Kubla Khan," so that scattered memories from Coleridge's immense reading and conflicting feelings and sensations seem to find their own order in his mind, without effort and without question, seems due to some such moment of inner release. And there is a similar exhilaration, in spite of all the horror, in the voyage of the Ancient Mariner, from the "free" movement of the ship in the wind at the outset to the release of the roaring wind and cascade of rain that bring his sufferings to an end. Whatever part opium may have taken in the process, Coleridge maintained that in both poems his rational mind was somehow held in abeyance. He said "Kubla Khan" was composed in a "dream" (when he published it in 1816) or a "reverie" (according to an earlier manuscript which has recently come to light). And although there is no question of dreaming in the actual writing of the other poem, which was planned deliberately and then revised and improved (1797, 1800, 1817), Coleridge called *The Ancient Mariner* also "A Poet's Reverie," until Lamb made him drop the title. Presumably "a poet's" reverie indicates some degree of rational control —but still imperfect control; for by "reverie" Coleridge meant expressly a state "akin to somnambulism, during which the understanding and moral sense are awake, though more or less confused."

Moreover, Coleridge classed nightmare with reverie, and published "The Pains of Sleep" (1803) together with "Kubla Khan," as if to point the connection. He found it difficult to square "Kubla Khan" and even, to some extent, *The Ancient Mariner*, with his doctrinal leanings and his increasing moral anxiety. As for "Kubla Khan," it was not a "poem" at all, but a "fragment," a "psychological curiosity." As for *The Ancient Mariner*, he found two ways of accounting for it, neither of them wholly satisfying. One was to deny that it contained any moral at all and to class it, by implication, with literature of escape such as the "Gothic" novels of the 1790s, the *Arabian Nights* and Coleridge's favorite "happy nightmare," *Robinson Crusoe*.[5] The other was to link it with Coleridge's intended essay on the preternatural in poetry—the essay which would have discussed "that willing suspension of disbelief for the moment, which constitutes poetic faith" and would no doubt have embodied Coleridge's life-long interest in occult "facts of mind" and his belief that an open-minded psychologist could find at least a "poetic faith," a vital if garbled revelation, by attending to popular superstitions and such abnormal psychic events as obsessions, presentiments and the hallucinations of mystics.[6] On this reading, the Ancient Mariner may resemble Macbeth, who, as Coleridge says, is forced into "a preternatural state" because he "tears himself live-asunder from nature." But as a text for his essay Coleridge preferred his unfinshed *Christabel* (1797–1801), in which he seems to have meant to include a more explicit religious teaching. And yet it is precisely the presence of a still undefined moral or sentimental purpose in *Christabel* that makes it a much slighter achievement than *The Ancient Mariner*.

There are haunting echoes of a moral struggle in *The Ancient Mariner*, but, as Wordsworth complained, Coleridge withholds from reducing them to a daylight morality. The tale is consistently irrational, with none of that effort of resistance typical of a nightmare allegory by Kafka. Although the Mariner speaks of his saint and his cross, the effective agents in his

story are the nature-spirits from Coleridge's Neoplatonic reading; and the effective morality, or binding-force, is an involuntary, spontaneous contact with nature. Symbolically, the
Mariner may resemble Macbeth; but he does not speak as a
moral agent. He is passive, in guilt and remorse. He acts when
he shoots the albatross, bites his arm, or blesses the watersnakes;
but he acts blindly, under compulsion, like Robinson Crusoe
(as Coleridge interpreted him) or like Coleridge himself in
"The Pains of Sleep," where

> all confused I could not know
> Whether I suffered or I did.

He invokes the nightmare of life-in-death blindly when he kills
the albatross and dispels it passively when he blesses the watersnakes "unaware." From this paralysis of his conscience, terri-
fying and yet refreshing, the Mariner has gained his mesmeric
authority, though he pays for it by remaining in the condition
of an outcast. Coleridge makes him spectator as well as actor
in the drama, so that he can recount even his worst terrors with
a calm after-thrill of lucid retrospection; and the crown of the
poet's achievement is his steadiness in preserving—even sharp-
ening—the sensations of nightmare (or "happy nightmare")
for their own sake, in spite of the emotional conflicts they
involve.[7]

Only one of Coleridge's poems, however, "Dejection: An
Ode"—in its original form a verse-letter to Sara Hutchinson—
answers fully to the ideal of poetical completeness that Coleridge came to define in Biographia as a condition of "judgement
ever awake and steady self-possession" as well as "enthusiasm
and feeling profound or vehement"; and, paradoxically, "Dejection" is one of the outstanding records of that ennui, that
loss of enthusiasm, which was the tragic malady of the Romantics. When he wrote it, in April 1802, Coleridge knew that his
marriage was near collapse and he was also afraid, like Wordsworth, that "the poet in him" was "dying." It was partly a
response to Wordsworth's ode on childhood and was echoed
in turn in "Resolution and Independence," so that the three
poems together form a kind of dialogue. The published version
of "Dejection" has less hope but also less self-pity than the
private letter;[8] it contains a remarkable effort at self-therapy.

In the first stanza of "Dejection" Coleridge is in the situation he often describes, looking at the sky and trying to find "a symbolical language" there for something in himself. But his usual sources of inspiration seem to fail him, and he is only dispirited by the noise of the wind-harp outside his room. Then, however, in the second stanza, he begins to reach his symbolical language as he approaches what is at once a self-judgment and a rounded ideal of poetry:

> A grief without a pang, void, dark, and drear,
>   A stifled, drowsy, unimpassioned grief,
>   Which finds no natural outlet, no relief,
>   In word, or sigh, or tear—
> O Lady! in this wan and heartless mood,
> To other thoughts by yonder throstle wooed,
>   All this long eve, so balmy and serene,
> Have I been gazing on the western sky,
>   And its peculiar tint of yellow green:
> And still I gaze—and with how blank an eye!
> And those thin clouds above, in flakes and bars,
> That give away their motion to the stars;
> Those stars, that glide behind them or between,
> Now sparkling, now bedimmed, but always seen:
> Yon crescent Moon, as fixed as if it grew
> In its own cloudless, starless lake of blue,
> I see them all, so excellently fair,
> I see, not feel, how beautiful they are!

"I see, not feel" is like Wordsworth's regret for vanishing glory or the Mariner's apathy before he blesses the watersnakes. But here Coleridge is searching for relief within himself, and he finds it in the rhythm of his stanza as he rises through images of solemn calm and friendly movement to contemplate the perfect self-centeredness and self-illumination of the lotus-like moon. More continuously than any other writer, Coleridge had admired Milton, the poet whose "self-possession" enabled him to "attract all forms and things to himself"; [9] and this whole stanza, with its emphasis on *seeing*, is a tribute to the great invocation in Book III of *Paradise Lost*, where Milton in his blindness prays for a "Celestial light" that may

> Shine inward, and the mind through all her powers
> Irradiate . . .

With Milton behind him Coleridge can resist his own despair. The first words of the next stanza are the words of *Samson Agonistes* but the rhythm is the triumphant rhythm of the "Nativity" hymn:

> My genial spirits fail;
> And what can these avail
> To lift the smothering weight from off my breast?
> It were a vain endeavour
> Though I should gaze for ever
> On that green light that lingers in the west:
> I may not hope from outward forms to win
> The passion and the life, whose fountains are within.

These lines imply a positive statement within their negation; in the published version of the poem, Coleridge builds on this at once:

> O Lady! we receive but what we give
> And in our life alone does Nature live:
> Ours is her wedding garment, ours her shroud!
>   And would we aught behold, of higher worth,
> Than that inanimate cold world allowed
> To the poor loveless ever-anxious crowd,
>   Ah! from the soul itself must issue forth
> A light, a glory, a fair luminous cloud
>   Enveloping the Earth
> And from the soul itself must there be sent
>   A sweet and potent voice, of its own birth,
> Of all sweet sounds the life and element!

This inner glory is "Joy," given only to those, like Sara Hutchinson, who are "pure of heart." For the poet himself, distress and the research he has resorted to for anodyne have "suspended" his birthright, his "shaping spirit of Imagination." Yet he can now turn his thoughts again to the Eolian harp and that "mighty Poet," the wind.

Admittedly, this later, bardic stanza about the wind is rather forced; and none of Coleridge's many subsequent poems have the same ease and power as the first parts of "Dejection." But it was no less important that he had gained a new insight into the imagination, which he identifies here for the first time with the creative and governing spirit of poetry. In an earlier poem, Coleridge had claimed "Energic Reason and a shaping mind"; but the muse he invokes before 1802 is neither Reason nor Imagination but Fancy, a "wild" or an "idle" Fancy in the manner of Collins.[10] In "Dejection" he took a long stride forward towards a new view of poetry, as he began to consider the imagination as both a state of inner harmony in the poet and the power that shapes the whole world of his poetry from within.

Before composing "Dejection," Coleridge had written of the imagination in conventional eighteenth-century terms, as the faculty by which we enjoy, recall, or combine images (typically visual images), or else as the faculty at work in "the fairy way of writing" and responsible for delusions and preternatural visions. In either case, it was subject to the laws of association; it was a "law of our nature," he wrote in 1797, by which we "gradually represent as wholly like" whatever is "partially like." In the last analysis, it was part of the automatic nervous system.

But while he was writing "Dejection," Coleridge was coming to revise his theories about associationism completely. The mind, he writes in 1801, is not "always passive—a lazy Looker-on on an external World." Nor does it always meet with separate atoms of experience, as Locke and his successors assumed. It is always active as well as passive, always contains the current of the past and an impulse towards continuity. Even memory, the stronghold of associationism, is not an automatic linkage of "ideas," * but the result of a "state of general feeling" (or a "state of affection or bodily Feeling") which resembles the past; and if so, he asserts towards the end of 1803, "Hartley's system totters":

I almost think that Ideas *never* recall Ideas—any more than Leaves in a forest create each other's motion—The Breeze it is that runs thro' them/it is the Soul, the state of Feeling. . . .

Similarly, Coleridge finds a potential continuity even in the sensation of the here-and-now:

How opposite to nature and the fact to talk of the "one moment" of Hume, of our whole being an aggregate of successive single sensations! Who ever felt a single sensation? Is not every one at the same moment conscious that there coexist a thousand others, a darker shade, or less light . . . ?

More and more, after 1803, Coleridge tends to emphasize wholeness and "continuity in . . . self-consciousness" as the ground of all mental experience and to absorb it all into a single dynamic source, the 'I' of every rational Being," the will.[11] This solution raises new problems, for it becomes diffi-

* *Ideas* here are images or traces of (separate) sense-impressions (i.e. Hume and Hartley's "ideas," not Plato's).

cult to distinguish between the will as a separate act of volition, a resolution of conflicting impulses, and the will as focus or expression of a unified personality. Coleridge tends to merge the first of these into the second. What are "motives," he asks, "but my impelling thoughts—and what is a Thought but another word for 'I thinking'?" At the same time, however, Coleridge does not deny that the mind is inclined to be passive and is subject in some ways to external laws of association; indeed, it is just this passivity that he now, from about 1803 onwards, wishes above all to resist. Just as we counteract the force of gravity in order to jump, he says, so does the "I" (which is synonymous with the moral will) counteract the force of association in order to perceive or think. Association of ideas, "idle flitting phantasies," indolence of will, are now very close to the roots of evil; there is a latent imperative in Coleridge's new psychology. Hence its inconsistencies and his continuous effort to overcome them—an effort that both enriches and complicates his new insight into the imagination.

This "shaping spirit" has already cast off the chains of the association theory in the writing of "Dejection." It is no longer passive towards Nature, for "in our life alone does Nature live." And it is no longer merely a more or less trustworthy instrument of cognition (and hence of detached enjoyment), but a part of the poet's vital emotions; indeed, the image-combining faculty can only come into force, the poem suggests, as the result of a state of enthusiasm or "Joy" that enables the poet to see *and* feel the beauty of nature. This state reaches back, in turn, through the whole of his past life: "To carry on the feelings of childhood into the powers of manhood," Coleridge writes later (with Wordsworth's "Homogeneity of character" in his mind, as it is in "Dejection")— ". . . this is the character and privilege of genius." [12] Imagination, then, gives the poet an undivided self in an undivided world. As Coleridge defines it in his important letter to Sotheby of 10 September 1802 (and again many times later), it is "the *modifying* and *co-adunating* Faculty." As such, moreover, it has no need of that external check by the judgment and rules of common assent so carefully provided by neoclassical theorists; in itself it is the "shaping spirit" of poetry. Ultimately, then, the "design" of a poem, its "machinery," its "ornament" —every part or aspect that matters for enjoyment and criticism

—find their coherence in the poet's state of feeling. This insight of Coleridge has made a lasting difference to literary thought.

But the imagination is much more for Coleridge than a state of inner harmony; it is also a reaching towards the Whole —a world view, a religious intuition—disguised as a psychological "faculty." This postulate of "faculties" in the mind, while necessary for one part of Coleridge's outlook, is inconsistent with another; and, in addition, the relationship of Self and Whole changes as he rejects his original nature worship.

In his pantheist letter to Sotheby, the imagination, exemplified by the Psalms (and by English poetry), unifies the poet's heart with his mind, and both with God and Nature; "we are all *one Life*." For the Greeks, "all natural Objects were *dead*—mere hollow Statues," unless there was "a Godkin or Goddessling *included* in each." "In the Hebrew Poets"—on the other hand—"each Thing has a Life of its own, & yet they are all one Life"; moreover:

> In God they move & live & *have* their Being—not *had*
> as the cold System of Newtonian Theology represents/but
> *have*. . . .

Taking this letter and "Dejection" together, then, the imagination is opposed to "that inanimate cold world" of "the poor loveless ever-anxious crowd" who regulate their lives by the ruling mechanistic theology of eighteenth-century society and its self-centered, utilitarian ethics; and at the same time it is opposed to Greek mythology—the stale reservoir of eighteenth-century poetic diction. One is the product of the creative faculty which at least "struggles" to reach the Whole, "modifies" and "co-adunates"; the other is at best "but Fancy, or the aggregating Faculty of the mind," which (according to *Biographia*, Ch. XIII) "has no other counters to play with, but fixities and definites." This opposition between two kinds of world view, the vital and the mechanical, the universal and the egocentric, becomes the central theme of Coleridge's later writing. After 1803, he even postulates another pair of mental faculties in order to explain it; he makes a division between Reason (which grasps eternal, absolute Ideas such as the definitions of mathematics and is identical, in its practical aspect, with the laws of the conscience) and Understanding, which can only record and classify the notices of the senses and is competent, at best, in matters of prudence. Coleridge's "Understanding" is much the same as the "reason" of eighteenth-century thinkers; but he holds that it can or should only operate under the control of the absolute Reason and by means of the Imagination which mediates between them.[13]

In Coleridge's original, pantheist scheme of Imagination and Fancy it is difficult to see, however, where Fancy comes in at all. For if we are, categorically, "all *one Life,*" why should we need a special faculty to recognize as much; and why should this faculty be shared by some races and not by others? Coleridge's later philosophy removes this objection to some extent (by making the imagination approach the Whole progressively, "struggle" to reach it); but only to introduce another. For if, as *Biographia* argues (Ch. XIII), the imagination (and the imagination alone) springs from the "primary Imagination" or power of perceiving, where does Fancy derive from? Either it also uses perception, in which case the distinction between the faculties here breaks down; or it is carried along entirely by the stream of associations, in which case it can have no active role in poetry at all. Sometimes Coleridge uses the term in a traditional way (much as Johnson had said that Cowley yoked "the most heterogeneous ideas" together "by violence"): for example, he finds Fancy, too, in Cowley's poetry, finds "fancy under the conditions of imagination" in Spenser, and fancy in the images of Shakespeare's line, "A lily prison'd in a gaol of snow." At other times the term carries a distinct edge of moral disapproval, as when Coleridge attributes fancy, but not imagination, to the verse of Scott, whom he thought of as typifying the cold-hearted upper-class religion of the day.[14] Apparently Coleridge retains his separation of faculties in order to claim a distinct and higher origin for the vision that seeks unity; but having done this, he cannot find any consistent place for the minor faculty in his criticism.

Moreover, as Coleridge drives a wedge between the moral will and the sensory appearances of nature, so, in theory, he gives the imagination itself more and more labor with less and less material. For example, in 1802 Shakespeare is a "metaphysician," but with the senses of "a wild Arab" or "a North American Indian"; by 1811, he works from observation, guided by self-knowledge; but by 1818 he is entirely "self-sustained," working from meditation alone, having no contact with the

environment or even the language of his time.[15] This bias towards the isolated consideration of the moral will is responsible
for the one-sidedness of Coleridge's criticism in general. He is
not interested at all in the plots or subject matter of Shakespeare's plays; and, in spite of his reputation as a psychological
analyst, he only considers with interest the characters he can
idealize or those like Hamlet, Richard III, and Edmund, in
whom he can trace an overbalance of intellect or meditation
and a defect of the moral will.

On the other hand, with his bias goes a search for living
principles of continuity in literature that makes Coleridge one
of the greatest and most original of critics. Whereas at first he
had paid more attention to the emotional, involuntary aspects
of poetic creation—the wind in the wind-harp—he gives more
emphasis later to character and education, so that imagination
becomes almost synonymous with "method." In one of his
finest essays, in *The Friend* (II 4; 1812), he praises the man of
method as one who calls time "into life and moral being"; this
is essentially the quality of mind and character that he admires
in Milton or in Wordsworth, the "homogeneity of character"
that enables Wordsworth to sustain his "original gift" of imposing himself on his material, of "spreading the tone, the *atmosphere* . . . of the ideal world around . . . situations, of which,
for the common view, custom had bedimmed all the lustre." And
when Coleridge differs from Wordsworth over poetic diction
(in *Biographia*, Chs. XVII–XVIII), he concentrates on
method, ignoring the original question of vocabulary; educated
speech and not rustic speech is the best for poetry, he says,
because the rustic can only "convey *insulated facts*," while the
cultivated mind seeks "*connexions*," a prospective view of a
subject, the subordination of its parts to "an organized whole."
Similarly, Coleridge prefers the "stately march and difficult
evolutions" of seventeenth-century prose, with its "cement of
thought as well as of style," to the "short and unconnected
sentences" of his own day; just as he prefers the movement of
Milton's verse to the movement of Pope's.

The most fruitful passages in Coleridge's criticism are
those where he distinguishes method and internal intercon-
nectedness as signs of the imagination. A famous example, from
his Shakespeare lectures of 1808, is his comment on two lines
from *Venus and Adonis*:

> Look! how a bright star shooteth from the sky,
> So glides he in the night from Venus' eye.

> How many images and feelings are here brought together
> without effort and without discord—the beauty of Adonis—
> the rapidity of his flight—the yearning yet hopelessness of
> the enamoured gazer—and a shadowy ideal character thrown
> over the whole.

It is Coleridge rather than Shakespeare here who provides a
"shadowy ideal character"; but probably no other critic had
so been able to demonstrate the instantaneous combination of
qualities in a poet's lines. The essay on *Method* in *The Friend*
provides a similar instance, this time of Coleridge's skill in
analyzing the sequence of Shakespeare's thought. Here he
demonstrates Shakespeare's judgment by examining two passages
of narrative, by Hamlet and by Mrs. Quickly, both immethodi-
cal but for opposite reasons—"Hamlet from the excess, Mrs.
Quickly from the want, or reflection and generalization." Mrs.
Quickly, he points out, has no pauses in her speech save those
enforced by "the necessity of taking breath, the efforts of
recollection, and the abrupt rectification of its failures"; and
no connectives, except "in the fusion of passion." On the other
side, with Hamlet, who is "meditative to excess," "all the digressions . . . consist of reflections . . . either directly expressed or
disguised in playful satire." From all this, Coleridge draws the
moral that method consists in a due balance "between our
passive impressions and the mind's own reactions on the
same." The whole essay is complementary to his debate with
Wordsworth over diction, and the moral, clearly, has some
reference to himself. But it is precisely this interest that gives
Coleridge his grip on those surface details of a passage that
lead directly to fundamentals; and it is here that the strength
of his criticism lies, not in character analysis.

As a third example of this strength, there is his discussion
of the music of verse in *Biographia*. In Chapter XVIII he suggests a biological explanation of the effects of meter in poetry.
Meter, he says, is the natural accompaniment to "language of
excitement" because it arouses expectancy and surprise in a
continuous, though barely perceptible, alternation; and because
it is determined by the balance of two fundamental human
tendencies, "*spontaneous* impulse" and "*voluntary* purpose."
Now this theory—a profoundly original one—is really an exten-

sion of Coleridge's thought at the time of the "Dejection" Ode, where he tries to derive the music of verse "from the soul itself," from the imagination conceived as an attunement of the conscious mind to the spontaneous wholeness of nature; and Coleridge shows how he applies it in his remarkable chapter on the first signs of genius in Shakespeare, where he begins by emphasizing the sense of musical delight (*Biographia*, Ch. XV). Striking images and interesting thoughts, he says there, may be acquired by a writer of talent:

> But the sense of musical delight, with the power of producing it, is a gift of imagination; and this together with the power of reducing multitude into unity of effect, and modifying a series of thoughts by some one predominant thought or feeling, may be cultivated and improved, but can never be learned.

Coleridge scrupulously refrains here from merging instinct into method; but he goes as far as he honestly can in bringing them together. Approaching poetry in this way, he gives a wholly new and far richer significance to the century-old praise of Shakespeare as the "child of Nature."

In developing these views, Coleridge took over from the German Romantics the theory that poetry is, or should be, an independent organic growth—organic growth, as opposed to mechanical construction.[16] Unlike a classical drama by Sophocles or Racine, he contends, a play by Shakespeare grows from within, as a tree does. In Shakespeare, contrasted this time with Beaumont and Fletcher, "all is growth, evolution, *genesis* —each line, each word almost, begets the following—and the will of the writer is an interfusion, a continuous agency, no series of separate acts"; and in Shakespeare (as contrasted with Massinger), changes in the characters are prepared for, because each of his characters "has indeed a life of its own . . . but yet an organ of the whole." In opposition to previous English critics, therefore, Coleridge claims that Shakespeare's plays are highly organized unities. Further—and here Coleridge's metaphysics or metabiology comes into play—this organizing power in Shakespeare was no gift of instinct but the reward of deliberate meditation. Shakespeare discerns the universal Idea, the "*I* representative," within his own personality; and through the dialectical interchange between the two poles of his own self (the individual ego and the universal self), he evolves solid and natural characters, whereas the characters of other playwrights, who lack this dynamic self-knowledge, have no more reality than ventriloquists' dolls. A modern critic here might speak more barely of the impersonality of Shakespeare's art. Coleridge's description, whatever its defects, has the advantage of stressing the complex union of living forces in the mind.

Coleridge could only describe such an organic unity on a purely abstract plane, because the world of his later thought was essentially a divided world, which the imagination "struggled" to unify. It was a world divided between "civilization," (including the industrial revolution), which was the sphere of Understanding, and faith, ethical values and "cultivation," the sphere of Reason. But how important the search for wholeness and the "cement of thought" were to Coleridge can be seen from his last work, *Church and State* (1830), where he argues that part of the Idea of the English constitution is a permanent national endowment for the advancement of learning and the provision of a schoolmaster in every parish. Here the residual Pantisocrat in Coleridge passes over into the first of the Victorian social prophets.

Notes

1. See *Miscellaneous Criticism*, p. 253; *Biographia Literaria*, I, 134; *Literary Remains* (ed. H. N. Coleridge), Vol. III, Ch. I. The best general account of Coleridge's early thought is in Hanson, Ch. X.

2. *Collected Letters* (ed. Griggs), p. 782 (cf. pp. 677ff.); *Essays on His Own Times*, II, 224, 494; House, *Coleridge*, pp. 42–45, 146–48; Potter, *Select Poetry and Prose*, p. 660; Snyder, *Logic and Learning*, p. 5. For Coleridge's later philosophy, see *Philosophical Lectures* (ed. Coburn and Muirhead), *Coleridge as Philosopher* (1930); A. O. Lovejoy, *Essays in the History of Ideas* (Baltimore, 1948); D. G. James, *The Romantic Comedy* (1948); B. Willey, *Nineteenth Century Studies* (1950). For his political thought, see *Mill on Bentham and Coleridge*, ed. Leavis; A. Cobban, *Burke and the Revolt against the Eighteenth Century* (1929). Many informative contemporary comments in Henry Crabb Robinson's diaries (ed. Edith J. Morley).

3. E.g., "Religious Musings," lines 88–104; cf. R. L. Brett, in *English Studies* (The English Association, 1949); M. H. Abrams, *The Mirror and the Lamp: Romantic Theory and the Critical Tradition* (New York, 1953), pp. 58–59. On Coleridge's imagery of motions, and his poetry in general, see House, *op. cit.*

4. *Collected Letters*, pp. 348–52. Elisabeth Schneider discusses Coleridge's views on reverie, giving strong reasons for doubting the opium-dream story about "Kubla Khan," and weaker reasons for dating it in 1800, in *Coleridge, Opium and "Kubla Khan"* (Chicago, 1953). On "reverie," see also R. C. Bald, "Coleridge and *The Ancient Mariner*,"

(*Nineteenth-Century Studies,* ed. H. Davies, New York, 1940) and House, *Coleridge.* Lowes, *The Road to Xanadu,* is indispensable on the literary sources of "Kubla Khan" and *The Ancient Mariner.*

5. See *Miscellaneous Criticism,* pp. 193, 299, 370–73, 405.

6. *Biographia,* I, 202; II, 6 (Ch. XIV); cf. *Poetical Works* (ed. Campbell), pp. 499, 590; *Shakespearean Criticism,* I, 151; *Miscellaneous Criticism,* pp. 191 ff., 321; *Philosophical Lectures,* pp. 44–47, 105, 239–40, 283; *Inquiring Spirit,* pp. 14–17, 45–58, 404–407; On *Christabel,* see A. H. Nethercot, *The Road to Tryermaine* (Chicago, 1939); cf. *Phil. Lect.,* 313–17.

7. See Bald, *op. cit.;* D. W. Harding, in *Scrutiny,* IX (1941); House, Ch. IV.

8. House, pp. 157 ff., reprints the original verse letter; cf. G. Whalley, *Coleridge and Sara Hutchinson* (1955); Lovejoy, *op. cit.* (Note 2, above), pp. 260–63.

9. *Biographia,* I, 23; II, 20; cf. *Poetical Works* (ed. Campbell), p. 540; *Collected Letters,* pp. 319–21. The early letters contain many more references to Milton than to Shakespeare.

10. See "Lines on a Friend," lines 39–40; and e.g., "Lines on an Autumnal Evening," "Songs of the Pixies," "Monody on the Death of Chatterton" (both versions), "The Destiny of Nations," lines 79–87.

11. Coleridge's psychology: see House, Ch. VI; *Inquiring Spirit,* pp. 14 ff., 30, 44, etc.; cf. Shawcross' Introduction to *Biographia;* I. A. Richards, *Coleridge on Imagination;* Notes 2, 4, 6, above.

12. *The Friend* (Bohn's Library edn.), pp. 22, 68; letter to Sotheby, 10 September 1802 (*Collected Letters;* extract in Raine, *Selected Letters*); letter to Sharp, 15 January 1804 (*Collected Letters;* extracts in Raine and in Potter). See Abrams, *The Mirror and the Lamp* and R. Wellek, *A History of Modern Criticism:* Vol. II, *The Romantic Age* (1955), on Coleridge's place in the history of critical ideas.

13. Reason and Understanding: see e.g., *Collected Letters,* pp. 1193–99; *The Statesman's Manual; Aids to Reflection* (Bohn's Library), pp. 143–71 (extract in Potter, pp. 456–58); *Church and State* (ed. H. N. Coleridge, 1839); p. 63; *Table Talk,* 4 January 1823; cf. Willey (Note 2, above), pp. 27–31.

14. *Shakespearean Criticism,* Vol. I, 214–17; *Miscellaneous Criticism,* p. 38 (see Potter, p. 335), pp. 323–35; *Biographia,* I, 15, 57–62, 202; II, 66–68. See discussions of Fancy and Imagination in Richards, Willey, *op. cit.,* and F. R. Leavis, "Coleridge in Criticism" *Scrutiny,* IX (1940); reprinted in *The Importance of Scrutiny,* ed. E. Bentley (New York, 1948).

15. *Collected Letters,* 810; *Shakespearean Criticism,* II, 117 (Potter, p. 347), p. 312; cf. *Statesman's Manual* (ed. White), p. 53.

16. *Miscellaneous Criticism,* pp. 44, 88, 95 (Potter, pp. 348, 411); cf. Raysor, *Shakespearean Criticism,* II, 117, note. On Coleridge's relation to German critical ideas, see Abrams, Wellek (Note 12, above); Shawcross, *Biographia;* Raysor, *Shakespearean Criticism;* J. Isaacs, "Coleridge's Critical Terminology" (*Essays and Studies by Members of the English Association,* 1935); G. McKenzie, *Organic Unity in Coleridge* (Berkeley, 1939); Sir Herbert Read, *Coleridge as Critic* (1949); also Brett (Note 3, above); Wilma L. Kennedy, *The English Heritage of Coleridge* (New Haven, 1947); cf. general studies, Note 2, above, and J. Needham, "Coleridge as a Philosophical Biologist" (*The Sceptical Biologist,* 1929); Carpenter, *The Indifferent Horseman,* pp. 312–33.

Elmer Edgar Stoll

8 · Symbolism In Coleridge

[The Cat, of the critics,] finding it all so
difficult, examining the thing as it were in-
conceivably arcanic.
—Marianne Moore, *My Apish Cousins*

THE LEARNED AND INGENIOUS symbolists dealing with *The
Ancient Mariner* whom I undertake to consider are Mr.
Kenneth Burke and Professor R. P. Warren. The symbolism
of Mr. Burke, who had discussed the poem in his *Philosophy
of Literary Form* (1941), is, as Mr. Warren says, "personal,"
preoccupied with Coleridge the man; and, consequently, the
critic practices psychology of a Freudian cast, with its *Ambivalenz* and *Identifizierung*, though not without some anthro-
pological notions derived from *The Golden Bough*. "The
Pilot's Boy," for instance, "who now doth crazy go" (but,
really, because of his having seen, as he thinks, the Devil or
his handiwork), becomes "the scapegoat," and that not only
for the Mariner but (still more remarkably) for the poet himself (pp. 39, 101, 287); and "the 'silly buckets' filled with
curative rain" (as the critic calls it)—upon which buckets
he "had pondered for years" though the word "silly" here
means only "paltry," "useless"—he takes for "a technical fore-
shadowing of the fate that befell" this quite episodic figure
in the poet (pp. 101, 287). But the autobiographical element
is more prominent; and as a whole the poem is held to be
a "ritual for the redemption of his drug" (*sic*, p. 96). The snakes
are "the synecdochic representatives of the drug" (isn't this con-

Reprinted by permission of the Modern Language Association of
America from PMLA, LXIII (1948), 214–33.

founded with another "habit"?); and since the critic has embraced *Ambivalenz*, and, like other "New Critics," is committed to paradox, the Mariner's blessing (though with a "gush of love") is really a cursing. To Mr. Knight [1] the snakes and the water mean something sexual; and in Mr. Burke that, too, is not wanting. In "the murder of the Albatross as a synecdochic representative of Sara" (72) there is more startling autobiography still; Coleridge here subsequently making "an explicit statement of a preference for church, prayer, and companionship over marriage" (pp. 24, 72, 95), though all the preference the Mariner himself expresses is that of a guest at such functions as the marriage-feast which he has just avoided. His preference is, indeed, not surprising. The Mariner passing, with his glittering eye, "like night from land to land," hymenean merriment, certainly, was not for him. But in fairness it must be added that for Mr. Burke synecdoche means, among other things, "the substitution of cause for effect and effect for cause"; and that, "if the Albatross is put there to be killed it could be said to 'participate in the crime,' in the sense that the savage [here *The Golden Bough*] after a successful hunt, thanks the quarry for its co-operation in the enterprise" (p. 28). And as for "kill" and "sacrifice," there is "important ambiguity in the scapegoat [here *The Golden Bough*, plus Freud, Hemingway, and Malraux] as in the stories of Christ and of Hamlet"; and "we might," he says, "call Hamlet the perfect liberal Christ, whose agony inaugurated the liberal era" (p. 46). From there the critic proceeds to "the 'criminal Christs' of gangster stories and hard-boiled fiction," in which "it is the evil that is featured, with promise of good as the frame." These various forms of disreputable character "die that we may live." Then from there to the Hemingway sacrificial bulls and wild game, which die in behalf of the slayer (that he may "live more intensely"). But again in fairness it must be added that some of these subsequent considerations are not quite explicitly connected with *The Ancient Mariner*. With little or no warrant in the text, Mr. Burke expounds and expatiates, dilates and divagates; but it must be remembered that according to Mr. Auden (and celebrating his "good sense" besides) he is "unquestionably the most brilliant and suggestive critic now writing in America." [2]

However that may be, Professor Warren,[3] in this matter, is perceptibly saner and more sensible; though he is considerably influenced by Mr. Burke, and (both being "New Critics") now and then treats his theories with more respect than those of critics hitherto more highly regarded (pp. 71–72, 137, 144). He thinks him, for example, "quite properly struck by the suggestive force of the phrase 'silly buckets' " (p. 112), though after (I trust) not pondering so long. Less engrossed with anthropology and autobiography, however, Mr. Warren is bent on importing into the poem, despite (as we shall see) Coleridge's own contrary principle, his basic theological and philosophical views as well as many of Mr. Warren's own. Not really much favoring Mr. Burke's and Mr. Fausset's treatment of the poem as a lurid personal confession, he turns to symbols more abstract. Like Professor Cleanth Brooks, he favors the word "meaningful"; and it suits his interpretation too.

Recognizing the distinction between allegory and symbolism, insisted upon by Coleridge (pp. 73–74, 78), which is practically that posited in my "Symbolism in Shakespeare" [4]— that allegory says one thing but means another, while symbolism means what it says and another thing besides—Mr. Warren rightly objects to "equating the Pilot with the Church and the Pilot's Boy with the clergy, or of the Hermit with the idea of an enlightened religion," and so on (p. 73), though he might well have included in his objection the snakes as opium and the Albatross as the poet's wife; but he then goes out of his way to call the reading of Professor Lowes (who keeps to the poem as, in Coleridge's own words, "pure imagination") a "merely literal reading" (p. 77). His own, like Mr. Burke's, is only too far from that. For Mr. Warren the killing of the Albatross symbolizes not uxoricide, indeed, but "Original Sin" (p. 84). Forsaking the usual and traditional way of thought, as represented even in the epigraph to the poem taken from Thomas Burnet's *Archaeologiae Philosophicae* (1692), he makes the Day evil and the Night good. Yet somewhat like Mr. Burke, and in his phrasing, he has the good events take place "under the aegis of the Moon," the bad events "under the aegis of the Sun"; though, as the critic candidly acknowledges, this is not always the case. The good moonlight, moreover, for him means the "Imagination"; the bad sunlight, "the reflective faculty." [5]

This is surely a strange and unhappily disturbing procedure, whereby a quite simple, long-established sort of symbolism in the epigraph, should, without any helpful hint to that effect in the marginal gloss provided, be "ironically" reversed in the poem itself. Irony (or Paradox, or Ambiguity), what critical crimes, nowadays, are committed in thy name! All that Burnet says in this connection (which, by the way, these critics, as such, might well have taken more to heart) is this: "But meanwhile must we diligently seek after truth, maintaining just measure, that we may distinguish certain from uncertain, *day from night.*" The last words are only a familiar expository metaphor, incidentally introduced: in any case, the poet, as a Romantic, a worshiper of Nature, would not, to use the critic's word, have "equated" the Day or the Sun with evil; and though as a Romantic preferring the imaginative to the reflective faculty, and the *Vernunft* to the *Verstand,* he, like Wordsworth, but unlike the later French and German Romantics, insisted on both morals and "good sense" [6] in poetry, and was, I think, rather incapable either of such a conception as the Sun ("the reflective faculty") being "the cause, symbolically speaking, of the acceptance of the crime" by the fellow-mariners (pp. 92–93), or as "the emotional equating of the Sun and the death-bark" (p. 94). The sailors, the critic hastens to add, here misunderstand:

> Nor dim nor red, like God's own head,
> The glorious Sun uprist;
> Then all averred, I had killed the bird
> That brought the fog and mist;

"they read God as justifying the act on the ground of practical consequence, just, as shall we say, Bishop Paley would have done" (p. 92). But how, then, without Mr. Warren's assistance, and until our distant day, was his own understanding of the matter to reach the reader; and why, on this theory, call the sun "glorious" or "equate" it with the reflective faculty, which "partakes of death"? Mr. Burke himself declares, a little less unplausibly, that the Sun, like God's *own head,* "avenges the murder" (p. 71). But by either interpretation Coleridge is trafficking in what Wordsworth (as quoted below) scornfully calls "hieroglyphics and enigmas," or in plain contradictions. The obvious meaning, appropriate enough in a fairy tale—in a *Percy's* "*Reliques*" ballad—is this, exempli-

fying a weathercock logic, in practical theology still widely
prevalent: that while the fog and mist lasted the sailors
thought the Ancient had done a hellish thing

> And it would work 'em woe,

but when

> Nor dim nor red, like God's own head,
> The glorious Sun uprist,

they, as the gloss has it, "justify the same." Spiritually blind
in both cases, however; the Sun itself, meanwhile, having
with their inner natures, or with celestial vengeance, either,
nothing at all to do. Nor has it when the death-bark appears;
or if it be to that "equated," is there then much of an event
—of a shudder—left for us

> When that strange shape drove suddenly
> Betwixt us and the Sun?

Moreover, Mr. Warren, as above, is flying in the face
of Coleridge's doctrine concerning symbolism, which he has
himself accepted, that, unlike allegory, it "partakes of the
reality which it renders intelligible" (p. 75). As Chesterton
says, "a symbol is not a disguise but a display; the best expression of something that cannot otherwise be expressed."
It is, in this respect, even like allegory when effective, which,
as Mr. C. S. Lewis observes, is "not to hide but to reveal."
Mr. Warren's own is not at all a symbolism like Tennyson's
in his "Ulysses" or Ibsen's in *The Master-Builder*, that of
a flesh-and-blood worthy who is voyaging and, at the same
time, philosophically exploring, or who is building and, at the
same time, romantically aspiring; and it does not render the
reality "intelligible." The critic himself properly insists that
symbols should not be "arbitrary" (p. 76), should be "rooted
in our universal natural experience" (p. 75), or else be "validated by the manipulation of the artist in a special context"
(p. 75). By neither test, surely, does the killing of the Albatross convey the meaning of "Original Sin." Moonlight, indeed, for the Romantics, might mean imagination, if the
poet indicated at all perceptibly that so he would have it,
and sunlight, possibly, the reflective faculty; but he couldn't,
at the same time, have the "crime, as it were, bring the
sun" (p. 92), the sun cause the acceptance of the crime by

the sailors (pp. 92–93), and itself "emotionally equate" with
the death-bark (p. 94). That seems regrettably like the
"paradoxical use of symbols" by Mr. Cleanth Brooks in interpreting *Macbeth*, which is far indeed from "revealing." [7]
In "Ulysses" and *The Master-Builder* the real and the symbolical, as they should, coalesce; but here, as often with the
French, "symbolism actually restricts the suggestive power of
the words themselves." [8] If the sun be the reflective faculty
and the moon the imaginative, how, then, can either, in addition, acceptably perform its natural and significant functions
in the itinerary, the one rising at first on the left, later on
the right, both also, in their movements, alternately lighting
up the scenery, and shining, as they actually would and do,
on both good and bad? Reflection and imagination alike,
meanwhile, reside more appropriately, of course, elsewhere. It
is partly the mere prominence of the two luminaries in the
poem that makes Mr. Warren and Mr. Burke take them for
symbols; like Mr. Knight, they are thus impressed by recurrence, reappearance; but in their own right and their sheer
reality sun and moon, on *terra firma* little noticed, are con-
spicuous and important, even on any ordinary voyage, over
unknown, empty seas, and particularly on a solitary one like
this. If the poet should look in his heart to write, so should
the reader in his own to read. Coleridge, cited by Lowes, tells
us, gratefully, that his Master, Bowyer, the same that flogged
him out of his upstart "infidelity," taught him, besides orthodoxy, that "poetry, even that of the loftiest, and seemingly
that of the wildest odes, had a logic of its own, as severe as
that of science." [9]

Now all these symbolist critics of *The Ancient Mariner*,
and of "Kubla Khan" as well, suffer, in my opinion, from at
least three fundamental failings: 1. They ignore the self-evi-
dent principle most neatly phrased by Alexander Pope, but
anticipated by Aristotle and echoed or independently asserted
by Goethe, Manzoni, Arnold, Pater, Sainte-Beuve, Taine, Poe,
Maupassant, Saintsbury, Curel, and no doubt others:

> A perfect Judge will read each work of Wit
> With the same spirit that the author writ.

Even by the French Vanguard, the New Critics should notice,
the principle is accepted. "L'idéal du critique," M. Benda says

of them in *La France byzantine* (p. 42), "est de coincider avec l'esprit du créateur ou romancier"; though this is, to be sure, by a mystical process, without allowing for the necessary later act of judgment. 2. They have not greatly profited by Coleridge's own utterances upon the critical principle and process. 3. They have not profited at all, apparently, by perusing *The Road to Xanadu*.

As for the first failing, the most obvious form of it is in the critics' manifest and besetting anachronism. *The Ancient Mariner* is in the style and meter of a medieval or early Elizabethan traditional ballad, with a superstitious Catholic background; it is a "literary fairy-tale," as Lowes calls it, an "old wives' tale," as Elton calls it; and what is present-day symbolism, with its "ambiguity" or Freudianism, doing in either? This is so incongruous that the Romantics of Coleridge's time would not have discovered it if there, and certainly would not have delighted in it. Plain allegory, which Mr. Warren rightly rejects, would have been less out of keeping.

As for the second failing, Coleridge in the *Biographia Literaria*, Chapter XIV, observes: "Nothing can permanently please which does not contain in itself the reason why it is so and not otherwise." "Every work of art," says even Poe, like Goethe before him, "contains within itself all that is necessary for its comprehension." A play or any other poem, that is, does not, in its own time, require prolegomena, footnotes, or appendices—the marginal glosses here appended, we shall see, are of a different order—whether from the author's or another's hand. Exposition, exegesis, properly comes generations afterwards—when the language presents difficulties, when the technique or conventions are obsolete—and in Shakespeare the other sort of comment, making, says Grillparzer the dramatist, "this most comprehensible of poets incomprehensible," is nowadays the chief difficulty itself. Furthermore, Coleridge's own practice as a critic of Shakespeare and other poetry is pretty much in keeping with his principle. He had, as in the case of *Hamlet*, not always sufficient knowledge of Elizabethan drama, or of Shakespeare's relations to his predecessors, for the right appreciation of his purpose; but he did not, like the Germans, overlay the text with philosophy, or, like our present-day antiquaries, with history or Elizabethan erudi-

tion, or, like our Freudians, with a psychology which the
dramatist could not have known (and would not have employed if he had). Of philosophy in poetry, indeed, when
really it is there, not simply imported or imputed, Coleridge
wrote to Wordsworth in 1815: "Whatever in Lucretius is
poetry is not philosophical; whatever is philosophical is not
poetry." He himself, of course, was a student of philosophy
and also a philosopher; but like Wordsworth, he kept art and
philosophy or science pretty much apart, and when he didn't
he generally fell under the same judgment as Lucretius. Like
Wordsworth, though the latter also did not always live up
to it, he certainly believed that "the Poet writes under one
restriction only, namely, the necessity of giving immediate
pleasure to a human Being possessed of that information
which may be expected from him, not as a lawyer, a physician,
a mariner, an astronomer, or a natural philosopher, but as
a Man." So, again: "Poets do not write for Poets alone, but
for Men." And yet again, speaking of abuses such as those
of the Metaphysicals or the Gongorists, though both Romantic
poets dreamt not of those to be perpetrated by the similar
sects today: "thrusting out of sight the plain humanities of
nature by a motley masquerade of tricks, quaintnesses, hieroglyphics, and enigmas." What is more, these symbolists fly
directly in the face of Coleridge's precise account in the *Biographia Literaria* of his own role as a partner in the *Lyrical
Ballads*: to deal "with persons and characters supernatural or
at least romantic; yet so as to transfer from our inward nature a human interest and a semblance of truth sufficient
to procure for these shadows of imagination that willing suspension of disbelief for the moment which constitutes poetic
faith." Now "a human interest" and the words following do
not mean symbolism and, still less, allegory. If anything, they
mean, make the supernatural, "for the moment"—for the
requirements of the occasion—natural, acceptable; as Shakespeare has the Ghost in *Hamlet* talk like a disembodied mortal
suffering in Purgatory—monotonously, relentlessly, with none
of the liveliness of life—

> Thy bones are marrowless, thy blood is cold—

or has Ariel talk lightly, impulsively, like a spirit of the air.
   If, moreover, allegory or symbolism had been intended,

why does some hint of that not appear in the marginal glosses? Why, indeed, were these added? They are not at all necessary for the understanding of the poem, are not like Mr. T. S. Eliot's notes appended to *The Waste Land*. In prose, they speak still, though more explicitly or philosophically, the language of superstition; they only amplify, and in explaining by no means explain away. Their purpose is but to heighten the illusion; they credibilize the marvels, providing an approach to them, a middle distance, which makes them, appropriately, more remote. In the poem itself this principle of perspective is happily observed. The marvels occur on unknown, distant seas within the meridian of marvels; and when the Mariner and his ship, equally bewitched, arrive, the effect of the mere sight of them on the normal, everyday Hermit, Pilot, and Pilot's Boy is startling, shocking. The effect of that, in turn, upon the Wedding-Guest and also the reader is convincing. And as important to the transition and the illusion is the effect upon the Mariner himself before that:

> Oh! dream of joy! is this indeed
> The lighthouse top I see?
> Is this the hill? Is this the kirk?
> Is this mine own countree?
> . . . .
> O let me be awake, my God!
> Or let me sleep alway.

It is like the ending of the *Midsummer Night's Dream*, as day breaks and the lovers wonder whether the adventures of the night were a dream or no. Dreaming without a waking is not dreaming. In the figurative sense of the word "perspective," to be sure, the Wedding-Guest, in his momentary, palpitating interruptions of the narrative—"Why looks't thou so?"—"I fear thee, Ancient Mariner"—represents the middle distance; and the marginal comment is the nearer distance, though still from us remote.

Furthermore, as everybody knows, 1798, the date of the publication, was near the high tide of English Romanticism, a period at which the interest in the superstitious and the supernatural—ghosts and other spirits, witchcraft and magic, omens and forebodings—was widely prevalent in not only poetry but the novel, and had reached the stage. In December, 1797, Monk Lewis's *Castle Spectre* was received at Drury Lane with great applause; and in June, 1798, Wordsworth, seeing it at Bristol, said "it fitted the taste of the audience like a glove." [10] Coleridge himself did not like it, as he says in his letter to Wordsworth, but not (of course) because it contained the supernatural. And none of the literary figures concerned with *The Ancient Mariner*, in its composition or on its appearance, seems to have detected allegory or symbolism in it; not William Wordsworth or Dorothy, not Lamb, Southey, or Hazlitt. Mr. Warren rightly insists that symbolism should be "necessary," or, as Arnold would say, "inevitable"; for symbolism that would mean, also, perceptible, as it is in "Ulysses" and *The Master-Builder;* and a symbolism that is not perceptible in its own day or for a hundred and fifty years after may well be considered illusory, nonexistent. Wordsworth himself at the outset suggested the killing of the Albatross, the "spectral persecution," the wandering of the Mariner, and the navigation by the dead men inspired. And Lamb, though he disliked the miraculous part of it, wrote to Wordsworth that he "was never so affected with any human tale." "After first reading it," he says, "I was totally possessed with it for many days." Apparently *The Ancient Mariner* was, though not well received by the reviewers, in the spirit of the time. Wordsworth in his repeated and rather extended discussions, in the 1800 edition of the *Lyrical Ballads* and by word of mouth to Miss Fenwick, gives no hint of an under-meaning. He finds fault with it freely enough; but the excellence he insists upon is purely poetical:

> Yet the Poem contains many delicate touches of passion, and indeed the passion is everywhere true to nature; a great number of the stanzas present beautiful images, and are expressed with unusual felicity of language; and the versification, tho' the metre is itself unfit for long poems, is harmonious and artfully varied, exhibiting the utmost powers of that metre, and every variety of which it is capable. It therefore appeared to me that these several merits (the first of which, namely, that of the passion, is of the highest kind) gave to the Poem a value which is not often possessed by better Poems.

Mr. Warren is, of course, right in insisting that for Coleridge, as for Wordsworth too, the word imagination was a sacred one (p. 67), and the poem in question "not to be read as an agreeable but scarcely meaningful effusion" (p. 69). But certainly Mr. Lowes was far enough from reading it

so; and Coleridge's answer (*Table Talk*, May 31, 1830) to
Mrs. Barbauld's objection that the poem had no moral the
critic, I think, misinterprets. "I told her," says the poet,

> that in my own judgment the poem had too much; and that the
> only or chief fault . . . was the obtrusion of the moral senti-
> ment so openly on the reader as a principle or cause of action
> in a work of such pure imagination. It ought to have had no
> more moral than the Arabian Nights' tale of the merchant's
> sitting down to eat dates by the side of a well and throwing
> the shells aside, and lo! a geni starts up, and says he *must* kill
> the aforesaid merchant, *because* one of the date shells had, it
> seems, put out the eye of the geni's son.

Undoubtedly the moral Coleridge had in mind was in lines
612–17:

> He prayeth well, who loveth well
> Both man and bird and beast.
> He prayeth best, who loveth best
> All things both great and small;
> For the dear God who loveth us,
> He made and loveth all.

And as also later fine critics have noticed, the moral is both
a little obtruded and not quite perfectly fitted to the poem
as a whole. Yet Coleridge's mere objection to that does not
exclude the possibility of a deeper, a more than literal, meaning. Such it has, as have all great poems or stories, from Eden
and Ilium down, and the poem now in question has more
of such meaning than many; but, as involved in the narrative, it should have been left to speak for itself. Not that as
spoken by the Mariner it can be considered objectionable.
Dramatically, the Mariner's farewell words are in keeping: he
has just spoken of walking to the kirk and of prayer. Besides, they are in keeping with the mediaeval spirit, which
was given to simple, open moralizing. They are not, however,
in keeping with Mr. Warren's sophisticated interpretation;
nor are the poet's words to Mrs. Barbauld; and that, once
on the subject of a meaning, Coleridge, so addicted as he was
to interpretation—to lecturing, or, as Lamb once jokingly said,
to preaching—should, if here there was anything like a symbolism—so weighty but cryptic a meaning—to lay bare, have
failed to profit by the opportunity, is almost entirely beyond
belief. The *bas bleu* after a moral—had *he* had a tale to tell
he would have held her with his own glittering eye.

And as for *The Road to Xanadu,* that inspired, prodigious volume of scholarship and critical perception, it would seem at times as if these critics now in question had not even read it. When Lowes wrote, the thoroughgoing symbolists had not yet tackled the poem, but the moralists had, either to misinterpret or to cavil; and his reply to them, as we shall see, nevertheless fits the latter-day symbolists remarkably well. But what should have impressed them still more is the great critic's re-creation of the poem from its origins. . . . Moreover, the critic not only recovers the original materials but also, after Coleridge, puts them together again. He perceives the artistry, for instance, in compacting and telescoping the story: as in passing lightly over the first crossing of the equator by means of the Wedding-Guest's interruption, when he beats his breast at the sound of the loud bassoon, and over the doubling of another cape, on the long voyage home, by means of the Mariner's collapse and spellbound sleep.

This all is but story, one of "pure imagination" as Coleridge calls it, though one poetically and structurally, not philosophically, anagogically significant. And now for Professor Lowes in his reply to the moralists. Like the symbolists, unless the poem was to be made deep and devious to their taste, the moralists such as Professor Babbitt objected to it because the Mariner "is relieved of the burden of his transgression by admiring the color of water-snakes"; or cried out upon "the ruthless slaying of the crew because the Mariner had killed a bird." But as the late Oliver Elton, quoted by Lowes, tersely puts it: "Coleridge is not . . . concerned with the prevention of cruelty to albatrosses." And as Lowes himself puts it, "art works through illusion—'that poetical and artistic illusion,' as Amiel has it, 'which does not aim at being confounded with reality itself' ":

> The shooting of a sea-bird carries in its train the vengeance of an aquatic daemon, acting in conjunction with a spectre-bark; and an impulse of love for other living creatures of the deep summons a troop of angels to navigate an unmanned ship. Moreover, because the Mariner has shot a bird, four times fifty sailors drop down dead, and the slayer himself is doomed to an endless life. The punishment, measured by the standards of a world of balanced penalties, palpably does not fit the crime. But the sphere of balanced penalties is not the given world in which the poem moves. Within *that* world,

where birds have tutelary daemons and ships are driven by
spectral and angelic powers, consequence and antecedent are
in keeping—if for the poet's moment we accept the poet's
premises [Xanadu, p. 300].

Or, as the critic says almost immediately after: "The *imaginative* use of familiar moral values, like the imaginative use of
the familiar outline of a voyage [as illustrated above], is
leagues away from the promulgation of edifying doctrine
through the vehicle of a fairytale." And as he says still later
(p. 301): "The fallacy of such criticism lies in its failure to
reckon with the very *donnée* of the poem." It is a matter,
in short, of a convention—of premises or postulates, and
such (by the way) as I have insisted upon, time and again,
in Shakespeare.

What, then, is the truth of "our inward nature" that
is transferred to this work of "pure imagination"? At bottom,
I think, there is convention again; which, when felicitous
and acceptable, is a convenience, "providing common ground
on which dramatist [or poet] and audience are mutually at
ease." [11] As in most fairy tales or old wives' tales, there is a
process of primitive or (as here) artistic simplification and
exaggeration. In most art, to be sure, there is; but in such
stories it is carried further. The punishment is far from
fitting the crime, whether the Mariner's or the crew's. But
this justice is not meant to be philosophical, nor, so far as
presided over by the Polar Spirit, Christian, but superstitious
and legendary. The fatality attaching to the House of Atreus,
making no distinctions, reaches beyond the original sinner,
like the wrath of Jehovah, "visiting the iniquity of the fathers
upon the children unto the third and fourth generation of
them that hate me." So it is often in Greek tragedy, in the
Iliad and the *Odyssey* as well as the Hebrew Scriptures. Both
the Hellenic and the Hebrew deity at times arbitrarily, irre-
sponsibly—"I will have mercy upon whom I will have mercy"
—permit and even ordain unnecessary slaughter of the con-
tending hosts, simply to satisfy their own wrath or fulfill their
inscrutable purposes; and in the *Odyssey* the hero was, as
Professor W. C. Wright [12] observes in drawing the parallel
with the poem in question, "abandoned by heaven because
he had . . . mutilated a certain primaeval creature beloved
of the Sea-god; and, secondly, he had to see his crew die

one after the other because in their turn they had killed certain creatures beloved of the Sun-god." Here the crew suffer because they had approved of the killing, but also as thus contributing to the punishment of the Mariner, who was first to blame. That retribution is greater, simpler, less regardful of distinctions, than in life we should have it, but yet has something of a natural movement: punishment, repentance, a gush of love for other living things, prayer and relief, yet further penance, for, as in ancient legend and somewhat as in life, "the train of cause and consequence knows no end." [13] And *"given that world,"* as Lowes says, one of tutelary Spirits and a retribution that is endless, and of a leading figure who, like the Wandering Jew and the Flying Dutchman, is immortal—"given that world, its inviolate keeping with itself becomes the sole condition of our acceptance, for the moment, of its validity" (p. 299).

For *The Ancient Mariner* is a structure, a perfectly ordered, a finely "complex, design wrought out through the exquisite adjustment of innumerable details" (p. 425). It is not an opium dream like "Kubla Khan"; and that is the answer to the symbolists of psychoanalytic and biographical bent. Both poems are exquisite; but the latter is not even by the canons of poetry a severely logical design; and old Bowyer, had he set eyes on it, might have reached for the birch.

What, then, is the importance of our poem, the symbolists may ask, if it carries no more meaning than is here allowed it? Why, that of beauty, which is a joy forever; a beauty "inviolate," self-contained; a beauty, in its six hundred lines, almost unrivalled in vision, in rhythm, melody, and narrative art. It is the traditional ballad of the supernatural raised to its highest potency; but it is also, as Professor Elton says, "a great, a concerted and complex composition, playing at once on the simplest matters of the heart and conscience, and on the strangest visions of the senses, with the depth of colour and changing, recurrent rhythms that we know." [14] Too simple for the symbolists; but neither that nor too complex for poetry, with which they are not content. Of Lowes Mr. Warren complains as now too "literal," now too "aesthetic." The symbolists themselves are, despite their intellectual and imaginative endowments, not sufficiently or discriminatingly either the one or the other.

One of the troubles with the symbolists and psycho-
analysts, as with the more unpretending "impressionists," is
that they do not look upon art as a communication, or on
criticism as an interpretation. They do not consider art as
in definite relation to the artist and his public; not inquiring,
as Goethe would have them do, "what his purpose was,
whether it was reasonable and intelligent, or in what measure it was achieved." They forget, indeed, that, not only a
communication, "all art is," as Synge, like Aristotle, Vernon
Lee, Abercrombie, and many another, has said, "a collabora-
tion"; and that it "exists not only in expressing a thing: it
equally exists [which, *vide supra*, is somewhat overstated] in
the receiving of the thing expressed." Instead, they in theory
look upon the work of art as having an independent and sub-
stantive existence, like an object in nature, yet, in practice, to
be examined and analyzed, understood and appreciated, at
the critic's own discretion; and they set their native imaginations a-work, instead of permitting them to respond to the
far more important imagination of the artist:

> If I contemplate, Nature with delight, I am certainly provid-
> ing material for the science of aesthetics, and I may consider
> myself to be in a poetical state of mind; but what is to be
> noted now is, that the experience is wholly *my own*. If, how-
> ever, I contemplate with delight a work of art—a poem, say—
> the experience is not wholly my own; another man's experience
> is involved with mine: namely, the poet's. This may not seem
> a very great difference; but in fact it is crucial: it is the vitally
> characteristic thing in poetry: for it is this that makes poetry
> one of the Arts. The theory of poetry, then, must take account
> not only of the quality of certain remarkable kinds of experi-
> ence, but also of the no less remarkable Art by which the poet
> has communicated his experience and enabled it to become
> ours as well.—Abercrombie, *The Theory of Poetry*, pp. 15–16.

On the view criticized by Abercrombie, then, either the poem
(the painting or the piece of music) "should not mean [so
they say] but *be*"; or else it has numerous meanings almost
any one of which has validity, though, in the upshot, the
symbolist, psychoanalyst, or impressionist critic is generally
not more tolerant of other people's interpretations than the
sensibly sensitive himself. But they do not so much interpret
as assimilate; and in assimilation, no doubt—in re-creation—
there are substantial satisfactions. Instead of "receiving," like

the Wedding-Guest, who "listens like a three years' child,"
the critic himself "has his will"—with the Albatross as Sara, the
Pilot's Boy as scapegoat, the snakes as opium, with sun and
moon. Whether he knows it or not, he is, so far, an egocentric, a solipsist, scarcely a critic; and what Saintsbury
years ago called "one of the commonest but most uncritical
faults of criticism—the refusal to consider what it is that the
author intended to give us," is now, in these days of symbolist
poetry, commoner than ever. Where so little meaning is im-
parted, it is, of course, not unnatural that some should be
imputed; but it is unnatural where there is no symbolism at
all.

.   .   .   .

The chief trouble with the symbolists, however, as critics
or as poets, is a sophisticated, an inflated conception of either
criticism or poetry. . . . "All art, indeed," as Pater says in
the essay on Giorgione, "constantly aspires towards the condition of music." But by these critics of *The Ancient Mariner*,
unwilling thus to "become as little children," the process—
this progress towards simplicity—is reversed. "The true drama,"
of course, whether in verse or in prose, is a higher, more complicated structure than the poem now in question; but here,
where the ballad is manifest, it is now almost ignored, dis-
owned. The poem in question, obviously, is, in form and
spirit, in style and meter, the ballad of tradition, though
glorified. Also, as both Lowes and Elton have said, it is a
"fairy-tale," "an old wives' tale," though (again) of a super-
lative sort. In the hands of the symbolists, however, it is "a
tale which holdeth children from play and old men from
the chimney-corner" now no more. It is a mystery, an enigma;
and, with or without a solution, no longer for young and
old alike, but for the learned alone, in the seminar or the
study.

Notes

1. G. Wilson Knight, *The Starlit Dome* (London, 1941), pp. 86–87.
2. Quoted from the *New Republic* in the *Book Review Digest*.
3. *The Ancient Mariner*, with an essay by Robert Penn Warren
(1946).
4. *Modern Language Review*, 1946, a reply to Mr. Brooks on *Macbeth*.
5. Warren, pp. 87–88. A little more in keeping with the text, perhaps,
Mr. Burke (p. 24) has it that the Mariner suffered his punishments under

the aegis of the Sun, and that his *cure* was effected under the aegis of the Moon; but out of this "meaningfulness" there is little indeed to choose, whether for philosophy or poetry. By psychological allegory the light of both sun and moon is darkened.

6. *Biographia Literaria*, Ch. XIV, last sentence; Wordsworth (1899), Preface, p. 852. And Coleridge's *Table Talk*: "Poetry is certainly more than good sense; but it must be good sense, at all events; just as a palace is more than a house; but it must be a house, at least."

7. Cleanth Brooks, *The Well Wrought Urn* (New York, 1947), pp. 22–49.

8. Lascelles Abercrombie, *Theory of Poetry* (London, 1926), p. 97.

9. *The Road to Xanadu* (1927), p. 298; *Biog. Lit.*, Ch. I.

10. *Ibid.*, p. 244.

11. H. Granville-Barker, *On Dramatic Method* (1931), p. 157.

12. *Xanadu*, pp. 566–67.

13. *Ibid.*, p. 297.

14. *A Survey of English Literature, 1780–1830* (1912), II, 108.

9 · "Kubla Khan," *Christabel,* and "Dejection"

IF COLERIDGE HAD NEVER PUBLISHED his Preface, who would have thought of "Kubla Khan" as a fragment? Who would have guessed at a dream? Who, without the confession, would have supposed that "in consequence of a slight indisposition, an anodyne had been prescribed"? Who would have thought it nothing but a "psychological curiosity"? Who, later, would have dared to talk of its "patchwork brilliance"? [1] Coleridge played, out of modesty, straight into the hands of critics.

Were it not for Livingston Lowes, it would hardly still be necessary to point out the poem's essential unity and the relation between its two parts. But Lowes's book has such deserved prestige for other reasons that his view may still have undeserved currency. He treats the relation between the parts as "inconsequential."

> With utter inconsequence, as the caves of ice glance and are gone, the Abyssinian damsel with a dulcimer is there, a tantalising phantom of a dream-remembered dream, unlocalized, without the slightest sense of unreality, in space; while the Tartar youth with flashing eyes is projected against the background of that twice phantasmal dome in air, dream-built within the dream. It is a bafflingly complex involution—dreams within dreams, like a nest of Oriental ivories, "sphere in sphere." [2]

He also talks of the "vivid incoherence" of the second part.[3] This shows, more clearly than anything could, the prejudice

Reprinted from *Coleridge* (1953, London) by Humphry House, by permission of Rupert Hart-Davis Ltd., London.

under which readers labor from having been told beforehand
that the poem was a dream, or the result of a dream. For
it is exactly on the relationship between these two parts that
the poem's character and the whole interpretation of it depend.

The "flashing eyes and floating hair" could only have
been attributed to a "Tartar youth" by somebody who had
momentarily forgotten the *Phaedrus,* say, and *A Midsummer
Night's Dream.* For this is poetic frenzy, and the "symphony
and song" are the emblemized conditions of poetic creation.
The unity of the poem focuses on just that transition from
the first part to the second, and the pivot of all interpretation is in the lines:

> Could I revive within me
> Her symphony and song,
> To such a deep delight 'twould win me,
> That with music loud and long,
> I would build that dome in air . . .[4]

For "Kubla Khan" is a poem about the act of poetic creation,
about the "ecstasy in imaginative fulfilment."[5] Interpretations have diverged to opposite poles of major meaning on
the treatment of the emphasis and rhythm of that single
line—"Could I revive within me." If a strong emphasis (and
therefore necessarily also a strong metrical stress) is put upon
"could," the word can be taken to imply "If only I could,
but I can't," and the whole poem can be made to appear
to be about the failure and frustration of the creative power.
But if the emphasis on "could" is slight, then the condition
is an "open" condition, like "Could you make it Wednesday
instead of Thursday, it would be easier for me"; and the
matter is the very possibility of creative achievement. The
word "once" in the line "In a vision once I saw" then also
becomes a light syllable, not implying "once, only once and,
I fear, never again," but rather indicating delight, surprise
and the sense of unique privilege.

In this choice I have no hesitation in taking the second
alternative; not only is it biographically relevant to point out
that in 1797–1798 Coleridge, so far from bemoaning the loss
of creative power, was only just discovering its strength; but
also the whole rhythmic character of the paragraph requires
this view. The meter is light and fast; the paragraph moves

from delight and surprise, through enthusiasm to ecstasy; no sensitive reader can read it otherwise. The verse is asserting, not denying, the ecstasy. If this were a poem of frustration and failure, the movement would be slow and the stresses heavy. Another verbal detail points the same way—"I would build *that* dome in air." What dome? Of course, the dome that has been described in the first part. And if it had not there been fully described, the music of the singing and the dulcimer would not have any substantial and evident power. It is just because the first part presents the dome and the river with all its setting so completely, beautifully, and finally, that we accept the authenticity of the creative impulse in the second part, and find in the last word "Paradise" a fact, not a forlorn hope. "Kubla Khan" is a triumphant positive statement of the potentialities of poetry. How great those potentialities are is revealed partly in the description of its *effects* at the ending of the second part and partly in the very substance and content of the first.

The precision and clarity of the opening part are the first things to mark—even in the order of the landscape. In the center is the pleasure-dome with its gardens on the river bank: to one side is the river's source in the chasm, to the other are the "caverns measureless to man" and the "sunless sea" into which the river falls: Kubla in the center can hear the *"mingled* measure" of the fountain of the source from one side, and of the dark caves from the other. The river winds across the whole landscape. Nobody need keep this mere geographical consistency of the description prominently in mind as he reads (though once established it remains clear and constant); but I suggest that if this factual-visual consistency had been absent, and there had been a mere random sequence or collocation of items, such as a dream might well have provided—items which needed a symbol-system to establish relations at all—then the absence *would* be observed: the poem would have been quite different, and a new kind of effort would have been needed to apprehend what unity it might have had. Within this main landscape, too, there is a pervasive order. The fertility of the plain is only made possible by the mysterious energy of the source. The dome has come into being by Kubla's decree: the dome is stately; the gardens are girdled round with walls and towers.

It is so often said that "Kubla Khan" achieves its effect mainly by "far-reaching suggestiveness," or by incantation or by much connotation, with little denotation, that it is worth emphasizing this element of plain clear statement at the outset, statement which does particularize a series of details interrelated to each other, and deriving their relevance from their interrelation and their order. Furthermore, the use of highly emotive and suggestive proper names is proportionately no large source of the poem's effect; it is only necessary to watch the incidence of them. Xanadu, Kubla Khan, and Alph occur once in that form within the poem's opening two-and-a-half lines: and none of them occurs again except for the single repetition of Kubla in line 29. Abyssinian and Mount Abora occur once each, in the three lines 39–41. There are no other proper names in the poem at all, unless we should count the final word Paradise.

Next, the mode of appraisal which relies on suggestiveness is likely to underestimate the strength and firmness of the descriptions. In particular, lines 17–24, describing the source of the river, do not in method employ "suggestiveness" at all.

> And from this chasm, with ceaseless turmoil seething,
> As if this earth in fast thick pants were breathing,
> A mighty fountain momently was forced:
> Amid whose swift half-intermitted burst
> Huge fragments vaulted like rebounding hail,
> Or chaffy grain beneath the thresher's flail:
> And 'mid these dancing rocks at once and ever
> It flung up momently the sacred river.

We may well believe that this is based on a combination of William Bartram's description of the "chrystal fountain" with his description of the "Alligator Hole," [6] but he did not provide the organization of the words to convey so fully the sense of inexhaustible energy, now falling now rising, but persisting through its own pulse. We have here in verse the counterpart to such later prose descriptions as that of the starlings or the "white rose of eddy-foam." The whole passage is full of life because the verse has both the needed energy and the needed control. The combination of energy and control in the rhythm and sound is so great, as in

> at once and ever
> It flung up momently the sacred river

that we are even in danger of missing the force of the imagery, as in "rebounding hail" and "dancing rocks." If we miss it, it is our fault not Coleridge's; and it sometimes appears as if readers are blaming or underestimating him because they have improperly allowed themselves, under the influence of the rhythm, to be blind to the "huge fragments" and "dancing rocks" which lay another kind of weight upon it, and to be blind to the construction of the thought, which holds together the continuity and the intermission.

A different kind of clarity and precision in the first part leads us nearer to the poem's central meaning—the consistency with which the main facts of this landscape are treated, the dome and the river. The dome (apart from the biographists' concern about its oriental connection with opium—all the more important to them because Purchas did not mention it and archaeologists have found no trace) is an agreed emblem of fulfillment and satisfaction, it is breastlike, full to touch and eye, rounded and complete. In the first part it is mentioned three times, as "a stately pleasure-dome" in line 2, as "the dome of pleasure" in line 31, and as "A sunny pleasure-dome" in line 36. Each time the word "pleasure" occurs with it. So too, the word *river* is used three times in the first part, and each time, without fail, it is "the *sacred* river": this is its constant, invariable epithet. The center of the landscape of this part is, as we have seen, the point at which the dome and the river join:

> The shadow of the dome of pleasure
> Floated midway on the waves.

Here, without possibility of doubt, the poem presents the conjunction of pleasure and sacredness: that is the core of Part One. And in Part Two the poet who has been able to realize this fusion of pleasure and sacredness is himself regarded as a holy or sacred person, a seer acquainted with the undivided life: and this part is clinched by the emphatic and final word Paradise. The conditional form of Part Two does not annul the presentation of Paradise in Part One, though it may hold out the hope of a future fuller vision.

What is this Paradise? Those who are intent on making "Kubla Khan" either a poem about imaginative failure or a document for the study of opium dreams, remind us that

many of the sources for Coleridge's details were descriptions
of false paradises; there was Aloadine's trick Mohammedan
Paradise to which young men were lured and entertained with
music and girls, so that they might be willing to die in battle
in the hope of winning such joys forever. There were, still
more notably, the pseudo-Paradises of Milton,

> that faire field
> Of *Enna*,[7]

and the place

> where *Abassin* Kings thir issue Guard,
> Mount *Amara*, though this by som suppos'd
> True Paradise under the *Ethiop* Line
> By *Nilus* head.[8]

Of course we have in "Kubla Khan" a fruit of Coleridge's
Miltonizing, but because the Abassin kings and Mount Amara
belong with one false paradise it does not follow that the
Abyssinian maid and Mount Abora belong with another.

There is only one answer to those who want to make
this a false Paradise—that is, an appeal to the poem as a
whole, its rhythmical development, its total effect as a poem
of fulfillment, and to say "If you still want to make that experience a spurious experience, do so: 'Thy way thou canst
not miss, me mine requires.'" Acceptance of the Paradise,
in sympathy, is the normal response, from childhood and un-
sophistication to criticism: to most people rejection would
mean a ruinous and purposeless wrench. But what is being
accepted?

Positively, it causes a distortion of the poem if we try
to approximate this Paradise either to the earthly Paradise
of Eden before the Fall or to the Heavenly Paradise which
is the ultimate abode of the blest. It may take its imagery
from Eden, but it is not Eden because Kubla Khan is not
Adam. Kubla Khan himself is literally an oriental prince with
his name adapted from Purchas. We may, if we persist in
hankering after formal equations, incline to say he *is* the
Representative Man, or Mankind in general: but what matters
is not his supposed fixed and antecedent symbolic character,
so much as his activity. Within the landscape treated as
literal he must be of princely scope, in order to decree the
dome and gardens: and it is this decree that matters, for it

images the power of man over his environment and the fact that man makes his Paradise for himself. Just as the whole poem is about poetic creation at the imaginative level, so, within the work of the imagination, occurs the creativeness of man at the ethical and practical levels. This is what the poet, of all men, is capable of realizing.

I have already noticed that the name Kubla is repeated only once after the first line; and the place of its repetition is significant:

> And 'mid this tumult Kubla heard from far
> Ancestral voices prophesying war!

This is essential to the full unity of the conception: the Paradise contains knowledge of the threat of its own possible destruction. It is not held as a permanent gift; the ideal life is always open to forces of evil; it must be not only created by man for himself, but also defended by him. It is not of the essence of this Paradise that it must be lost; but there is a risk that it may be lost.

About the river, again, we need not aim to be too precise and make equations. Its function in the poem is clear. The bounding energy of its source makes the fertility of the plain possible: it is the sacred given condition of human life. By using it rightly, by building on its bank, by diverting its water into his sinuous rills, Kubla achieves his perfect state of balanced living. It is an image of these nonhuman, holy, given conditions. It is not an allegorical river which would still flow across that plain if Kubla was not there. It is an imaginative statement of the abundant life in the universe, which begins and ends in a mystery touched with dread, but it is a statement of this life as the ground of ideal human activity.

The "caves of ice" need special attention. Some discussions of the poem seem to imply that they belong with the "caverns measureless to man"; but there surely can be no doubt that in the poem they belong closely and necessarily with the dome.

> It was a miracle of rare device,
> A sunny pleasure-dome, with caves of ice!

The very line shows the closeness by the antithesis, the convex against the concave, the warm against the cold. It is not

necessary to invoke Coleridge's own statement of the theory
of the reconciliation of opposites in art [9] ("the heat in ice"
is even one of his examples) to see that it is the holding
together of these two different elements in which the miracle
consists. They are repeated together, also within the single
line, 47, in Part Two. Lowes shows clearly how in Coleridge's
memory the caves of ice came to be associated with the
sacred river; [10] and in his sources the ice does not indicate
terror or torment or death (as Miss Bodkin [11] seems to think
Coleridge's ice does here), but rather the marvellous, and
the delight which accompanies the marvellous; the ice is
linked specifically to the fountains sacred to the moon. This
marvellousness is present also in "Kubla Khan," but there
is more: ice is shining, clear, crystalline, hard: and here it
adds greater strength and austerity to what would be otherwise the lush, soft, even sentimental, core of the poem. As
it is, the miracle of rare device consists in the combination
of these softer and harder elements. And when this is seen
in relation to the act of poetic creation, in the light of which
all Part One must be understood, its function is still plainer:
such creation has this element of austerity in it.

For this is a vision of the ideal human life *as the poetic
imagination can create it*. Part One only exists in the light
of Part Two. There may be other Paradises, other false Paradises too: but this is the creation of the poet in his frenzy.
And it is because he can create it that he deserves the
ritual dread.

II

The critique of *Christabel* is an entirely different matter:
for not only is it inescapably a fragment, but the two parts
differ so much from each other, that they scarcely seem to
belong to the same poem. The unlikeness here would have
been altogether apparent even if Coleridge had not himself, as
usual, used a Preface to explain that the two parts were written in different years, with the visit to Germany between
them, and even if all his letters and other comments on the
business were unknown.

One of the most obvious differences between the two
parts is caused by his physical move from Somerset to the
Lake District. In Part I there is the castle in the woodland,

with oak and moss and mistletoe, a landscape which has its
function only in relation to the persons and the atmosphere.
There are no proper names but those of the three main
persons. In Part II we plunge straight into the detailed geog-
raphy of the region; Wyndermere, Langdale Pike, Dungeon-
ghyll, Borodale and the rest, organize the reader's attention
as if this were matter of history rather than of imagery.

It is generally agreed that the experience of reading the
first part of *Christabel* is more an acquaintance with an atmosphere than the apprehension of a poetic unity. This atmosphere is achieved partly through description of the setting,
partly by the mystery surrounding Geraldine.

One of the familiar examples of description will illustrate
the relationship between Coleridge's descriptions and Dorothy
Wordsworth's.

Dorothy, 25 January 1798:

> The sky spread over with one continuous cloud, whitened by
> the light of the moon . . .[12]

Dorothy, 31 January:

> When we left home the moon immensely large, the sky scat-
> tered over with clouds. These soon closed in, contracting the
> dimensions of the moon without concealing her.[13]

Coleridge, Gutch Memorandum Book:

> Behind the thin
> Grey cloud that covered but not hid the sky
> The round full moon looked small.[14]

Coleridge, *Christabel*, Part I, lines 14–19:

> Is the night chilly and dark?
> The night is chilly, but not dark.
> The thin gray cloud is spread on high,
> It covers but not hides the sky.
> The moon is behind, and at the full;
> And yet she looks both small and dull.

We do not know whose original observation this may
have been, but one thing is clear—that Coleridge did more
than merely take over an existing observation of Dorothy's or
his own, and transfer it straight into *Christabel*; because he
has very much modified his own first verse draft in the Gutch
book. Especially by adding the moon's dullness—perhaps he

even did pronounce the word "dull" to rhyme with "full"—
he has increased the mysteriousness and vagueness of the
midnight light, and has reached an effect which is altogether
absent from Wordsworth's lines in "A Night-Piece," which
also belong with the same entry in Dorothy's Journal. Wordsworth wrote:

> The sky is overcast
> With a continuous cloud of texture close,
> Heavy and wan, all whitened by the Moon,
> Which through that veil is indistinctly seen,
> A dull, contracted circle, yielding light
> So feebly spread that not a shadow falls,
> Chequering the ground.[15]

The difference of atmosphere from *Christabel* is very marked.
The whole Wordsworth poem is an attempt to expand, rather
in the manner of Cowper, according to a method in which
rhythm has little part; to win assent to the delight by mere
accumulation of circumstance and detail. But in the result
there is no particularity of mood. The Coleridge lines, by
contrast, suggest both by vocabulary and rhythm that cloud
and moon are behaving oddly and ominously, just out of the
way of ordinary behavior, as if proportion is thrown out and
normal vision perplexed. At point after point in *Christabel*
descriptions are used to heighten the mystery by such suggestions of slight distortion in behavior, or of contrast, or
surprise—

> And wildly glittered here and there
> The gems entangled in her hair.
> In moonshine cold
> The brands were flat, the brands were dying,
> Amid their own white ashes lying;
> But when the lady passed, there came
> A tongue of light, a fit of flame;
> And Christabel saw the lady's eye
>
> The silver lamp burns dead and dim.

But it is all fragmentary and finally unsatisfying because it
leads up to a mystery which is both incomplete and clueless.
The enigmatic Geraldine entirely swamps Part I. I do not
propose to go into the questions of how far she was a vam-
pire or a Lamia or whether she was a victim of metempsychosis.[16] But Ernest Hartley Coleridge was surely right when

he said that there are a number of indications that in Part I Geraldine is "at the mercy of some malign influence not herself." [17] She is in "sore distress" and asks for pity (l. 73); "in wretched plight" (l. 188); she first (apparently without irony) wishes Christabel's mother were there, and even after the malignant wish for the mother to be off, she will still try to requite Christabel well; she must even pray: "for I Must pray, ere yet in bed I lie" (ll. 233–34). The critical act of revealing her bosom is approached with extreme reluctance. She acts "drawing in her breath aloud, / Like one that shuddered." Then comes the main passage on which Ernest Hartley Coleridge comments:

> Ah! what a stricken look was hers!
> Deep from within she seems half-way
> To lift some weight with sick assay,
> And eyes the maid and seeks delay;
> Then suddenly, as one defied,
> Collects herself in scorn and pride,
> And lay down by the Maiden's side! [18]

These lines did not occur in the original version of 1816; they were not published till 1828; and that edition is the basis of the *textus receptus*. They occur in none of the main manuscripts. Their insertion seems rather to underline what was already implied, than to declare a later change of purpose; and they were, further, a protection against the misrepresentation of critics.

The whole of this scene has unquestionably a genuine horror in it: the mitigating explanatory lines were absent from the version reviewed so malignantly in *The Examiner* (very probably by Hazlitt) on 2 June 1816:

> There is something disgusting at the bottom of his subject, which is but ill glossed over by a veil of Della Cruscan sentiment and fine writing—like moon-beams playing on a charnel-house, or flowers strewed on a dead body.

An anonymous pamphlet later "pronounced poor Christabel 'the most obscene Poem in the English Language' "— which prompted Coleridge's comment: "I saw an old book at Coleorton in which the Paradise Lost was described as an 'obscene Poem,' so I am in good company." [19]

There are three extant accounts of how *Christabel* was to have been finished that are near enough to Coleridge him-

self to have serious claim to be considered authentic. Two
come from Gillman, in whose house at Highgate Coleridge
lived from 1816 till his death; the other from Coleridge's
son Derwent. The shorter Gillman account is this:

> The story of Christabel is partly founded on the notion,
> that the virtuous of this world save the wicked. The pious and
> good Christabel suffers and prays for
>
> > The weal of her lover that is far away,
>
> exposed to various temptations in a foreign land; and she thus
> defeats the power of evil represented in the person of Geraldine.
> This is one main object of the tale.[20]

The Derwent Coleridge account is also short and general:

> The sufferings of Christabel were to have been repre-
> sented as vicarious, endured for her "lover far away"; and
> Geraldine, no witch or goblin, or malignant being of any kind,
> but a spirit, executing her appointed task with the best good
> will, as she herself says:
>
> > All they, who live in the upper sky,
> > Do love you, holy Christabel, &c.
> >
> >   (ll. 227–32)
>
> In form this is, of course, accommodated to "a fond super-
> stition," in keeping with the general tenour of the piece; but
> that the holy and the innocent do often suffer for the faults
> of those they love, and are thus made the instruments to bring
> them back to the ways of peace, is a matter of fact, and in
> Coleridge's hands might have been worked up into a tale of
> deep and delicate pathos.[21]

The longer Gillman account of the projected third and fourth
parts is this:

> Over the mountains, the Bard, as directed by Sir Leoline,
> "hastes" with his disciple; but in consequence of one of
> those inundations supposed to be common to this country, the
> spot only where the castle once stood is discovered—the edifice
> itself being washed away. He determines to return. Geraldine
> being acquainted with all that is passing, like the Weird Sisters
> in *Macbeth*, vanishes. Re-appearing, however, she waits the
> return of the Bard, exciting in the mean time, by her wily arts,
> all the anger she could rouse in the Baron's breast, as well as
> the jealousy of which he is described to have been susceptible.
> The old Bard and the youth at length arrive, and therefore she
> can no longer personate the character of Geraldine, the daugh-
> ter of Lord Roland de Vaux, but changes her appearance to

that of the accepted though absent lover of Christabel. Next ensues a courtship most distressing to Christabel, who feels— she knows not why—great disgust for her once favoured knight. This coldness is very painful to the Baron, who has no more conception than herself of the supernatural trans- formation. She at last yields to her father's entreaties, and con- sents to approach the altar with this hated suitor. The real lover returning, enters at this moment, and produces the ring which she had once given him in sign of her betrothment. Thus defeated, the supernatural being Geraldine disappears. As predicted, the castle bell tolls, the mother's voice is heard, and to the exceeding great joy of the parties, the rightful mar- riage takes place, after which follows a reconciliation and ex- planation between the father and daughter.[22]

James Dykes Campbell said in his edition of the poems (1893) that he suspected and hoped Coleridge was merely quizzing Gillman with the shorter account of the ending.[23] Dante Gabriel Rossetti took the longer Gillman ending seriously.[24] In two modern American articles it has been accepted as highly probable.[25] But the chief objection against the long Gillman ending is plain—that, as it is presented, it makes the story seem like a vulgar, trivial Gothic Romance; and Donald R. Tuttle has virtually accepted the idea that it is simply as a Gothic Romance that the poem is to be read. The shorter Gillman account of the ending, and the account given by Derwent Coleridge, both agree in making Christabel the center of the main interest; and agree moreover on the view that the primary subject of the poem was Christabel's vicarious suffering for her lover.

This leads to the one other interesting recorded remark made by Coleridge himself about the poem—that Crashaw's verses on St. Theresa beginning

> Since 'tis not to be had at home,
> She'l travel to a martyrdome

were ever present to my mind whilst writing the second part of Christabel; if, indeed by some subtle process of the mind they did not suggest the first thought of the whole poem.[26]

Now since the central theme of the Crashaw poem is the desire for martyrdom, and since the traditional view of mar- tyrdom, and of the virtue in the blood of martyrs, includes the idea of the value to others of vicarious suffering, this one remark of Coleridge's tends strongly to reinforce the evidence

of Derwent Coleridge and the shorter account given by Gillman.

A. H. Nethercot, whose book *The Road to Tryermaine*
contains the fullest and fairest modern attempt to interpret the
poem, found himself forced in his conclusion to the belief that
its theme was relatively "simple and straightforward." He
argues that *Christabel* was to exemplify the "preternatural,"
just as *The Ancient Mariner* was to exemplify the "supernatural." Coleridge used the word "preternatural" at the beginning
of his critique of *The Monk*: in 1801 he was planning to
publish *Christabel* with two essays prefixed, one on the preternatural and one on meter.[27] Nethercot links this to the lines
on Joan of Arc in "The Destiny of Nations," which speak of
"Beings of higher class than Man," who take on human form
for their own purposes, and make

> Of transient Evil ever-during Good
> Themselves probatory, and denied
> Confess'd to view by preternatural deed
> To o'erwhelm the will, save on some fated day.[28]

Geraldine, Nethercot argues, is such a being as this, in Derwent
Coleridge's words, "a spirit, executing her appointed task with
the best good will." She is the agency through whom Christabel (whose name has "Christ's name in 't") is to be brought
to "an abbreviated but concentrated form" [29] of martyrdom at
her father's castle. By this means Christabel would make atone-
ment for the wrongs committed by her absent lover.

This is neat, and consistent with various evidence; but
as Nethercot fully admits, it is hard to reconcile with Coleridge's overwhelming difficulties in completing the poem, his
references to his "vision" of it, all the suggestions that the
theme was subtle and complicated. The underlying fact is that
none of Coleridge's poems at this period can be covered by a
short, neat statement of their theme, any more than *The Ancient Mariner* is explained by quoting the epigrammatic moral
at its end. In view of Coleridge's statement about the importance to him, in a "subtle" way, of Crashaw's poem on St.
Theresa, there seems a strong likelihood that he was hampered
by problems which belong to the psychological borderland
where matters of religion overlap with matters of sex:

> Shee never undertooke to know,
> What death with love should have to doe

> Nor has shee ere yet understood
> Why to show love shee should shed blood.

In the seventeenth century such double references could be carried together in the mind without any intellectual unease, and without any moral shame or awkwardness. In 1800 that was not so. Yet Coleridge, of all Englishmen then living, was the one most likely to have had some understanding of this borderland, and to have known intimately the difficulties of using that, perhaps dim, understanding at the center of a narrative poem. He was not writing an elementary story of Gothic horror, but was trying to explore more deeply the serious psychological areas which such stories just touched in their own trivial way.

III

For nearly sixteen years now the original full text of "Dejection: An Ode" has been known.[30] But the current editions and selections of Coleridge's poems still necessarily print the *textus receptus,* and consequently the relation between the various versions is not widely known and its import not generally understood. The *textus receptus* is called An Ode; it is divided into eight stanzas, which altogether amount to 139 lines. But the original version was written as a verse letter to Sara Hutchinson on 4 April 1802, in 340 lines.

The whole matter of these original "verses" and of the resulting Ode belongs closely to an entry in his Note-Book: the passage is a long meditation on personal unhappiness, with this at its center:

> O Sara wherefore am I not happy! Why for years have I not enjoyed one pure & sincere pleasure! one full joy!—one genuine Delight, that rings sharp to the Beat of the Finger!—all cracked, & dull with base Alloy!—

Here, in the rough, is the kind of personal experience from which there grew his insistence on the distinction between the primary and the secondary imagination: and that the secondary imagination appears not in its achievement—for the "recreation" is here "rendered impossible"—but in its "essentially vital" activity, as it "*struggles* to idealise and unify." In such prose passages we are watching a half-act of artistic creation.

In the various stages of "Dejection: An Ode" we can, I

think, see these "struggles" working on very similar material, carried into further stages towards artistic creation, towards unity. I think it is the opinion of many readers of the Ode, that brilliantly successful as most of it is, as *parts*, yet it fails to achieve complete artistic unity. By comparison with "Frost at Midnight" or *The Ancient Mariner* or "Kubla Khan" it is not a whole poem.

In the received text, the opening of stanza vii especially, and its placing and relevance, are serious obstacles to accepting the poem as a whole. The stanza opens with a sudden twist of thought, in very awkward language:

> Hence, viper thoughts, that coil around my mind,
>   Reality's dark dream!
> I turn from you, and listen to the wind,
>   Which long has raved unnoticed.[31]

And the "viper thoughts" against which this revulsion occurs are the famous meditative stanza about the loss of his "shaping spirit of Imagination," ending with the lines:

> Till that which suits a part infects the whole,
> And now is almost grown the habit of my soul.

The phrase "reality's dark dream" then applies to the firm, sad honesty of self-analysis which makes the greatness of that stanza. This result has come about by taking over the word "dream" from the original version (l. 185), where the "dark distressful Dream," from which he turns, is the thought of his misery if Sara were ill in body or in mind and he, necessarily absent, were unable to comfort her. The "dream" was not the honest self-analysis at all. And in the original version the passage about the loss of "the shaping spirit of Imagination," though substantially the same in wording, follows, instead of preceding, the vital change in the weather: it follows the groans, and smarting wounds, and the screams of the lost child. The "tender lay" is not Otway's, but William's. The course of the weather is very important to the argument, and they move parallel.

Another major change is this: in the published Ode the praise and description of "joy" is divided between stanza v and the end of stanza viii, at the end of the poem. In the original verses these two parts are undivided and form one long strain, at the end of the poem, a strain of forty-four lines, beginning

O Sara! we receive but what we give,

including the images of the wedding garment, the shroud, the
luminous cloud, the light, the glory, the fair luminous mist;
and these images focus not on Coleridge and his loss of joy,
but on Sara and her possession of it. It is thus a paean to her
happiness, not a wail over his misery. Moreover, this long
strain contains one important and beautifully developed image
which was dropped altogether in the published version:

> Thou being innocent and full of love,
> And nested with the Darlings of thy Love,
> And feeling in thy Soul, Heart, Lips, and Arms
> Even what the conjugal and mother Dove,
> That borrows genial warmth from those, she warms,
> Feels in the thrill'd wings, blessedly outspread—[32]

The loss of this from inside the praise of joy is perhaps the
worst the poem has suffered. "Thy Soul, Heart, Lips, and
Arms" and "the thrill'd wings" make the union of the physical
and emotional in the mood of joy more concrete than anything
retained in the public poem. In its original place the "conjugal
and mother Dove" stood as a contrast to a long explicit passage
about Coleridge's unhappiness in his own marriage,

> those habitual Ills
> That wear out Life, when two unequal Minds
> Meet in one House and two discordant Wills;

about the fact

> that my coarse domestic Life has known
> No Habits of heart-nursing Sympathy.

In the light of these passages the line "Our's is her Wedding
Garment, our's her Shroud" acquires its force: the two gar-
ments may be the same.

The main theme of the unpublished passages of the verses
was the contrast between Sara Hutchinson's "joyous" member-
ship of the Wordsworth group, with its permanency of gladness
and affection, and Coleridge's own separation from it, and lack
of an equivalent—

> To *visit* those, I love, as I love thee,
> Mary, and William, and dear Dorothy,
> It is but a temptation to repine—
> The transientness is Poison in the Wine,
> Eats out the pith of Joy, makes all Joy hollow,
> All Pleasure a dim Dream of Pain to follow!

All this personal detail had to be cut out before publication, and in the cutting the sequence of the poem was altered as well as its direction and tone.

As the poem originally stood, the relation of the change in weather to the sequence of mood was quite different. The crescent moon and the "Green Light that lingers in the West" were the setting of the "stifling, drowsy, unimpassion'd Grief"; of "I see, not feel, how beautiful they are"; of

> I may not hope from outward Forms to win
> The Passion and the Life, whose Fountains are within!

just as they are in the received text; the first, more quiet, mood of self-analysis. This passes on to the pain that he has caused Sara, to the happiness of the Wordsworth group, and to the dream of his absence from Sara in illness. The change in the wind has been happening "unnoticed" during these thoughts. The fierce, active variable wind then breaks in, and governs all the rest of the poem. The wind that is the "Mad Lutanist," the "Actor, perfect in all tragic Sounds," the "mighty Poet, even to frenzy bold," is the wind which leads into the lines about the suspense of imagination, the "abstruse research," and into the final forty-four lines about the power of joy inside the soul itself, the "strong music in the Soul,"

> This Light, this Glory, this fair luminous Mist,
> This beautiful and beauty-making Power!

This wind has several different aspects: as tragic actor, and bold mighty poet it may express the wounds and groans of a host in rout together with a "Tale of less Affright, / And tempered with Delight": but it is also the destructive wind from which regeneration may follow, at once destroyer and creator. The line:

> And be this Tempest but a Mountain Birth

which now, slightly altered, comes in stanza viii, originally preceded the "Imagination" lines: the imagination has not come into the matter before that point.

A case cannot be made out for the full coherence of the original version; but this major difference is important. For it is under the stimulus of this strong creative wind that the deepest self-analysis occurs, and also the fullest realization of the power of joy, as it is actually achieved in Sara herself.

In the longer version, too, the Eolian harp is less prominent; the lines given to it are in length and substance virtually the same as in the shorter poem; and its function is rather to declare the character of the wind than to pose the doubtful question of the passivity or activity of the wind. I. A. Richards's long discussion of the harp image in *Coleridge on Imagination* [33] was written before the longer text was available; but he has since expressed (more or less) his adherence to what he then said.[34]

I would now suggest that the emphasis on the harp image and on Coleridge's modes of imagining the relation between the mind and external nature, the treatment of his poems too much as embryo philosophy, has tended to obscure the place of the affections and feelings in them. "Dejection: An Ode" is not primarily a poem about modes of perception. It is a poem about unhappiness and about love and about joy. Of the later autobiographical poems there is least of self-pity in it, the self-analysis being all the clearer and more mature therefore, because the sense of love and of joy is so strong. This idea of joy was a guiding principle of Coleridge's life.

The "joy" of "Dejection" must be understood as involving the "deep delight" which "Kubla Khan" shows at the center of creative happiness. To give some further indication of what "joy" meant to Coleridge I shall quote two entries in one of his Note-Books: the first comes before the writing of "Dejection" and describes a particular kind of joy in his son Hartley with splendid distinction:

> Sunday, November 1, 1801. Hartley breeched—dancing to the jingling of the money—but eager & solemn Joy, not his usual whirl-about gladness—but solemn to & fro eager looks, as befitted the importance of the aera.[35]

That belongs partly with the "Conclusion to Part II" of *Christabel*, and partly looks forward to "Dejection" in the following year. The other note was written after "Dejection," probably in October 1803, and applies to himself:

> I write melancholy, always melancholy: you will suspect that it is the fault of my natural Temper. Alas! no.—This is the great Cross in that my Nature is made for Joy—impelling me to Joyance—& I never—never can yield to it.—I am a genuine *Tantalus*—[36]

That is one of the most awful things he ever wrote.

There are passages in the later autobiographical poems where one can put one's finger on a word, phrase, or rhythm which declares, in its poetic weakness, an emotional weakness which suddenly obtrudes, as if it came there through a lack of alert attention. This weakness is often due to self-pity. It is the Tantalus who cannot reach his Joy.

Self-pity is exceedingly hard to sympathize with, to understand, to assess; it is easy to sweep it all away as undignified whining, lacking control and decorum, as evidence of a deep and distasteful psychological malaise. There are many parts of Coleridge's published writings, especially in his letters, which it is tempting to treat in this way. And he does suffer by comparison with others. There are many parallels, for instance, between his circumstances and those of Hopkins: both suffered from ill health, the sense of isolation, and from a thwarting of the creative impulse; both planned or began many works which were never finished; both were faced, though in rather different ways, with the problem of bringing their creative poetical powers into relation with their scholarship and their technical interest in philosophy. Coleridge might well have taken as the motto or the basis of a poem that passage from the twelfth chapter of Jeremiah which opens Hopkins' sonnet:

> Thou art indeed just, Lord, if I contend
> With thee; but, sir, so what I plead is just.
> Why do sinners' ways prosper? and why must
> Disappointment all I endeavour end? [37]

In fact, this very idea is expressed in the ending of Coleridge's "The Pains of Sleep," of 1803—

> Such punishments, I said, were due
> To natures deepliest stained with sin—
> For aye entempesting anew
> The unfathomable hell within,
> The horror of their deeds to view,
> To know and loathe, yet wish and do!
> Such griefs with such men well agree
> But wherefore, wherefore fall on me? [38]

And his sonnet "Work without Hope" exactly parallels Hopkins's contrast of the fertility and life of nature with its own eunuch-like unproductiveness: "birds build, but not I build," wrote Hopkins; and Coleridge—

> All Nature seems at work. Slugs leave their lair—
> The bees are stirring—birds are on the wing—

> And Winter slumbering in the open air,
> Wears on his smiling face a dream of Spring!
> And I the while, the sole unbusy thing,
> Nor honey make, nor pair, nor build, nor sing.[39]

The parallels in the circumstances, the ideas, even the images are striking. But the comparison is in Hopkins's favor, because he avoids just that kind of weakness. In that stanza from "The Pains of Sleep," it is only in the last line that they appear. Where Hopkins twice boldly uses the strong interrogative "Why":

> Why do sinners' ways prosper? and why must . . .

Coleridge twice side-by-side uses the weak interrogative "wherefore":

> Wherefore, wherefore fall on me?

It is a tone which his admirers have to face.

But the ending of the verses to Sara as a paean of joy was not an isolated break from a lasting mood of self-pity. She was for several years his focus point and stay, and I should like to end this essay by quoting without comment the sonnet he wrote to her in 1801:

> Are there two things, of all which men possess,
> That are so like each other and so near,
> As mutual Love seems like to Happiness?
> Dear Asra, woman beyond utterance dear!
> This Love which ever welling at my heart,
> Now in its living fount doth heave and fall,
> Now overflowing pours thro' every part
> Of all my frame, and fills and changes all,
> Like vernal waters springing up through snow,
> This Love that seeming great beyond the power
> Of growth, yet seemeth ever more to grow,
> Could I transmute the whole to one rich Dower
> Of Happy Life, and give it all to Thee,
> Thy lot, methinks, were Heaven, thy age, Eternity! [40]

Notes

1. P. H. B. Lyon, *The Discovery of Poetry*, p. 101.
2. J. L. Lowes, *The Road to Xanadu* (London, 1931), p. 409.
3. *Ibid.*, p. 363, where it is called an attribute of dreams.
4. *The Complete Works of Samuel Taylor Coleridge*, ed. E. H. Coleridge (Oxford, 1912), I, 298. (Hereafter referred to as *PW*.)
5. Maud Bodkin, *Archetypal Patterns in Poetry* (London, 1951), p. 95.
6. Lowes, pp. 367–69; *PW*, I, 297.

7. *Paradise Lost*, IV, 268–69.

8. *Ibid.*, 280–83.

9. "On Poesy or Art," printed in *Biographia Literaria*, ed. J. Shaw-cross, 2 vols. (London, 1907), II, 255–56; *cf. BL*, II, 12.

10. Lowes, pp. 379–80.

11. *Archetypal Patterns in Poetry*, p. 135.

12. *Journals of Dorothy Wordsworth*, ed. E. de Selincourt, I, 4.

13. *Ibid.*, I, 5.

14. Quoted in *Christabel*, S. T. Coleridge, Illustrated by a Facsimile of the Manuscript, and by Textual and other Notes, by E. H. Coleridge (1907), p. 3.

15. *Poetical Works*, ed. E. de Selincourt, II, 208.

16. For an exhaustive exploration of these questions, see A. H. Nethercot, *The Road to Tryermaine* (Chicago, 1939), Bk. II.

17. *Christabel*, p. 76 n. 2. But Gillman (p. 284) calls her "an evil being, not of this world"; James Gillman, *The Life of Samuel Taylor Coleridge*, 1838.

18. Ll. 256–62; the earlier versions read, simply, for these lines:

> She took two paces and a stride,
> And lay down by the maiden's side.

19. *Unpublished Letters of S. T. Coleridge*, ed. E. L. Griggs (London, 1932), II, 247; To Southey, February 1819. The letter also says: "It seems that Hazlitt from pure malignity had spread about the Report that Geraldine was a Man in disguise."

20. Gillman, p. 283.

21. *Christabel*, p. 52, n. 1: from *The Poems of Samuel Taylor Cole-ridge*, ed. Derwent and Sara Coleridge, [?] 1870. This undated issue first contained an introductory essay by Derwent Coleridge. I have not seen a copy of it, and *Christabel* is my only authority for the quotation.

22. Gillman, pp. 301–302.

23. *Ibid.*, p. 604.

24. Hall Caine, *Recollections of Dante Gabriel Rossetti* (1882), p. 154.

25. B. R. McElderry, Jr., "Coleridge's Plan for Completing *Christ-abel*," *Studies in Philology*, XXXIII (1936); Donald R. Tuttle, "*Christa-bel* Sources in Percy's *Reliques* and the Gothic Romance," *PMLA*, LIII (1938).

26. *Letters, Conversations and Recollections of S. T. Coleridge*, edited by Thomas Allsop, 3rd edn. (1864), pp. 104–105.

27. *Letters*, etc., I, 349; "To Thomas Poole, 16 Mar. 1801." See Nethercot, pp. 200–201.

28. *PW*, I, 136 n. The text is that included in Southey's *Joan of Arc*, 1796. See Nethercot, pp. 201–205.

29. Nethercot, p. 210.

30. Ernest de Selincourt, "Coleridge's *Dejection: an Ode*," *Essays & Studies*, XXII (1937); and also de Selincourt, *Wordsworthian and other Studies*, pp. 57–76.

31. Ll. 94–97; *PW*, I, 367.

32. *Cf.* for both theme and imagery these lines from "To Two Sisters" (1807), ll. 1–5; *PW*, I, 410:

> To know, to esteem, to love,—and then to part—
> Makes up life's tale to many a feeling heart;

> Alas for some abiding-place of love,
> O'er which my spirit, like the mother dove,
> Might brood with warming wings!

33. Esp. pp. 150 ff.

34. *The Portable Coleridge*, ed. I. A. Richards (New York, 1950), pp. 15–16, 41–42.

35. MS Note-Book No. 21. British Museum Additional Manuscripts 47518, ff. 34V–35.

36. MS Note-Book No. 21. Add MSS 47518, ff. 70V–71.

37. *Poems*, 3rd edn., ed. W. H. Gardner, p. 113.

38. Ll. 43–50; *PW*, I, 390–91.

39. Dated in first draft 21 Feb 1825; *PW*, I, 447 and II, 1110–11; Hopkins may well have known this sonnet, and also "The Pains of Sleep."

40. *PW*, I, 361–62. First published 1893. This sonnet was prefixed to the MS of *Christabel* which Coleridge presented to Sara Hutchinson.

Part Four   Byron

Wilfred S. Dowden

10 · The Consistency in Byron's
Social Doctrine

IF WE WERE TO APPLY Emerson's maxim of the foolish consistency to the mind of Lord Byron, we should find that it was neither small nor plagued with hobgoblins. His lordship was nothing if not inconsistent. His career bears witness to this fact, for his life was full of radical changes. His poetry, too, is inconsistent. For example, he experimented with many metrical forms, trying established measures of his own country (such as the heroic couplet of the school of Pope), as well as measures formerly used almost exclusively by foreign poets (such as the *ottava rima* of Pulci). In content, too, this inconsistency is manifest. His habit of changing, within a single paragraph or stanza, from a mood of high seriousness to one of light banality cannot be overlooked by even the most casual reader of his poetry. Yet, there was one point on which he never varied in his thinking.

In his study of Byron, Professor Paul Trueblood explains that the poet's medium was satire and that he began his career with satirical verse, turned from it to sentiment in *Childe Harold* and other poems, and finally returned to it in *Don Juan, The Vision of Judgment,* and works of the later period. He also explains that Byron became increasingly serious in political and social doctrines from December, 1820, when he broke off the composition of *Don Juan* after completing the fifth canto, to June, 1822, when he took up the poem again. He

Wilfred S. Dowden, "The Consistency in Byron's Social Doctrine," *The Rice Institute Pamphlet,* XXXVII (October, 1950), 18–44. Used by permission of Rice University and the author.

says, too, that there is evidence in the last eight cantos of *Don Juan* of revolutionary indoctrination, which was not apparent earlier.[1]

There can be no doubt that Byron exhibited maturity and found his poetic medium in the satire of *Don Juan, The Irish Avatar,* and other of these later poems. In them he could attack cant, religious, political, and moral, as he had never been able to attack it in verses of the *Childe Harold* type. His nature was basically satirical, and he returned to that form of verse as a natural consequence of this nature.

If, however, he turned away from satire in the poems of the middle period, he did not turn away from the principles of his satiric verse, or from the abuses at which he directed it. He did not wield the cudgel so effectively in sentimental verse as in satire, but he wielded it, nevertheless, against the same enemy which he attacked in the later cantos of *Don Juan.*

This consistency in Byron's social doctrine is indicated best, I think, by an entry in his journal on January 16, 1814:

As for me, by the blessing of indifference, I have simplified my politics into an utter detestation of all existing governments; and, as it is the shortest and most agreeable and summary feeling imaginable, the first moment of an universal republic would convert me into an advocate for single and uncontradicted despotism. The fact is, riches are power, and poverty is slavery all over the earth, and one sort of establishment is no better nor worse for a *people* than another. . . . I have no consistency, except in politics; and that probably arises from my indifference on the subject altogether.[2]

After we have loosed this statement from its tangle of Byronic facetiousness, one fact is clear: Byron's consistency was not in his politics, as he maintained. His interest in government was in what it would do for a people, and his consistent theme in his poetry, as in his life, was a relentless fight against oppression and for freedom. He was no more serious in thought and purpose in this respect in 1823 than he was in 1812.

Byron's political career was brief and unprofitable; his active interest in politics soon waned and was thenceforward admittedly small. But Byron was first of all a poet; so it will be well for us to turn our attention from his brief and stormy political career in order to examine his literary productions. We look first at *Childe Harold,* because it is, I think, a key poem. In the first place, it covers a large part of Byron's creative period. He began work on it early in his career and did not finish it until 1818, six years before his death; and his mind was occupied with it during much of that time. In the second place, it contains many ideas on the subject of liberty, which he developed more fully in other poems and dramas. It is, therefore, a kind of catch-all and carry-all of Byron's thoughts on social doctrine.

It is a significant fact, I think, that Byron returns again and again to the love of freedom in his description of each of the places Childe Harold visits. This fact is true, not only of the first two cantos, published in 1812, but also of cantos three and four, published in 1816 and 1818 respectively. In Lisbon, for example, he notes with horror the poverty and slavery which abound there. In Spain he sees that Seville is free but must soon fall to the tyrant. The history of Spain indicates that the fight for freedom has been a long one, and he regrets that the tree of liberty is not yet planted in Spanish soil. The sons of Spain, who never knew freedom, fight on for their country, even though at this time (1812) they have no king or state for which to fight, Charles IV and Ferdinand VII having abdicated in favor of Napoleon.

He also laments for Greece when he compares her present state with her past glory. He regrets that Greece is a "sad relic of departed worth." He laments the fact that the people are slaves from birth to death, and that every "carle can lord it o'er the land." He dreams that the hour is near which shall give Greece back the heritage that is hers—her lost liberty. "What spirit," he asks, "shall call thee from the tomb?" The Greeks themselves cry for foreign arms and aid. But he calls indignantly to these hereditary bondsmen: Do they not know that they who would be free must strike the blow themselves? Help from outside may "lay their despoilers low," but that will *not* win freedom's flame. He ends this plea by calling on Greece to change her lords; her "glorious day is o'er, but not [her] years of shame."

We are not surprised by the first significant fact exhibited in this passage. Byron shows here a deep love for liberty. He had shown that in the first canto and in some early poems and letters as well. We note, however, that in calling upon the hereditary bondsmen of Greece to rid themselves of their present lords, and in admonishing them that they alone can achieve the freedom they deserve, he is anticipating revolutionary indoctrination, which, as Mr. Trueblood points out, is part of the essence of the latter cantos of *Don Juan*. Byron was indoctrinated with revolutionary fervor a good while before the appearance of the great satires of the later period, or, for that matter, before the appearance of *Childe Harold*, Canto IV, in 1818. Had he found a more suitable means of expression in his earlier career, he would have raised a stronger voice on behalf of these principles.

Revolution, Byron would say, is the means by which a country might rid itself of tyrants and achieve the freedom it deserves. The idea of revolution versus tyranny was much on his mind, and the thought of one seemed to lead to an expression of the other. Thus there are several discussions of each in *Childe Harold*.

For example, he speaks of the tripartite war of Spain, France, and England, and regrets the loss of life which paves the way for the tyrant. He deplores the outcome of Waterloo for the same reason. The world is not more free because Gaul is in fetters. There is no reason for man to pay homage to the wolf which struck the lion down. The result of Waterloo seems to him to be a revival of thralldom, which is to be the "patch'd-up idol of enlightened days."

The tendency toward revolution is expressed in a letter to Tom Moore, dated April 20, 1814. Byron explains that he refused to see Louis XVIII make his triumphal entry into London; but he says, "In some coming year of Hegira, I should not dislike to see the place where he *had* reigned, shortly after the second revolution and a happy sovereignty of two months, the last six weeks being civil war." [3]

The "Ode to Napoleon Buonaparte," which was published in 1814, is in keeping with the spirit of this letter. The ode is an occasional poem, written at the time of Napoleon's first exile. Byron indicates the power which Napoleon held when tyrants of Europe had bowed to him and thanked him for a crown. He had both France and the rest of the world in his possession. Why, then, did he fail? One reason for his failure is best summed up in these lines:

> But thou, forsooth, must be a king
> And don the purple vest
> As if that foolish robe could wring
> Remembrance from thy breast. [4]

Now Napoleon's return in 1815 placed Byron's ode in a very strange light. In a letter to Moore the poet says that he can forgive the rogue for utterly falsifying every line of the poem, and calls to mind the story of the abbé who wrote a treatise designed to prove that the Swedish Constitution was indissoluble and eternal. He had no sooner corrected the last sheet than word came that the government had been destroyed by Gustavus III. "The King of Sweden may overthrow the *constitution*," said the abbé, "but not *my book*." [5] What is there about Byron's ode that is like the abbé's book?

Napoleon had the opportunity of being something other than a tyrant, but he had to don the purple and tyrannize, as had those whom he conquered. Thus, he was doomed to failure. We note that Byron did not include his name with those who he thought were leaders "in talent and truth": Washington, Franklin, Penn, Mirabeau, or Saint-Just. Napoleon's return, then, falsified the ode in only one sense; in another it made the poem even more durable than the abbé's book, for his return, signifying desire for supreme rule, bore out Byron's thesis that tyrants are conquered only by tyrants, as he expresses it later in *Childe Harold*.

Another passage in *Childe Harold* gives an excellent analysis of the attitude which drives men to tyrannize. It is significant here in that Byron is again expressing the same idea that he voiced two years earlier in the ode. He is still speaking of Napoleon:

> But quiet to quick bosoms is a Hell,
> And *there* hath been thy bane; there is a fire
> And motion of the Soul which will not dwell
> In its own narrow being, but aspire
> Beyond the fitting medium of desire;
> And, but once kindled, quenchless evermore,
> Preys upon high adventure, nor can tire
> Of aught but rest; a fever at the core,
> Fatal to him who bears, to all who ever bore. [6]

Such agitation leads these men on, and they become so accustomed to conflict and strife that, after they have conquered all, their lives are empty, filled with sorrow and supineness; and they die like a flame unfed. Once they have attained the tyrannical heights they seek, these men are destined to look down thenceforward on the hate of those below.

We trace this vein through the remainder of the poem. Byron points out that a contributing factor to Napoleon's downfall was one weakest weakness—vanity. However, this fault alone did not comprise the chief error or cause the failure of the emperor. One less sensitive than Byron to the needs and desires of a suffering humanity would have failed to see that, as the poet says in a note:

> The great error of Napoleon, "if we have writ our annals true," was a continued obtrusion on mankind of his want of all community of feeling for or with them; perhaps more offensive to human vanity than the active cruelty of more trembling and suspicious tyranny. Such were his speeches to public assemblies as well as individuals; and the single expression which he is said to have used on returning to Paris after the Russian winter had destroyed his army, rubbing his hands over a fire, "This is pleasanter than Moscow," would probably alienate more favor from his cause than the destruction and reverses which led to the remark.[7]

And what is the result of Napoleon's lack of community of feeling with mankind? What do we reap from this "barren being"? The result is oppression of the worst kind. Men fear lest their own judgments become too bright and their free thoughts be crime. Thus, they plod in sluggish misery from generation to generation, begetting inborn slaves, who wage war for their chains rather than be free. They fall in the same worn-out causes in which they have seen their fellows fall and do not realize, as he indicates in many places, that their hope lies within themselves.

The continuation of Childe Harold's pilgrimage in the last two cantos of the poem gives the poet more opportunities to expound his favorite theme. For example, when he visits the Rhine, he regrets the "evil will" of the robber barons who built the castles along the banks of the river. He laments their power, which kept so many people in subjection for so long.

He eulogizes the soldier Marceau, not for his prowess in battle, but because

> . . . He was freedom's champion, one of those
> The few in number, who had not o'erstept
> The charter to chastise which she bestows
> On such as wield her weapons; he had kept
> The whiteness of his soul—and thus men o'er him wept.[8]

This picture is in striking contrast to the description of Napoleon in the same canto.

In a similar manner he contrasts Waterloo with Morat and Marathon. Perhaps time had obliterated the less heroic, more terrible memories of the two ancient battlefields, but, nevertheless, Byron believed that

> They were true Glory's stainless victories,
> Won by the unambitious heart and hand
> Of a proud, brotherly, and civic band.[9]

The poet is led to a brief discussion of the French Revolution, and herein lies much of Byron's philosophy of "revolution in the right cause." The French people made themselves a fearful monument, the wreck of old opinions. They went too far and overthrew good with evil; hence they left ruins and only the foundations upon which to renew dungeons and thrones. In short, tyrants were conquered by tyrants. Note how closely this idea is related to the "Ode to Napoleon" and to other passages in *Childe Harold*, to which attention has already been called.

But all hope is not lost, for man has felt his strength. He might have used it better, but Byron does not place too much blame upon those who have been oppressed so long, if, at times, they mistake their prey.

The cause of liberty and laments for its loss are no less ardent in the last canto of the poem than they had been in the first three. Italy is the object of the poet's description, and he leads off with an account of his impressions of Venice. After a few introductory remarks he returns to his old theme. He regrets that Venice, after thirteen hundred years of freedom, is now in submission to foreign foes. Possibly Byron had not learned enough of the history of the city to form as definite an opinion about its freedom as he did at a later date. At any rate, in a drama which we shall examine presently, he began to realize that in the instance of the Venetian Government of the fourteenth century the word "republic" was not synonymous with "freedom."

He also expresses another idea which he was to elaborate in a later poem. In one stanza he states that in her love for Tasso, Venice should have cut the knot which bound her to a foreign tyrant. He speaks of Petrarch as one who arose to raise the language of his country from her barbaric foes. He also suggests that "Tully's voice, Virgil's lay, and Livy's pictured page" will bring about the resurrection of fallen Rome. The idea that the hope for Italy lay in her art was reiterated and developed more fully in *The Prophecy of Dante*.

In 1819, before he had completed the fifth canto of *Don Juan*, Byron was writing another poem, which, though not as well known, is nevertheless important to the problem at hand. On February 21, 1820, he wrote to John Murray that he had not done more than six hundred lines of "Dante's Prophecy." [10] Something must have incited him to work, however, for on March 14, 1820, he enclosed four cantos of "*Dante's Prophecy, vision, or what not*" in a letter to the publisher. If these cantos were approved, he intended to go on "like Isaiah." [11]

The Prophecy of Dante was not published until April 12, 1821; but since Byron first mentions it early in 1820, we may assume that it was on his mind the year before. If this assumption is correct, then, the composition of the poem was not far removed in time from that of the last canto of *Childe Harold*, and would naturally contain many of the ideas expressed in the earlier work.

The theme of the *Prophecy* is the unification and freedom of Italy. Byron views the country through the eyes of the great Italian poet, who has been exiled from his native Florence. Dante laments that Florence and Italy would not struggle for freedom and would not listen to his voice, which was raised on behalf of freedom. The history of Italy is then presented as if it were being prophesied by Dante. Italy, he says, will succumb to each tyrant who invades her. She has already fallen to the Goth and German; Frank and Hun are yet to come. But Italy still has "hearts, and hands, and arms" with which to fight oppression.

Dante again asserts his love for his country and prophesies her literary future. Poets shall rise and follow in the path he has made. Some, he says, shall sing of liberty, and Italy will hear their voices.

Finally, Dante predicts that Italy will become great through her art and that warring nations will pause in their conflict to cast envious eyes upon her. In this poem, as in the conclusion of *Childe Harold*, Byron takes occasion to eulogize the great Italian poet and artists. The nationalism of these men interested him most, and he found his own theme of liberty in the poetry of each.

Italy will, in the end, honor the name of the great poet

who thus prophesies her future, and the vengeance of his verse
will outlive all the pride and wealth that Florence and Italy
hold dear. It shall also outlive the worst of all evils, the sway
of petty tyrants in a state. The second canto ends on the theme
of the poem and explains how Italy might gain her freedom:

> What is there wanting then to set thee free,
> And show thy beauty to the fullest light?
> To make the Alps impassable; and we
> Her sons may do this with *one* deed—*unite!* [12]

The consistency in Byron's social doctrine is exemplified
in his dramas as well as in his poetry. On April 9, 1820, he
wrote to Murray that he had begun work on *Marino Faliero,
Doge of Venice*. The drama was completed in July 1820, and
published with *The Prophecy of Dante* the following year. He
found the story in Marin Sanuto's *Lives of the Doges*.

The plot is motivated by the action of Michele Steno, who,
having been affronted by the Doge, wrote on the chair of state
an offensive lampoon on Marino and his wife. The man was
tried and given a sentence which Marino felt was inadequate.
Discontented with this action and with his lot in general, the
Doge entered into a conspiracy with a group of men who
wanted to overthrow the Venetian Constitution and the rule
of the governing body, called the Council of Ten, which they
felt was oppressive and tyrannical. They set up Marino Faliero
as their sovereign. The plot was discovered, the conspirators
captured, and the Doge executed.

Although the tragedy was not completed until 1820, it was
on Byron's mind a long time before that date. In the preface
to the drama he says, "It is now four years that I have meditated this work." [13] His first idea was to make the tragedy hinge
on the jealousy of the Doge. However, he was dissuaded from
this policy by his friend Matthew Gregory Lewis, with whom
he discussed his intention in Venice in 1817. Lewis assured
him that if he should make the Doge jealous, he would have
to contend with established writers, to say nothing of Shakespeare, and that he would be better advised to shift the
emphasis.[14]

The emphasis was shifted accordingly, and Byron takes
the opportunity of striking a blow on behalf of freedom and
another against the ambition and excessive pride which make
tyrants. For the Doge seems to be a split personality. He did

not want to be made Doge of Venice. The position was thrust upon him while he was happiest in his work as leader of his army. Nor does he like the restrictions placed upon him by the Council of Ten, who are the petty tyrants of whom Byron spoke in *The Prophecy of Dante*. Moreover, he sees the oppression of the people of his city and sympathizes with the conspirators who solicit his aid. But he is overcome with personal ambition and desires to exchange his Doge's cap for a crown. As far as the conspirators are concerned, he may have his wish, but such overwhelming ambition and desire for guilty glory can, in Byron's philosophy, bring him "naught but grief and pain." His plot is detected and fails, thus again expressing Byron's idea, first seen in *Childe Harold*, that revolution to gain freedom is worth while; but when revolution is staged for personal ambition, as in the case of that fostered by the Doge, it results in more tyranny and is doomed to failure.

Blind obedience to a state, on the other hand, is as wrong as desire for personal gain and glory, and it can lead to nothing better than that which is the final goal of tyranny. This idea is nowhere so apparent as in *The Two Foscari*, which was published in 1821. In *Marino Faliero* Byron had condemned a cause which had gone too far and resulted in tyranny, the evil which it fought. In *The Two Foscari* he condemned a blind obedience which obviates the possibility of fighting for any cause at all.

The elder Foscari, Doge of Venice, is compelled by the Council of Ten to sit in judgment on his only son, who is accused of treason. Tossing aside all bonds of parenthood, the old man watches as his son is put to torture in order that a confession might be wrung from him. The father is not unmoved by the trial, but his oath of allegiance to the state, he feels, compels him to witness and condone it. The son is equally adamant, in that his great love for Venice will not let him explain that he is guilty of a betrayal which he thought was for the good of the city. Confession would mean exile. In the absence of the Doge, the council finds Foscari guilty and orders that he be banished. It is also decided that the Doge must be removed from office, even though he has been loyal to the city and has won her many conquests. This final action is too much for the old man, who dies of a broken heart.

The Council of Ten of this drama is the same council

against which Marino Faliero revolted. Venice, presumably, is a republic, but Byron makes clear here, as in *Marino Faliero*, that the populace of the city is not free in any respect, and that, though the Doge or prince is not the supreme ruler of the city, he might as well be, for totalitarianism already is represented by the dreaded Council of Ten. These men have become as tyrannical as any monarch. Thus, we have the expression of the idea which he first stated in the journal of 1814, *viz.*, "One establishment is no better for a *people* than another"—that is, he would have added, if that government begins to tyrannize.

The Doge's blind obedience to the laws of the state, and to his own oath of allegiance, regardless of mitigating circumstances, is a philosophy which has seldom failed to bring about disorder. History, from the time of the fall of the Roman Empire to the fall of the Fascist states, illustrates this fact. The Doge's own words best sum up this concept:

> [Venice has] subdued the World; in such a state
> An individual, be he richest of
> Such a rank as is permitted, or the meanest,
> Without a name, is alike nothing, when
> The policy, irrevocably tending
> To one great end, must be maintained in vigour.[15]

The Doge's error was in adhering to the principles of a government which had so perverted its aim as to make, not its citizenry its primary concern, but the glory of the city itself.

Here, then, are the two extremes, and the mean was what Byron sought. It is what men who would be free have sought through the ages. Byron would be willing that men serve a state only that the state might serve men.

These three works on Italian history, all of which dealt with the problem of Italian freedom, were published at a time when unification was the primary question and the Carbonari were secretly active. They could not have escaped official notice. Byron's letters to friends in England at this time are full of allusions to the situation in Italy and of his own active participation in these affairs. He harbored the ammunition and arms of the liberals in his home, offered to defend any who were in danger of arrest by the authorities, offered his house as a kind of fort to be used by the liberals until the countryside could be aroused, and at one time wrote out an address to the Italian people, in which he proffered both money and services to their cause. This address is supposed to have fallen into the hands of the Pontifical Government, thereby causing Byron trouble with the authorities. In short, the fact that the Carbonari attempted no general uprising at this time probably saved him from being arrested as a leader in the liberation movement.

The satires of the later period are much more powerful than the verses of the earlier and middle years; but they continue the theme which the poet adopted in 1812, in his speeches in Parliament and in *Childe Harold*. The difference in his attitude seems to lie in the fact that he has lost patience, not with the people, but with their willingness to continue in servility. Note, for example, the poem entitled *The Irish Avatar*, which was written on the occasion of the triumphal entry of George IV into Dublin, ten days after the death of Queen Caroline. He was greeted with an outburst of enthusiastic loyalty, which Byron abhorred because of the oppression of the Irish people. This poem is a satire on the king, it is true; but it is also a bitter denunciation of the courtesy extended him who was the cause of their oppression.

Consider also *The Vision of Judgment*, 1821, which was occasioned by Southey's poor eulogy of George III, in the preface to which Southey bitterly attacked Byron and his works. Byron retaliated with this the best of travesties, which alone is responsible for the fact that Southey's poem is remembered. Byron goes far beyond attacking Southey in the satire; he takes occasion to denounce the policies of the king. He holds George III responsible for the oppression of countless millions, and while he grants that the king is an excellent example of virtue in private matters, he cannot forgive the fact that George constantly warred with freedom and the free. His virtue was adequate for *him*, but not for the millions who found in him the cause of their oppression.

With the exception of the last eight cantos of *Don Juan*, *The Vision of Judgment* was Byron's last great work. All that he had to say in earlier writings, however, is summed up in *Don Juan*, which is one of the best satires in our language. In this poem Byron attacks the faults of mankind: hypocrisy, cant, pride, the vanity of glory, the evils of needless warfare; and in an unusually subtle yet significant manner, he returns to his consistent theme—freedom from oppression.

Byron changes his tactics in these stanzas. Formerly, he

had always viewed the situation from the standpoint of the oppressed. Now he places Don Juan, not with the masses, but in the company of those who are responsible for oppression. Juan first fights in the Russian Army under Suvoroff in the siege of Ismail. He then proceeds to the Russian Court at Moscow, where he becomes a favorite of Empress Catherine. From there he goes, as Catherine's ambassador, to England and mingles with the nobility and court periphery. There, amid the petty intrigues and trivial happenings of English high society, the poem breaks off.

The poet does not lose sight of his theme in the latter part of this poem, for he keeps it constantly on the mind of Don Juan. In order to trace this idea, we must go back to Canto VIII and the siege of Ismail. Juan fights valiantly in this bloody battle and is beginning to feel a little of the thirst for glory which comes to those who wage war successfully, when he is reined in sharply. He sees two Cossacks, bent on murdering a ten-year-old Turkish girl. He saves the child as she tries to hide among the bodies of her parents and friends. From that time on, Don Juan's first thought is for the safety and well-being of his charge. He takes her with him to Russia, where she serves as a contrast to the pomp of court life. She goes with him on his journey through the countries of Europe to England, where her innocence is again juxtaposed to the banality and trivial intrigues of society. And Juan

> Loved the infant orphan he had saved,
> As patriots (now and then) may love a nation;
> His pride too felt that she was not enslaved
> Owing to him.[16]

For the child stands as a symbol of oppression. At a time when Don Juan was about to fall heart and soul into the pattern of tyranny, he was rescued by the act of rescuing this child. It is she also who is before him at the Russian Court and in England as a reminder of his love of liberty. It is true that Byron disposes of her in the twelfth canto by placing her under the tutelage of a stately, precise, and virtuous old lady, but the child is not forgotten by Don Juan or the reader; and we cannot be sure that Byron did not have plans for her in subsequent lines.

The fact that the girl is a Turk, against whom Don Juan, as a soldier in the Russian Army, is fighting, bears witness to the fact that the poet was interested in the cause of liberty for all people, not just for the Greeks, Italians, or others with whom he was in sympathy. In short, what Byron says is:

> I wish men to be free
> As much from mobs as kings—from you as me.[17]

The part Byron played in the Greek fight for independence is too well known and too complex to be discussed here. Suffice it to say that we now know that he did not go to Greece out of any feeling of boredom or philhellenic enthusiasm. Richard Edgecumbe and Harold Nicholson, in their studies of Byron's activities in Greece, did away with that misconception long ago. Indeed, some of his contemporaries realized the importance of his part in the Greek fight for liberty, as witness this statement taken from an article in *The Gentleman's Magazine* for June 1824:

> Lord Byron had succeeded . . . in stirring up among the people of the part of Greece in which he resided, an almost inconceivable enthusiasm. His exertions were incessant in their cause, and the gratitude of the people was proportioned to them. His influence was not lessened by being employed often to procure humane, even kind treatment towards the Turkish captives.[18]

This statement, from a letter from Mavrocardato to the secretary of the Greek Committee in England, indicates the attitude of the Greek patriots: "I shall attempt to perform my duty towards this great man: the eternal gratitude of my country will perhaps be the only true tribute to his memory." [19]

No better proof of the truth of these statements can be found than in the following quotation, taken from an article which appeared in *Times Literary Supplement* for May 13, 1949:

> It was Byron . . . who morally re-armed the defeated and disunited little nation. . . . [T]he Greeks owe English poets and poetry a great debt. And they are deeply conscious of the fact. To the Greek peasant of to-day every Englishman is in some sort a great-grandchild of the famous Byron, and he reaps in terms of friendship and hospitality the love and reverence that the poet himself did not live to enjoy.[20]

"Close thy *Byron*; open thy *Goethe*," said Carlyle with characteristic vehemence. Now I should not like to reverse that statement, but in an age which is characterized by a struggle

for the freedom of the individual, more than by any other one
thing, I should like to suggest that we open our Byron and
read what he has to say. It is true that he was a product of
his age and that he stands with Shelley, the young Coleridge
and Wordsworth, Leigh Hunt, Tom Moore, and others as a
poet of reform. But does he not also have a philosophy which
is characteristic of our time?

An article entitled "Byron in Our Day" appeared in 1907,
and I assume that each generation has thought of Byron as
having aspects peculiarly suited to its own age. The reason for
this fact is, I suppose, that basic human problems, hopes, and
desires are, like the abbé's book, "indissoluble and eternal."
The poet or dramatist who treats these social problems is not
writing for his own, but for all ages. Thus we can, in one very
real sense, speak of "Byron in Our Day" and present evidence
substantiating the fact that his doctrines are as suitable to 1949
or 1950 as they were to 1907, or, for that matter, 1812 or 1823.

But do we not have more reason for opening our Byron?
Are not his ideas on freedom, tyranny, slavery, and oppression
applicable to this day of the United Nations Organization with
its Declaration of Human Rights? Now, when "freedom from
oppression" and "human rights" are key phrases, Byron speaks
to us again; and there are indications that we are turning to
him with new interest and understanding. We may laugh at
the aspects of musical comedy heroism in his life, or at his
clever satire of current social, economic, and political questions;
but we can also be strengthened by the fact that his hopes for
the future of man were the same as ours, and that he was un-
relenting in his efforts to help secure the freedom he advocated.
Shades of the Byronic hero have haunted the poet from the
time of the publication of the *Turkish Tales* to the present.
They have colored our reading of *Childe Harold* and other
poems and have influenced our attitude toward his life and its
achievements on behalf of humanity. To see Byron only in
terms of the Byronic hero, however, is to take a fleeting glimpse
of him. Other glimpses reveal the subjectivism caused by the
personal tragedy of 1816, the disillusionment of 1819, and the
valor of 1823. But if we are to understand Byron, we have to
take, not glimpses, but an over-all view of the man and the
poet. Such a view will reveal to us one who never wavered in
the pursuit of his objective. He began his career with expres-

sions of hope for the freedom of man. He continued to express
this hope, which is a dominant element in most of his poetry,
and he ended his days striving, successfully, to instill that hope
and love of liberty in the hearts of a suffering people.

Notes

1. Paul Graham Trueblood, *The Flowering of Byron's Genius* (Stanford, 1945), pp. 6–25.
2. Rowland E. Prothero (ed.), *The Works of Lord Byron: Letters and Journals* (London, 1902), II, 381.
3. *Ibid.*, III, 72.
4. George Gordon, Lord Byron, *Complete Poetical Works* (New York, 1907), p. 389.
5. Prothero, *op. cit.*, III, 187.
6. Byron, *op. cit.*, p. 226.
7. *Ibid.*, p. 241 n.
8. *Ibid.*, p. 230.
9. *Ibid.*, p. 231.
10. Prothero, *op. cit.*, IV, 409.
11. *Ibid.*, p. 418.
12. Byron, *op. cit.*, p. 544.
13. *Ibid.*, p. 568.
14. *Ibid.*
15. *Ibid.*, p. 744.
16. *Ibid.*, p. 1173.
17. *Ibid.*, p. 1155.
18. "Memoir of the Late Lord Byron," *The Gentleman's Magazine*, CXXXV (1824), 565.
19. *Ibid.*
20. "Hellene and Philhellene," *The Times Literary Supplement*, May 13, 1949, p. 1.

11 · Childe Harold's Pilgrimage:
Cantos III and IV

"LORD BYRON," Scott wrote in May 1816, ". . . has Child Harolded himself and Outlawed himself into too great a resemblance with the pictures of his imagination." [1] This fusion of the poet with the hero-type he had created is the central feature of *Childe Harold*, Canto III, which was written to give utterance to his deep obsessive mood that summer. He was not, of course, continuously wretched, and the poem is not a full account of his experiences: here again there is no mention of his travelling companions, or of, say, his jokes at the expense of Polidori; but it *is* true to his dominating and recurrent thoughts and feelings of this period.

An immediate result of his new state of mind was the obliteration of his earlier distinction between hero and narrator. Byron begins by speaking unmistakably in his own person, and then breaks off to introduce Childe Harold and insist on the latter's fictional status:

> In my youth's summer I did sing of One,
> > The wandering outlaw of his own dark mind;
> > Again I seize the theme, then but begun,
> > And bear it with me, . . .[2]

But his account of his poetic motives makes it clear that his relation to this character is unique and intimate:

> 'T is to create, and in creating live
> > A being more intense that we endow
> > With form our fancy, gaining as we give

Reprinted from *Byron* by Andrew Rutherford by permission of Oliver & Boyd Ltd. and the author. Copyright 1961 by Oliver & Boyd Ltd.

> The life we image, even as I do now—
> What am I? Nothing: but not so art thou,
> Soul of my thought! with whom I traverse earth,
> Invisible but gazing, as I glow
> Mixed with thy spirit, blended with thy birth,
> And feeling still with thee in my crushed feelings' dearth.

Some such mixing and blending takes place almost at once, for even in the summary of Harold's recent fortunes we become aware that it is really Byron who is being described. By adopting this transparent fiction he gains first of all a means of avoiding direct treatment of his own domestic circumstances— this seemed promised by the opening stanzas with their explicit references to his wife and child, and to his wounded feelings, but with the transition to Childe Harold he can leave the quarrel and the separation wrapped in mystery: he can appeal for sympathy, in fact, without disclosing or discussing the real causes of his suffering. And secondly, he can be much more laudatory about Harold than he could about himself, without antagonizing readers at the very outset of his poem. Having achieved these aims, however, Byron allows the distinction between Harold and himself to lapse. He may choose to present his idealized self-portrait in the first or the third person, but the portrait remains virtually the same: in passing from autobiographical statement to professed fiction, one finds only a change of grammatical number, with no corresponding change in personality, for there is no difference in mood, temperament or opinion between the new Childe Harold and the "I" of the narrator. In this canto, as Jeffrey wrote in reviewing it,

> . . . it is really impracticable to distinguish them.—Not only do the author and his hero travel and reflect together—but, in truth, we scarcely ever have any notice to which of them the sentiments so energetically expressed are to be ascribed; and in those which are unequivocally given as those of the Noble author himself, there is the same tone of misanthropy, sadness and scorn, which we were formerly willing to regard as a part of the assumed costume of the Childe.[3]

The new protagonist, who thus combines the functions of both hero and narrator, shows a marked advance on all his predecessors. The main characters in the verse tales had been melancholy, misanthropic, lonely, proud, and passionate, but their lives were set in distant countries, often in past or unspecified periods; and although they embodied some of Byron's daydreams and desires, they were remote from most of his immediate interests. The earlier Childe Harold had been a contemporary figure, in spite of his pseudo-medieval trappings, but his *ennui* and self-sufficiency had shut him off from the life around him, and he remained a detached spectator, little moved by what he saw. The new Harold retains most of the qualities which had appealed to Byron in these earlier heroes, but he has nothing of his namesake's *ennui*. Like the original narrator he responds readily to natural beauty, and is interested in modern life and politics—passionately aware of the state of Europe, and feeling intensely his own grief and grievances, he emerges as "the orator of the world's woes and his own." [4] The figure of the melancholy Wanderer is modified by Byron's own experiences, thoughts and feelings, and also by his reading of "Alastor," so that it becomes a picture, no longer of the Sinner or the Outlaw, but of the Poet—the wronged and suffering Romantic Genius.

All objects and events are seen through the eyes of this narrator-hero, and the reflections they give rise to are as alive and personal as the passages of introspection: as Scott notes in his review of Canto IV, "His descriptions of present and existing scenes however striking and beautiful, his recurrence to past actions however important and however powerfully described, become interesting chiefly from the tincture which they receive from the mind of the author." [5] It is this assimilation of facts to the poet-hero's personality and interests that gives Canto III its unity, and prevents it from degenerating into a mere travelogue. Battlefields, monuments, history, characters, and scenery are all viewed in relation to one or another of Childe Harold's main preoccupations—his own wrongs and sorrows, the fate of genius, the liberty of peoples, the value and significance of Nature; and these four major themes are not presented separately, but linked and interwoven so that they figure as related aspects of the hero's mind and character, imposing a coherence on his multitude of observations and reflections.

This new *persona* brings with it a distinctive mode of utterance. When we read this canto after Cantos I and II we get a general impression of much greater power and competence: there is none of the former uncertainty, the fumbling experiments with humor or archaic diction, or the awkward changes of tone. Byron seems to have much more definite ideas of what he wants to do and how to do it: he is aiming now not at variety and inclusiveness—ideals which he had abandoned in the verse tales—but at a stylistic elevation corresponding to his own intensity of feeling; and he does often achieve this. Yet while one can readily agree with those readers who thought Canto III his best work up to now, it is far from being wholly successful. The Spenserian stanza is too elaborate and difficult a verse form to lend itself to Byron's slapdash way of writing— he may seem to use it easily and fluently, but the ease and fluency often depend on carelessness in composition: in spite of the revisions which appear in his first draft, he seems to be improvising, catching at words and phrases which will carry on the stanza, without always thinking of their precise significance. This may result only in minor faults of craftsmanship, like the misrelated participle in

> Awaking with a start,
> The waters heave around me . . .

but it can sometimes have more serious effects. Thus Byron often writes a striking opening for a stanza, and then lets it tail off in a succession of weak lines or phrases loosely strung together: this collapse of the rhetorical pitch which he began by setting himself is due partly to artistic carelessness or incompetence, partly also to a tendency to overstate even his strong feelings, and thus aim at a more elevated tone than he could easily sustain. The attempt at a high style is unfortunate in other ways as well. It can lead, for example, to a rather unscrupulous manipulation of the reader's responses—the comparison of Harold wrapped in his thoughts to a corpse wrapped in its shroud seems designed merely to evoke a vague sense of the terrible and the mysterious; and although this is an exceptionally blatant case, there is very often an imprecision in the diction and the imagery which makes Byron's style appear inflated rather than impressive. Occasionally, too, the tone of public utterance seems inappropriate—it is quite suitable for his thoughts on Waterloo, but not for his apostrophes to his infant daughter, and there is indeed a certain vulgarity in his orating on his own parental love.

Although such blemishes do not appear in every stanza, they soon force us to modify our first favorable impression of

Canto III, since we are increasingly aware of faults, in taste as
well as craftsmanship, which point to weaknesses in Byron-
Harold's character and sensibility. From the very opening of
the poem, indeed, one finds some causes for dissatisfaction
with the central figure, through whose consciousness we apprehend the meaning. In addition to the faults already noted,
there is Byron's irritating love of "mystifying" the reader—
hinting at his sins and sorrows without ever stating clearly
what they were, and thus achieving cheap effects of horror or
of pathos:

> Yet must I think less wildly:—I *have* thought
> Too long and darkly, till my brain became,
> In its own eddy boiling and o'erwrought,
> A whirling gulf of phantasy and flame:
> And thus, untaught in youth my heart to tame,
> My springs of life were poisoned. 'Tis too late! . . .
> Long absent Harold re-appears at last;
> He of the breast which fain no more would feel,
> Wrung with the wounds which kill not, but ne'er heal; . . .

A more fatal flaw appears in the account of Harold's distaste
for his fellowmen. The alienation of the poet or genius from
society is a common enough theme in romantic literature, but
it can be treated on very different levels of moral seriousness
and integrity. A good example, which will serve as a touch-
stone, is provided by Wordsworth's description of his anguish,
his conflicting loyalties, when England went to war with revolutionary France:

> . . . I felt
> The ravage of this most unnatural strife
> In my own hearts; there lay it like a weight
> At enmity with all the tenderest springs
> Of my enjoyments. I, who with the breeze
> Had play'd, a green leaf on the blessed tree
> Of my beloved country; nor had wish'd
> For happier fortune than to wither there,
> Now from my pleasant station was cut off,
> and toss'd about in whirlwinds. I rejoiced,
> Yea, afterwards, truth most painful to record!
> Exulted in the triumph of my soul
> When Englishmen by thousands were o'erthrown,
> Left without glory on the Field, or driven,
> Brave hearts, to shameful flight. It was a grief,
> Grief call it not, 'twas anything but that,
> A conflict of sensations without name,

> Of which he only who may love the sight
> Of a village steeple as I do can judge
> When in the Congregation, bending all
> To their great Father, prayers were offer'd up,
> Or praises for our Country's Victories,
> And 'mid the simple worshippers, perchance,
> I only, like an uninvited Guest
> Whom no one own'd sate silent, shall I add,
> Fed on the day of vengeance yet to come? [6]

Here Wordsworth succeeds in conveying both the intensity and the complexity of his feelings, and in the circumstances both these qualities command respect. His isolation was reluctant and unhappy, for although his deepest beliefs about human nature and society forced him out of sympathy with England, his basic love for her was still strong. Indeed his very feelings about France owed something to his upbringing: the "green leaf" metaphor, as well as emphasizing his close natural attachment to his country, also reminds us that it was English Nature which had helped to form his moral being; while the Village Steeple and Congregation suggest not only the simple pieties now perhaps being misapplied, but the whole context of rustic life which had done so much to develop his love and respect for human nature. The passage deals, then, with the clash between his major loyalties at that time, and it gains from being read as part of the poem in which these loyalties are fully discussed, but even taken by itself it can be seen to give an honest, sensitive, and convincing record of an agonizing inner conflict. When we pass from this to Byron's presentation of Childe Harold, we find thoughts and feelings of a very different order:

> But soon he knew himself the most unfit
> Of men to herd with Man, with whom he held
> Little in common; untaught to submit
> His thoughts to others, though his soul was quell'd
> In youth by his own thoughts; still uncompell'd,
> He would not yield dominion of his mind
> To Spirits against whom his own rebell'd,
> Proud though in desolation—which could find
> A life within itself, to breathe without mankind.

In place of Wordsworth's scrupulous precise description of his feelings, Byron offers us flashy paradox and large rhetorical gestures expressing a shoddy kind of self-approval. He complacently accepts isolation as the natural lot of genius—indeed as something rather creditable; no conflict is involved because "mankind" is lumped together as a homogeneous mass of dullness and stupidity, to be easily rejected by the great or sensitive soul; and this rejection is based simply on a firm conviction of his own spiritual superiority. One sees here the baneful influence of Shelley's notions of the difference between poets and other men—notions which were all too easily reconciled with certain favorite attitudes of Byron's own; and the combination had an irresistible attraction for him at that time. The long account of Harold is thus as much of an indulgence, a dream fantasy, as anything in the verse tales; and it culminates in a passage of almost ludicrous exaggeration, which shows how completely Byron's critical intelligence is in abeyance:

> Self-exiled Harold wanders forth again,
>   With nought of Hope left—but with less of gloom;
>   The very knowledge that he lived in vain,
>   That all was over on this side the tomb,
>   Had made Despair a smilingness assume,
>   Which, though 'twere wild—as on the plunder'd wreck
>   When mariners would madly meet their doom
>   With draughts intemperate on the sinking deck,—
> Did yet inspire a cheer, which he forbore to check.

Canto III, however, is not all like this. It is a remarkable blend of public and private interests, and we pass from thinly veiled autobiography to a meditation on the results of Britain's final victory over Napoleon:

> Fit retribution! Gaul may champ the bit
>   And foam in fetters;—but is Earth more free?
>   Did nations combat to make One submit?
>   Or league to teach all Kings true Sovereignty?
>   What! shall reviving Thraldom again be
>   The patched-up Idol of enlightened days?
>   Shall we, who struck the Lion down, shall we
>   Pay the Wolf homage? proffering lowly gaze
> And servile knees to Thrones? . . .

In stanzas such as these one finds fully developed some of the ideas on war and politics which Byron held for the remainder of his life. He hated despotisms of every kind, and sympathized with peoples who were subject to domestic or to foreign tyrants. He believed in liberty, for other men as well as for himself, and his views on the French Revolution were like those later expressed by Shelley in the preface to *The Revolt of Islam*: in this canto he deplores the worst excesses of the revolutionaries, but argues that men warped by oppression could not be expected to behave with perfect justice, and far from being appalled by their mistakes, he looks forward eagerly to another more decisive revolution. His views on war were closely related to these few basic ideas: he detested wars of conquest or aggression, or mere clashes between rival powers, stressing their futility and the human misery which they involve—thus in his thoughts on Waterloo he emphasizes the sterility of Britain's victory, the waste of life, and the sorrow which it brought to thousands. But, like Godwin, he approved of battles fought for liberty: young Marceau, as a general of the French Republic, is commemorated as a champion of Freedom; and the field of Morat, where the Swiss defeated the Burgundians, is viewed with reverence instead of horror:

> While Waterloo with Cannae's carnage vies,
> Morat and Marathon twin names shall stand;
> They were true Glory's stainless victories,
> Won by the unambitious heart and hand
> Of a proud, brotherly, and civic band,
> All unbought champions in no princely cause
> Of vice-entailed Corruption; they no land
> Doomed to bewail the blasphemy of laws
> Making Kings' right divine, by some Draconic clause.

All these beliefs were not newly conceived in 1816—they had appeared in some of Byron's poems and letters before now; but his sudden severance from English life and his resentful hostility to public opinion made him voice his views more openly and more intransigently than he had ever done before. There is therefore an emotional connection between his private grievances and Harold's politics,[7] but in spite of this the quality of feeling differs greatly in his presentation of these subjects. The political stanzas can be prejudiced and unfair; they can also degenerate from eloquence into stilted rhetoric or frigid cliché; but they are never contaminated by the arrogance and self-pity which so often vitiate the speaker's treatment of his personal affairs.

Byron resists, too, the temptation to depict the lives of men like Rousseau and Napoleon as mere types or analogues of his own case. He is aware of similarities between his lot and theirs, and this awareness helps to give the poem its unity

and strength of feeling; but he avoids crudely identifying them
with himself. He sees Napoleon, for example, as another great
man dragged down and humiliated by inferior beings, but he
does not oversimplify and sentimentalize his story: ever since
his schooldays Byron had felt an inclination to idealize the
Emperor, but the inescapable facts of his hero's career forced
him to recognize the complexity of his character; and though
he still admires Napoleon, he does not attempt to minimize
his weaknesses:

> Oh, more or less than man—in high or low—
>   Battling with nations, flying from the field;
>   Now making monarchs' necks thy footstool, now
>   More than thy meanest soldier taught to yield;
>   An Empire thou couldst crush, command, rebuild,
>   But govern not thy pettiest passion, nor,
>   However deeply in men's spirits skill'd,
>   Look through thine own, nor curb the lust of War,
> Nor learn that tempted Fate will leave the loftiest Star.

Some parts of this analysis remind one of his antithetical
descriptions of the verse-tale heroes—

> In him inexplicably mixed appeared
> Much to be loved and hated, sought and feared—

but there is an important difference: Byron has to acknowledge
in Napoleon some traits—notably cowardice—which cannot be
glossed over or romanticized. He is faced with the complexity
of life itself, which restricts the characteristic workings of
his imagination and forbids him to reduce real people to a
stereotyped formula. With this greater respect for truth there
sometimes comes increased maturity of judgment: in Rousseau
Byron finds another romantic genius who felt that those around
him were his enemies, but instead of treating him with the
uncritical indulgence shown to Harold, he proceeds to comment on his errors and delusions:

> His life was one long war with self-sought foes,
>   Or friends by him self-banished; for his mind
>   Had grown Suspicion's sanctuary, and chose,
>   For its own cruel sacrifice, the kind,
>   'Gainst whom he raged with fury strange and blind. . . .

Through these more objective (although sympathetic) analyses
of real individuals, who resembled him in one way or another,
Byron achieves momentarily a sounder understanding of him-

self and of the problems of "greatness" than he arrived at by direct consideration of his own predicament. Thus when he comes to relate Napoleon's character and situation to his own, he writes about the restless romantic temperament with far more penetration than he showed in his account of Harold:

> But Quiet to quick bosoms is a Hell
>   And *there* hath been thy bane; there is a fire
>   And motion of the Soul which will not dwell
>   In its own narrow being, but aspire
>   Beyond the fitting medium of desire;
>   And, but once kindled, quenchless evermore,
>   Preys upon high adventure, nor can tire
>   Of aught but rest; a fever at the core,
> Fatal to him who bears, to all who ever bore.
>
> This makes the madmen who have made men mad
>   By their contagion; Conquerors and Kings,
>   Founders of sects and systems, to whom add
>   Sophists, Bards, Statesmen, all unquiet things
>   Which stir too strongly the soul's secret springs,
>   And are themselves the fools to those they fool;
>   Envied, yet how unenviable! what stings
>   Are theirs! One breast laid open were a school
> Which would unteach Mankind the lust to shine or rule.

This is admirable, but Byron cannot stay long at this level—in the very next stanza we are conscious of a falling-off, for when he turns from the exceptional psychology of these men to their relations with ordinary mortals, his reflections are more limited and personal, with a hint of self-pity; and his pretentious metaphor suggests perhaps an over-facile opposition between genius and mediocrity:

> He who ascends to mountain-tops shall find
>   The loftiest peaks most wrapt in clouds and snow;
>   He who surpasses or subdues mankind,
>   Must look down on the hate of those below . . .

The imagery of this stanza points to the important part that Nature plays in Canto III. It is no longer described for its own sake, as it had been in the earlier *Childe Harold*, but it figures largely in the presentation of the poet-hero's emotional and spiritual states. Conscious of his wrongs and sorrows, and his own innate superiority, he flies to solitude among the mountains, where he sometimes looks on his surroundings simply as a refuge from the crowd and the turmoil of life:

> Is it not better, then, to be alone,
>> And love Earth only for its earthly sake?
>> By the blue rushing of the arrowy Rhone,
>> Or the pure bosom of its nursing Lake,
>> Which feeds it as a mother who doth make
>> A fair but froward infant her own care,
>> Kissing its cries away as these awake;—
>> Is it not better thus our lives to wear,
> Than join the crushing crowd, doomed to inflict or bear?

Here one sees in the opening lines Byron's ability to give new and vigorous expression to quite commonplace ideas, but the effect is spoiled by the long simile, which may have originated in his feelings about Ada and her mother, but which is developed with so little reference to the actual relation of lake to river that it seems a crude sentimentalizing of physical Nature. In the next stanza Byron passes without any explanation from his loving Earth only for her earthly sake to a kind of Nature mysticism which is not strictly that of Shelley or of Wordsworth, but which obviously owes a good deal to these authors. This peculiarly abrupt transition may lend substance to the view that he was not writing from his own experience, but exploiting various ideas that had already received literary treatment, and a curious imprecision in his phrasing sometimes gives the same impression.[8] Probably, however, he is speaking of things he had really felt or thought he felt when under the influence of Shelley's talk and Wordsworth's poetry, and any vagueness in his account of the experience is due, not to its being a deliberate fake, but to its never having been much more than a vague yearning emotion:

> I live not in myself, but I become
>> Portion of that around me; and to me
>> High mountains are a feeling, but the hum
>> Of human cities torture: I can see
>> Nothing to loathe in Nature, save to be
>> A link reluctant in a fleshly chain,
>> Classed among creatures, when the soul can flee,
>> And with the sky—the peak—the heaving plain
> Of Ocean, or the stars, mingle—and not in vain . . .

> Are not the mountains, waves, and skies, a part
>> Of me and of my Soul, as I of them?
>> Is not the love of these deep in my heart
>> With a pure passion? should I not contemn
>> All objects, if compared with these? and stem

> A tide of suffering, rather than forego
> Such feelings for the hard and worldly phlegm
> Of those whose eyes are only turned below,
> Gazing upon the ground, with thoughts, which dare not glow.

These last few lines suggest (what one suspected all along) that the primary function of such fine "poetic" sentiments may simply be to differentiate Childe Harold from the herd, and demonstrate his great superiority of soul. The build-up of his character seems more important than the actual "religion" he asserts here, and throughout the poem Nature provides him not so much with a system of beliefs as with a symbolism by means of which he can present more fully his own personality and feelings. In the scenes which he surveys he can find emblems, as it were, of his present situation: [9] the castles of the Rhine suggest the lofty mind's relation to the crowd; the river itself makes him wish that it were Lethe, though it would flow in vain over *his* memory; and a storm over Lake Léman seems to parallel his own emotional turmoil:

> Sky—Mountains—River—Winds—Lake—Lightnings! ye!
>> With night, and clouds, and thunder—and a Soul
>> To make these felt and feeling, well may be
>> Things that have made me watchful; the far roll
>> Of your departing voices, is the knoll
>> Of what in me is sleepless,—if I rest.
> But where of ye, O Tempests! is the goal?
> Are ye like those within the human breast?
> Or do ye find, at length, like eagles, some high nest?

> Could I embody and unbosom now
>> That which is most within me,—could I wreak
>> My thoughts upon expression, and thus throw
>> Soul—heart—mind—passions—feelings—strong or weak—
>> All that I would have sought, and all I seek,
>> Bear, know, feel—and yet breathe—into *one* word,
>> And that one word were Lightning, I would speak;
>> But as it is, I live and die unheard,
> With a most voiceless thought, sheathing it as a sword.

While, therefore, there are several foci of interest in this canto, the central interest always is the poet-hero himself. Byron has chosen to present his criticism of life, his meditations on his own experience, through this character, and our final judgment on the poem will depend, presumably, on what we think of "Harold" in his new role. I myself find him un-

satisfactory: he is too histrionic and self-pitying a figure, and
the admiration Byron obviously feels for him (as for the verse-
tale heroes) seems excessive and unjustified. Harold lays claim
to exceptional nobility of soul, but neither the greatness of his
nature nor the fineness of his sensibility is sufficiently established by the poem itself; and while his thoughts are often
interesting, they hardly warrant his conviction of their elevation
above those of ordinary men. This self-flattering, self-drama-
tizing self-deception is his greatest weakness, which appears
again and again, producing some of the most famous, but most
questionable, purple passages in Canto III:

> I have not loved the World, nor the World me;
> I have not flattered its rank breath, nor bowed
> To its idolatries a patient knee,
> Nor coined my cheek to smiles,—nor cried aloud
> In worship of an echo: in the crowd
> They could not deem me one of such—I stood
> Among them, but not of them—in a shroud
> Of thoughts which were not their thoughts, and still could,
> Had I not filed my mind, which thus itself subdued.

Here we have the Byronic Byron at his best and worst. There
is a natural temptation to adduce biographical evidence to
prove that he is lying at this point—that he *had* loved "the
World" and courted its approval with remarkable success; but
confining ourselves to more reputable critical procedures, we
may point not only to some loosenesses of thought and of expression, but also to the presentation of humanity as a crowd
of base, hypocritical, rank-breathed idolators, forming a single
monolithic entity ("the World") which is contrasted with the
one great individual—himself. The vanity and petulance of
this are obvious and deplorable; and yet the stanza cannot be
rejected out of hand: one has to admit that these feelings are
successfully created for us by the verse, in spite of—or rather
by means of—its stylistic defects; so that it would probably be
fairest to describe this passage (and the many others like it)
as extremely good bad poetry, highly competent though
vicious. Then again, as I have tried to show, this aspect of
Childe Harold is not always in the foreground, for when
Byron's interest was sufficiently engaged in other characters or
other subjects he could escape almost completely from his
worst faults and write poetry of a higher order, even though
the balance he attains is a precarious one, and he is constantly

in danger of lapsing into the cheap attitudes he nearly always strikes when considering his recent history or his relation to his fellowmen.

There is, moreover, some confusion in the actual conception of Childe Harold's character: his total detachment from mankind, his retreat to solitude and Nature, and his arrogant contempt for ordinary humanity, are difficult to reconcile with his professed enthusiasm for Revolution and Freedom for the People. Byron was trying for the first time to combine romantic liberalism with the "Byronic" attributes of pride, misanthropy, and isolation, and the result is not convincing psychologically. The conflict is never fully recognized, and it is far from being resolved by the glib formula "To fly from, need not be to hate, mankind"; so that we see reflected here a contradiction in the author's own beliefs and feelings.

Clearly, then, in spite of the increased creative power that Byron shows in Canto III, he had not yet solved the two closely related problems of his style and his poetic personality.

Canto III of *Childe Harold* [shows] the limitations of the Byronic hero as *persona* or protagonist, and it seems unnecessary to examine Canto IV in the same detail. Yet this poem contains new elements as well as familiar weaknesses, for there are some changes and developments which constitute a real departure from Byron's mood of 1816, and look forward to the coming revolution in his whole poetic manner and technique. It should be seen, then, as essentially transitional in nature, using themes and attitudes which had appeared before, but sometimes modifying them in important ways, especially by coming closer to his normal everyday feelings and idiom.

For the most part he adopts the same conventions as he had evolved for Canto III: his journey from Venice to Rome provides the basic structure of the work, just as his route through Belgium, Germany and Switzerland gave him the framework for the former poem; and he now abandons even the pretense of a distinction between poet and hero:

> With regard to the conduct of the last canto [he writes], there will be found less of the pilgrim than in any of the preceding, and that little slightly, if at all, separated from the author speaking in his own person . . . and the very anxiety to preserve this difference, and disappointment at finding it un-

availing, so far crushed my efforts in the composition, that I
determined to abandon it altogether—and have done so.

In the poem itself then he speaks openly in his own person
mentioning the Pilgrim only as a once-convenient fiction, or
a fancy of the past.

This does not mean, however, that he has abandoned the
whole complex of ideas and feelings associated with Harold.
Byron's mood had changed during his months in Italy, but he
had not altogether lost his melancholy and resentment, or his
desire to voice them to the world, and in some new stanzas
his tone is indistinguishable from that of the most violent,
emotional, and self-regarding passages of Canto III:

> . . . There are some feelings Time can not benumb,
> Nor Torture shake, or mine would now be cold and dumb.

> Existence may be borne, and the deep root
>   Of life and sufferance makes its firm abode
>   In bare and desolated bosoms: mute
>   The camel labours with the heaviest load,
>   And the wolf dies in silence—not bestowed
>   In vain should such example be; if they,
>   Things of ignoble or of savage mood,
>   Endure and shrink not, we of nobler clay
> May temper it to bear,—it is but for a day.

One cannot help noticing that Byron's own endurance, on
which he so prides himself, is far from being as silent as this
might suggest. He breaks out, just as in the former canto, in
wild indignation and self-pity; and even when he speaks about
Forgiveness, our impression is not one of genuine emotional or
spiritual change, but rather of his continued self-approval—of
his admiration for his own superior deportment in adversity:

> And if my voice break forth, 'tis not that now
>   I shrink from what is suffered: let him speak
>   Who hath beheld decline upon my brow,
>   Or seen my mind's convulsion leave it weak;
>   But in this page a record will I seek.
>   Not in the air shall these my words disperse,
>   Though I be ashes; a far hour shall wreak
>   The deep prophetic fulness of this verse,
> And pile on human heads the mountain of my curse!

> That curse shall be Forgiveness—Have I not—
>   Hear me, my mother Earth! behold it, Heaven!—
>   Have I not had to wrestle with my lot?

Have I not suffered things to be forgiven?
Have I not had my brain seared, my heart riven,
Hopes sapped, name blighted, Life's life lied away?
And only not to desperation driven,
Because not altogether of such clay
As rots into the souls of those whom I survey.

"Why do you indulge this despondency?" asked Shelley, and his choice of verb shows critical and psychological perception, for there is a kind of relish and self-satisfaction in the gloom with which Byron surveys his fate; and the same is true of some of his more general reflections about human life:

Our life is a false nature—'tis not in
The harmony of things,—this hard decree,
This uneradicable taint of Sin,
This boundless Upas, this all-blasting tree,
Whose root is Earth—whose leaves and branches be
The skies which rain their plagues on men like dew—
Disease, death, bondage—all the woes we see,
And worse, the woes we see not—which throb through
The immedicable soul, with heart-aches ever new.

This ranting pessimism, which provoked Peacock's amusing satire in *Nightmare Abbey*, is one of the characteristic notes of Canto IV, yet it does not pervade the whole poem. And while Byron's treatment of his wrongs and sorrows often resembles that of Canto III, his poetic personality has changed in other ways. This can be seen, for example, in his attitude to Nature. His passing from Switzerland to Italy made in itself for a change of emphasis—the new poem, he told Murray, "necessarily treats more of works of art than of Nature": [10] but his own approach is different too. Once freed from the immediate influence of Shelley, Byron threw off his vague mysticism, and except for two stanzas added at a very late stage, we hear nothing in this canto about mingling with the Universe,[11] and very little about flying from Men to Solitude. When he turns to scenery he is not searching for a refuge or religion—he is interested in Nature simply for its beauty, or its associations, literary and historical. He has returned in fact to the viewpoint of an ideal tourist, even if he departs from it at times to reappear as a Romantic Genius. Byron's mood—in spite of all the "darkness and dismay"—has ceased to be obsessive, and though he can still work up his grief and indignation to a high pitch, they are no longer fused in a single intense emotional state, governing the selection and use of material throughout the poem. We find as a consequence that the narrator's personality does not always blend and unify his observations as it did in Canto III, for some things, like the Falls of Terni, are described in detail only because Byron saw them and thought they were beautiful and interesting—not because they have any bearing on his main emotional or intellectual preoccupations. And the same centrifugal tendency appears in his handling of other topics such as War and Liberty.

Of course one must not try to force this canto into the mould of its predecessor; here we have a new mood and new theme—the elegiac—which could hardly be avoided in Italy, and which is more important than the subjects carried forward from 1816. All around him Byron saw the ruins or the relics or achievements of past civilizations, and he began to see his own fall in relation to that of great cities and great geniuses of former ages. Indeed Canto IV is best regarded as a long meditation on Time's works, defeats, and victories, culminating in the address to Ocean, which for Byron is a symbol of Eternity. This meditation is not simply a long melancholy musing on the impermanence of earthly glory: for all Byron's pessimism he can see that true nobility and greatness triumph over mutability and death—poets, for example, who had been disgraced, exiled or imprisoned by their countrymen or rulers are now reverenced, while their enemies (despots or populace) are remembered only with contempt. Here was another aspect of "the fate of genius"—one that brought some consolation to his wounded pride, while the long perspectives which Italian history provided helped him to adjust emotionally to his own changed circumstances.

Even when we do full justice to this new and central theme, however, we must acknowledge Canto IV to be the most loosely organized as well as the longest section of *Childe Harold's Pilgrimage*. This is partly a consequence of his additions to the poem: his second thoughts are often admirable in themselves, but they detract occasionally from the work's coherence. Stanzas 51 and 52 add little to what Byron has already said, but interrupt the argument which runs naturally on from stanza 50 to stanza 53; stanzas 27–29, which he wrote after seeing a wonderful sunset on his evening ride, form an isolated piece of natural description; and there are other examples of unskillful dovetailing of new with old. But most of the sixty stanzas added to the original one hundred and twenty-six are worked in very well, and the looseness of construction is due less to the stages in which Canto IV was written than to some confusion in the poet's own feelings, and in the aims he sets himself. In Canto III he had created a particular narrator-hero, and presented his account of his surroundings through this character: here his purpose is ostensibly the same, but he finds it much more difficult to maintain the personality he had assumed, while his interest in the scenes around him tends to get out of control. There were so many things to see and to describe in Italy—Byron himself says that "the text, within the limits I proposed, I soon found hardly sufficient for the labyrinth of external objects, and the consequent reflections" [12]—and he comes nearer here than he had ever done before to the methods of a guide-book, trying to include everything of interest to the tourist.[13] And this eagerness to comment and describe, together with a certain instability in his own feelings, leads him to neglect the characterization of the narrator-hero.

When the poem opens the speaker is as much an object of attention as the scene which he surveys—he is an important figure in the foreground of his own composition, which would hardly be complete without him there as an observer and participant:

> I stood in Venice, on the "Bridge of Sighs;"
> A Palace and a prison on each hand:
> I saw from out the wave her structures rise
> As from the stroke of the Enchanter's wand:
> A thousand Years their cloudy wings expand
> Around me, . . .

We remain aware of this narrator's personality, but it seems to vary as the poem progresses—sometimes he is less a meditative tourist than a sufferer and victim, for whom sad surroundings are an appropriate and congenial setting:

> But my Soul wanders; I demand it back
> To meditate amongst decay, and stand
> A ruin amidst ruins. . . .

In discussing his own ruin, too, he can lapse (as we have seen) into anger and self-pity, and an exaggerated pessimism couched

in violent and turgid rhetoric. At other times, however, as he
gazes on the real ruins around him, his own sorrows are
dwarfed and his mood becomes much calmer, though still
melancholy:

> Upon such a shrine
> What are our petty griefs?—let me not number mine . . .

> Tully was not so eloquent as thou,
>   Thou nameless column with the buried base!
>   What are the laurels of the Caesar's brow?
>   Crown me with ivy from his dwelling-place.
>   Whose arch or pillar meets me in the face,
>   Titus or Trajan's? No—'tis that of time:
>   Triumph, arch, pillar, all he doth displace
>   Scoffing; and apostolic statues climb
> To crush the imperial urn, whose ashes slept sublime,

> Buried in air, the deep blue sky of Rome,
>   And looking to the stars: they had contained
>   A Spirit which with these would find a home,
>   The last of those who o'er the whole earth reigned,
>   The Roman Globe—for, after, none sustained,
>   But yielded back his conquests:—he was more
>   Than a mere Alexander, and, unstained
>   With household blood and wine, serenely wore
> His sovereign virtues—still we Trajan's name adore.

Here, even as he celebrates Time's triumph, Byron shows how
virtue triumphs over time, and there are many other passages
like this, propounding views of life quite different from the
vision of futility and gloom which Harold sometimes gives us;
and the style, significantly, is much less pretentious and extrava-
gant than in his wilder outbursts—it can become stilted and
awkward, but at best he has a dignified descriptive-meditative
manner admirably suited to his elegiac theme. Then there are
stanzas where the emotional temperature is lower still—where
Byron seems not frenzied, grief-stricken, or even mildly melancholy, but normal and contented as he enjoys the scene before
him, though too often in such moods he tries to work up his
ideas and observations into "poetry," giving them a factitious
and unnecessary elevation. Sometimes, on the other hand, he
seems to be feeling his way towards a more familiar style of
easy discourse, and this can approximate for brief moments to
the colloquial pungency of satire:

> Was she as those who love their lords, or they
>   Who love the lords of other? . . .

Occasionally one feels that Byron is trying to achieve in this not very suitable verse-form some effects of contrast and deflation like those of his own later satires:

> "While stands the Coliseum, Rome shall stand:
>   When falls the Coliseum, Rome shall fall;
>   And when Rome falls—the World." From our own land
>   Thus spake the pilgrims o'er this mighty wall
>   In Saxon times, which we are wont to call
>   Ancient; and these three mortal things are still
>   On their foundations, and unaltered all—
>   Rome and her Ruin past Redemption's skill—
> The World—the same wide den—of thieves, or what ye will.

The failure represented by the trailing weak conclusion was due mainly to the structure of the Spenserian stanza; and it was soon to be transformed into success when he discovered the potentialities of *ottava rima*, with its crisp epigrammatic final couplet to replace the needless Alexandrines of *Childe Harold*.

There is, then, no one style in Canto IV. The tone is governed neither by a firmly-held conception of the narrator's character, nor by singleness of feeling in the author. Byron could pass at this time from gloom and despondency to a delighted interest in the world around him, and these contradictory emotions are reflected in the poem.

Notes

1. *The Letters of Sir Walter Scott*, ed. H. J. C. Grierson, D. Cook, W. M. Parker and others, (London, 1932–1937), IV, 234.

2. *The Works of Lord Byron: Poetry*, ed. E. H. Coleridge (London, 1904–1905), II, 217. All subsequent references to *Childe Harold's Pilgrimage* are from this volume.

3. *Edinburgh Review*, XXVII (December, 1816), 293.

4. H. J. C. Grierson, *The Background of English Literature* (London, 1925), p. 88.

5. *Quarterly Review*, XIX (April, 1818), 228.

6. *The Prelude*, ed. E. de Selincourt, 2nd edn, rev. Helen Darbishire, (Oxford, 1959), p. 382.

7. This is particularly clear in letters of the period 1816–1817, where he looks on revolution as a means of getting his revenge on the Society which had cast him out.

8. Wordsworth himself thought that Byron's enthusiasm for Nature was assumed or borrowed. Moore tells (*Memoirs*, III, 161) of a visit which the older poet paid to him in October, 1820:

[Wordsworth] spoke of Byron's plagiarisms from him; the whole third canto of "Childe Harold" founded on his style and sentiments. The feeling of natural objects which is there expressed, not caught by B. from nature herself, but from him (Wordsworth), and spoiled in the transmission. "Tintern Abbey" the source of it all; from which same poem too the celebrated passage about Solitude, in the first canto of "Childe Harold," is (he said) taken, with this difference, that what is naturally expressed by him, has been worked by Byron into a laboured and antithetical sort of declamation.

And Wordsworth expressed the same views in his letters.

9. The same habit of thought is to be found in *Manfred*, and in Byron's journal for September 1816: "Passed *whole woods of withered pines, all withered*; trunks stripped and barkless, branches lifeless; done by a single winter,—their appearance reminded me of me and my family." *The Works of Lord Byron: Letters and Journals*, ed. R. E. Prothero (London, 1898–1901), Vol. III, 360.

10. *Letters and Journals*, IV, 153.

11. "There are no metaphysics in it; at least I think not," he told Murray (*L.J.*, IV, 155).

12. II, 323.

13. Hobhouse supplemented this endeavor with his voluminous notes appended to the poem, and with his volume of *Historical Illustrations of the Fourth Canto of Childe Harold*.

C. M. Bowra

12 · Don Juan

IN THE HISTORY of the English Romantics, Byron has a peculiar place. From a European point of view, he is the chief exponent and most renowned figure of the whole movement, the man who summed up in himself its essential qualities and by his inspiring example imposed them on the civilized world. From the usual English point of view, he is hardly a Romantic at all, but a survival from the eighteenth century and an enemy of much that the true Romantics thought most holy. His European reputation was already great in his lifetime and has not been seriously shaken since. Just as Goethe regarded him as "the greatest genius of the century" and said: "He is not antique and not modern; he is like the present day," so Mazzini said: "He gave a European role to English poetry. He led the genius of England on a pilgrimage through Europe."

This reputation was matched by an influence no less remarkable. There was hardly a country whose leading poets in the thirties and forties of the nineteenth century were not in some sense Byronic, in their rejection of established systems, their aggressive self-assertion, their love of liberty, and their cult of love. When Russian poetry found its first full strength about 1820, Byron was its chief model and its most powerful inspiration. To him Pushkin owed not only the ideas and the form of such poems as *The Prisoner of the Caucasus* and *Poltava*, but intended his *Evgeny Onegin* to be a Russian counterpart of *Don Juan*; and if there was ever a case of nature

Reprinted by permission of the publishers from C. M. Bowra, *The Romantic Imagination*, Cambridge, Mass.: Harvard University Press, Copyright, 1949, by The President and Fellows of Harvard College.

imitating art, it can be seen in the startling resemblances between Lermontov and the Byronic heroes. From Byron, Lermontov learned to speak of himself as he really was, in his
strange contradictions of affection and hatred, of delight and
boredom, of sentiment and irony, of love of society and love of
solitude. Throughout Europe poets looked to Byron because
he had given voice to something which they recognized and
prized in themselves. Of course, his fame was all the greater
because he was thought to be a victim of English hypocrisy
and because he died heroically for the liberation of Greece.
But that was fortuitous. What mattered was that he put into
poetry something that belonged to many men in his time, and
that he was a pioneer of a new outlook and a new art. He set
his mark on a whole generation, and his fame rang from one
end of Europe to another.

In his own country Byron's reputation has been quite different. In his lifetime he was not admired by his reverend
seniors. Wordsworth not only thought his style very slovenly,
but regarded him as "a monster . . . a Man of Genius whose
heart is perverted." [1] Though Coleridge did not scruple to
enlist Byron's support in getting his plays acted, he had no
high opinion of his work and thought his later poetry
"Satanic." [2] Even Keats, who was much less prejudiced than
Wordsworth and Coleridge, dismissed *Don Juan* as "Lord
Byron's last flash poem," [3] and was outraged by its description
of a storm at sea:

> This gives me the most horrid idea of human nature, that
> a man like Byron should have exhausted all the pleasures of
> the world so compleatly that there was nothing left for him but
> to laugh and gloat over the most solemn and heart rending
> [scenes] of human misery.[4]

Blake was less violent and seems to have felt some tenderness
for Byron because he was a rebel and an outcast. That is
perhaps why, in 1822, he dedicated *The Ghost of Abel* "To
Lord Byron in the Wilderness." Yet he too felt that something
was wrong with Byron, that he was an erring, if not a lost,
soul, and that he had surrendered to the false lures of naturalism. *The Ghost of Abel* is an answer to Byron's *Cain* and
shows how far apart the two poets were in their convictions.
In return, Byron felt no regard for the poets who criticized him.
He thought Wordsworth a bore, and says so more than once

in *Don Juan.* Apart from *Christabel,* he had a low opinion of Coleridge's work, and thought the man himself "a shabby fellow." [5] Nor did Shelley's advocacy of Keats persuade Byron to think well of him. Some of Byron's remarks in his letters about Keats are too indecent to be printed, and though he recanted somewhat after Keats's death, his epitaph on him shows no more than a contemptuous pity:

> 'T is strange the mind, that very fiery particle,
> Should let itself be snuffed out by an article.[6]

Of Blake, Byron says nothing, and the probability is that he never heard of him.

In both the European and the English views of Byron there is a mixture of truth and error. Goethe, Mazzini, Pushkin, and others were right to see in Byron the representative of a new age. When the French Revolution broke the equilibrium on which the civilization of the eighteenth century had rested, a new type of man came into existence, and Byron was the supreme example of it in his rejection of estabilshed ties, his cult of the self, his love of adventure, and his ironical distrust of his own emotions and beliefs. He was an aristocratic rebel when aristocrats were leaders of new movements and new ideas; in him the poet became a man of action because the creative spirit, long discouraged and constricted, found that words alone were not enough for it and that it must display itself in generous gesture and gallant risk. At the same time, Byron's Continental admirers did not distinguish the false from the true in his work or his personality. They were so fascinated by his early poems that they continued to prize them even when he had begun to compose in a different and more truly creative spirit. The dream worlds of escape in his early romances answered a dissatisfaction in many men, who accepted as great poetry what was in fact often false or feeble. Until he left England for the second and last time, Byron lacked the experience which alone could make his subjects convincing, and though he dallied with Romantic notions, he did not really believe in them and for that reason was not master of them. Much of Byron's earlier poetry is deficient both in art and in truth. It did indeed open new prospects, and it is extraordinary what the passionate sincerity of a great genius like Pushkin could make of them. But many others were so entranced by

Byron's poses that they were content to write a poetry of pose, and it is this, more than anything else, which is so disturbing in much that was written in Latin countries during the Romantic age. The Byronic affectations were ubiquitous, but they are usually neither attractive nor convincing, and even when they are embodied in a man of real talent, they remain an obstacle to our full enjoyment of his work.

Byron's English critics misjudged him in a different way. If Wordsworth and Coleridge were so shocked by his morals that they were blind to the merits of his poetry, the same cannot be said of Keats. Keats condemned Byron because their conceptions of poetry were different, and the chief difference lay in their opposite views of the part to be played by the imagination. In September 1819, Keats wrote to his brother George:

> You speak of Lord Byron and me—There is this great difference between us. He describes what he sees—I describe what I imagine. Mine is the hardest task. You see the immense difference.[7]

This is a fair comment, and Keats was not the only man to make it. In dedicating *The Ghost of Abel* to Byron, Blake says:

> What doest thou here, Elijah? Can a Poet doubt the Visions of Jehovah? Nature has no Outline, but Imagination has. Nature has no Tune, but Imagination has. Nature has no supernatural and dissolves: Imagination is Eternity.[8]

In Blake's view Byron's error is to follow nature instead of the imagination. With this Byron would not have quarreled. For, as he wrote in his first letter on Bowles's *Strictures on Pope:*

> It is the fashion of the day to lay great stress upon what they call "imagination" and "invention," the two commonest of qualities: an Irish peasant with a little whisky in his head will imagine and invent more than would furnish forth a modern poem.[9]

On the central article of the Romantic creed, the importance of the imagination, Byron was regarded as a heretic by such good judges as Keats and Blake, and he would not have denied the accusation. It is not surprising that among his contemporaries he was treated as an undesirable alien in the world of English poetry. But he worked by different standards and would not have been troubled by such criticisms. In rejecting the imagination he obeyed a deep conviction, and this rejection inspired his best work and won him a special place among the poets of his time.

In this chorus of disapproval there is one distinguished exception. Shelley liked Byron as a man and admired him as a poet. It is true that the two men were drawn together by circumstances. They belonged to the same social class and had alike come into conflict with it and suffered from it. But there was no call for Shelley to admire Byron's poetry unless he really thought it good, and that, with some reservations, he sincerely did. Shelley met Byron soon after he had left England and begun to discover where his real gifts lay. Even so, Shelley distinguished between the better and the worse poems. When Byron showed him *The Deformed Transformed*, Shelley saw where the faults lay and said so frankly. But when Byron began *Don Juan*, Shelley gave unqualified praise. He saw "the power and the beauty and the wit" of the poem and admired the portraiture of human nature "laid on with the eternal colours of the feelings of humanity." [10] At a time when poets and critics alike poured abuse on *Don Juan* as slovenly and immoral, Shelley saw that it was the great poem which Byron alone could write, and that it was the sincere reflection of his complex nature and alive with human feelings.

Don Juan is Byron's masterpiece because into it he put the whole of his real self and nothing of the false self which he had manufactured for his earlier poems. And just because it is true to experience, the technique is entirely adequate and cannot be blamed for carelessness. In it Byron speaks not in a slack version of the grand manner, but with the rich ebullience of his conversation and his incomparable letters. He uses the whole living language as he himself knew it and spoke it. It is wonderfully natural and unaffected, and the tone of the words responds with perfect ease to Byron's wayward moods. If he derived his form from Pulci's *Morgante Maggiore*, he showed excellent judgment in doing so. For Pulci has something of Byron's careless gaiety and of his ability to temper seriousness with mockery. The *ottava rima* with its easy progress is well adapted to story-telling, and the clinching couplet in each stanza gives excellent opportunities for epigram such as were denied by the Spenserian stanzas of *Childe Harold*. The easy flowing stanzas suit Byron's different effects, and though they

lack polished art, they are a perfect vehicle for what he has to
say. They are so flexible that in them Byron's carelessness does
not matter and indeed becomes a virtue, since it is part of his
conversational manner. All kinds of elements pass easily into
this style. It is equally suited to lyrical description and scurri-
lous satire, to sustained narrative and personal outbursts, to
stately declamation and slapdash slang. The brilliantly ingenious rhymes keep it fresh and lively, and the sprightly,
uninhibited movement of the stanzas is in perfect accord with
the darts and flashes of Byron's mind.

In *Don Juan* Byron speaks as freely and as candidly about
himself as Wordsworth does in *The Prelude*. Of course, *Don
Juan* is cast in the form of objective narrative and deals with
imaginary incidents, but what holds it together and provides
its amazing vitality is Byron's personality, and the contrast with
Wordsworth's self-portrait shows how far apart the two men
were. Their differences of taste and of temperament are matched
by their differences of outlook on the nature of poetry. When
Wordsworth conceived the idea of *The Prelude*, he was entirely
absorbed in his Romantic creed and believed that his was a
dedicated task which must be fulfilled through communion
with nature. In his earlier work Byron had assumed some of the
airs appropriate to such a creed without feeling its mystical
appeal. But when he wrote *Don Juan*, he wished to do something different. He decided that he must tell the truth in the
hope of making men better. He was not surprised that *Don
Juan* shocked a large number of people, but he held that he
himself was not to blame. As he wrote to Murray:

> I maintain that it is the most moral of poems; but if
> people won't discover the moral, that is their fault, not mine.[11]

His purpose was to expose the hypocrisy and the corruption of
the high society which he knew so well, and in his hero to
depict

> a vicious and unprincipled character, and lead him through
> those ranks of society, whose high external accomplishments
> cover and cloak internal and secret vices.[12]

Byron knew his subject from the inside, and though his moral
earnestness may sound impertinent to those who think that they
are better men than he, there is no doubt of his sincerity. He
wished to expose a disgraceful sham by telling the full truth
about it.

In other words, Byron turned from his own kind of Romantic escape to satirical realism. At the outset nothing could be more alien to the serious Romantic spirit, the essence of which was to concentrate on some mysterious corner of existence and to extract the utmost possible from it. In writing *Don Juan*, Byron was no doubt moved by more than one reason. In the first place, he seems to have seen that his early art was not worthy of his real capacity, and he wished to replace it by something which satisfied the artist in him. In the second place, he was outraged by the behavior of English society, which had first petted and idolized him and then turned malignantly on him. He felt that such behavior deserved punishment, and he knew how to inflict it. In the third place, he was compounded of so many elements that he had, sooner or later, to find a poetry which should contain them all. His earlier work reflected something in himself, especially his discontent and his longing for some dramatic splendor of circumstance and character. But in him the dreamer and the solitary were countered by the wit and the man of the world, and these could not be kept permanently out of his work. His creative spirit moved not on a single, straight line like that of Wordsworth or Shelley, but by devious and circuitous paths. But when he wrote *Don Juan*, he had found his direction. He wished to tell the truth as he saw it with all the paradoxes and contradictions of his nature. The result is an extremely personal document in which the whole of Byron is contained. The exaggerations and the fantasy of the story only serve to bring into prominence and set in a clear perspective his individual views of existence and his conflicting feelings about it.

Byron differs from the authentic Romantics not merely in his low estimate of the imagination but in the peculiar quality and power of his wit. Indeed, his wit rises largely from his loss of belief in the imagination. Once he ceased to believe in the reality or the relevance of his wilder inventions, he turned on himself and laughed. All these fine ideas, he seems to say, are rather ridiculous: we have only to look at them in practice to see what they mean and how unlike the reality is to the dream. Of course, such a point of view was a natural product of the high society in which Byron had lived. The world of the Regency pursued its pleasures in an atmosphere of malice and mockery, and Byron had his fair share of both. But there was something else deep in his nature. His emotions and his intelligence were at war, and through wit he found some sort of reconciliation between them. If one side of him was given to wild dreams, another side saw that these could not be realized, and he resolved the discord with mockery. Indeed, the conflict was deeper than this. Even his emotions were at war with one another, and he would pass by sudden leaps from love to hatred and from admiration to contempt. He was a true child of his age in the uncertainty of his temperament and its wayward responses to experience. But since he was extremely intelligent and observant, he did not deceive himself into thinking that all his responses were right. He marked their inconsistencies and treated them with ironical disdain as part of our human imperfection. At the outset *Don Juan* is a criticism of the Romantic outlook because it says that human beings may have beautiful dreams but fail to live up to them.

In embarking on this realistic and satirical task, Byron was careful not to exaggerate on certain matters which concerned him. He saw that though he had largely outlived his wilder notions or seen their limitations in actual life, they still counted for something and could not altogether be rejected. His aim was to put them in a true setting, to show both their strength and their weakness, to assess them at their right worth. So his poem moves, as it were, on two lines. On the one hand he gives an abundance of delightful poetry to some subjects which the Romantics would approve and which still appealed to him. On the other hand he stresses with wit and irony the defects and contradictions and pretenses which belong to these subjects. His acid temper works on his material and destroys anything false or pretentious in it, with the result that his Romantic longings are countered by a searching irony and are not allowed to claim too much for themselves. If the special successes of Wordsworth and Shelley were possible because humor never raised its head in the sacred places of their imagination, Byron's success comes from the opposite cause, that through humor he gave a new dimension and a greater truth to his creations. His poetry comes closer to the common man because it is more mixed and more complex than was allowed by his great contemporaries in their austere devotion to ideal worlds.

Byron's dual approach to his subject is reflected in a mannerism which is extremely common in *Don Juan*. He will begin to discourse seriously of a subject and speak nobly and finely about it, only to end with some calculated anticlimax, which makes us think that after all he does not care very much about what he has said. We almost feel that he has tricked us by making us respond to a serious topic, only to say that there is nothing in it. But this is not a correct analysis of what Byron does. When he treats of love or nature or liberty in this way, it is not because he has seen through them or wishes us to think that he has. The moods of admiration and of mockery exist concurrently in him and are merged in his outlook. As a poet he feels the one strongly and writes about it with all his powers, but as a man of the world he sees that other men may ridicule him, and he forestalls them by getting in the first laugh. His mockery is partly protective, partly the expression of a sincere conviction that few things in life are what they appear to be and that most things, however noble in some aspects, are ridiculous in others. Byron makes no attempt to harmonize the two points of view, but is content that life should be like this. Nor can we say that he is wrong. Laughter is entitled to have its way where it will, and nothing is ultimately the less serious because in some moods and in some times we make fun of it.

Byron differed from his Romantic contemporaries in the complex character of his response to experience. In his earlier poetry he had tried to look at things from almost a single point of view, but in *Don Juan* he abandoned this and exploited the whole range of his feelings. Whereas the other Romantics tended to follow a single principle in their approach to life, Byron followed his own wayward, changing moods. Just as the Romantics were in their own way perfectly true to themselves, so was Byron in his, but his nature was more complicated than theirs and could not be confined to a single channel. If he lacks their simplicity and the special power which comes with it, he makes up for this by the range of his tastes and the wonderful variety of his responses. Of course, the result is that he misses the peculiar intensity of the great Romantics, but he makes much of many themes which are beyond their reach, and gives in *Don Juan* a panorama of contemporary life which is much richer than anything they could have produced. Those who saw in *Don Juan* the epic of the age were not entirely wrong. It touches many facets of actual life and gives an appropriate poetry to each. Byron had an omnivorous taste for experience and tried most things that came his way. The result is that his great poem provides a vivid and searching commentary on the contemporary scene.

Though Byron abandoned the Romantic view of the imagination and practiced a new realistic art, he did not altogether abandon some themes and ideas which meant much to the Romantics. He seems rather to have applied his critical mind to their favorite topics and to have kept only what he thought to be real and true. If he had no sense of a transcendental order behind reality, he did not forsake all the subjects in which his contemporaries looked for it. Rather, he felt that matters like nature and love were sufficient in themselves to inspire poetry, and that he need not look beyond them for something else. Though he had little interest in the work of Wordsworth, Coleridge, and Keats, and had a genuine admiration for Dryden and Pope, he was in fact a child of his time, and his poetical powers were brought into action not by the refined sentiment and economical fancy of the Augustans, but by wild and vaulting ideas which came from the French Revolution. If in some ways he looks like a counter-revolutionary who tried to confine poetry in its old discipline, he is actually closer to Rousseau and Chateaubriand than to Pope and Johnson. The new age had formed in him tastes which he could not abandon and which dictated the course of his life. He was more typical of his time than either Wordsworth or Shelley; for while their outlooks were limited by their private philosophies, Byron absorbed the life around him and expressed what thousands of his contemporaries felt. Indeed, so wide was his understanding that he is a poet not merely of England but of all Europe.

Byron's position with regard to the other Romantics can be seen in his attitude towards nature. He loved it beyond question, and was perhaps happiest when he was alone with it. But his conception of nature lacked the mystery which Wordsworth, Coleridge, and Keats found in it. Or rather, he found a different mystery, more immediate and more homely, which absorbed his being and engaged his powers without opening doors into some unknown world. In his own way perhaps he had a religion of nature, and we need not disbelieve him when he says:

My altars are the mountains and the Ocean,
Earth—air—stars,—all that springs from the great Whole,
Who hath produced, and will receive the Soul.
(III, civ, 6–8)

But though Byron might hold such a belief, it was not what inspired his poetry of nature. His genius was set to work not by a sense of immanent divinity but simply by what he saw and by the appeal which it had for him. He marked the appearances of nature with an observing eye, and he was delightfully free of conventional prepossessions about what he ought to look for and like in it. He had been brought up in the English country, and in early manhood he had traveled in Greece. His knowledge of nature was different from Wordsworth's, and in some ways wider. He certainly responded to it in a different way. While Wordsworth sought vision or moral inspiration, Byron took nature as he found it and appreciated much that Wordsworth missed. His poetry of nature is instinctive and immediate, free from theory or ulterior intention. He liked it, and that was enough for him. But because he liked it as much as he did, he differed from his predecessors of the eighteenth century who saw it through a haze of literary associations and preferred it in its sentimental aspects. Byron knew it as it is and wrote abundantly about it.

Byron of course often speaks of nature's more attractive aspects, and it is characteristic of *Don Juan* that some of its best passages of description are taken from Greece and the Aegean, from the land and the sea which Byron loved because in them he had escaped from ties and responsibilities which harassed him. If he wrote some of his finest cantos at Ravenna when he was under the spell of La Guiccioli, his memory turned back to his first voyage in Greece and to the days when, alone with a few friends and the simple Suliotes, whose natural nobility won his admiration, he had not yet tasted of success and failure. Now Greece was again in his mind because of the revolt against the Turks, and before long he was to obey her irresistible summons. In the interval he put into *Don Juan* scenes which come from his first delight in Greek islands, sunlit and solitary and washed by an azure sea. The island to which Juan swims as a castaway is authentically Greek in its roughness and its wildness no less than in its moments of magical calm:

It was a wild and breaker-beaten coast,
  With cliffs above, and a broad sandy shore,
Guarded by shoals and rocks as by an host,
  With here and there a creek, whose aspect wore
A better welcome to the tempest-tost;
  And rarely ceased the haughty billow's roar,
Save on the dead long summer days, which make
The outstretched Ocean glitter like a lake.

                                              (II, clxxvii)

The description is truthful and accurate. This is just how many Greek islands look to the visitor, and Byron shows his sterling sense when he sketches the scene as he himself has known it. There was no need to make more of it, and the straightforward description has its own full poetry. Each detail is given with a sure eye to its significance, and the scene lives not merely for the sight but for the imagination.

Byron of course had more enchanting memories of Greece than this. In no country does the evening come with more unexpected splendors, when the whole landscape changes from color to color and the light reflected from the sea gives a limpid purity to the outlines of the mountains and to the inlets of water which pierce them. It is this incomparable beauty which Byron uses as an appropriate setting for his young lovers:

It was the cooling hour, just when the rounded
  Red sun sinks down behind the azure hill,
Which then seems as if the whole earth it bounded,
  Circling all Nature, hushed, and dim, and still,
With the far mountain-crescent half surrounded
  On one side, and the deep sea calm and chill
Upon the other, and the rosy sky
With one star sparkling through it like an eye.

                                              (II, clxxxiii)

The ancient Greek poets were not concerned to praise the beauties of their country with words so precise as these, but Byron, bred in a northern clime where colors are dimmer and outlines less clear, catches the brilliant hues of the Greek evening, when the red sun, the azure hills, and the rosy sky unite to form a perfect harmony. The scene, as he paints it, has a peculiar charm because he writes from loving memory and recalls what this miraculous land once meant to him. He does not look for a soul in nature, but in its company he is entirely absorbed and happy. It is the setting for moments in

which his spirit has been at peace and all his attention caught
in the delight of visible things. He pays nature more notice
than the Greek poets ever did, but he owes something to them
in his feeling for it as a background to human life—even more
than a background, for nature provides the frame in which we
live and shapes our feelings to suit it.

If Byron's greatest love was for Greece, his love for the
English landscape was hardly less powerful, and in this too he
went his own way and found his own kind of poetry. In Canto
XIII he describes a Norman abbey, which is of course Newstead, where he spent his childhood. When he wrote these
lines, he had not seen Newstead for eight years, and he was
never to see it again. But time and separation have not dimmed
his memory; they have rather sharpened and refined it. Byron,
exiled in Italy, recalls this characteristically English scene in
its tranquil beauty and gracious ease. He catches the charm of
an old English country house in surroundings where nature
has been tamed but only to become more truly itself. He, who
knew the sunlit splendor of the Aegean, felt also the appeal of
quiet waters and liked to recall the lake near his own home:

> Before the mansion lay a lucid Lake,
>   Broad as transparent, deep, and freshly fed
> By a river, which its softened way did take
>   In currents through the calmer water spread
> Around: the wildfowl nestled in the brake
>   And sedges, brooding in their liquid bed:
> The woods sloped downwards to its brink, and stood
> With their green faces fixed upon the flood.
>
> (XIII, lvii)

This is perhaps nature as a country gentleman of the Regency
might admire it in his own domain, but it has its own charm
and beauty, and Byron's account reflects his typically English
pleasure in nature as it works for the comfort of man.

Because he had no gospel of nature and did not seek any
special revelation through it, Byron was able to face its cruel
and inhuman aspects as most of the Romantics could not. It is
true that in "Ruth" Wordsworth suggests that a childhood
spent in the violent climate of Georgia may not be entirely
beneficent to the character, but he shied away from this painful
topic and found in the quiet hills of Cumberland and West-
moreland a nature which suited his theories. It is also true
that in his last years Keats began to be troubled by the savage

side of nature and the system by which life exists by preying
on other life, but he did not survive long enough to develop
his doubts. With Byron it is different. He sees nature as it is
and is not afraid of dwelling on its sinister side. He does so
without comment and without complaint, but he knows what
he is talking about. For instance, the storm in *Don Juan*
stands in marked contrast to the storm in *The Ancient
Mariner*. While Coleridge catches the alluring magic of a wild
moon and dancing stars, Byron dwells on the sullen, brooding
atmosphere before the storm comes:

> 'T was twilight, and the sunless day went down
>   Over the waste of waters; like a veil,
> Which, if withdrawn, would but disclose the frown
>   Of one whose hate is masked but to assail.
> Thus to their hopeless eyes the night was shown,
>   And grimly darkled o'er the faces pale,
> And the dim desolate deep: twelve days had Fear
> Been their familiar, and now Death was here.
>
> (II, xlix)

The helplessness of man before nature was a subject from
which the Romantics shrank, but Byron saw it and spoke sincerely about it; and his words come with a sudden fresh
breath at a time when nature was too often seen only in its
gentler moods.

Byron's keen eye for the world about him took him beyond
nature to human dwellings and great towns, and he was one of
the first poets to feel the magic of modern London. It had
been the scene of his glittering triumph, and he was well
acquainted with the haunts where society took its pleasures,
but it meant more than that to him. He liked its bustle and
its crowds, its lights and noise and stupendous air of life, its
dirt and its magnificence. His view of London may be contrasted with Wordsworth's. Wordsworth had his moment of
vision, when from Westminster Bridge he saw the Thames and
the giant city in the calm of the early morning:

> silent, bare,
> Ships, towers, domes, theatres, and temples lie
> Open unto the fields, and to the sky;
> All bright and glittering in the smokeless air.

That shows how even in a great city Wordsworth's genius could
be inspired to its finest rapture, but nonetheless what inspires

him is not the bustle of the city but its temporary quiet. For a moment in London he feels as if he were among the silence of his lonely hills. Byron looks at a similar sight and finds something quite different:

> A mighty mass of brick, and smoke, and shipping,
>   Dirty and dusky, but as wide as eye
> Could reach, with here and there a sail just skipping
>   In sight, then lost amidst the forestry
> Of masts; a wilderness of steeples peeping
>   On tiptoe through their sea-coal canopy;
> A huge, dun Cupola, like a foolscrap crown
> On a fool's head—and there is London Town!
>
>   (X, lxxxii)

Byron sees in London what most men see in it, but with a more observant and more malicious eye. His is a realistic art of topographical poetry. Instead of looking for some manifestation of the ideal in the actual, he is quite content with the actual and says what he thinks about it.

Byron created what was in effect a new poetry of the visible world, both in country and in towns, by the variety of his responses to it. Where be began, other poets have continued, until we are now familiar with a poetry of cities and suburbs as well as of all kinds of countryside. His triumph was to pass beyond his early love of pathless woods and lonely shores to more common and familiar scenes, and to prove that they too have their fascination. His conception of the world in which we live grew from his delighted observation of it, but this observation was itself shaped by the new outlook which belonged to his generation and lay behind all its poetry. Byron differs from the other Romantics in his interpretation of nature and his lack of interest in any ulterior significance to be found in it, but he agrees with them in thinking that it is a primary subject of poetry and plays a large part in human life.

A second Romantic subject to which Byron gave great attention is love. In this he was far more adventurous than Wordsworth and more experienced than Keats. If he had an equal in the importance which he attached to love, it was Shelley, but Shelley's view of it was quite different. For Shelley love is a union of souls, foreordained in some celestial scheme of predestination, and guided by the powers which move the universe. Byron saw nothing in such speculations. He lacked

Shelley's gift of thinking that every woman with whom he fell in love was an incarnation of heavenly virtues. Nor is it clear that Byron ever fell completely in love with anyone. He needed the support and the society of women; he liked to be admired and petted and comforted by them; he found that with them he could unburden his troubles. But of the several women whom he is thought to have loved, there is hardly one for whom he felt an absorbing and dominating passion. Perhaps the strongest affection which he knew was for his half-sister, Augusta, and for that he had to pay in scandal and calumny, with the result that he came to believe that the noblest devotions are doomed to come to a violent or an ignoble end. His other chief devotion was for La Guiccioli. She awoke his political ambitions and made him a man of action, and there is no doubt of his affection for her. But even in the happy years which he spent with her, he yearned for something else, complete and innocent. He seems indeed to have been haunted by two dreams. One was of some woman older than himself who would give to him the affectionate care of which his stern, strong-minded mother was incapable; the other was of an ideal first love, tender and natural, and not at all like what he had felt for Lady Caroline Lamb. When he dealt with love in *Don Juan*, Byron, despite his realism, could not but describe something which he had never actually known, an ideal condition which he was always seeking but never found.

The love of an older woman for a young man is sketched in Julia's love for Juan. Despite the elements of mockery and farce which enliven the episode, Byron puts into Julia's passion his ideal of what such a thing should be. Her husband means nothing to her, and she pines both to give and to receive affection. In her own way she fights against a passion which she thinks wrong, but Juan is eager for her, and his proposals are more than she can resist. So Byron, in his most engaging manner, sums up her surrender:

> A little while still she strove, and much repented,
> And whispering "I will ne'er consent"—consented.
> (I, cxvii, 7–8)

For Juan it is perhaps no more than an exciting experience, the first adventure in an amorous career, but for Julia it is different. She has staked everything on an act which she feels to be wrong and yet desires with all her being, and in the end she fails. What most concerns Byron and draws out his best poetry is the pathos of her failure, the tragic dilemma of a woman who gives her whole nature to something which is not really for her. It is his imaginative sympathy which gives such power to the letter which Julia writes to Juan, and especially to those words in it which record her defeat and her unwilling and perfect acceptance of it:

> You will proceed in pleasure, and in pride,
>   Beloved and loving many; all is o'er
> For me on earth, except some years to hide
>   My shame and sorrow deep in my heart's core:
> These I could bear, but cannot cast aside
>   The passion which still rages as before,—
> And so farewell—forgive me, love me—No,
> That word is idle now—but let it go.

(I, cxcv)

This is of course a poetry of sentiment, but of genuine and noble sentiment which is nonetheless fine because it rises not from actual experience but from longing for an ideal. It is not surprising that when, a few years later, Pushkin wrote *Evgeny Onegin* and made his heroine, Tatyana, write a declaration of love to a vain and insensitive man, he should have learned something from Byron's tenderness and understanding.

Byron's other haunting obsession, of an ideal, first love, is presented in the love of Juan and Haidée on a Greek island. Haidée is a child of nature in the sense that she has not been corrupted by society but follows her instincts without questioning their worth or their consequences. She has a noble heart and a noble style, as befit one who is in her own small world an important person. She presents an implicit contrast to the young aristocratic English women who pursued Byron when he was in fashion. She begins by saving Juan from death and, because she has nursed him, falls in love with him. Such a love comes suddenly and naturally and needs no explanation. Nor has the moralist in Byron anything to say against it, since it is entirely sincere and single-minded. He is content to contrast Haidée's trustful surrender with the false protest of constancy made by more sophisticated young women. This love finds and fulfills itself in natural surroundings which show how natural it is:

They were alone, but not alone as they
  Who shut in chambers think it loneliness;
The silent Ocean, and the starlight bay,
  The twilight glow, which momently grew less,
The voiceless sands, and dropping caves, that lay
  Around them, made them to each other press,
As if there were no life beneath the sky
Save theirs, and that their life could never die.
                                    (II, clxxxviii)

This may be a dream, but it is a dream enhanced by authentic
emotions and an ideal of what first love ought to be. It may
be closer to actual life than Shelley's Platonic visions, but it
is more truly Romantic than any love poetry written by Wordsworth or Keats.

In these two love affairs, with all their ideal quality, Byron
does not forget his critical self. He, who felt the claim of such
passions and wrote his finest poetry about them, was well aware
that there was another side to the question, and he shows this
in more than one way. In the first place, each love leads to
disaster. Julia goes to a convent, and Haidée dies of grief. Byron
may dream of ideal love and show what a woman may feel
for a man, but he knows that the woman will pay for it and
that the world will not be indulgent to her. Society, whether
in the form of Julia's husband or of Haidée's father, will exact
its punishment. Under his cynical exterior, Byron was tender-
hearted and chivalrous, and his two ideal love affairs reveal
how well he understood the woman's point of view. In the
second place, Byron takes a lower view of men than of women,
and seems to think that men are incapable of real constancy
and devotion. Juan is certainly much attracted by Julia, and he
is truly in love with Haidée. But in both cases, when the end
comes, he takes it lightly. After Julia he goes away on his voyage without much thought of her, and after Haidée he uses his
natural charms to improve his worldly position. As his career
proceeds, he learns to exploit more fully his physical advantages,
and Byron describes with a sharp insight his motives when he
yields to the demands of the Empress Catherine of Russia:

He, on the other hand, if not in love,
  Fell into that no less imperious passion,
Self-love—which, when some sort of thing above
  Ourselves, a singer, dancer, much in fashion,
Or Duchess—Princess—Empress, "deigns to prove"

('T is Pope's phrase) a great longing, though a rash one,
For one especial person out of many,
Makes us believe ourselves as good as any.

(IX, lxviii)

Though Byron felt the claims of ideal love and longed for it,
he believed that it is inevitably frustrated by society and spoiled
by the corrupt instincts of men. He shows how life blunts a
man's finer feelings and obliterates even his memories of the
purest love. He tempers his Romantic ideal with realistic considerations, but the result is that the ideal remains as alluring
as before.

In his treatment of nature and of love, Byron shows what
he gained from the common outlook of his age and what
affinities he had with his Romantic contemporaries. But deeper
perhaps than his interest in these two subjects was something
else which lay at the center of his being and determined much
that was best in him. Byron was representative of his generation in his belief in individual liberty and his hatred of tyranny
and constraint, whether exercised by individuals or by societies.
He wished at all costs to realize his powers, to be truly and fully
himself, not to compromise with convention or to hide behind
cant. While Blake wished for an unimpeded freedom in the
activity of the imagination, Byron wished for something similar
in the familiar world. For him, as for some of his contemporaries, the failure of the French Revolution was a challenge
to put its ideals into action, and chief of these was the belief
in personal liberty and in the importance of the individual man.
More fortunate than Pushkin or Lermontov, who felt the same
urgent need but were prevented by circumstances from realizing it, Byron found a way to say what he pleased and to do what
he liked. If he sometimes followed mere whims and impulses,
if some of his ambitions were no more than affectations, he was
not without guiding principles, and his death at Missolonghi
shows that he was not an actor but a soldier, a man of affairs,
and a master of men. Despite all his self-mockery, he knew
that he had a star and that he must follow it, that there was
something in himself which must be translated into fact and
that he must be true to it. No doubt his conception of liberty
was more instinctive than intellectual, and he did not see
what difficulties and contradictions it contained. It was an ideal,
a driving power, a summons to make the best of certain

possibilities in himself. Much more than Wordsworth and Coleridge, who after their first enthusiasm for the French Revolution surrendered to caution and skepticism, more even than
Keats, whose love of liberty was hardly developed to its full
range, Byron wished to be free and insisted that other men must
be free too.

This ideal Byron shared with Shelley, but though he shared
Shelley's passion, he did not share his vision of an ideal future;
he was content to do his best for the moment by attacking
tyrants wherever they existed and pleading the cause of oppressed humanity. Not that he was pessimistic about the future.
He could not believe that men would for long tolerate the senseless restrictions to which they were subjected. He wished to
stir them to revolt, to make them get rid of their monarchs, and
he says frankly:

> For I will teach, if possible the stones
> To rise against Earth's tyrants. Never let it
>   Be said that we still truckle unto thrones;—
> But ye—our children's children! think how we
> Showed *what things were* before the World was free!
>   (VIII, cxxxv, 4–8)

Byron was on the side of liberty against the Holy Alliance
and the government of George IV. He was not afraid to attack
so popular a hero as the Duke of Wellington as the "best of
cut-throats"; he covered Brougham with abuse; his treatment
of the European monarchs is delightfully contemptuous:

> Shut up the bald-coot bully Alexander!
>   Ship off the Holy Three to Senegal;
> Teach them that "sauce for goose is sauce for gander,"
>   And ask them how *they* like to be in thrall?
>   (XIV, lxxxiii, 1–4)

At a time when his countrymen were proclaiming their cham-
pionship and love of liberty, Byron accused them of being its
most violent enemies. England, on whom such great hopes
were once placed, has now betrayed them:

> How all the nations deem her their worst foe,
>   That worst than *worst of foes,* the once adored
> False friend, who held out Freedom to Mankind,
> But now would chain them—to the very *mind.*
>   (X, lxvii, 5–8)

In Byron the ideals of 1789 were still a living force. He saw
that the free fulfillment of the human self would be possible

only when the powerful obstacles of thrones and courts were removed, and that the cruelest of tyrannies is that which seeks to enslave the mind.

In the great appeals for liberty which ring through *Don Juan*, and in the attacks which Byron makes on its enemies, we can see the fundamental purpose of the poem. Byron set out to tell the truth, but his views were determined by a powerful and positive belief in the worth of individual man. He resembled Blake in his condemnation of senseless cruelty and of the hypocrisy which it breeds for its support. He was appalled by the habits of high society which claimed to do one thing and did another, and hid its vices under good manners and high-sounding principles. It evoked his sharpest irony:

> Oh for a *forty-parson power* to chant
> Thy praise, Hypocrisy! Oh for a hymn
> Loud as the virtues thou dost loudly vaunt,
> Not practise! Oh for trump of Cherubim!
> (X, xxxiv, 1–4)

He hoped that by telling the truth he would awake the world to the evils which blighted its happiness, and expose its respected social system as a corrupt and corrupting sham. On the positive side, what he liked was the free play of the affections as he depicted it in his ideal love scenes and in the carefree happiness of his Greek island. Much more than any other poet of the time, he had a keen appreciation of the natural man and thought his ordinary pleasures right and worthy of protection. He might not agree with the moral code of his age and his country, but he had his own values. Above all, he thought that truthfulness is a paramount duty, and that only through it can mankind be liberated from many ugly and degrading bonds.

Though *Don Juan* stands almost alone among poems of the Romantic age, it belongs to it and is in its own way a true product of it. Though Byron rejected the Romantic belief in the imagination, he was true to the Romantic outlook in his devotion to an ideal of man which may have been no more than a dream, but nonetheless kept his devotion despite the ordeal of facts and his own corroding skepticism. He knew how difficult this ideal was to realize and what powerful obstacles it met in the corruption of society and the contradictions of human nature. He made many discoveries, seldom creditable, about himself and other men, and that is why at times he seems

cynical and disillusioned. Disillusioned perhaps he was, in the
sense that he had few hopes that all his dreams would come
true; but cynical he was not, at least about the matters which
lay nearest to his heart. It was not their worth which he questioned, but the possibility of translating them into fact. Of
course, he rejected any suggestion that he treated his task seriously, and no one could accuse him of being solemn. But serious
he is, not merely when he speaks directly about his convictions,
but when he presents them with irony and mockery. He made a
bold attempt to put the whole of himself into *Don Juan*, and
the result is something quite outside the range of his great contemporaries. The alternations of his moods are matched by the
extraordinary range of his subjects. There seems to be almost no
topic on which he has not got something interesting or witty
or penetrating to say. The story is only half the poem; the
other half is a racy commentary on life and manners. *Don Juan*
is the record of a remarkable personality, a poet and a man of
action, a dreamer and a wit, a great lover and a great hater, a
man with many airs of the eighteenth century and yet wholly
of the nineteenth, a Whig noble and a revolutionary democrat.
The paradoxes of his nature are fully reflected in *Don Juan*,
which is itself both a romantic epic and a realistic satire, and
it owes the wide range and abundant wealth of its poetry to
the fact that Byron had in himself many Romantic longings,
but tested them by truth and reality and remained faithful only
to those which meant so much to him that he could not live
without them.

Notes

1. *Letters of William and Dorothy Wordsworth: The Later Years*, ed.
by E. de Selincourt, 3 vols. (Oxford, 1939), II, 640.
2. Coleridge, *Biographia Epistolaria*, ed. by A. Turnbull (London,
1911), p. 169.
3. *Letters of John Keats*, ed. by M. B. Forman (London, 1952), p.
405.
4. H. E. Rollins, *The Keats Circle*, 2 vols. (Cambridge, Mass., 1948),
II, 134.
5. *The Works of Lord Byron: Poetry*, ed. by Ernest Hartley Coleridge,
6 vols. (London, 1903), IV, 171. See also pp. 272, 484.
6. Byron, *Don Juan*, XI, LX, 7–8.
7. *Letters of John Keats*, p. 413.
8. Blake, *The Ghost of Abel*, in *Poetry and Prose*, p. 584.

9. *The Works of Lord Byron: Letters and Journals*, ed. by Rowland E. Prothero, 6 vols. (London, 1901), V, appendix 3, p. 554.

10. Letter of May 25, 1820, quoted by N. I. White, *Shelley*, 2 vols. (London, 1947), II, 186.

11. *Works of Lord Byron: Letters and Journals*, letter of February 1st, 1819, in Vol. IV, 279.

12. Quoted by E. de Selincourt, *Wordsworthian and Other Studies*, p. 122.

Part Five   Shelley

Richard Harter Fogle

13·The Imaginal Design of Shelley's "Ode to the West Wind"

SUCH AN EXPOSITION as I am about to attempt requires some justification, especially when the poem to be expounded is almost universally known, widely recognized as a masterpiece, and reprinted in hundreds of anthologies of English poetry. Only a few years ago this enterprise would have been reckoned quite unnecessary. Today, however, the situation is somewhat changed. The gentle—or ungentle—art of explication is enjoying a still-increasing vogue, while at the same time our most influential explicators have been categorically, and to me unwarrantably, hostile to Shelley. John Crowe Ransom considers him merely feeble, Allen Tate indicts him for confusion of metaphor—a terrible charge in contemporary criticism, despite the immortal evidence of the "To be or not to be" soliloquy—and Cleanth Brooks in *Modern Poetry and the Tradition* consigns him to limbo posthaste as "a very unsatisfactory poet," sentimental and guilty of "poor craftsmanship." Those, on the other hand, who know Shelley best have generally been too much occupied with learning still more about him to heed the attackers, who are frequently, as in the instances I have cited, critics of unquestionable influence and power. A detailed defense, as this is intended to be, of a lyric generally accepted as representative of Shelley at his best, should therefore fill a genuine need.

The general standards employed here, I am confident, would be approved even by Shelley's most uncompromising dis-

Reprinted by permission of the author and the editor from *ELH* [*Journal of English Literary History*], Vol. 15, No. 3 (1948), pp. 219–26. Published by The Johns Hopkins Press.

approvers, being, in fact, their own; although it might be remarked that they used to belong to Samuel Taylor Coleridge. Broadly, I assume that a good poem should impose an imaginative unity upon diverse materials; that it should provide a complex human problem with a satisfactory solution; that through the medium of artistic form it should give coherence to the intellectual, emotional, and sensuous experience of the poet.

My method, however, is unlike theirs in being deliberately tentative, eclectic, and impure. Undoubtedly the poem itself is the important issue, but despite much contemporary opinion it should not be isolated from the mind of the poet, his environment, his artistic theories, and the body of his poetry. To do so, in my opinion, is to deprive the poem of its legitimate background, leaving only general criteria which can too easily be manipulated to serve the prejudices of the critic. It is interesting, by the way, that those who are austerest in approaching Romantic poetry are often less abstemious in other situations. Professor Cleanth Brooks, for example, advances upon Shelley equipped only with his standards and his bare fists. He has, however, given us excellent expositions of the esoteric background of Eliot's *Waste Land*, and of the eccentric historicocosmogony of Yeats, with no apparent feeling that these are irrelevant.

No explication, fortunately, can entirely account for a poem. One may dilute, expand, and appreciate, but full explanation is impossible. Interpretation, I believe, must be tentative, and frankly metaphorical. Some method must obviously be found, and some standard of judgment applied, but no method or standard dare claim unique validity. I shall attempt to define what I see in the poem in its own particularity, rather than, as has become the predominant practice, what I do not see. My standards, save in the general sense, which has earlier been specified, derive from the poem itself, and I introduce whatever material seems calculated to advance understanding and appreciation of it. In order to speak fully of the imagery, which is perhaps most vital, I am regretfully compelled to omit consideration of the stanzaic, rhetorical, syntactical, and sound patterns, although these are well worthy of thorough study. Finally, my immediate purpose is to demonstrate that the "Ode to the West Wind" is a lyric of great complexity and consummate artistic design.

On the most elementary level, the poem deals in the first three stanzas with the action of the West Wind upon the leaf, the cloud, and the wave. Through this action Shelley steps progressively toward an imaginative examination of the possibility of identifying himself with the wind, and what it stands for. These first three stanzas are, at any rate on the surface, objective descriptions of natural phenomena. In stanza iv the identification is suggested, tentatively and provisionally, through Nature, in terms which bind the natural pattern of leaf-cloud-wave firmly to the emerging personality of the poet:

> If I were a dead leaf thou mightest bear;
> If I were a swift cloud to fly with thee;
> A wave to pant beneath thy power . . .

and culminates in stanza v—"Be thou, Spirit fierce, My spirit! Be thou me, impetuous one!"

This identification represents, so to speak, the unity which the poem is to win from variety. The individual is to be merged with the general; Shelley is to become the instrument through which speaks the universal voice. The medium by which this unity is imaginatively achieved is the nature imagery of the three beginning stanzas—the action upon and the interrelationship of the West Wind with the leaf, the cloud, and the wave.

The stress, or structure, or problem of the "Ode" may also be defined as the "death and regeneration" contrast, which has been discussed by I. J. Kapstein, Newman Ivey White, and others. For the West Wind is both destroyer and preserver; it shatters established structures that new ones may be built from their ruins; it scatters the withered leaves, but in order to "quicken a new birth." This contrast, like the individual-general contrast earlier mentioned, needs and gets a poetic reconciliation, a unification concretely and emotionally satisfying.

This theme is partially developed in stanza i, in which the wind scatters and disperses the forms of Nature, but preserves its order and continuity by spreading the "winged seeds" where at the propitious time they may issue forth anew. Stanza i, we may add, has a dual function of design. It introduces the contrast of death and rebirth, Autumn and Spring, but it also serves to introduce the leaf image of the leaf-cloud-wave pattern. Here we must notice a difficulty in our terms. Reference to the "death and regeneration" theme is likely to be misleading unless we point out that the West Wind of Autumn, while both destroyer and preserver, is not also regenerator. The difference is more than a technicality, for it will fundamentally affect our notion of what Shelley is writing about: what he claims for the Wind and for his own poetry.

It is left for another West Wind, the Zephyrus or Favonius of Lucretius and Virgil, "thine azure sister of the Spring," to blow "Her clarion o'er the dreaming earth," and recall to life the dead who do but sleep. The West Wind of Autumn is a power of destruction, which nevertheless preserves whatever of the existing order is vital and promising. Fruition, however, is left to another power, kindred but still distinct. Shelley, in fact, is more modest, even amidst affirmation, than would appear at a glance. Indeed, it might be pointed out that not merely here but even in the earlier and less mature *Revolt of Islam* (IX, xxi–xxix) the same personal modesty tempers revolutionary confidence and hope.

Predominant, then, is the expression of a dynamic force, the tremendous power of revolutionary change. In stanza ii the wind is both architect and wrecker of "the approaching storm," whose "congregated might of vapors" will give vent to the bursting forth of "Black rain, and fire, and hail." The mingled menace, power, and beauty of the clouds, agents of the unseen wind, are symbolized in complex personifications: "*Angels* of rain and lightning," and the "*bright hair* uplifted from the head of some *fierce Maenad*." Images of height and motion artfully contribute to the attraction—and repulsion—aroused by the scene: "the *steep* sky's *commotion*" (a richly synthetic term); "even from the dim verge of the horizon to the Zenith's height": along with the motor and kinesthetic force of "Loose clouds . . . *shed*"; "*Shook* from the tangled boughs . . ."; "Black rain . . . will burst." The scene is full of movement and force, applied to the solid structure of the "vaulted dome" of the sky. The suggestion that the change may be beneficent and fruitful is subtly implied by the linking of the clouds to the "decaying leaves" of stanza i, carried further in the "*tangled boughs* of Heaven and Ocean," with their connotations of cyclical and reciprocal interfertilization.

In stanza ii Shelley has viewed the revolutionary process complexly, as at once beautiful and terrible, fruitful and destructive; and he has reconciled these opposites, has unified and given them form, by the widely inclusive picture of wind, storm, and sky, simultaneously visible and harmoniously interrelated. In stanza iii another difficulty is to be met and conquered.

Change and reform, in their iconoclastic vigor, destroy good as well as evil, for in the fabric of society the two are inextricably interwoven. The exquisite calm of the blue Mediterranean must be rudely shattered, although it frames in its motionless and idealizing medium ("the wave's intenser day") the loveliest forms of the past. The mellow patina of the centuries has its own attractions. We must also consider that the scene is Baiae, with its mingled associations of social splendor, amenity, and injustice. These "old palaces and towers," spiritualized by their medium (itself an emblem of the perspective of Time), and softened by their clothing of Time and Nature, are almost overpowering to sensibility; "so sweet the sense faints picturing them."

If it is suspected that I am overreading these lines, I would refer the doubter to Shelley's *Philosophical View of Reform*, in which he takes account in explicit and abstract prose of the problem here expressed poetically and imaginally. "Tyranny," he remarks among other things, "entrenches itself within the existing interests of the best and most refined citizens of a nation and says 'If you dare trample upon these, be free.'" Or note the subtly blended delight and reprehension projected in the "Lines Written Among the Euganean Hills," as the poet looks down at the "Column, tower, and dome, and spire" of beautiful and dishonored Venice. Or examine in "Adonais," the atmosphere of lovely, decadent Rome,

> . . . at once the Paradise,
> The grave, the city, and the wilderness.

Shelley has, in my opinion, harmonized and reconciled the discordances and difficulties of the theme: not by proposing a complete solution, indeed—the only possible solution is to let the West Wind have its way—but by understanding, accepting, and realizing the dilemma in art.

In order fully to comprehend the complexity which Shelley resolves, the weight of intellect and emotion which the poem must carry, it is well to consider more thoroughly the central symbol of the West Wind. In the context of the "Ode" it stands for the spirit of revolution, or for revolutionary change; and we have seen that, like Moses, it opens the way to the promised land, without itself being permitted to enter. Its qualities, however, betray its relationship with more universal and more gracious meanings. An unseen, irresistible power, it is a single door which opens upon the central unity of all things, the very fulcrum of Shelley's thought. It is an aspect of the master concept of his most significant poetry.

The West Wind is an absolute and hidden power which informs all things, while it is perceptible and to be imaged only in its effects, like "the one Life within us and abroad" of Coleridge, or Wordworth's

> A motion and a spirit, that impels
> All thinking things, all objects of all thought,
> And rolls through all things.

In the poetry of Shelley it is akin to the secret fire which inwardly illumines "the visioned maid" of *Alastor*. It is related to the "awful shadow" of Intellectual Beauty, which floats though unseen among us"; and to the "imageless, deep truth" of *Prometheus Unbound*. In "Adonais" it becomes the Eternal, the "burning fountain" whither shall return the creative genius of Keats:

> . . . that sustaining Love
> Which through the web of being blindly wove
> By man and beast and earth and air and sea,
> Burns bright or dim, as each are mirrors of
> The fire for which all thirst.

In another guise, it is the skylark, the symbol of the poet, unseen, but inundating the sky with "profuse strains of unpremeditated art." Again, it has affinities with the unaccountable power of poetic inspiration as it is described in the *Defence of Poetry*: "the mind in creation is as a fading coal, which some invisible influence, like an inconstant wind, awakens to transitory brightness." The symbolism of the West Wind, in short, opens out into far-reaching associations, rich and deep in their freight of intellect and emotion.

Likewise rich in its imaginative ramifications is Shelley's development of the "death and regeneration" theme, into which is woven the myths of the seasons; of Christ, his resurrection, and of Judgment Day; and the imagery of the pastoral; all so skilfully harmonized that the shift from one to another is almost imperceptible. The leaves and the "winged seeds" will play their part in the great cyclical rebirth of Spring, and the image of the seeds leads us also into the Christian resurrection of Easter. They "lie cold and low" until awakened by the gentle wind of Spring, which suggests both the Resurrection and Judgment Day as she blows "her clarion o'er the dreaming earth." The pastoral enters also, blended with the wind, "Driving sweet buds like *flocks* to *feed* in air," linked to the Christian by the shepherd-sheep image, and merging once more with the rebirth of Spring and Nature, as the wind fills "With living hues and odors plain and hill." It may not perhaps be too fanciful to suggest yet another enriching association, harmonizing with the seasonal and religious myth alike: the West Wind is both Siva and Vishnu of the Hindu triad, destroyer and preserver together. Only Brahma, the creator, it is not.

Consequently, when in stanza iv Shelley turns to the subjective and individual, his problem is given meaning and reference not merely by his attempted self-identification with the West Wind, but also by his relation of the individual to the ideological, cultural, religious, and national wholes. By using the symbol of the West Wind, and by describing its effects upon leaf, cloud, and wave, he has realized and objectified the revolutionary ideal in Nature; and by introducing the seasonal, religious, and pastoral myths he has softened and humanized a conception in itself perhaps a little rigorous. Then, in culmination, the personal binds the two aspects of the theme together. From the nature imagery of leaf-cloud-wave arises the prayer to be united with the wind: a union which will provide the means for the only sort of regeneration which Shelley—I should say modestly—deemed personally possible. That is, filled with an inspiration not of his own making or owning, his thoughts should be driven "Like withered leaves to quicken a new birth"; his words should be scattered among mankind.

There has arisen of late years a strange disposition to deny a place to the subjective in poetry. This view I confess I do not fully understand; it would appear to lead to a hopeless confusion of the genres. An objective lyric seems to me as much a contradiction in terms as an actionless narrative, or a plotless drama. For those who are dismayed by the entrance of the poet upon the scene, however, it may be pointed out that in the "Ode to the West Wind" the personal element is an integral part of the design, as presumably could be established of any good lyric. The "Ode" is about self-abnegation, the absorption of the individual Ego into a larger unity. It is, I think, then, more than a mere play on words to demand that there should be the imaginative realization of a self to be abnegated and absorbed. If the offering is to have significance, let it be prized by the giver.

The lines "I fall upon the thorns of life . . ." and "A heavy weight of hours has chained and bowed / One too like thee," which some have found objectionable, are obviously part of the imaginal design. The West Wind is free and uncontrollable. Shelley calls for a like though a lesser freedom—not egotistically, but through the power of self-dedication to a cause—to become the fitting instrument and medium of a voice, the trumpet of a prophecy not his own. That he introduces his own emotions, his sufferings, frailties, forebodings— serves to intensify the stress and increase the voltage of the poetic argument, to broaden its scope. Poems should end in reconciliation, but a unity too easily won is lacking in value. The personal stanzas of the "Ode to the West Wind" round out the expression of a problem that is felt and real. This reconciliation, to conclude, has as its materials the stress between the individual and the general, the actual and the ideal, each given its "ample room and verge enough." The resolvent is hope—hope tempered with humility—hope firm-based in the revolutionary idealism symbolized by the West Wind, and in the immemorial logic of seasonal, religious, and pastoral Myth.

Carlos Baker

14·The Heart of the Cosmos:

Prometheus Unbound

> Man, one harmonious soul of many a soul,
> Whose nature is its own divine control,
> Where all things flow, as rivers to the sea.
> —*Prometheus Unbound*

> Let us believe in a kind of optimism in
> which we are our own gods.
> —Shelley to Maria Gisborne

BETWEEN THE AUTUMN of 1818 and the winter of 1819–1820, Shelley devoted infinite labors to the composition of the ethical and psychological drama which has ever since been regarded, except by a few unreconstructed dissenters, as his masterpiece. Shelley himself said that it was the best thing he ever wrote, and there is no reason to doubt the statement. He managed to combine in it, for the first though not for the last time, his two most persistent themes, the necessity of social reform and the necessity of societal love, in such a way that they supplement and complement one another. The vehicle for these themes is a poem of the greatest subtlety, ambitious in conception, simple in its larger outlines, imbued with moral grandeur, alive with splendid lyrics, and virtually unmarred by those weaknesses of conception of execution which so often weakened the fabric of his visions. The critical history of *Prometheus Unbound* is replete with minor squabbles as to whether or not it has a meaning and, if it has, what that meaning is. Yet the critical history shows, above all, that the poem partakes of the nature of mythology in being (the phrase is from I. A. Richards) relatively inexhaustible to meditation. Of no other poem by Shelley can this be so truly said; of few other poems by Shelley can it be said at all.

There was a time, in his vegetarian or salad days, when Shelley thought of Prometheus as a villain. The myth, as he assured readers of *Queen Mab*, was everywhere accepted as allegorical: Prometheus represents the human race. Having effected a tragic change in his natural habits, man used fire for culinary purposes, in order to forget, as he gorged on roasted flesh, the antecedent horrors of the slaughterhouse. Henceforth "his vitals were devoured by the vulture of disease," and all vice arose. Jupiter and the rest of the gods, foreseeing the unhappy consequences of Prometheus' action, were "amused or irritated" by the Titan's shortsightedness, yet allowed him to continue his vicious practice though they presumably knew that it would act to the ultimate detriment of all men. This, at least, was the gospel according to John Frank Newton.

The passage of five years produced a complete reversal in Shelley's sympathies. When he wrote the preface for *Prometheus Unbound*, though he still attached a moral meaning to the myth, the protagonist had become a suffering and enduring hero and Jupiter a "perfidious adversary." [1] Shelley may, indeed, have begun to turn away from Newton's interpretation almost as soon as it was incorporated into the notes to *Queen Mab*. Some months before *Queen Mab* was ready for the printer, he ordered a copy of the plays of Aeschylus, with translation subjoined.[2] If he read *Prometheus Bound* at this time, however, it had no discernible effect, and though he soon began to show signs of knowing Aeschylus, it was not until roughly 1817 that the plays of the Greek tragedian began to be felt as a major stimulant to Shelley's literary imagination.[3] As at Chamonix in the summer of 1816 he had thought of Peacock's Ahrimanes, enthroned among perpetual snows and preparing to loose avalanches with his right hand, so the ascent of Les Echelles in the early spring of 1818 reminded him of the Golgotha of the Aeschylean Prometheus: "vast rifts and caverns . . . wintry mountains . . . and walls of toppling rocks, only to be scaled as [Aeschylus] described, by the winged chariot of the ocean nymphs." [4] Six months later, after four or five weeks of intermittent labor, Shelley completed the crucial first act of his *Prometheus Unbound*. Far from being the carnivorous villain of Newton's argument, the reformed Prometheus at least remotely approached, in majesty and moral excellence, the stature of Jesus Christ, or so Shelley appears to have thought.

It is not difficult to account for Shelley's reversed interpretation of the character of Prometheus. Few students of Shelley's earlier poetry could fail to see that the Aeschylean Titan is a natural prototype for the Shelleyan hero, ready to be adopted whenever Shelley, in the fullness of his literary wisdom, can apprehend him.[5] Once so apprehended, he rapidly displaces Milton's Satan in the forefront of Shelley's affection. "In addition to courage, and majesty, and firm and patient opposition to omnipotent force," wrote Shelley, Prometheus is "exempt from the stains of ambition, envy, revenge, and a desire for personal aggrandizement, which, in the hero of *Paradise Lost*, interfere with the interest." Laon is more Promethean than Satanic, a lonely benefactor of mankind who has endured torture for what may be described as a social principle, and defied established power out of a hope (for Prometheus it is a conviction) that at some future date this power will be overthrown. At the same time, Shelley's Titan is an almost awesome improvement over Laon, being conceived in what Keats might have called "a more naked and Grecian manner," and possessed of a grandeur (partly the result of his Aeschylean heritage) to which the hero of *The Revolt*, sired by the Oriental heroes of Southey and Peacock, could hardly aspire. The measure of the advance may be suggested by saying that Laon is a Gothic man and Prometheus a Greek myth—or, better, that Laon suffers from Shelley's determination to make him a creature of flesh and blood, where Prometheus is at all times a typical rather than a realistic figure, a pure mythological character uninhibited by history or by the need of being human. By Shelley's estimate, Prometheus is "the type of the highest perfection of moral and intellectual nature impelled by the purest and truest motives to the best and noblest ends." [6]

Shelley's mature dramatic and philosophical purpose is nowhere better shown than in his conception of Prometheus' character. As in Newton's version of the fable, Prometheus represents mankind, or more specifically, as we shall see, the mind of mankind. But instead of introducing fire, and hence cookery, and hence the reprehensible practice of meat eating, and hence disease and corruption into the world, the Prometheus of 1818–1819 has at last succeeded in casting corruption forth. The process no longer has anything to do with what man puts, or does not put, into his stomach, but it has everything to do with what man allows, or does not allow to exist in his mind. . . . *The Revolt of Islam* enunciates a relatively simple moral and metaphysical conviction: the furtherance of good cannot be entrusted to superior powers, but is primarily the obligation of man, who can fulfil this obligation only by expunging hatred from his mental processes and admitting love or sympathy in its place. The same principle governs the decisions of the protagonist in the first act of *Prometheus Unbound*, upon which all subsequent developments depend. But instead of showing the world at an exemplary way station in its slow progress towards perfection, as he had done in *The Revolt*, Shelley chose now to show man at a single symbolic hour—the hour of the world's redemption through man's act of self-reform.

The advance shown in the respective treatments of Laon and Prometheus is paralleled by the marked superiority of Asia over Cythna. Here, however, the advancement has less to do with Cythna's being a woman and Asia a goddess than with the fact that Asia is the realization of the conception towards which Shelley was still groping when he wrote *The Revolt of Islam*. It should be recalled that the Asia-concept had been taking gradual shape in Shelley's mind at least from 1815 onwards. Towards the end of "Alastor" the visionary maiden had been purged of those fleshly attributes which Mrs. Campbell deplores as more nearly relevant to "some scantily dressed beauty at a costume ball," [7] and had taken on a symbolic condition. In the following year, 1816, Shelley had projected a completely depersonalized ideal of spiritual power in the "Hymn to Intellectual Beauty." The dedicatory poem to *The Revolt of Islam*, composed in the fall of 1817, contains Shelley's attempt to elevate Mary to the Asia-status. Her presence is said to have fallen on Shelley's "wintry heart" like "bright Spring upon some herbless plain," an image that is developed with great subtlety in *Prometheus Unbound*. But the attempted apotheosis of Mary, while no doubt sincere, is largely

abortive, and the full realization of the significance of the
Asia-symbol probably did not come until 1818, when, among
other tasks, Shelley prepared his translation of Plato's *Symposium*.

Somewhere between the completion of *The Revolt* in
September, 1817, and his beginning the first act of *Prometheus
Unbound* in September, 1818, Shelley seems also to have
passed the equatorial belt between the immature turbulence
of a long poem in the tradition of Southey's *Thalaba* and the
comparatively simple classical lines of his Promethean story.
The Revolt is cluttered, while *Prometheus Unbound* displays
a clean symmetry, as if in abandoning forever the extended
metrical narrative, Shelley had discovered in the lyrical drama
his true medium. An accession of subtlety is likewise evident.
The violent melodrama of *The Revolt*, arising at least in part
from Shelley's conviction that he must diversify his plot with
"moving and romantic adventure," made way for the drama
of mind as one finds it in *Prometheus*, a drama deep and intense, like the deliberate struggle of serpents at the bottom of
the sea, leaving hardly a ruffle of overt action upon the surface
of the play.

Shelley's powers of conception and expression were never
at a higher point than they were in 1818–1819 while he was
at work on what is certainly his greatest poem. Perhaps there
is greater ease and fluency in such later works as *The Witch
of Atlas*, but there is also a kind of autumnal languor. In *The
Masque of Anarchy* and *Oedipus Tyrannus*, born of the weekly
political press, he designedly did not attempt the high style or
the cosmic conception. Finally, there are signs of mounting
fatigue and either self-doubt or *ennui* in his failure to bring
to completion such potentially magnificent poems as *Charles I*
and *The Triumph of Life*, or to develop fully the fragmentary
prologue to *Hellas*. But at this earlier date Shelley stood, fresh
and active, in the dawn of his maturing powers.

II

The dramatic tensions of *Prometheus Unbound* originate
in two related situations: the separation and reunion of Prometheus and Asia, and the ancient enmity between Prometheus
and Jupiter. The first of these is a version of the Psyche-
Epipsyche theme developed for the first time on what may be

called a cosmic scale. The second, though couched in terms of Greek rather than Zoroastrian mythology, is clearly another and greatly superior treatment of the good-evil antithesis as employed in the first and final cantos of *The Revolt of Islam*. The fourth of the major figures, Demogorgon, has occasioned much dispute, largely because, like such earlier characters as Queen Mab and Ahasuerus, he has a particularized name which calls up many associations besides the primary one intended by Shelley. . . . [H]e represents Necessity—an enigmatic amoral law in terms of which the struggle between the powers of good and those of evil has been carried on since the beginning.

One way of expressing the fundamental aim of the drama is to say that it is directed towards a situation in which it will be ethically possible for the reunion of Prometheus and Asia to occur. But all spirits are secretly affected by "Demogorgon's mighty law" (II, ii, 43), and in Shelley's conception the fate of Jupiter is closely linked with that of Prometheus and Asia. That is to say, as soon as Prometheus and Asia are genuinely ready to be reunited, the reign of Jupiter must end. This consummation is the more fitting in that Asia's second-act exposition of the background of the present action strongly suggests that she was separated from Prometheus at, or soon after, the time of Jupiter's accession to the throne.

Three thousand years before the opening of the drama, Prometheus

> Gave wisdom, which is strength, to Jupiter,
> And with this law alone, "Let man be free,"
> Clothed him with the dominion of wide Heaven.
>
> (II, iv, 44–46)

But Jupiter kept "faithless faith" (III, iii, 130). In putting on omnipotence, as is usual with the Shelleyan tyrant, he abandoned love and law (II, iv, 47–48). Under his sovereignty, famine, toil, disease, and strife appeared upon the earth. Although Prometheus granted man hope and love, and equipped him with knowledge of the sciences and the arts in order partially to alleviate his multiple woes, Jupiter's reign continued and was destined to continue so long as man's will gave sanction to it by continuing in hatred (II, iv, 50–100). Prometheus, the altruistic though as yet imperfect champion of man, was chained in a ravine of icy rocks among the mountains of the Indian Caucasus, while Asia, until then his inseparable companion, went into exile in a far-distant Indian vale, a place as "desolate and frozen" as the scene of her erstwhile consort's agony (I, 826–28). The torture and the exile, the immortal hatred of Prometheus for Jupiter, and the mournful longing of Asia for reunion with Prometheus have endured, as the action opens, for thirty centuries.

In *The Revolt* Shelley anticipated more closely than in any preceding poem the careful allegorical scheme which he worked out in *Prometheus Unbound*. Close companions in childhood and lovers in their youth, Laon and Cythna are separated through the machinations of Othman—a kind of parallel to the Prometheus-Asia-Jupiter situation,[8] though the former is much more crude. Later on Shelley grants Laon and Cythna a brief night of reunion, replete with passionate embraces which have, however, no place in *Prometheus Unbound*; and, following their death at the stake, he gives them an eternity of shared joy in the Temple of the Spirit, along with their "winged child"—again a pattern which is carried out, even to the inclusion of the child, in *Prometheus Unbound*. But in 1817 Shelley was so involved with his intention to write a "mere human story" that he fought as shy as possible of allegory. Therefore the separation and reunion of Laon and Cythna, having little determinable significance in a symbolic sense, seems in the main to be adventitious, the result of chance and accident, of forces applied from without instead of deriving from the mental attributes of the hero, upon whose growth and eventual ripeness the denouement of *Prometheus Unbound* depends.

The relatively compact structure of *Prometheus Unbound* may be ascribed in part to the fact that the whole of the poem is the biography of an Hour (the "all-nameless hour" as has been pointed out, of man's redemption through Prometheus' act of self-reform) together with the events immediately preceding it, and those which directly ensue upon its arrival. At the proper time, emphasis is placed upon the Hour itself; yet the primary stress, because this is a drama of mind rather than of outward action, is on the preparatory circumstances. Everything is made to hinge upon the readiness of Prometheus. The Hour is even said to be "of many, one"—which suggests that it is not a particular predestined time, but any hour at which

Prometheus reaches the point of growth which he has now reached.

Shelley's main task in Act I was to make Prometheus' ripeness dramatically convincing, somewhat as Shakespeare had first to render almost, if not quite, palpable the deep electric unrest which is present under the quiet demeanor of Denmark in order to raise the responses of Hamlet to the point at which he is ready for action. In *Hamlet*, the ghost is of course the immediate agent of shock; in *Prometheus Unbound* it is something even less tangible than a ghost: the consciousness that the Hour is imminent, that things are about to happen.

It is perfectly plain that the protagonist has not always been what Shelley calls him in the preface, "the type of the highest perfection of moral and intellectual nature." He has always, of course, had saving graces. Unlike Milton's Satan, with whom Shelley contrasts him, he has been free of envy, malice, and self-aggrandizing ambition. Yet he has shared at least two traits of mind with that otherwise inferior fellow rebel: an immortal hatred of Omnipotence which has given him the necessary courage never to submit or yield; and a kind of unregenerate pride [9] which can make him exultantly say, even after three thousand years of torture, that when the great Hour arrives, it will drag Jupiter from his throne, "as some dark Priest hales the reluctant victim," to kiss the blood

> From these pale feet, which then might trample thee
> If they disdained not such a prostrate slave.
>
> (I, 51–52)

It is true that Prometheus immediately denies that he has spoken in exultation or in proud disdain:

> Disdain! Ah, no! I pity thee. What ruin
> Will hunt thee undefended through the wide Heaven!
> How will thy soul, cloven to its depth with terror,
> Gape like a hell within! I speak in grief,
> Not exultation, for I hate no more,
> As then ere misery made me wise. The curse
> Once breathed on thee I would recall.
>
> (I, 53–59)

Yet the very suddenness of this recantation, as if he had momentarily forgotten himself into the past and given way once more to a pride intellectually but not emotionally ab-

jured, serves to emphasize the comparative recency of his
conversion.

When Prometheus fulfils his promise to recall his curse
upon Jupiter, Shelley is able to use the occasion even more
effectively than in the opening apostrophe to emphasize the
hero's conversion from pride to pity. Summoned from the vale
of shadows beneath the grave, the Phantasm of Jupiter is made
to repeat the curse; torn by some inner compulsion which it
is unable to resist, and even imitating Prometheus' original
gestures, the ghost echoes the dire and ancient words:

> Heap on thy soul, by virtue of this Curse,
> Ill deeds; then be thou damned, beholding good;
> Both infinite as is the universe,
> And thou, and thy self-torturing solitude.
> An awful image of calm power
> Though now thou sittest, let the hour
> Come, when thou must appear to be
> That which thou art internally;
> And after many a false and fruitless crime,
> Scorn track thy lagging fall through boundless space and time!
>
> (I, 292–301)

"Were these my words?" says Prometheus to the Earth-mother,
and her affirmative response leads directly to the second recantation:

> It doth repent me; words are quick and vain;
> Grief for awhile is blind, and so was mine.
> I wish no living thing to suffer pain.
>
> (I, 304–306)

The moral reformation of Prometheus is now complete, and
the way for his reunion with Asia has been prepared, so that
he is able to endure with equanimity almost all the remaining
tortures, the most cruel and subtle excoriations of mind, which
Jupiter, out of a vengeful determination to requite him for
having had the curse repeated, now heaps upon him. Even if
Shelley had not contrasted Prometheus and Satan in his pref-
atory remarks, readers could hardly miss the ironic suggestion
of *Paradise Lost* in the words of Prometheus' original curse.
Like Milton's Satan, Jupiter will heap ill deeds upon his own
soul; like him also he will be damned in the most excruciating
fashion—"beholding good," knowing the bliss of heaven but
being unable to share in it; like Satan, too, though majestic in
his power, he will be shown to be outwardly what he is inter-

nally, an image of all evil; and like Satan, he will fall through boundless space and time down to "the wide waves of ruin . . . into a shoreless sea" (III, i, 71–74).

Somewhat more obvious, because it is instrumental in the temptation scene which immediately follows the second recantation, is Shelley's attempt to develop the resemblance between Jesus Christ and Prometheus in both being impervious to temptation, and serene in self-mastery. When Mercury appears as an emissary from Jupiter, with the legioned furies snarling at his heels, he comes ostensibly from Heaven rather than from Hell. But he shortly asserts that whenever in the past he has left the side of Prometheus and returned to Jupiter's domain, Heaven, by comparison, "seems Hell" (I, 358). Even now, he says, the Torturer Jove (Shelley uses the names interchangeably) is arming the "subtle, foul, or savage fiends," who people the abyss, with more slow agonies for Prometheus (I, 367–70). Unlike Satan on the Mount of Temptation, Mercury pities his prospective victim; yet, being under the compulsion of a higher power, he executes Jupiter's commands, offering "benefits" if Prometheus will submit, and even suggesting the possibility that instead of enduring the tortures now in prospect, Prometheus might

> dwell among the Gods the while,
> Lapped in voluptuous joy.

(I, 425–26)

Like Jesus Christ, however, Prometheus refuses to quit his Golgotha in the bleak ravine, and the agonies which yet must come, because he knows that the reign of evil will end, after the agony.

With the messenger's departure, the unleashed furies are enabled to begin their subtle torture, all of them designed to scarify the mind of Prometheus rather than his body. It is noteworthy that he succeeds in withstanding them through serene self-dominance (I, 430, 492). And it is especially remarkable, in view of Shelley's youthful recriminations against Jesus and in view of the parallelism between the Christ and Prometheus which he has been developing, that the really climactic and almost unendurable torture is a vision of Jesus Christ's agony upon the Cross. When all the other furies have done their worst and returned to the depths, one remains to display this most heartrending of all emblems. The worst of

it is that the faith Jesus kindled has been abused, and his words
have acted like "swift poison, withering up truth, peace, and
pity," so that crimes have been ever afterwards perpetrated
under the protection of his name (I, 549). When Prometheus'
eyes have been directed to the emblem of the crucifixion, which
the Fury evidently displays like a tableau, the Fury explains
its significance in words whose bearing cannot be lost upon
the Titan:

> . . . those who do endure
> Deep wrongs for man, and scorn, and chains, but heap
> Thousand-fold torment on themselves and him.
>
> (I, 594–96)

Quite as bad as this fact, says the Fury, is the deep ignorance
of human society:

> [Men] dare not devise good for man's estate,
> And yet they know not that they do not dare.
> The good want power, but to weep barren tears.
> The powerful goodness want; worse need for them.
> The wise want love; and those who love want wisdom;
> And all best things are thus confused to ill.
>
> (I, 623–28)

The Fury ceases with an ironic echo of the words of Jesus:
"They know not what they do." But, as the Saviour's words
were spoken out of an infinite pity, so Prometheus reacts with
pity for man's ignorance. "Thou pitiest them?" says the last
of the Furies. "I speak no more!"—and he disappears.[10]

The first act of *Prometheus Unbound* ought thus to be
seen as preparatory in purpose, designed to show that the
Titan, having cast out pride and hatred while remaining firm
and calm in his opposition to the evil principle, is now ready
for the arrival of the great hour of man's redemption. A com-
mentator bent on showing the classical symmetry of the act
might point out that Shelley has balanced the visitation of the
Furies, at the close of this section, with a chorus of fair spirits,
who prophesy that love and unselfishness will in the end
prevail. It may be assumed that this prophecy provides a salve
for the still aching mental wounds of Prometheus. The act
closes with a speech of Panthea's which, as it refers to the
place of Asia's exile, may be regarded as transitional, since
Act II is to deal with Asia's visit to Demogorgon. But these
are formal matters. The most striking aspect of the first act

is that Shelley, like the author of the *Beowulf* and many another envisioner of gods and heroes in the great tradition of English literature since the Middle Ages, has suffused a myth of pagan origin with deeply felt Christian symbolism. He has begun with Aeschylus and ended by the representation of an ethic which is close to that of the New Testament.

III

When Peacock made the second prose outline for his *Ahrimanes*, he supposed that the universe was governed by Necessity. Under its rule two antagonistic spirits, Oromaze and Ahrimanes, did unending battle. Shelley, as we know, adopted this mythological pattern for his *Revolt of Islam*. As in Peacock's poem, Necessity dwells apart, taking no discernible hand in the action, yet ready, if the world were ready, to usher in a new order. In Shelley's *Revolt* as in Peacock's poem the world is still dominated by the evil spirit, yet not utterly so, since it is possible for Laon and Cythna to produce a revolution which proves, albeit temporarily, what the world might be like under the rule of the good spirit. Further, as both Peacock and Shelley no doubt told each other in their conversations on mythology, the laws of Necessity required that the spirit of evil would one day be cast down, and that a new age would come, in which the spirit of good would endure through a historical cycle. Laon and Cythna, in their immortal transfigurations, awaited the advent of the new age, the roll of the cycle, in their south polar retreat.

With certain differences, partly the result of his merger of the Greek and the Zoroastrian schemes, Shelley follows a similar plan in *Prometheus Unbound*. In *Ahrimanes* and *The Revolt* the spirits of good and evil join battle under the eye of Necessity. But where the earlier poems of Peacock and Shelley showed a world not yet ready for the return of the Good, the world in *Prometheus Unbound* has at last reached that status, and Prometheus' unbinding can occur. Where the revolution failed in *The Revolt*, having been superinduced by outward action, that in *Prometheus Unbound*, having involved and taken place in man's whole mental constitution, must succeed.

Prometheus' opening apostrophe to Jupiter proves that Shelley had something like the foregoing mythological pattern in mind. Jupiter is:

> Monarch of Gods and Daemons, and all Spirits
> But One, who throng those bright and rolling worlds.

The "One" is probably Prometheus, who has placed Jupiter in the seat of power.[11] Prometheus' controlling secret is that Necessity must eventually institute what are in effect proceedings of impeachment against Jupiter, for this monarch has been guilty of high crimes, misdemeanors, and malfeasance in office from the moment he assumed the throne. Precisely when this impeachment will occur, Prometheus does not appear to know, but he does know that "it must come." As we have seen, the determining factor is Prometheus' capacity for self-reform, a capacity potentially present, but not successfully invoked, among the human beings who participated in *The Revolt of Islam*.

The second and third acts of *Prometheus Unbound* are the inevitable consequence of the first. As the preparatory act closes, Panthea has alluded to Asia, waiting in "that far Indian vale / The scene of her sad exile"—a place once cold and desolate but now, because of Prometheus' accession of pity, "invested with fair flowers and herbs / And haunted by sweet airs and sounds," for the winter of Prometheus' suffering has ended, and Asia's transforming powers are accordingly released.

During the first act, which opens in the dark night of Prometheus' soul, morning has broken. Now dawn and the spring have come to Asia's vale, and as she awaits the arrival of her sister-nymph, Panthea, she knows that the long-looked-for Hour is at hand.

> This is the season, this the day, the hour;
> At sunrise thou shouldst come, sweet sister mine,
> Too long desired, too long delaying, come!
>
> (II, i, 13–15)

The significance of Asia's "sisters," Ione and Panthea, like the meaning of Demogorgon, has been variously debated, but it seems plain that Shelley intended them to represent, in mounting order, degrees of love and perceptiveness within the human mind.[12] The lesser of the two is clearly Ione, who is subconsciously aware of the approaching change in the heart of the cosmos without being able to define what it is that vaguely disturbs her usual calm.[13] The unfocused awareness which wakes and inwardly stirs Ione is both focused and much more fully developed in Panthea, to whom, in the course of a dream, comes a clear vision of Prometheus, transfigured with the love he has learned through long suffering.[14] Panthea's perceptions are thus far clearer than those of her sister and it is this quality which enables her to act as the intermediary between Prometheus (representing the mind of man) and Asia (representing the idea of divine love). Panthea is "more fair" than any other except Asia, being the lesser "shadow" or imperfect representation of the ineffable radiance of her elder sister.[15]

As he develops the dream sequence which fills the first scene of Act II, Shelley again emphasizes the gradations of the sisters. Panthea's excuse for her tardy arrival in Asia's valley is that her wings were faint with the delight of her "remembered dream," the first of the two which came to her as she and Ione slept at the feet of Prometheus. Her words are inadequate, but by gazing into her eyes Asia herself sees the vision of Prometheus joyously transfigured. It should be noticed that Panthea merely saw and remembered the vision; only Asia can interpret its meaning, and this she immediately does:

> Say not those smiles that we shall meet again
> Within that bright pavilion which their beams
> Shall build o'er the waste world? The dream is told.
>
> (II, i, 124–26)

Two other dreams, precisely alike in their significance, have come to Panthea and Asia respectively, and Shelley uses them to start Asia's pilgrimage from her place of exile. In her second dream, Panthea has read the words, "Follow, follow," upon the fallen leaves of an almond tree; in Asia's dream the same enigmatic message seemed to be stamped on every herb and written in shadows on the morning clouds. When Asia repeats the message, echoes take it up, and give the sisters a clue to their destination:

> In the world unknown
> Sleeps a voice unspoken;
> By thy step alone
> Can its rest be broken;
> Child of Ocean!
>
> (II, i, 190–94)

The slumbrous spirit in the world unknown is of course Demogorgon or Necessity. Prometheus' recantation has made it possible for Asia and Panthea to begin their descent to the unknown world of Demogorgon.

Since Asia's interview with Demogorgon, in scene iv, is the major objective of Act II, the short intervening descriptive and lyrical scenes may be quickly passed over. Scene ii is chiefly memorable for the colloquy of fauns, who speak somewhat after the manner of Caliban at those times when Shakespeare allows him to describe the enchanted island, and whose dramatic function is to predict. One of them mentions his delight in

> . . . those wise and lovely songs
> Of Fate, and Chance, and God, and Chaos old,
> And Love, and the chained Titan's woful doom,
> And how he shall be loosed, and make the earth
> One brotherhood.
>
> (II, ii, 91–95)

In scene iii, Asia and Panthea reach a pinnacle of rock above the realm of Demogorgon, and in one of Shelley's most majestic lyrics are beckoned by a song of spirits:

> To the deep, to the deep,
>   Down, down!
> Through the shade of sleep,
> Through the cloudy strife
> Of Death and of Life;
> Through the veil and the bar
> Of things which seem and are,
> Even to the steps of the remotest throne,
>   Down, down!
>
> (II, iii, 54–62)

On the steps of that remote throne, Asia's questioning of Demogorgon elicits answers which are oracular, yet penetrable enough to anyone sufficiently familiar with the combination of Hellenic and Zoroastrian mythology which Shelley uses throughout his poem. Asia begins with a kind of catechism. Who made the living world? Who made all that it contains? Who made the powers of the human mind: thought, passion, reason, will, imagination? Who made that sense of ecstasy so strong that it fills the eyes with tears and leaves the earth a solitude when it departs? [16] Demogorgon's answer is always the same: God. If the sudden interjection of God the Creator into a hierarchy of gods already accepted is at first somewhat puzzling, the puzzle is easily solved when it is recalled that in the early version of Peacock's *Ahrimanes* Necessity began by delegating power to El Oran the Creator. But in Peacock, as now in Shelley, God the Creator has done his work long ago and takes no part in the current action.[17]

Asia next inquires into the origin of mental evils, the sundry ways in which the powers of the human mind are perverted and abused. Who made terror, madness, crime, remorse, despair, hatred, self-contempt, pain, and the fear of Hell—in short, all horrors which unsettle the human mind? Once more Demogorgon's answer is always the same: He reigns. Since Jupiter reigns, and since the first act has already shown him to be a past master in the art of mental torture, there can be no doubt of Demogorgon's meaning.

The reader now learns, through Asia, of the events preceding Jupiter's reign and the manacling of Prometheus. Heaven, Earth, Light, and Love were all that existed in the epoch before the birth of time. This age was succeeded by a primitivistic period, under Saturn, in which earth's "primal spirits" merely vegetated, having neither knowledge, power, thought, self-governance, nor love.[18] The Age of Saturn ended when Prometheus taught man science and art, medicine, astronomy, and navigation, but at the same time gave wisdom and power to Jupiter, with what disastrous results we already know.

As she concludes her mythological account, Asia importunately returns to the problem of the origin of evil, urging Demogorgon to name the real culprit. Who rains down evil, "the immedicable plague," which drives man until his will is wrecked, and he becomes a lonely outcast, the scorn of earth? Could it be that Jupiter who trembled like a slave at Prometheus' original curse? Who is Jupiter's master? Is Jupiter also a slave? "All spirits are enslaved," says Demogorgon, "which serve things evil." If Jupiter does so, then he is a slave. But Asia still seeks the culprit's name. "Whom called'st thou God?" she asks, as if she half-suspected that God the Creator and Jupiter had some alliance.[19] "I spoke but as ye speak," says Demogorgon, "for Jove is the supreme of living things"— a remark which might well imply that God the Creator has had nothing to do with the origin of evil, which arose with the reign of Jupiter, long after the Creator's work was done. Who, then, *is* the master of Jove, if God is not? Demogorgon begs this question: "The deep truth is imageless." [20] But he does assert that all things are subject to Fate, Time, Occasion, Chance, and Change, except eternal Love. The presumption is therefore that Jupiter is somehow subject to Fate (or Necessity), and that the occasion has now arrived when through the happy chance of Prometheus' self-mastery the great change can take place, and eternal Love can be reunited with mankind.

This occasion is now at hand, for to Asia's final question —"When shall the destined hour arrive?"—Demogorgon responds by pointing to a throng of charioteers. These are the immortal Hours, one of whom awaits Asia. Actually there are two especially nominated charioteers, one dark and of a dreadful aspect, the other bright and with dovelike eyes which may predict the coming peace. The dark hour represents, of course, the fall of Jupiter, and the bright hour the simultaneous "rise" of Asia and Prometheus, for what to the protagonists is an hour of joy is to their antagonist one of gloom. The first, who describes himself as "the Shadow of a destiny" even more dreadful than his own aspect, has come to bear Demogorgon to Olympus. The task of the second is to carry Asia to Prometheus. The two charioteers will arrive at their respective destinations at the same time, or, to put it another way, the reunion of the mind of man and eternal love will coincide with the casting-down of Jupiter, the originator of all those evils of the mind which Demogorgon has earlier enumerated.

The second act closes with a scene descriptive of Asia's transfiguration. The sisters are *en voyage* in the chariot of the Hour. Although the sun has not yet risen, being estopped with the wonder of the approaching miracle, Panthea observes in the clouds around them an awesome spread of light.[21] It emanates from Asia at this hour of her second birth, as aeons ago, among the Aegean islands, when she first uprose, like sea-born Aphrodite, standing within a veined shell,

> love, like the atmosphere
> Of the sun's fire filling the living world

burst from her, and permeated all living things. Now the period of her eclipse is over, and the air is filled with the voices of all articulate beings seeking Asia's sympathy. In one of the two final lyrics of the second act, a corporate voice chants a hymn to Asia, addressing her as "Life of Life,"

"Child of Light," and "Lamp of Earth"; in the second, Asia herself takes up the strain, comparing her soul to an enchanted boat, upborne upon the sound waves of the hymn, and wafted back to the paradise of a diviner day.[22]

Act III begins on the crest of Olympus, in the midst of the *hybris* of Jupiter, who is rejoicing at the approaching hour of his omnipotence. He imagines, having wrongly interpreted Prometheus' secret, that Demogorgon's arrival will be immediately followed by the extinction of man's defiance, which for centuries has threatened the foundations of his fear-buttressed empire.[23] But when Demogorgon alights from the chariot of Jupiter's dark hour, the casting-down of the Torturer is swift and sure. This event, which in dramatic terms ought to be climactic, does not seem to have been so conceived by Shelley. The mental reform achieved when Prometheus casts hate from his heart in Act I is not only a symbolic anticipation of the cosmic reform achieved by Demogorgon in dethroning Jupiter, but also a direct cause of it. To all intents and purposes the expulsion of Jupiter really took place during Prometheus' first-act recantation. For this play, despite its mythological fabric, is a drama of the inner mind, and evil is represented as a deformity of the mind. What is extirpated there can survive nowhere else in the universe. Or, as Demogorgon puts it in his final words to Jupiter:

> The tyranny of heaven none may retain,
> Or reassume, or hold, succeeding thee.
>
> (III, i, 57–58)

From this point on it remained to Shelley to explore the consequences of Jupiter's fall from dominance.[24] In scene iii Hercules unbinds Prometheus. Thus, says he, does strength minister to "wisdom, courage, and long-suffering love." Now the Titanic psyche is reunited to his epipsyche, and Prometheus assures Asia that from this time forth they will never be separated. Now the Spirit of the Hour, an Ariel with one more task to do before his freedom is earned, is told to circumnavigate the great globe itself, proclaiming everywhere, through the music of a great conch shell, the glad news of man's redemption. Now Mother Earth, as the warmth circles down through her marble veins, details a spirit in the likeness of a winged child to conduct Asia and Prometheus, as Laon and Cythna were in the end conducted, to a far-off temple beside

a windless pool, past Nysa, birthplace of Bacchus, and beyond
Indus. There the Spirit of the Earth tells the assembled company of the miraculous effects of the skyborne shell music,
and how "with little change of shape or hue" all things had
put their evil natures off. Now the Spirit of the Hour appears
to report the success of his last journey, and to describe finally
the state of man under the new dispensation:

> The painted veil, by those who were, called life,
> Which mimicked, as with colours idly spread,
> All men believed and hoped, is torn aside;
> The loathsome mask has fallen, the man remains
> Sceptreless, free, uncircumscribed, but man
> Equal, unclassed, tribeless, and nationless,
> Exempt from awe, worship, degree, the king
> Over himself; just, gentle, wise; but man
> Passionless?—no, yet free from guilt or pain,
> Which were, for his will made or suffered them;
> Nor yet exempt, though ruling them like slaves,
> From chance, and death, and mutability,
> The clogs of that which else might oversoar
> The loftiest star of unascended heaven.
>
> (III, iv, 190–203)

For many readers the foregoing summarization is the real
ave atque vale of the drama, and there has accordingly been
some division of opinion as to whether the concluding act,
long known as Shelley's "afterthought," has any legitimate
excuse for being. Grabo quite properly describes Act IV as a
"philosophical epilogue," and one is inclined to regard it, like
many epilogues, as a kind of addendum rather than as an
integral part of the drama.[25] But those who are less interested
in the play as a play than as a vehicle for Shelley's philosophical ideas would be loath to part with the fourth act: it
presents several ideas not hitherto made explicit, and it develops and re-emphasizes ideas which receive less extended
treatment elsewhere in the drama.

Act IV consists of three successive choric movements,
each introduced and interpreted by Panthea and Ione. The
first movement represents the confused departure, heard from
afar off, of the outworn prereformational hours "to the dark,
to the past, to the dead," and the arrival of the bright nascent
hours of the new order. These last are fittingly accompanied by
the powers of might and pleasure "from the mind of human-
kind." Until Prometheus' reformation, they lay trammeled in

the dark, but they are now celebrating a new freedom, which they owe to the rebirth of love and light in the human mind.

The second movement in the act is a fanciful love dialogue between the feminine Moon and the masculine Earth. The conceit, which Shelley carefully develops in sexual imagery, is that the rebirth of love in the Earth has kindled a response in the cold bosom of the Moon, his "crystal paramour," the effect of which is that she is warmed and rendered fruitful. The development of the conceit is the more remarkable in that Shelley equates gravitational attraction with the sympathetic powers of love, and compares the moon's movement around the earth to that of an aroused and "insatiate bride," half-dementedly circling her lover in order to gaze on his form from every side. Since the praise of love is intended here, the equation may be symbolically justified, although the idea that the moon is warmed and fertilized by the proximity of the earth would scarcely gain the assent of astronomers.

In the third movement, which is first antiphonal then hortatory in character, Demogorgon invokes the spirits of men both living and dead, of the earth, moon, and stars, of all fauna and flora, and of all the elements, to hear a final proclamation upon the significance of this great day in the evolution of the universe.

IV

The difficulty in the interpretation of *Prometheus Unbound* arises chiefly from the fact that the leading characters are both characters in a drama and symbolic universals. In reading or describing the play, as in earlier sections of this [essay], one must adopt Shelley's dramatic terminology and follow his conduct of the action as if these personified universals were living people. Yet if one thinks in terms of the philosophical meaning of the play rather than in terms of objective, dramatic representation (Shelley's phrase would be the "impersonation" of "visions"), Prometheus is not a "character" at all but rather an image of the mind of man.[26] By the same token, Jupiter and Asia are ideas in the mind of Prometheus, although one should not speak of the "mind of Prometheus" without remembering that in philosophical terms the designation is inexact, since Prometheus himself is *mind*, that is, the human mind seen in its universal aspect. Two other "characters," God the Creator (who is merely alluded to and remains passive in the play) and Demogorgon (who is Necessity conceived as amoral law) stand somewhat apart from, though they are closely linked to, the mind of man. The first has endowed that mind with invaluable faculties; the second is linked closely enough to the mind to respond to any major changes which occur there. In other words, Prometheus would be perfectly justified in saying, by Act III, that once his self-reform was complete, the rest happened "by Necessity." So long as this fundamental dualism between dramatic representation and symbolic function has been recognized, it can be held in critical abeyance. The foregoing sections of this [essay] have followed through in detail the development of the action conceived as dramatic action. The symbolic values which Shelley attached to Prometheus, Jupiter, Asia, Demogorgon, and the unseen and essentially inactive God of creation have just been indicated in general terms. It remains to show what the development of the action signifies in more or less philosophical terms.

The essential meaning is fairly simple: the removal of that repressive force which now manacles and tortures the human mind would not only provide an opportunity for the rebirth of the power of love in that mind, but would also enable man to realize his tremendous potential of intellectual might and spiritual pleasure (or blessedness, as Carlyle would translate it) which has for so long been stifled by fear, hate, selfishness, and despair. The conditional mood of this statement is quite intentional: Shelley is not suggesting that these things have happened, but only that they ought to happen. The *Prometheus* is one of those "dreams of what ought to be or may be" in the distant future.

Shelley works out his vision of man's achievement of ethical perfection in a broad, pseudohistorical perspective, the groundwork for which is provided by Asia's second-act exposition. As in *The Revolt of Islam*, he pays no attention to specific historical details, but moves upon a highly imaginative mythological plane. The mind of man in the Saturnian Age was undeveloped, and man simply vegetated. At a subsequent period, The Age of Prometheus, he acquired knowledge and power. But at the same time "fierce wants," "mad disquietudes and shadows idle of unreal good" began to appear, levying mutual war and "ruining the lair [the human mind] wherein they raged." As partly compensatory "alleviations of his state" man's mind evolved the creative arts and the useful sciences. Prometheus' granting Jupiter dominance upon only one condition, namely that man is to be free, means in effect that the mind of man suffered its fierce wants and mad disquietudes to assume command, while at the same time retaining the power of freedom of choice. Mind may at any time shake off these agonies if the inward conditions of that mind can be made right. Yet the paradox has been that the mind's capacity for self-deception is so strong that the almost limitless possibilities inherent in an act of self-reform have long been lost to sight. Hence the mind of man has been subjected to the severest tortures. Eventually, however, the great hour arrives. The mind resolves to rid itself of the attitudes which, as in Plato's myth of the cave, have kept it chained in the darkness. With this resolution the way for the expulsion of the mind's daemon is prepared. This resolution and this preparation provide Shelley with the ethical scheme of Act I.

Precisely at the moment of the expulsion (represented in a preliminary way by the departure of the last of the Furies, and finally by the fall of Jupiter), the way is made ready for the entry into the human mind of a harmonizing power long since lost (dramatically represented by Prometheus' reunion with Asia). Until the great hour of its enlightenment, the human mind in its self-induced blindness and self-torture has not been able to comprehend this higher love except as a "shadow of beauty unbeheld." [27] It has had to remain content with imperfect degrees of love (Ione and Panthea). Mind is ultimately released by its own strength (Hercules). We are given to understand that the mad disquietudes may return, although such a contingency is for the time being unlikely. (Prometheus is resolved never again to part with Asia, while Jupiter is safely caged under the bars which cover the abyss.) [28]

The obvious question raised by the play is one of the oldest in philosophic literature: How far is man able to control his own destiny? Since *Prometheus Unbound* was conceived and developed as an ethical and psychological drama, Shelley answers the question in these terms: if the mind of man can rid itself of hatred and vengeance, that mind will be cleansed of "fear and pain," and consequently receptive to the harmonizing power of love. Supreme mental well-being will then ensue; order will succeed disorder; harmony will inform chaos. As one of Shelley's images indicates, man will resemble the leprous child who, having drunk of the healing waters of a secret spring, returns home so completely transformed that its mother does not recognize it.

In describing Shelley's view of the problem of evil, Mary asserted that he thought it necessary only for mankind to will "that there should be no evil, and there would be none." With certain qualifications this is true, although the qualifications must be explicitly stated. For Shelley, in his increasingly strong conviction that matter is a function of mind, evil is largely, though by no means entirely, a remediable defect of spiritual vision, an inability to break through the clouds into the sunlight of moral truth. As such, evil is a daemon which can be exorcised, or a gloomy veil which can be dispelled, by a vigorous act of the virtuous will. Man can then realize his full potentialities or, in Shelley's phrase, he can become "king over himself" because his mind is freed from the tyranny of guilt and pain which his uneducated will formerly suffered to exist there.

But Shelley's Magna Carta contains two restraining clauses or qualifications which make it plain that his beatific vision did not blind him to certain exigencies of life on earth. One of these is that, even under the new dispensation (assuming, as he does, that it were achieved on a worldwide scale), man will still have to contend with "chance and death and mutability." Being king over himself, he can rule these incontrovertible facts as if they were his slaves. Yet change, and chance, and death, if not the poor, we shall have always with us. To this extent, at least Shelley's earlier belief in a mechanical necessitarianism had survived into the 1818–1819 period. The survival was fortunate. It acted, as Solve rightly says, "as a sort of balance wheel upon his too enthusiastic faith in the regenerative power of mind." [29]

The second restrictive clause in Shelley's scheme of the new moral order may be inferred from Demogorgon's final exhortation to the assembled cosmic hosts, namely, that there is no absolute guarantee of a permanent expulsion of moral evil.

> Gentleness, Virtue, Wisdom, and Endurance,
> These are the seals of that most firm assurance

> Which bars the pit over Destruction's strength;
> And if, with infirm hand, Eternity,
> Mother of many acts and hours, should free
> The serpent that would clasp her with his length,
> These are the spells by which to reassume
> An empire o'er the disentangled doom.
>
> (IV, i, 526–69)

Jupiter, the spiritually destructive force, has been cast down into the pit. The named powers of the human mind seal up the "firm assurance" that he will remain there. But the chthonic force is strong, and though the assurance is now firm enough, there is always the possibility that in the long stretch of future "acts and hours," some infirmity will develop which will set this force free once more. The serpent would clasp Eternity with his length: moral evil would perpetuate itself through all eternity.[30] If the torturing force should gain its freedom, the same powers of the human mind that now seal it in the abyss are the "spells" by which man may reassume

> An empire o'er the disentangled doom

which now lies coiled and tangled, in durance vile, under the throne of Eternity.

The place of Demogorgon in Shelley's philosophic scheme should now be evident. Demogorgon is the eternal law of amoral necessity which requires an act of mind in order to be set in motion. In *The Revolt of Islam* Shelley had concluded that the furtherance of good in the cosmos is ultimately man's problem, and that the only way in which the forces of moral good can be activated is through a regeneration in the mind of man. This is "Demogorgon's mighty law." Until the great hour of Prometheus' change of heart, Demogorgon is only a potential or holding force, shapeless and inert. Under his throne the happier destiny of man, a "snake-like Doom," has been coiled since Prometheus first gave power to Jupiter. The spirits who guide Asia down to the steps of that remote throne assert that "such strength" is in "meekness" (or in other words, love is so strong a force) that under its compulsion the Eternal (Demogorgon) must unloose man's happier destiny through "life's portal" (II, iv, 94–98). Asia does not urge Demogorgon to free Prometheus because there is no need for her to do so. Love has already been reborn in the mind of man, and by "Demogorgon's mighty law" the release of Prometheus must follow. There is, however, another side to this law. At the end of

Act IV, we are told that man's darker destiny of suffering is coiled under the throne of Demogorgon where formerly the happier destiny of man lay unfulfilled. If the forces of moral good were capable of being set in motion only through a regeneration in the mind of man, the forces of moral evil can reassume their former dominance only through a degeneration in the strength of that mind. This, one may infer, is the other side of Demogorgon's mighty law. But as long as gentleness, wisdom, virtue, and endurance remain in man, he will always have weapons with which to combat moral evil.

Prometheus Unbound is in most ways a beautifully exact and skilfully devised piece of work. The structure is carefully wrought, though it must be understood that the stress throughout is less on action than on revelation, that one of the problems is to offer a timeless event in dramatic time, and that the ordinary rules of dramatic organization have, on the whole, comparatively little relevance. Particularly in the first act, but often enough elsewhere, Shelley achieves a sonorous and masterful blank verse which shows that, if he had gone to school to Wordsworth at the time of "Alastor," he had not neglected Milton in the meantime. The interspersed lyrics contain a quality of lightness without sacrifice of dignity, which serves admirably to relieve the austerity of the rolling iambs, of which they frequently seem a distant echo, like wind in trees after thunder. Nor are these lyrics, as is sometimes said, mere musical interludes without significant relation to the progress of the play. Their function is roughly that of a dramatic chorus: to mourn or rejoice as occasions require, to mark transitions, to introduce or close the scenes, or to provide commentary on the course of the action. They are, moreover, carefully related to the deep and detailed complexities of the myth Shelley has evolved.

The pertinence of the drama as a treatment of one aspect —as Shelley saw it, the crucial aspect—of the problem of evil, the great care with which the original myth has been modified to meet the demands Shelley places upon it, the psychological subtleties and distinctions of character, and the clean exactness with which the whole is seen, as soon as its purpose is grasped, to fit together—these qualify *Prometheus Unbound* as an imaginative achievement of the first order. One may find the Hell of Act I more satisfactory than the Heaven of Act IV, but

this means only that more is always known of Hell than can
be imagined of Heaven, as even Dante and Milton, out of their
respective experiences in the imaginative reaction of both,
would have freely admitted.[31]

As a myth of moral regeneration, the *Prometheus* needs
rather to be understood than to be justified. One has only to
grasp the respective psychological attitudes of the self-enslaved
and the self-liberated man in order to understand Shelley's
meaning. The opening scene shows man's mind as it now is,
with reasons. The rest is an image of the mind of man set free,
made perfect, made whole:

> One harmonious soul of many a soul
> Whose nature is its own divine control.[32]

Shelley's drama provides poetic affirmation for his belief in
"a kind of optimism in which we are our own gods," although
that optimism is tempered by his appreciation of the radical
imperfections which now exist in both the physical and the
moral world.

Notes

1. *Prometheus Unbound*, preface, paragraph 2. All citations and quotations from Shelley's poetry are from *The Complete Poetical Works of
Percy Bysshe Shelley*, ed. G. E. Woodberry, Cambridge Edition (Boston,
1901).
2. *Letters*, IX, 36. Dec. 24, 1812. All references to Shelley's prose
works and letters are from *The Complete Works of Percy Bysshe Shelley*,
ed. Roger Ingpen and W. E. Peck, Julian Edition, 10 vols. (London,
1926–1930).
3. Shelley quoted *Prometheus Bound* with humorous intent in a letter
to Mary, Oct. 25, 1814. *Letters*, IX, 100. Mary's list of his reading for
1816, in White, *Shelley*, II, 542, shows that he read the play in that year.
An extensive reading of Aeschylus occurred in 1817. See Mary's journal and
the 1817 reading list in White, I, 524 and II, 544.
4. *Letters*, IX, 186 and IX, 293.
5. Shelley of course makes the Aeschylean Prometheus over in terms
of the Shelleyan hero. For a careful contrasting of Aeschylus and Shelley,
see O. W. Campbell, *Shelley and the Unromantics* (London, 1924), pp.
197–202.
6. See the preface to *Prometheus Unbound*.
7. O. W. Campbell, *Shelley and the Unromantics, op. cit.*, p. 190.
8. On the former closeness of Prometheus and Asia, see Prometheus'
statement (I, 122–23):

> I wandered once
> With Asia, drinking life from her loved eyes.

9. Panthea later remarks (I, 336) that "The Titan looks as ever, firm, not proud." Yet the Phantasm of Jupiter has not long since addressed Prometheus as "proud sufferer" (I, 245). Cf. also Mercury's reference to Prometheus' "haughty heart" (I, 378). In the unreformed Prometheus, there is a clear indication of the sin of pride.

10. An observation which one is glad to see has gained no acceptors is that of C. E. Jones, "Christ a Fury?" *Modern Language Notes*, L (January, 1935), 41. The notion is that the last remaining Fury is Christ, but it should be plain from the discussion above that the Fury only displays the Crucifix as a device to deepen the suffering of Prometheus. "Behold an emblem," says the Fury (I, 594). Prometheus then addresses the vision. He is not, as Mr. Jones alleges, speaking to the Fury, but rather to the silent figure which the Fury is exhibiting. If Shelley thought of *Prometheus Unbound* as in any sense a stage play, he would no doubt have wished to have the emblem placed in a curtained recess, backstage center, where the Fury could have pulled the curtain aside, and revealed, within, the Christian image.

11. According to Grabo, the One is "The hypostasis which is truth, beauty, perfection" (*Prometheus Unbound: An Interpretation*, Chapel Hill, 1935, p. 13).

12. Grabo, *op. cit.*, p. 52, calls the sisters "aspects of love," defining Asia as "passionate creative love," Panthea as "sympathetic love," and Ione as "the spirit of Love in Beauty." Douglas Bush, *Mythology and the Romantic Tradition in English Poetry* (Cambridge, Mass., 1937) echoes Grabo in saying that "in some vague way" the sisters represent "aspects of love," while observing that the family in the play—a man, his wife and two sisters-in-law—is a "typical Shelleyan household." Vida Scudder implies that the three sisters may be Faith (Panthea), Hope (Ione), and Charity (Asia), of whom the greatest, as in Paul, would be the last. Kenneth N. Cameron, "The Political Symbolism of *Prometheus Unbound*," PMLA, LVIII (1943), 740, believes that Ione is Memory, Panthea Hope, and Asia, of course, Love.

13. See Panthea's account II, i, 56–106, but especially lines 93–99.

14. Shelley's description of Correggio's "Christ Beatified," which he saw in a gallery in the fall of 1818 while he was at work on Act I, has a number of points in common with this vision of Prometheus transfigured. See *Letters*, IX, 342, November 9, 1818.

15. Whether or not he owned the conception to Plato, Shelley habitually thought of Divine Love (or as he called it in 1816, Intellectual Beauty) as too bright for the human eye to bear. Only the "shadow" of Intellectual Beauty fell upon him on that memorable occasion in his youth, yet the shadow was enough to produce his ecstatic reaction. In view of the sun and moon imagery used in "Epipsychidion," one might suggest that Panthea is a kind of moon to Asia's sun, borrowing reflected light. The conception of Asia as sunlike is clearly in Shelley's mind: the vernal phenomena at the beginning of Act II occur when Asia's power is released, and at the end of this act, Asia is compared to the "sun's fire filling the living world" (II, v, 27–30). In one of the Homeric Hymns, which Shelley translated in 1818, there occurs the name Pandeia, "a bright maid of beauty rare," whose mother is the moon.

16. Shelley evidently has in mind here some such experience as that described in the "Hymn to Intellectual Beauty," when, in rapt ecstasy, his eyes streamed with tears. See especially stanzas v–vi of that poem.

17. This agrees with Grabo, *op. cit.*, p. 74: "It is evident that God the Creator does not reign in man's universe."

18. Shelley employs a somewhat pseudohistorical strategy in his "Ode to Liberty," published in the volume with *Prometheus Unbound* in 1820. Before the coming of the spirit of Liberty

> This divinest universe
> Was yet a chaos and a curse.

War and despair raged among men and beasts "without truce or terms." Man had not learned the fine arts or even the simpler arts of cultivation, and tyranny hung like a fierce cloud over a waste of waves. This state of things continued until Athens arose.

19. Asia means, in effect, "who was it that you called God some moments ago?" The rather awkward preterit, "called'st" is required here, since if the form were "call'st," Asia would be asking, "Who is your God?" This last question is neither asked nor answered in the play.

20. Shelley could easily have caused Demogorgon to answer this question forthrightly. The master of Jupiter is the reformed Prometheus.

21. The great hour, according to the time scheme of the drama, is high noon. "We shall rest from long labors at noon," says the charioteer (II, iv, 173). Shelley evidently intends that Acts I and II fill the time from night to noon. The stage directions for the first act state that while the act is in progress "morning slowly breaks," but do not mention sunrise. The time of Act II, scene i, is given as "morning," but the sun is still below the horizon, and it is only "crimson dawn." In II, v, Panthea remarks that the sun "is yet unrisen." Since, however, the noon hour is so close at hand that Asia's transfiguration has already come, it would appear to be Shelley's intention that on this day of days the sun is to be stationary at the dawn position until the great noon hour arrives. In reply to Panthea's remark, the Spirit of the Hour says that "the sun will not rise until noon," for Apollo is "held in heaven by wonder." It would seem, therefore, that Shelley has been consistent in the application of his idea, though perhaps unintentionally deceptive at one or two points. Thus Asia (II, i, 14) says that Panthea is to arrive "at sunrise." When Panthea arrives, Asia gently upbraids her for being late, which would suggest that she has arrived after sunrise. Despite such slips, however, it is impossible to agree with Woodberry (Cambridge Edition, p. 623) that the remark of the Spirit of the Hour is "not to be taken literally."

22. On the probable derivation of the final stanza of Asia's song from the myth in Plato's *Statesman*, see the letter by E. M. W. Tillyard in *The Times Literary Supplement* (Sept. 29, 1932), p. 691.

23. Shelley has very considerably altered the original myth at this point in order to bring Demogorgon into his theogony. One of the frequent passages of sexual imagery in Shelley is that in which Jupiter boastfully recalls Thetis' passionate words at the moment of their union (III, i, 37–42). Shelley perhaps has in mind some sort of balance between the Prometheus-Asia relationship and that of Jupiter and Thetis, but he does not develop it. It is in any case an element of Jupiter's *hybris* that he imagines that he has begotten Demogorgon upon Thetis. Actually, of course, Jupiter's whole character is destructive rather than creative, so that the child he thinks he has begotten has no existence except in his prideful imagination.

24. I pass over the pleasant idyl of scene ii in which the sun-god describes Jupiter's fall to the god of the ocean, and both rejoice in the event.

25. In one particular, and probably in one only, the writing of the fourth act was dramatically obligatory, for it satisfies the reader's natural

curiosity as to whether Jupiter's threat to drag Demogorgon down with him to the pit was ever carried out. That the threat was empty is indicated by Demogorgon's reappearance at the close of Act IV.

26. See Melvin T. Solve, *Shelley: His Theory of Poetry* (Chicago, 1927), p. 91. Among earlier commentators, W. M. Rossetti, J. A. Symonds, and H. S. Salt are in substantial agreement that Prometheus represents the human mind.

27. It is, of course, the beauty itself which is "unbeheld." Prometheus was able to see the shadow of that beauty in Panthea's eyes. The phrase should be understood as if written, "shadow of beauty-unbeheld."

28. Lesser characters: Mercury, Jupiter's unwilling emissary, may represent half-enslaved and indecisive intellect disconsolately unleashing further tortures within the mind. Thetis, consort of Jupiter, is some sort of whoredom, probably a personification of lust. Jupiter, being destructive and hence uncreative evil, could beget nothing upon her, as O. W. Campbell points out, *op. cit.*, p. 219.

29. *Shelley: His Theory of Poetry*, p. 87.

30. The source both of this figure and of Shelley's conception of Demogorgon was observed some years ago by H. G. Lotspeich, "Shelley's 'Eternity' and Demogorgon," *Philological Quarterly* XIII (1934), 309–11. The pertinent passage is Book I, Chapter I of Boccaccio's *Genealogia Deorum Gentilium*. Shelley's Demogorgon says that his name is Eternity. In Boccaccio Eternity is the *socia* or companion of Demogorgon. The cave of Demogorgon in Shelley has its prototype in Boccaccio. There, too, Eternity is represented as an aged goddess encircled by a snake. Those who are troubled by Shelley's apparent inconsistency in speaking of Demogorgon in the masculine gender, of Demogorgon as Eternity, and of Eternity in the feminine gender, will doubtless find an explanation in the fact that Shelley was combining the "companions" of Boccaccio into a single concept. He may have done so in the interests of dramatic unity. He may have wished to suggest that Demogorgon partook of both the male and the female, thus standing as a kind of ancestor to the Hermaphrodite in *The Witch of Atlas*. Finally, he may have intended to imply that the law of amoral necessity was eternal, an idea which could be figured forth with dramatic economy by making Demogorgon and Eternity one.

31. Shelley well knew how much more skill was needed to make poetry of beauty, virtue, and harmony than of injustice, deformity, and discord. "Better verses," said he, "have been written on Hell than [on] Paradise." *Prose*, VII, 101.

32. Josiah Royce finds an instructive parallel between Shelley's poetic expression of this idea and Hegel's concept of a "concrete universal." See his *The Spirit of Modern Philosophy* (Boston, 1931), pp. 225–26.

Stewart C. Wilcox

15·The Sources, Symbolism, and Unity of Shelley's ''Skylark''

THE SOURCES and influences which stimulated Shelley's imagination when he composed the "Skylark" are not merely significant in themselves, but also essential in understanding its meaning. In particular, his use of the myth of the soul from Plato's *Phaedrus,* a source hitherto mentioned only incidentally,[1] needs to be elucidated. Woven into the imagery of the poem are three main threads of development: observations of nature and the skylark mainly suggested by the spot in Italy which, John Gisborne tells us, he associated with Shelley and skylarks; suggestive references to the poet's own state of mind in early summer of 1820 when he composed the poem;[2] and philosophical ideas, principally embodied in the bird as a Platonic symbol of the ideal spirit of poetry. These three strands of meaning—natural, personal, and philosophical—Shelley so blends in his design that they bring artistic wholeness to its structure and unity to its ideas. Let us turn first to the natural observations which led Shelley to compose his poem.

From June 15 to August 5, 1820, Shelley, Mary, and Claire Clairmont stayed at Casa Ricci, the Leghorn home of John and Maria Gisborne. In a note of 1839 Mrs. Shelley says:

> In the spring we spent a week or two near Leghorn, borrowing the house of some friends, who were absent on a journey to England. It was on a beautiful summer evening while wandering among the lanes, whose myrtle hedges were the bowers of the fireflies, that we heard the carrolling of the skylark, which inspired one of the most beautiful of his poems.[3]

Reprinted by permission of the author and the University of North Carolina from *Studies in Philology,* Vol. XLVI, No. 4 (October 1949), pp. 560–76.

Additional evidence is John Gisborne's refreshingly natural description, written in 1827, of the fields he connected with Shelley and skylarks:

> We passed by the side of the brook, over those breezy and luxuriant meadows of which one in particular was most dear to our remembrance. It is the favourite resort of innumerable larks, and other sweet-voiced birds! How often, pursuing our early morning walks over this lovely expanse, we have beheld the speckled songsters, burst forth from their bed of rich herbage and soar fluttering–gladdening the very air with their incessant and thrilling notes–to a height at which the straining eye could scarcely ken the stationary and diminutive specks into which their soft and still receding forms had at length vanished. The steep banks of the brook were overgrown with myrtles and other sweet shrubs and embellished with an infinite variety of gaudy, delicate and odorous flowers. . . . We returned home . . . by the Conduits, which recalled mournfully to our remembrance a delightful walk we had once taken in that direction with a dear friend who no longer lives but in the indelible sympathies of his surviving and enthusiastic admirers.[4]

Shelley's life in 1819, however, was far from being as happy and joyous as such a reminiscence might lead us to believe.

During the first half of this year, as Newman I. White emphasizes, Shelley was suffering from the effects of a severe winter in Florence.[5] His nervous energies were depleted, and he bore the burdens of Godwin's financial difficulties, Mary's frantic worry over them, the domestic discord between her and Claire, and Mary's continuing grief over the loss of Clara and William. To these troubles were added the death of Elena Adelaide Shelley, the mysterious Neapolitan child, as well as the previous attempts at blackmail by Paolo, Shelley's discharged servant. Moreover, the English reviewers' condemnations of his ideas in his poetry aroused his hatred and plunged him into discouragement, for he was concerned far less about public recognition of his genius than about acceptance of his moral precepts for reform. In the midst of these trials he remained relatively unproductive. What is perhaps surprising is that he wrote at all. Hence to see in the concluding stanzas of the "Skylark" a contrast between the joy of the spirit of the ideal poet embodied in the bird and the depression of the earthly poet still longing for the moral regeneration of men's minds is but to recognize Shelley's growing despair that man would ever realize anew a world's great age. Doubtless he took momentary delight in the surroundings of Casa Ricci, for his resiliency of spirit was remarkable. But the "Skylark" is basically not joyous—indeed, it is a poem of yearning for the ecstatic joy of the skylark-poet, the unattainable perfection of the ideal. This, Shelley's sources, to which we now come, help disclose.

The heart of this discussion of sources and influences is that Shelley used Plato's myth of the winged soul in the *Phaedrus* as the philosophical basis of his symbolism of the bird "Skylark." If he did, it then follows that the poem should be Platonistically interpreted. Moreover, its unity—its steady progression to climax in imagery, structure, and meaning—will be clearly seen to depend upon the consistency of the ideas suggested by the skylark as a symbol.[6]

First we should observe that Shelley read both the *Phaedrus* and the *Phaedo* during his stay at Pisa during the first half of 1820, and that during the previous two years he had translated the *Ion, Symposium, Menexenus,* parts of the *Republic,* and the notes on Socrates.[7] Even the brief, though important, essay *On Love* was probably composed in 1820.[8] Thus Shelley's mind was full of Platonic concepts and images. Perhaps the most famous and striking of all these is the myth of the charioteer in the *Phaedrus,* wherein is found the figure of the winged soul as well as observations upon the soul itself and its divine inspiration.

Concerning inspiration and the nature of man's soul, Plato says, "To him who is rightly mad, rightly possessed the madness brings release from his present ills . . . " and "the poetry of common-sense [i.e., poetry based upon art without inspiration] fades into nothingness before the poetry of the madmen." [9] He then goes on to say that the gods gave men madness [i.e., inspiration] as a blessing; but proof of this rests upon our knowledge of the real nature of the soul. Suffice it here that this nature is the soul's immortality which derives from its essence, movement. After launching into the magnificent poetry of his myth in which the soul is "likened to the conjoint nature of a team of winged horses and a charioteer," Plato adds:

> Now with the gods the horses and the charioteers are noble, all of them, both in themselves and by descent, whereas with other races there is a mixture. With us [i.e., men], note first, the driver has to guide a pair of horses. and, secondly, one of

them is beautiful and good, the other reverse in character and
stock. And hence for us the driving must needs be different
and vexing. Now comes the question why a living creature is
called mortal or immortal, and this we must try to explain.
Soul in its totality has the care of all that is inanimate, and
traverses the whole heaven, appearing now in one shape, now
in another; when it is perfect, and fully winged, it soars on
high, and regulates the entire world. But the soul that has
lost its wings is borne along until it fastens upon something
solid, and there finds a dwelling place, taking on an earthly
body which seems to be self-moving—but the cause of motion
is the power of the soul. The conjoint whole, soul and the body
thereto knit, is called a living creature, and has the added name
of "mortal."

Now the natural function of a wing is to soar, to go upward to
the region where dwell the gods, those whose souls are wholly
immortal and who gaze upon the eternal essences. But man's
wing, of all bodily elements, is nearest the divine. And the
divine, which is Beauty, Wisdom, Goodness, nourishes the
wings of the soul.

Plato next adds that mortal souls which fail in their attempt to gaze upon the essences, or which are misused and
become filled with forgetfulness and evil, shed their wings and
fall to earth. In their first birth such souls become men, those
of the fullest vision becoming lovers of wisdom or beauty, or
servants of the Muses and Eros.

Omitting here Plato's discussion of the time required for
a soul to "return to the place from which it comes," we arrive
at the part of the *Phaedrus* which specifically suggested to
Shelley the philosophical basis of his symbolism:

And now it is that a human soul may pass into the existence
of a beast, and also from a beast he who once was human may
pass back again into a man; for the soul that never had a vision
of the truth, never can pass into our human shape. Why not?
Because Man necessarily has intelligence according to "ideal
form" as it is called, which proceeds from many sense-percep-
tions into one concept of reflection. But this act of thought
is recollection, a remembrance of those things which once our
soul beheld when it went in the procession with its God, when
on high it viewed the things we now say *are*, when it lifted up
its head towards true existence. Wherefore rightly is the mind
of the lover of wisdom only winged; for with all the power he
has he gives himself in memory to those things by communing
with which God is divine. And a man who makes right use of
memories like these is ever being initiated into perfect mys-

teries, and he alone becomes truly perfect. But since he turns away from the concerns of men, and cleaves to the divine, the world rebukes him for a madman; the many see not that he is a man inspired.

Here, then, is the point we have reached with our whole discourse in the fourth kind of madness. This kind it is that causes a man to be held for mad, who, when he sees the beauty here below, in remembrance of the veritable beauty is fledged with wings, and, quivering, would fain mount upwards; but he cannot, and only gazes up, like a bird indifferent to everything below. . . . Small is the remnant of the souls in whom is present the needful share of memory; but these when they behold some semblance of the things that are yonder are amazed, and lose possession of themselves, but what it is so moves them, that they do not know, because they cannot clearly make it out.

In addition, continues Plato in his discourse upon him who has lately gazed upon the eternal essence of Beauty,

. . . when he beholds a face of aspect divine well copying the Beautiful, or an ideal bodily form, first he shudders, and something of the terror he then had comes over him; anon, as he gazes at the object, he reveres it as if it were a god, and if he were not afraid that men would think him downright mad, he would bow down to his love with offerings as if it were a graven image and a god indeed. While he looks the shuddering passes, and he is taken with sweating and unwonted heat; for he has received the effluence of beauty through his eyes, and is made hot, and with that effluence his wing is bathed to life. And with the warmth are melted the parts where sprout the wings, which parts, long since grown hard, were tightly sealed, and kept the plumes from budding forth. And as the nourishment streams in, the quills of the feathers swell, and begin to grow from the root, underneath, all over the form of the soul—for of yore the entire soul was feathered.

Of the foregoing passages Lane Cooper has remarked that ". . . the *Ion* contains nothing so odd to the modern reader as the detailed description . . . of the growth of the wings and the feathers for the upward flight of the soul." [10] Yet Shelley, steeped in Plato's poetical imagery, evidently found the figure more provocative than odd. Let us, then, proceed to an examination of the structure, imagery, and symbolism of the "Skylark" in the light of the myth, Shelley's personal life in 1820, and the influence of real skylarks.

Shelley clearly indicates his three main divisions. The first six stanzas are the proem, which is followed by a transitional stanza apostrophizing the skylark, "What is most like thee?" This stanza and the following four that answer Shelley's question in as many figures lead up to a second stanza of transition in which the skylark's music is said to surpass "All that ever was / Joyous, and clear, and fresh. . . ." Both transitional stanzas, it should be remarked, belong in division two, which is bounded by them, and both are skillfully constructed to look both forward and backward: the first effects the change from the natural, real skylark to a being apprehensible only through figurative comparisons that reveal aspects of hidden beauty; the second summarizes part two and carries us over from its comparisons to the third, philosophical part of the poem, which accomplishes the skylark's metamorphosis into a symbol representing the soul, the spirit, of the ideal poet, and the soaring spirit of poetry which is his essence. The subdivisions of this philosophical part ". . . emphasize the symbolic value of the skylark first to the poet in general, and then to the particular poet Shelley." [11]

Indeed, the extraordinary care that Shelley took to prepare the reader for the three main as well as the lesser parts of his poem is revealed in the very first stanza. Here the skylark is both a real bird and a spiritual symbol. Yet we soon perceive that Shelley is going to begin relatively close to the ground with natural particulars. The natural skylark is not of course described. Nevertheless its spiral, evermounting flight is vividly suggested by the lilting rhythm of the line "And singing still dost soar, and soaring ever singest." The verse, as Elizabeth Nitchie has pointed out, overflows its bounds. The image of the "flood of rapture" (l. 65), which is repeated many times in the poem, is reflected in the stanza form. The long fifth line of the stanza, especially, gives the effect of a swift cascade of sound overflowing the rim of the quatrain, for the "profuse strains" cannot be confined within narrow limits. They rush over into the wider space, often with no pause indicated by punctuation, or possible in the reading.

We are next given the setting (the sunset, stanza 3) and its background (purple evening, stanza 4). In addition the similes of these stanzas suggest the ethereal nature of the skylark, for it is like an "unbodied joy" [12] or a "star of Heaven" but dimly seen in daylight. Stanza five, which Mr. T. S. Eliot has perhaps willfully said he does not understand, carries us skillfully on by its metaphor. Like Venus, the morning star whose "intense lamp narrows" until it is hardly seen and is but *felt* still to be in the sky, so is the skylark still heard, though become invisible:

> Keen as are the arrows
> Of that silver sphere,
> Whose intense lamp narrows
> In the white dawn clear
> Until we hardly see—we feel that it is there.[13]

This preparation, moreover, is peculiarly necessary, for Shelley is not going to appeal primarily to our sight, but to our hearing —a departure from Plato's emphasis upon our vision as the faculty through which we best apprehend essential forms and beauty. It may be remarked further that Plato's emphasis upon vision occurs in the very passage which sets forth the figure of the "feathered soul." Hence if Shelley did use the myth, he was doubtless aware of the significance of this change in sensory appeal and developed his metaphors and imagery accordingly. The next stanza, the last in part one, veritably rings with the bird's song:

> All the earth and air
> With thy voice is loud,
> As, when night is bare,
> From one lonely cloud
> The moon rains out her beams, and Heaven is overflowed.[14]

Here, then, is the reversal in order of emphasis designed to reinforce the shift from vision to hearing, for it is now the light which is in the simile. That is, instead of describing the visual, as do the early lines of the third, fourth, and fifth stanzas, the first two lines describe the aural. In succeeding stanzas a consummately handled shift from appeal to one sense to another has prepared us for part two.

The second part (stanzas 7–12) begins with the first of the two transitional stanzas:

> What thou art we know not;
> What is most like thee?
> From rainbow clouds there flow not
> Drops so bright to see
> As from thy presence showers a rain of melody.

Most striking here is the coalescence of the appeals to our sense perceptions. In the previous stanza the moon has rained

out her beams from a cloud to overflow Heaven with light.
Here, however, the liquid notes of the skylark showering a rain
of music are like bright drops seen descending from a rainbow
cloud. The suggestion of the colors of the spectrum, of the
brilliant refraction of the raindrops, and the organic inclusion
of these elements in the metaphor "rain of melody" produce
a coalescent imagery of the highest order. Without mixing his
sense references Shelley works his imagery forward from his
comparison into the active word *showers*. Sound, color, light,
all are blended into one phrase. We are now fully prepared
for the similes describing the skylark, the answers to the poet's
rhetorical question "What is most like thee?"

The first reply compares the skylark to the Poet, who, if
he is "rightly mad" (Plato's phrase) like the skylark itself in
stanza one, sings "hymns unbidden" from the divine inspiration of "unpremeditated art." [15] In this conception of the ideal
poet, who in Shelley's figure is hidden "In the light of thought,"
just as the bird is unseen in its airy spiral upward, is to be perceived the core of his moral philosophy. For through his imagination the poet becomes "the great instrument of moral
good," [16] a disseminator of love, "that powerful attraction
towards all that we conceive, or fear, or hope beyond ourselves,
when we find within our own thoughts the chasm of an in-
sufficient void, and seek to awaken in all things that are, a
community with what we experience within ourselves." (*On
Love*)

The "maiden . . . / Soothing her love-laden / Soul in secret hour / With music sweet as love" (stanza 9) arouses two
trains of reflection: first, that the arts of poetry and music were
to Plato, as to all Greeks, practically one; [17] second, that the
maiden is, figuratively, an aspect of Intellectual Beauty, Love,
the soul of the type-Poet. Thus the skylark's music, which overflows Heaven, is like the maiden's, which "overflows her bower." [18]
Though the reference is hardly more than a hint, in its organic
imagery it is correspondent with the development of the whole
poem so far as the poem relates to Shelley's ideas on Love.

The comparison of the skylark to a glowworm in the grass,[19]
which reminds the admirer of Marvell of "The mower to the
glowworms," was undoubtedly prompted by the fireflies Shelley
saw among the myrtle hedges at Leghorn. External nature is
again used for comparison in the next stanza, where the bird

is compared to a rose. And then in the next, the last stanza of part two, the use of simile is abandoned and the previous stanzas unified. In *showers* we are reminded of the same word in the first stanza of this second part. Here also Shelley creates organically, for the showers *sound* on the grass that is twinkling with the phosphorescent fireflies, and the flowers, in contrast to the rose with its sweet odor [20] in the stanza before, are brightly awakened by the refreshing rain. Finally, the previous images, though there seems to be no necessary order in their arrangement, are summed up in the word *All* of the last two lines:

> All that ever was
> Joyous, and clear, and fresh, thy music doth surpass.

In their figures the Poet, maiden, glowworm, and rose are hidden beauty, and since to Shelley beauty was an aspect of Love, concealment becomes the mode of its suggestion. This motif is implicit, to be sure, yet that makes no less effective the use of hidden beauty as a preparation for part three, for which we are now ready.[21]

"I have never heard," says Shelley of the skylark in the first stanza of the last part,

> Praise of love or wine
> That panted forth a rapture so divine.

This, I believe, harks back to Plato's *Symposium*, the subject of which is Love, the occasion a feast at which the wine is partly symbolical.[22] In the succeeding stanzas the superiority of inspiration to artistry is again indicated in the comparison of the divine notes of the skylark to such lesser music, "wherein we feel there is some hidden want," as a marriage chorus or mere chant of triumph. Moreover, the objects that evoke the bird's song (stanza 15) give pause for question; and unlike man, says Shelley, the bird loves its own kind and knows no pain. It would seem that the contrast is to his own worldly tribulations in 1820, bound down as he is in the earthly prison-house of his mortal form, as it is also in the next stanza, where the skylark's spirit is said to be free of weariness (*languor*) and annoyance. Nor is the skylark's ethereal spirit subject to the satiety of earthly love as is the mortal poet, who must suffer from the soul's mixture of earthly and heavenly love, knowing not the pure perfection of the beauteous forms gazed upon by nonmortals whose souls are fully winged.

In stanza seventeen the poem reaches its climax. The apotheosis of the skylark becomes complete:

> Waking or asleep,
>   Thou of death must deem [23]
> Things more true and deep
>   Than we mortals dream,
> Or how could thy notes flow in such a crystal stream?

In the mythopoeic sense the skylark is now a symbol of spirit and as if it were a fully winged soul must be able to see behind the veil that prevents mortals from apprehending pure form. Man comes into the world "trailing clouds of glory"; but his recollections are a dim, shadowy memory. Moreover, he yearns for life-in-death, to see what the idealized skylark can see. Using Plato's poetic fable, Shelley has made the skylark a symbol of exultation and spiritual desire. Benjamin Kurtz concludes that the poem here ascends a climax to a synthesis of life-in-death, to the same "true and deep" intuition that "The Cloud" attains in its culmination, "I change, but I cannot die." [24] But our realization is not purely joyous, for

> We look before and after,
>   And pine for what is not:
> Our sincerest laughter
>   With some pain is fraught,
> Our sweetest songs are those that tell of saddest thought.

Significantly, the first line of this stanza is an echo of a phrase in the fragment "on Life" (1819?).[25] There Shelley asks,

> For what are we? Whence do we come? and whither do we go? Is birth the commencement, is death the conclusion of our being? What is birth and death?

> The most refined abstractions of logic conduct to a view of life, which, though startling to the apprehension, is, in fact, that which the habitual sense of its repeated combinations has extinguished in us. It strips, as it were, the painted curtain from this scene of things. I confess that I am one of those who am unable to refuse my assent to the conclusions of those philosophers who assert that nothing exists but as it is perceived.

> It is a decision against which all our persuasions struggle, and we must be long convicted before we can be convinced that the solid universe of external things is "such stuff as dreams are made of [sic.]." The shocking absurdities of the popular philosophy of mind and matter, its fatal consequences in

morals, and their violent dogmatism concerning the source of all things, had early conducted me to materialism. This materialism is a seducing system to young and superficial minds. It allows its disciples to talk, and dispenses them from thinking. But I was discontented with such a view of things as it afforded; man is a being of high aspirations, "looking both before and after," whose "thoughts wander through eternity," disclaiming alliance with transience and decay; incapable of imagining to himself annihilation; existing but in the future and the past; being, not what he is, but what he has been and shall be. Whatever may be his true and final destination, there is a spirit within him at enmity with nothingness and dissolution. This is the character of all life and being.

That man's "thoughts wander through eternity" is from Belial's harangue in *Paradise Lost* (II, 148). The previous phrase is from Hamlet:

> Sure, he that made us with such large discourse,
> Looking both before and after, gave us not
> That capability and god-like reason
> To fust in us unus'd.

> (IV, iv, 37)

But Shelley's use in the "Skylark" of "large discourse [i.e., reasoning power] looking both before and after" undoubtedly goes back not only to Shakespeare but also to the foregoing argument in which man is considered "not what he is, but what he has been and shall be." Thus the central mood of yearning aspiration in the poem is fulfilled in the joy of the ideal bird. Shelley is saying that we are mortals, with the capacity, to be sure, which the bird does not have, of looking before and after, but without the ability of the bird or of the winged soul to fly straight to heaven. We merely pine for it, for what is not, and consequently sorrow and joy are blended in our human song. This paradox of pain and sadness in human pleasure he discusses in *A Defence of Poetry*:

> . . . from an inexplicable defect of harmony in the constitution of human nature, the pain of the inferior is frequently connected with the pleasures of the superior portions of our being. Sorrow, terror, anguish, despair itself, are often the chosen expressions of an approximation to the highest good. Our sympathy in tragic fiction depends on this principle; tragedy delights by affording a shadow of the pleasure which exists in pain. This is the source also of the melancholy which is inseparable from the sweetest melody. The pleasure that is in sorrow is sweeter than the pleasure of pleasure itself. And

hence the saying, "It is better to go to the house of mourning, than to the house of mirth." Not that this highest species of pleasure is necessarily linked with pain. The delight of love and friendship, the ecstasy of the admiration of nature, the joy of the perception and still more of the creation of poetry, is often wholly unalloyed.

The production and assurance of pleasure in this highest sense is true utility. Those who produce and preserve this pleasure are poets or poetical philosophers.

Hence the "Skylark" reflects Shelley's keen awareness of the mixture of his personal sorrows and his yearning for the pure joy of imagination in its most exalted mood. This I think he makes clear in the next stanza:

> Yet if we could scorn
>   Hate, and pride, and fear;
> If we were things born
>   Not to shed a tear,
> I know not how thy joy we ever should come near.

Of it Mr. Ellsworth Barnard says,

> The meaning . . . is somewhat obscure. Shelley may mean that even if man were not subdued by suffering, he still, in the happiest state conceivable, could not come near perfect joy of the skylark; or he may mean that by virtue of that very suffering man becomes able to experience a joy that *does* come near the skylark's.[26]

Perhaps the obscurity can be resolved by remembering what Blake said, that if it were not true that

> Joy and woe are woven fine,
> A clothing for the soul divine,

we could not even approach the joy of the aspiring soul, we should have no comprehension of it. There is something of a paradox, but that is not to be wondered at, for Shelley pictured man in the millennium as not free from, though master over, "labor and pain and grief":

> Passionless? no: yet free from guilt or pain,
> Which were, for his will made, or suffered them,
> Nor yet exempt, though ruling them like slaves,
> From chance, and death, and mutability,
> The clogs of that which else might oversoar
> The loftiest star of unascended heaven. . . .
>
> (*Prometheus Unbound*, III, 198–203)

Again man's longing for the perfection of the skylark-poet is emphasized in the next stanza, where Shelley suggests that the skylark's skill makes it the ideal for a poet to follow: neither the loveliest music nor the finest poetry can equal the mad ecstasy of the songbird. And finally in the last stanza Shelley appeals to the skylark for personal inspiration of divine madness. Like Coleridge in the corresponding lines of "Kubla Khan," he is drawing upon the ancient concept of *furor poeticus*.[27] The poem has come full turn, for here too is the "unpremeditated art" of the first stanza. The concluding line emphasizes once more the moral function of the poet—here Shelley himself—who, if only he were as divinely joyous (*blithe*) as the skylark, would gain the ear of the world.

Once more may I draw upon Newman I. White, who says:

> In the *Ode to the West Wind* Shelley the prophet of reform seeks to become one in spirit with the destroying and preserving west wind; in *To a Skylark* the lyric side of his genius seeks to become similarly identified with the spirit of "unbodied joy." Together they represent almost perfectly the two aspects of Shelley's poetry. Both overflow from the optimism of the third act of *Prometheus Unbound*, modified by personal sorrows and disillusion. Both reveal Shelley's intense desire that the world should listen to him. The last line of the latter (emphasizing the "then" and "now") unconsciously reveals that the antagonism of the general public caused Shelley more depression than his letters admit.[28]

The "Ode to the West Wind" may perhaps be technically superior in its threefold structure and unique versification to the "Skylark." Nevertheless the latter poem reveals extraordinary skill in the handling of its imagery and in its structural and symbolic development, for its meaning gives it an underlying, coherent unity. Its internal consistency thus becomes its own evidence, external support to which is given by the Platonic patterns of so much of Shelley's verse and prose and by his own life in 1820.

Notes

1. By Lane Cooper in *Two Views of Education* (New Haven, 1922), p. 158, and in *Plato* (New York, 1938), p. 6. He says in the latter volume:

> The Platonic order is rigorous. Shelley glories in a democratic disorder of similitudes starting with a manifest untruth: "Bird thou never wert." His lark is a spirit; it is like a poet, a maiden, a glow-worm.

Further his doctrine of "unpremeditated art" confutes itself by its conscious echo of Milton, who also knows and uses this interesting rhetorical commonplace.

Mr. Cooper is following Benjamin Jowett here (*The Dialogues of Plato*, tr. Jowett, 1892, l. 472). In his adverse criticisms of Shelley's good sense and technique (*Two Views*, pp. 159–60) Mr. Cooper is following J. M. Robertson (*New Essays towards a Critical Method*, 1897, pp. 210–22). May I add, however, that my disagreement with Mr. Cooper over the merits of Shelley's poem is entirely apart from my admiration of his translations of Plato, parts of which appear below. Here also I gratefully acknowledge the help given me in this paper by Newman I. White and Elizabeth Nitchie.

2. Newman I. White, *Shelley* (New York, 1940), II, 594, n. 54, says,

In an article entitled "Probable Dates of Composition of Shelley's 'Letter to Maria Gisborne' and 'To a Skylark,'" in *Studies in Philology*, XXXVI (July, 1939), 524–28, I have shown from the chronology of letters, journals, and the *Prometheus Unbound* volume that the "Letter" was in all probability written June 15 and "To a Skylark" June 22 or soon afterwards.

3. As quoted by G. E. Woodberry, *The Complete Poetical Works of Percy Bysshe Shelley* (Cambridge, Mass., 1892), Vol. III, Part 2, p. 515. Mrs. Shelley also says:

. . . the *Ode to the Skylark*, and *The Cloud* . . . in the opinion of many critics, bear a purer poetical stamp than any other of his productions. They were written as his mind prompted, listening to the carolling of the bird, aloft in the azure sky of Italy, or marking the cloud as it sped across the heavens, while he floated in his boat on the Thames. (So Woodberry, p. 515)

4. Quoted by White, *Shelley*, II, 594, n. 54, from the unpublished journal of John Gisborne formerly in the Ashley Library, now in the British Museum, entry for October 20, 1827.

5. In this discussion I depend upon White, *Shelley*, Ch. XXIV and his *Portrait of Shelley* (New York, 1945), Ch. XXI.

6. I. T. Richards's "A Note on Source Influences in Shelley's *Cloud* and *Skylark*," *PMLA*, L (1935), 562–67, suggests that the "by no means improbable" source of the "Skylark" is "the well-known melodious verses, 'On Paradise Lost,'" by Andrew Marvell. The parallels therein offered, however, could as well be coincidental as necessary.

It is of interest to observe that previous bird poems do not seem to have deeply influenced Shelley. Doubtless he recollected some of them— Shakespeare's "Hark, hark! the lark at heaven's gate," the last lines of his sonnet "When in disgrace with fortune . . . ," or Hogg's "The Skylark," in which the bird is an "Emblem of happiness." Gray's "Ode on the Pleasure's arising from Vicissitude" may likewise have had some influence. At their closest, however, such relationships seem similar to that which Shelley's poem bears to Wordsworth's "To the Cuckoo" (1807): ". . . shall I call thee Bird / Or but a wandering Voice? . . . No bird, but an invisible thing, / A voice, a mystery . . . ." See below n. 27 for reference to Wordsworth's "To a Skylark" (1807). In his own turn, Shelley apparently influenced Wordsworth's "To a Skylark" of 1825, and the myrtle hedges and field of skylarks at Casa Ricci in Hardy's little poem, "Shelley's Skylark."

7. See J. A. Notopoulos, "The Dating of Shelley's Notes and Translations from Plato," *Modern Language Review*, XXXIV (1939), 245–48.

8. See Frederick L. Jones, "The Vision Theme in Shelley's *Alastor* and Related Works," *Studies in Philology*, XLIV (1947), 115–16, for excellent proof that *On Love* was written late in 1820 or early in 1821. The exact date of course makes little difference here. J. A. Notopoulos, "The Dating of Shelley's Prose." *PMLA*, LVIII (1943), 491–92, suggests the date 1818–1819. Rossetti's guess of 1815, therefore, seems highly unlikely.

9. These quotations and the ones which follow are from Cooper's *Plato*, pp. 27 ff.

10. *Ibid.*, p. 77. Apparently the origins of the little bird as a symbol of the soul are hidden in the dim mists of antiquity. During the Renaissance, however, painters of the Madonna and Child regularly included the bird-as-symbol in their representations. See Herbert Friedmann, *The Symbolic Goldfinch, Its History and Significance in European Devotional Art*, The Bollingen Series VII (New York, 1946). One of Mr. Friedmann's comments is especially illuminating (p. 7):

> The goldfinch (or other small bird) represents the Soul as opposed to the Body, the spiritual in contrast to the earthly part. The soul being the loftier, more aspiring part was early connected with the idea of being winged and came to be pictorialized in the form of a bird, or at least in a form approximating that of a bird. Such icons appear to derive from the oldest of catacomb decorations, and may even go back to Egyptian hieroglyphics. This is the interpretation stressed by several writers, of whom we may mention in particular Yrojö Hirn, who, in his learned book *The Sacred Shrine*, A Study of the Poetry and Art of the Catholic Church (1912), p. 373, so disposes of the motif of the little bird. St. Ambrose explains the two sparrows of the Gospel as signifying the Body and the Soul "for both are lifted up to God by spiritual wings."

11. Newman I. White, *The Best of Shelley* (New York, 1932), p. 488.

12. Although the Harvard MS clears up the once-disputed emendation of *embodied* for *unbodied*, it may be noted that the latter, correct reading fits perfectly into the interpretation of the poem offered here. Compare Byron's *Manfred*, I, ii, 52–55: "Oh, that I were / The viewless spirit of a lovely sound, / A living voice, a breathing harmony, / A bodiless enjoyment."

13. Mr. Eliot's comment, which appears in his essay on Crashaw in *For Lancelot Andrewes* (New York, 1929), pp. 135–36, is quoted by A. Eiloart, "Shelley's 'Skylark': The 'Silver Sphere,' " *Notes and Queries*, CLXI (1931), 4–6. This article convincingly identifies the *silver sphere* as Venus rather than the moon. Hence some of Empson's interesting remarks on this stanza in *Seven Types of Ambiguity* (London, 1930), pp. 197 ff., are beside the point.

14. Echoes of the first part of Wordsworth's "Ode: Intimations" seem to linger in this and the next stanza. Aside from the obvious Platonic connections between Shelley's and Wordsworth's two poems, are rhythmical and verbal resemblances which, though difficult to anatomize, persistently strike a common chord: "Night is bare" (S) and "the heavens

are bare" (W); "rainbow clouds" and "rainbow" are in both, as is the
moon; and the trimeter of the two poems reinforces the effect of resemblance.

15. The significance of Lane Cooper's comment, previously quoted,
that Shelley's "doctrine of 'unpremeditated art' confutes itself by its
conscious echo of Milton, who also knows and uses this interesting
rhetorical commonplace . . ." is, to say the least, puzzling. Milton's
phrase is in *Paradise Lost*, IX, 24:

> Of My Celestial Patroness, who deigns
> Her nightly visitation unimplor'd
> And dictates to me slumb'ring, or inspires
> Easy my unpremeditated Verse . . .

Though the echo is obvious, I fail to see how Shelley confutes himself,
for Milton here is appealing to Urania, who, he and tradition say, enlightened him in the night when he was composing. Urania's is the
creative inspiration of wisdom, the inner illumination which compensates
him in the darkness of his loss of physical sight. In the Miltonic phrase
Hebraic-Christian and Platonic-Neoplatonic references have complicatedly
fused, whereas Shelley's phrase would seem to imply the contrast already
indicated between mere art and divine inspiration. For Milton, when he
was, apparently, in a state of mental tranquillity, Urania was a direct link,
a source of divine knowledge. Shelley was elevated by joy and divine
madness above the mundane: poetical composition lifted him "above the
stormy mist of sensations" of the ordinary world. (See following comment
on stanza 14 of the "Skylark" and the quotation below from the *Ion*.) For
discussion of Milton's "unpremeditated" first drafts, which in their
method contrast so strongly with Keats's, for example, see John S. Diek-
hoff, "Critical Activity of the Poetic Mind: John Milton," *PMLA*, LV
(1940), 748–72.

16. From *A Defence of Poetry*. Shelley's famous passage at the end of
this essay in which occur the lines "Poets are the unacknowledged legis-
lators of the world," and "the hierophants [Cf. the Greek, meaning "priests
of the Eleusinian mysteries"] of an unapprehended inspiration," is to be
connected with the purely divine soul which "in its totality has the care
of all that is inanimate, and traverses the whole heaven, appearing now in
one shape, now in another; when it is perfect, and fully winged, it soars
on high, and regulates the entire world." *Phaedrus*, Cooper, *Plato*, p. 29.

17. See Cooper, *Plato*, p. xlix. The veiled maiden is of course a frequent appearance in Shelley. See E. W. Marjarum, "The Symbolism of
Shelley's 'To a Skylark,' " *PMLA*, LII (1937), 911–13, who relevantly
discusses the theme, as does F. L. Jones, "The Vision Theme in Shelley's
Alastor and Related Works," *Studies in Philology*, XLIV (1947), 108–
25.

18. In the Harvard MS this line reads "With music which is love. . . ."
Evidently Shelley substituted *sweet as* while he was entering the "Skylark"
in his copybook. The significance of the deletion is that he first identified
literally the maiden's *music* with *love*.

19. Marjarum, *op. cit.*, p. 913, says of this glowworm image that it

> . . . is analogous to the maidens of the other poems, except that
> here the flowers and grass form the veil. It has the same juxtaposition
> of elements as the veiled and luminous maiden of *Alastor*, or *The
> Witch of Atlas*, who took threads of mist and light and starbeams,

> And with these threads a subtle veil she wove—
> A Shadow for the splendour of her love.   (151–52)

If the adjective *aereal* (1. 49) is interpreted to mean ethereal in the sense of celestial, the consistency of the meaning suggested by the imagery here is apparent—the ideal in the actual.

20. Ellsworth Barnard, editor of *Shelley: Selected Poems, Essays, and Letters*, Odyssey Series in Literature (New York, 1944), p. 381, n. to 1. 452 of "Epipsychidion":

> Locock compares Shelley's letter to Peacock, March 23, 1819: "Odour, which . . . produces sensations of voluptuous faintness"; and the letter to Clare, January 16, 1821: "the smell of a flower affects me with violent emotions." Compare also 11. 108–10 of the present poem, *Alastor*, 1. 453 ("a soul-dissolving odour") . . . and Pope's *Essay on Man*, I, 200: "Die of a rose in aromatic pain."

21. Hoxie Neale Fairchild kindly pointed out to me this motif of part two. I have found E. Wayne Marjarum's article "The Symbolism of Shelley's 'To a Skylark'" helpful. He does not, however, find readily apparent a logical unity between the earlier "descriptive" stanzas and the later "reflective" ones. Rather he seeks for the poem "a native unity born of common origin in a unique personality" (p. 913). The thesis of this paper of course is that Shelley's imagery is artistically woven into a carefully developed structural plan, the whole being unified by a (1) natural (2) figuratively compared (3) symbolic skylark which in the poem is correspondent with the winged soul in Plato's myth.

22. See Cooper, *Plato*, p. 212. Shelley translated the *Symposium* in July, 1818. See also below, note to last stanza of the "Skylark."

23. *Deem* here means *think*, evidently.

24. *The Pursuit of Death* (New York, 1933), p. 226.

25. J. A. Notopoulos, "The Dating of Shelley's Prose," pp. 489–91, supports Dowden's conjecture of 1819. However, F. L. Jones, "Shelley's *On Life*," PMLA, LXII (1947) 774, n. 2, agrees with W. M. Rossetti and H. B. Forman that the essay is of 1815–1816.

26. *Shelley: Selected Poems, Essays, and Letters*, p. 322, n. to 1. 91.

27.   Could I revive within me
>   Her symphony and song
>   To such a deep delight 'twould win me
>   That with music loud and long,
>   I would build that dome in air . . .
>   And all should cry, Beware! Beware!
>   His flashing eyes, his floating hair!

That poetic inspiration for Coleridge had its roots in joy, Elisabeth Schneider points out in "The Dream of *Kubla Khan*," PMLA, LX (1945), 784–801, an article deserving of the closest attention. For Shelley, the poet-seer, delight or joy also was essential. No more than Miss Schneider do I wish to labor the obvious. Yet probably the most famous passage of the *vates* with "eye in a fine frenzy rolling," a description in which Plato doubtless borrowed much from accounts of individuals possessed by the god in worshipping Dionysus, suggests its own parallels:

> In like manner the Muse first of all inspires men herself; . . . For all good poets, epic as well as lyric, compose their beautiful poems not by art, but because they are inspired and possessed. And as the

Corybantian revellers when they dance are not in their right mind, so the lyric poets are not in their right mind when they are composing their beautiful strains: but when falling under the power of music and metre they are inspired and possessed; like Bacchic maidens who draw milk and honey from the rivers when they are under the influence of Dionysus but not when they are in their right mind. And the soul of the lyric poet does the same, as they themselves say; for they tell us that they bring songs from honeyed fountains, culling them out of the gardens and dells of the Muses; they, like the bees, winging their way from flower to flower. And this is true. For the poet is a light and winged and holy thing, and there is no invention in him until he has been inspired and is out of his senses, and the mind is no longer in him; when he has not attained to this state, he is powerless and is unable to utter his oracles.

As quoted by Schneider, p. 800, from Jowett's translation of the *Ion, Dialogues of Plato* (Oxford, 1942, 3rd ed.), I, 501–502.

Phaedrus himself was among the speakers of the *Symposium*, a fact which links it to the *Phaedrus*. The doctrine of inspiration and art, openly discussed in the *Phaedrus*, is implicit in the *Symposium*. Both dialogues are on the art of love, whence springs eloquence and poetry. See Cooper, *Plato*, pp. xlvii; 212.

Compare also here Wordsworth's "To a Skylark"; he is addressing the bird: "Where is madness about thee, and joy divine / In that song of thine; / Lift me, guide me high and high / To thy banqueting-place in the sky." Likewise compare Byron's *Childe Harold*, III, xcvii: "Could I embody and unbosom now / That which is most within me. . . ."

28. *The Best of Shelley*, p. 488.

Part Six   Keats

Bernard Blackstone

16·The Mind of Keats in His Art

THAT KEATS'S VALUES were organic and what I have ventured to
call "biological" I have shown in another place;[1] I have no
wish to repeat myself in this paper but anything I now say must
be based on those findings. Keats, insofar as we can speak of his
"philosophy," is an existential thinker in the broadest sense of
the word; truth is no truth unless it is "proved on the pulses."
Meaning is deeply integrated with living; relationship rooted
in family ties and friendly intercourse is the only nexus of those
odd moments of illumination (what Wordsworth called "spots
of time") that come to the artist, or the ordinary man, who has
learned to lean upon his "negative capability," his capacity of
not making up his mind. Here Keats is closer to the social-
minded and skeptical eighteenth century, and above all to
Pope, than he is to the dogmatism of Wordsworth and Shelley.
He is closer too to Byron.

For Keats's is the philosophy of no-philosophy, the doctrine of the undoctrinaire. For him years could never bring
the philosophic mind. Truth is neither an accumulation nor
a progressive understanding; truth opens out from moment to
moment, and what is true today may not be true tomorrow,
and what is true for one man may not be true for another.
The celebrated "Beauty is truth, truth beauty" is not an enigma
or a banality: it is a concentration of a variety of Keats's original
intuitions, placing truth in the same organic framework as the
patterns of the natural order, as the growth and symmetry of
trees or tigers, and with all their capacity for change and decay.

Written especially for this book.

For this reason I have never been able to agree with those who see Keats as a Neoplatonic thinker. That he was deeply influenced by Neoplatonism is evident, and I have elsewhere tried to show that his month at Oxford in the company of Benjamin Bailey was crucial for his development. But all that was earthy, coarse, sensual, and greedy in him (beauty as that which is to be *eaten*) revolted against the abstractions of Plotinus and Porphyry, all that was amoral in him flinched from Plato's ethical dogmatism (he would have echoed Blake's "If morality is religion, then Socrates is the Saviour"). Shelley's devout acceptance of Plato's dual authority was impossible for Keats.

This is not to say that Keats's mind was without its problems. His first recorded letter (in verse, to his brother George, of August 1816) opens with troubled confession of spiritual dereliction; a later verse letter (to Haydon, November 1816) celebrates Wordsworth, Hunt, and Haydon himself as "Great Spirits" who "will give the World another heart / And other Pulses." There is no lack of social concern. That Keats was indeed one of those "to whom the miseries of the world / Are misery, and will not let them rest" (*The Fall of Hyperion*, I, 148–49) is manifest from both prose and poetry. The letters themselves are a paradigm of early nineteenth century sensibility. But Keats was not a reformer as Blake and Shelley were. A letter to Bailey (January 23, 1818) may suggest that for him the moral question, even the question of suffering, was a *superficial* one: we should not ask it if we could go a little deeper:

> One saying of your's I shall never forget—you may not recollect it—it being perhaps said when you were looking on the surface and seeming of Humanity alone, without a thought of the past or the future—or the deeps of good and evil—you were at the moment *estranged from speculation* and I think you have arguments ready for the Man who would utter it to you—this is a formidable preface for a simple thing—merely you said: "Why should Woman suffer?"

In asking "Why should woman suffer?" Bailey had posed a superficial objection to the doctrine of universal good, and Bailey would himself have had arguments ready to refute this objection if it had been made to *him* at a moment when he was not "estranged from speculation," i.e., not in a nonmetaphysical mood. Thus Keats clearly distinguishes the moral or humanitarian from the metaphysical approach, and gives the palm to the latter. Yet with his peculiar honesty he has already considered (in a letter to Bailey of October 1817) the possibility that laziness has crept in, and a shrinking from the contemplation of suffering—perhaps Wordsworth is in the right after all? A recent letter from Bailey had moved him to altruistic feelings:

> . . . and I wish I had a heart always open to such sensations —but there is no altering a Man's nature and mine must be radically wrong for it will lie dormant a whole Month. This leads me to suppose that there are no Men thoroughly wicked —so as never to be self spiritualized into a kind of sublime Misery—but alas! 'tis but for an Hour—he is the only Man "who has kept watch on Man's Mortality"[,] who has philanthropy enough to overcome the disposition to an indolent enjoyment of intellect—who is brave enough to volunteer for uncomfortable hours.

The fact is of course that Keats's life span was far too short for him to develop any consistent and firmly held "philosophy," and still less any ethical system. Like Shelley he plays about with systems and ideas, but unlike Shelley he never gives himself wholeheartedly to any. Shelley's intellectual progress is a saga of devoutly embraced nostra passionately jettisoned for their polar opposites; Keats's is a wavering pattern of delicate adjustments, afterthoughts, and caveats, an almost molelike working underground towards consistency. Yet beneath it all there are foundations (or, better, roots) which are steady enough. If I have mentioned the moral aspect first it is in order to get it out of the way; ethics is always posterior to metaphysics.

With all his admiration of Wordsworth, Keats objected to the preachifying aspect of his poetry. In a letter to Reynolds of 3 February 1818 he asks:

> . . . for the sake of a few fine imaginative or domestic passages,[2] are we to be bullied into a certain Philosophy engendered in the whims of an Egotist—Every man has his speculations, but every man does not brood and peacock over them till he makes a false coinage and deceives himself. Many a man can travel to the very bourne of Heaven, and yet want confidence to put down his half-seeing. Sancho will invent a Journey heavenward as well as any body. We hate poetry that has a palpable design upon us—and if we do not agree, seems to put its hand in its breeches pocket. Poetry should be great and unobtrusive, a thing which enters into one's soul, and

> does not startle it or amaze it with itself, but with its subject.
> —How beautiful are the retired flowers! how would they lose
> their beauty were they to throng into the highway crying out,
> "admire me I am a violet!—dote upon me I am a primrose!"

This tentative approach to *la condition humaine* sets Keats
off not only from Wordsworth but also from all the other great
Romantics except Byron. Speculation, the Keatsian word for
uncommitted metaphysical thinking, is also a Byronic word.
(Perhaps it was because they were so near in many of their
approaches and their findings that Keats [after a hero-worship-
ping early period] attacked the cynicism of *Don Juan*; perhaps
a stifled resentment that Keats had kept his child's heart
touched off Byron's gross attack in the October 1820 letter
to John Murray.) Speculation is the *exercise* of "negative capability": it springs from questioning.

A Question is the best beacon towards a little Speculation
(letter to Bailey of October 1817). It is the free play of imagination (reason in its most exalted mood) around a point of intense human interest. Keats applies the term to ponderings on
immortality (letter to Bailey of November 1817), to *intensity*
of artistic impact [3] (letter of December 22, 1817 to George and
Georgiana Keats) and to the relation between passion and
beauty (letter to Bailey of November 22, 1817). Because this
last is the most crucial of his references, and because it leads
us to the heart of his poetry, we shall do well to linger over it.

This November letter to Bailey has long been recognized
as a *locus criticus* for Keats's view of the imagination. He writes
it midstream of the great creative effort of *Endymion*; something of the passion of that effort spills over into the prose
statement:

> . . . I must say of one thing that has pressed upon me lately
> and increased my Humility and capability of submission and
> that is this truth—Men of Genius are great as certain etherial
> Chemicals operating on the Mass of neutral intellect—but
> they have not any individuality, any determined Character—I
> would call the top and head of those who have a proper self
> Men of Power—

Here we have the first tentative statement of the principle he
was a month later to define as "negative capability." The man
of genius has no "character"; he is a catalyst, a "chameleon
poet," relishing the dark side of things as much as the bright,

for "both end in speculation" (letter to Woodhouse, 27 October 1818). Morality, then, is already on the way out.

But Keats "long[s] to be talking about the imagination":

> I am certain of nothing but of the holiness of the Heart's affections and the truth of Imagination—What the imagination seizes as Beauty must be truth—whether it existed before or not—for I have the same Idea of all our Passions as of Love they are all, in their sublime, creative of essential Beauty. In a Word, you may know my favorite Speculation by my first Book and the little song I sent in my last—which is a representation from the fancy of the probable mode of operating in these matters.

The statement points us forward to the close of the "Grecian Urn" and backward to recently completed stretches of *Endymion*. There is a link with Blake—"every thing possible to be believ'd is an image of truth"; [4] there is a stretching out to Nietzsche's and Lawrence's doctrine of the wisdom of the blood. Passion "in its sublime" is the soil of *essential* beauty; and essential beauty of truth. We think of Blake again: "The road of excess leads to the palace of wisdom." [5] To understand what Keats meant by "essential beauty" we have to know what he meant by *essence:* and that takes us directly to where Keats himself points us, "my first Book and the little song" which is the "Sorrow Song" in Book IV.

The passage from Book I to which he refers comprises lines 777 to 842. We are sure of this not only because of the key word "essence" but also because he quotes the passage a month later in a letter to his publisher (January 30, 1818):

> My dear Taylor,
>   These Lines, as they now stand, about Happiness have rung in my ears like a "chime a mending." See here,
>
>   behold
>
> Wherein Lies happiness Poeona? fold—
> This appears to me the very contrary of blessed. I hope this will appear to you more eligible.
>   Wherein lies Happiness? In that which becks
>   Our ready Minds to fellowship divine;
>   A fellowship with essence, till we shine
>   Full alchymized and free of space. Behold
>   The clear Religion of heaven—fold. &c—

These corrections and additions passed into the text as we now know it. Keats apologizes for "such a preface . . . to the subject"—which must strike Taylor, who is "a consequitive Man, as a thing almost of mere words"—but, Keats assures him,

> when I wrote it it was a regular stepping of the Imagination towards a Truth. My having written that Argument will perhaps be of the greatest Service to me of any thing I ever did. It set before me at once the gradations of Happiness even like a kind of Pleasure Thermometer—and is my first Step towards the chief attempt in the Drama—the playing of different Natures with Joy and Sorrow.

Once again we are struck by the concreteness of Keats's "philosophy"; it springs from "speculation," but is intensely practical in its findings—a guide to here-and-now living and, from the artist's point of view, not fully real until it can be embodied in the human give-and-take of the drama.

The passage is too long to quote in its entirety. Happiness, which Keats sees with Pope as "our being's end and aim," [6] is to be sought in "fellowship with essence." And how is such a fellowship to be attained? By living life from its center, by burning with Pater's "hard gem-like flame," by living in the past as freely as in the present, in the distant as wholly as in the near: in short, by dropping the barriers, the "mind-forged manacles," [7] which hold us back from pure empathy, from the "in-feeling" with all that is. If Keats were alive today he would recognize in the modern craze for Zen (or what the West imagines to be Zen) an exacerbation of his own urge in *Endymion*; exacerbation, because science, while giving us almost unlimited control over our nonhuman environment, has alienated us almost irreparably from any creative relationship with it. It is this creative relationship that Keats is after in *Endymion*, and really the crux of his philosophy lies in this single question: How is man, through *the representative man*, the poet, to regain his lost identity with the All? This is a theme that resounds in his letters to Bailey, and which is presented, in a rather naively "Hermetic" form, in "The Poet." [8] The "essence" with which man must be in fellowship, if he is to be happy, is the spark of life itself (hence the reference to alchemy), to be recognized as intensely in Mrs. Reynold's cat as in the bright star,[9] to be sought as ardently in savoring a cup of claret as in listening to the sea's music.[10] Again we are reminded of Pater and Wilde. They derive from this aspect of Keats, but shirk his massive commitment to reality. The warmth of relationship is absent from their praises of the flame and the rose; Keats would share what they would hoard in ivory tower or seraglio. These are men without brother George or sister-in-law Georgiana, and well satisfied with their lack. They are also, in St. Paul's phrase, "without God in the world."

Let us continue with Keats's argument. As instances of "the clear religion of heaven," which is "a fellowship with essence," he gives us a well-spaced list: the touch of a rose leaf, the wind's music, old ditties and battle songs.

> Feel we these things?—that moment have we stept
> Into a sort of oneness, and our state
> Is like a floating spirit's.

But there are experiences beyond these. Keats would not be Keats if he did not go on from the solitary to the companionable. Love and friendship are approaches to essence richer and deeper than the data of sense, though rooted in sense; love in particular has an influence which

> Thrown in our eyes, genders a novel sense,
> At which we start and fret; till in the end,
> Melting into its radiance, we blend,
> Mingle, and so become a part of it . . .

The terms are firmer, maturer, than anything Wordsworth or Coleridge would have given us in a like context. All these poets were inhibited and thrown off balance by want of a sexual experience which had come as by right to Shakespeare and Donne and was as by right abjured by Herbert and Milton. Shelley, however maritally precocious, is in as bad a case. Keats's fantasies, though verbally more outrageous,[11] have a touch of salt which may come from his medical experience, his native good sense or his eclectic reading.[12] That none of these palliatives could stand up against Fanny Brawne need cause us no surprise.

The "novel sense" bestowed on the lover is a total function embracing body, soul, and spirit (or whatever other division we or the poet may adopt for the moment) and through its exercise "Life's self is nourish'd by its proper pith"—a dramatic phrase not easily explicable but clearly restressing the preoccupation with "essence." The search appears to be for some experience, or perhaps some technique of dealing with experience (again we are reminded of Zen), which will equip us to live our life from its existential center. The famous phrase in the November 22, 1817 letter to Bailey—"O for a Life of Sensations rather than of Thoughts!"—is a plea not for hedonism but for the direct contact with reality, the living at the fingertips of the senses, which "thought" (discursive thinking, concepts, verbal counters for the pure gold of immediately sensed experience) deflects us from. Keats is not unique here: the return to immediacy is part of the Romantic platform. Coleridge's reference to the "film of selfish solicitude" (in more modern terms, of egocentric anxiety),[13] Blake's sustained assault on "the selfish center," Shelley's choice and celebration of a life of insecurity—all these manifest the Romantic bid to jolt the early nineteenth century out of the complacency which had landed it in the slough of "living and partly living."

But Keats *is* unique in the drive and direction of his assault. He had not (and knew he had not) the intellectual equipment which made it possible for Coleridge and Shelley and Byron [14] to summon Plato and Porphyry, the Fathers and Doctors and the Cambridge Platonists to their aid in the fight against unthinking conformism. But he *had* (and knew he had) a native equipment of tingling senses and supercharged perception (boosted, maybe, by the fever of his hereditary disease) which put him streets ahead of his more academic confreres in the quest for "the Real." The evidence of his letters shows that he was anxious to fill up the gaps imposed by defective schooling, but he was conscious enough of his own powers, of their scope and intensity, to know that reading could not add to, though it might serve to elucidate and order, the intuitions granted in the free play of what he and Coleridge called "imagination."

Yet here too danger lay. If, as I believe is almost certain, Thomas Taylor's translation of *Parmenides* lay open to Keats's eye on Bailey's shelves at Oxford in that seminal month of 1817, he could not fail to be struck by this admonitory paragraph from the Introduction:

> But if we are desirous, after having bid adieu to corporeal vision, and the fascinating but delusive forms of the phantasy, which, Calypso-like, detain us in exile from our father's land; and after having through a long and laborious dialectic wandering gained our paternal port, and purified ourselves from the baneful rout of the passions, those domestic foes of the soul; if after all this we are desirous of gaining a glimpse of the

surpassing simplicity and ineffable union of this occult and
astonishing light, we must crowd all our conceptions together
into the most profound indivisibility, and, opening the greatest eye of the soul, entreat this all-comprehending deity to
approach: for them, preceded by unadorned Beauty, silently
walking on the extremities of her shining feet, he will suddenly
from his awful sanctuary rise to our view.

Keats visited Bailey in September; it was not until the end of
November that the draft of *Endymion* was completed, and not
until January 1818 that it was sent to press. We know that the
interval was one of almost feverish corrections and additions.
Bailey's conversation, and the Platonic ideas to which he introduced Keats, had their share in all this. If we accept the conventional (and rather too crude) interpretation of *Endymion*
as an allegory of the quest for ideal Beauty, it is easy to see how
Plato's distinction between the two Aphrodites, Pandemos and
Urania, struck and shook Keats; how the Platonic image of life
as a quest jibed with the already determined pattern of *Endymion*, yet threw it slightly askew, so that later critics have felt
a trepidation in the last two books, as if Keats were readjusting
his ideas; how, finally, the consummation so devoutly wished
in the opening books as a species of Hampstead harem becomes,
in the event, more of a university extension lecture or spiritual
picnic (lines 991–96) to which external students might be
readily admitted.

Love, beauty, wisdom—Keats's thought, early and late,
revolves about these three centers (which usurp, for him, the
place of the traditional triad of goodness, truth, and beauty).
His aim is their reconciliation—not simply in the abstract, but
within the pattern of everyday living. He seeks a unity of experience abjured by Byron (for whom life and thought were a
kaleidoscope of fleeting impressions) and achieved by Wordsworth only through a severe restriction of the free play of impulse and experience. In this, again, he is closer to Blake than
to any other of his contemporaries; but he had not the advantage, or disadvantage, of Blake's "orthodoxy," or conformity
with the metaphysical norm represented in the West by Christianity and in the East by Vedanta. "The philosophy of the
East taught the first principles of human perception," Blake
had said—and it is through perception, or "sensation" (which
we have shown to mean direct sensuous contact, undiluted by
concepts) that Keats too would approach reality. Like Blake

(though without Blake's tremendous *balance*—which, ironically, earned him the reputation of insanity in his own day, like the seer in the country of the blind) he fixes on love as the center of his triad. Love, he tells us (in this same *Endymion* passage) "genders a new sense": and Keats means by this, quite literally, a sense or organ of perception additional to the usual five. Love, again, upsets our scale of values; we see the paltriness of ambition. And, finally, love introduces us to an experience of empathy which is active rather than passive. Through the experience of love we not only share in the pulse of the universe, of life in its "essence," but we contribute to that pulse: the center of experience is also the center of dynamism:

> Just so may love, although 'tis understood
> The mere commingling of passionate breath,
> Produces more than our searching witnesseth:
> What I know not: but who, of men, can tell
> That flowers would bloom, or that green fruit would swell
> To melting pulp, that fish would have bright mail,
> The earth its dower of river, wood, and vale,
> The meadows runnels, runnels pebble-stones,
> The seed its harvest, or the lute its tones,
> Tones ravishment, or ravishment its sweet,
> If human souls did never kiss and greet?

Despite the imperfections of this passage (the penultimate line is nonsense, since the first use of "ravishment" includes the "sweet" of the second), and despite its logical self-cancelling-out (of course none of these events could occur—*esse est percipi* —if the human race committed suicide) its impact is far from negligible; one is uneasily conscious that the Hampstead surgeon's apprentice is raising issues best left to Central Africa ethnologists or to Professor C. G. Jung.

The Romantics learned from the speculative historians of myth [15] that they were not isolated in time. From the myth itself they learned that they were not isolated in space. The myth enforced on the dramatic plane lessons they had learned from the Hermetic writers. Plato, Plotinus, Hermes Trismegistus, and Cornelius Agrippa talked of the web of being woven, not blindly, between sun, moon, and planets, between earth, air, water, and fire, between the animal, vegetable, and mineral kingdoms, and between the worlds of nature and supernature. In this web of correspondences man is the dynamic center, as certain plates in Agrippa's *Occult Philosophy* abundantly show.

The Romantic poets moved out of the world of the coffee-house, the salon, the study, the garden—outside the world of the Cowperian Sunday morning ramble during which the wise and Christian poet walked "between the various ranks of varied green" ignorant of their names and natures, viewing these "hedgerow beauties numberless" as moral emblems or gay decoration—into a sphere of relationships and correspondences, of "signatures" and analogies, in which

> The starres have us to bed;
> Night drawes the curtain, which the sunne withdrawes;
> Musick and light attend our head.
> All things unto our flesh are kinde
> In their descent and being; to our minde
> In their ascent and cause.

In such a world man need no longer feel himself isolated (the long nightmare of the eighteenth century, which drove Smart and Collins and Cowper mad):

> For Man is ev'ry thing,
> And more: He is a tree, yet bears more fruit;
> A beast, yet is, or should be more:
> Reason and speech we onely bring.
> Parrats may thank us, if they are not mute,
> They go upon the score.
>
> Man is all symmetrie,
> Full of proportions, one limbe to another,
> And all to all the world besides:
> Each part may call the farthest, brother:
> For head with foot hath private amitie,
> And both with moons and tides.[16]

Endymion is precisely a poem of this "symmetry," the "fearful symmetry" of Blake's tyger which draws its awesomeness from its creation and its locus, its framing under God's hand and its exquisite aptness to the human totality, the universe viewed humanwise under the poet's eye. The song and dance which open *Endymion* are reflections, in the mythical mirror, of the first day of creation, when the morning stars sang together, and all the sons of God shouted for joy. Keats came late to Milton (if we can talk of "early" and "late" in a life so woefully foreshortened) but it is not difficult to see that *Endymion* is a lyrical *Paradise Lost* and *Regained*. To this extent at least Keats is the link between Milton and Shakespeare, that the "metaphysical" in Milton and the "human" in Shakespeare met in him, clashed, and (long before the clash was recognized) evolved amalgams of astonishing range and depth.

The "Sorrow Song" to which Keats also refers in his crucial letter to Bailey is almost grotesquely "Hermetic." If it has not appeared so hitherto it is because most commentators on Keats have been content to admire his verbal felicities (he is in actual fact one of the clumsiest of English poets in huge stretches of his output) and quietly ignore what he is trying to say. The "Sorrow Song" is a compressed version of the "Happiness" passage we have just considered, and presents what Blake would have called the "contrary" of that argument (we remember Keats's definition of the drama as "the Playing of different Natures with Joy and Sorrow") translated into lyrical terms— like one of Shakespeare's clowns' songs. A pithy reappraisal. By Book IV Keats (he is learning all the time) has had time to enlarge his experience. The "Sorrow Song" presents us with the theme of metamorphosis.

There is something very Celtic about Keats's poetry. Yeats and Ellis, who did their best to prove Blake an Irishman, would have been better employed in making Keats out to be Welsh. His idea of the poet is bardic. Take his constant celebration of great men and national heroes—a recognized function of the bard. Take his hatred, at the same time, of war: the Druids, as Davies tells us, were eminently peaceloving.[17] Add his love of "riddling," a unique facet of his poetry. Has it ever been noticed how many of his lines and paragraphs end with a question mark? It is not simply that his mind *was* questioning, non-assertive, content with "half-seeings." He delights to pose enigmas, to speak darkly. His verse is by no means easy. Most pervasive, most Celtic, and most Keatsian, is the theme of metamorphosis. A theme familiar to us from our childhood (it is the stock-in-trade of most fairy tales) it runs through the whole corpus of myth and legend. In this realm everything keeps changing into something else with a vim and gusto bewildering to the Anglo-Saxon mind; but the changes are not fortuitous. There is a purpose and a progression. The journey of the psyche through the forms leads into the world of the Mysteries. And here, too, we shall find Keats at home.

There are other correspondences. In tracing his own transformation

When through the old oak forest I have gone

in the sonnet "On Sitting Down to Read *King Lear* Once Again" he is specifically identifying himself with the Druid or *derwydd*, the oak-seer.[18] When he uses the mistletoe bough in *Endymion* for purposes of transmutation, and when he writes in *Hyperion* of "tall oaks, those green-robed senators of mighty woods," he is again drawing on Davies. Mistletoe was the Druidic plant, the Druids wore green, and their dignity was in fact that of senators.

The theme of metempsychosis is central in Keats. We find it in his earliest writing, and in a host of shapes, serious and whimsical. His "Nebuchadnezzar's Dream" is dated "circa 1817" by Garrod; we have a still earlier date, November 1815, for the verse epistle "To George Felton Mathew," which traces that very indifferent poet's progress through the forms of vegetable, fish, bird, and man. The Circe episode dominates Book IV of *Endymion*. We perceive that there are evil transformations as well as good ones (*Lamia* and "La Belle Dame Sans Merci" are examples).

The key word is "intensity." When any situation reaches boiling point, as it were, it suffers a dialectical change, an "enantiodromia": water becomes steam. "The excellence of every Art is its intensity, capable of making all disagreeables evaporate, from their being in close relationship with Beauty and Truth," he writes in a letter of December 1817. "Intensity" produces a kind of crystallization, often by means of a catalysis which brings about a fusion, as in his ode "On Seeing a Lock of Milton's Hair." [19] "Ailsa Crag" and the "Grecian Urn" provide better known examples. "I know not your many havens of intenseness," he writes in a letter to Haydon of 8 April 1818, but "when a Schoolboy the abstract idea I had of an heroic painting—was what I cannot describe I saw it somewhat sideways large prominent round and colour'd with magnificence— somewhat like the feel I have of Anthony and Cleopatra. Or of Alcibiades, leaning on his Crimson Couch in his Galley, his broad shoulders imperceptibly heaving with the Sea. . . ." Sensation is again the shorthand for thought; Keats is conveying his ideas through ideograms. At the same time he is indicating how the visual idea can pass over into the thought which is more than a thought; painting, at its greatest, becomes metaphysics. So Aldous Huxley describes the plays of Shakespeare (the least "metaphysical" of artists) as adding up to a vast *Summa*.

But the *Summa* is unsystematic. Things cohere, but with an alogical, tentative magnetism or polar attraction. Participants in the cosmic dance often change partners. Art exists to trace these fluctuations as well as to probe to the basic pattern which underlies them. Keats admires Shakespeare because, above all other poets, he can hold the One and the Many, the permanent and the fleeting, within the flexible framework of his art; and it all comes without effort. "I ne[v]er found so many beauties in the Sonnets—they seem to be full of fine things said unintentionally—in the intensity of working out conceits," he writes to Reynolds on 22 November 1817. This effortless hitting upon the truth, and the congruence of one truth with another (he calls it "dovetailing"), is a faculty he finds in himself when his perceptive powers are stretched to their uttermost.

> I had not a dispute but a disquisition with Dilke, on various subjects; several things dovetailed in my mind, and at once it struck me what quality went to form a Man of Achievement especially in Literature and which Shakespeare possessed so enormously—I mean *Negative Capability*, that is[,] when a man is capable of being in uncertainties, Mysteries, doubts, without any irritable reaching after facts and reason—Coleridge, for instance, would let go by a fine isolated verisimilitude caught from the Penetralium of mystery, from being incapable of remaining Content with half knowledge.[20]

Coleridge is a systematizer; he is not content with glimpses of truth, momentary illuminations: he is even prepared to reject any intuition which will not fit into a pattern of received ideas. But for Keats the intuitions, fleeting and contradictory as they may be, are the very stuff of wisdom.

How do such intuitions come? We may end this enquiry, which has, alas! led us little further than to the point where we can say that such "philosophy" as we find in Keats consists of a series of half-seeings and guesses revolving round the poles of Beauty, Love, and Wisdom, by deciding (and this at least should be possible from the evidence of the poems and the letters and the testimony of friends) what were the conditions, interior and exterior, under which Keats most favorably achieved his insights. The passage quoted above shows that they could come in the rough and tumble of debate, and again we are reminded that of all the Romantics Keats was the most sociable, the nearest, we may say, to Dr. Johnson and the circle of the coffeehouse. As his disease grew upon him, with its resultant hypersensitivy, he withdrew; in one terrible phrase, towards the close of his life, he laments that he should be "forc'd to walk through the City and hate as I walk." But this is far from his normal response to the claims of society. His thinking grew and flourished within the pattern of friendship. Contemplation proceeded *pari passu* with action. And even, according to Woodhouse's testimony,[21] *pari passu* with composition.

> He has repeatedly said in conversation that he never sits down to write unless he is full of ideas. . . . He is impatient of correcting, and says he would rather burn the piece in question and write another or something else—"My judgment (he says) is as active while I am actually writing as my imagination. *In fact all my faculties are strongly excited, and in their full play*[22] —And shall I afterwards, when my imagination is idle, and the heat in which I wrote has gone off, and sit down coldly to criticize, when in Possession of only one faculty, what I have written when almost inspired?"

Here again we have the picture of the whole man *writing*, and consciously writing, from his center and with the ensemble of his faculties; as he *thought* and *felt*, with like consciousness, in the dynamic interplay of the social circle.

Yet there is no truth without its opposite; and no one knew better than Keats that frantic need for withdrawal that descends upon the creative mind at unpredictable intervals. We have already seen something of his doctrine of "identity."[23] The poet "has no identity" because he is all the time identifying himself with the objects of his contemplation; yet there are "unpleasant human identities" which clash if not with the poet's own identity yet with the sensitive creative vacuum which serves him for one;[24] and the "identity" even of a beloved brother can become unbearable.[25] The letter to George and Georgiana of 14 February – 3 May 1819 brings three pragmatic terms together, and points forward to one of the most crucial (in this connection) of the odes.

> An indolent day—fill'd with speculations even of an unpleasant colour—is bearable and even pleasant alone . . . but to have nothing to do, and to be surrounded with unpleasant human identities . . . is a capital punishment of a capital crime. . . .

The "Ode on Indolence" which was the direct outcome of this passage in the journal-letter leads us into the heart of

Keats's doctrine of creative leisure. The significant epigraph "They toil not, neither do they spin" pinpoints its theme. An aspiration to be like "the retired flowers" had already been expressed; without this reference we might have missed its closeness to the divine message, as so much that is Christian in Keats *is* missed by his commentators. (There is more real Christianity in Keats, even in his callowest Huntian phase, than in all Wordsworth's *Ecclesiastical Sonnets*.) What Keats is saying through his epigraph (and it's almost a cryptogram, bearing in mind the readers he might expect) is this: "Look below the surface of what may seem an idle poem and glimpse the forces at work; *connect* John Keats lazing on a Hampstead lawn with a moment of truth achieved some two centuries ago on a Palestine hillside; connect, once again, *that* moment of truth with the whole majestic movement of Greek art and thought expressed in my poem by the figured urn—and then judge my poem."

It is Keats's most difficult and most complex poem; and it has never had the attention it deserves. "You will judge of my 1819 temper," he writes to Miss Jeffrey (June 9, 1819) "when I tell you that the thing I have most enjoyed this year has been writing an ode to Indolence." Why should he "enjoy" it so much, in this most crucial year of his life? Simply because, like a certain passage in *Endymion* in another crucial year, it stands to him as a "thermometer" distinguishing the gradations of that truth which is also the beautiful. But now it isn't simply a *pleasure* thermometer: the three mysterious figures come to reinforce the message of insight through suffering which had already been meditated in the Cave of Quietude of *Endymion* Book IV:

> Enter none
> Who strive therefore: on the sudden it is won.
> Just when the sufferer begins to burn,
> Then it is free to him; and from an urn,
> Still fed by melting ice, he takes a draught—
> Young Semele such richness never quaft
> In her maternal longing! Happy gloom!
> Dark Paradise! where pale becomes the bloom
> Of health by due; where silence dreariest
> Is most articulate; where hopes infest;
> Where those eyes are the brightest far that keep
> Their lids shut longest in a dreamless sleep.[26]

Once again the theme of *sudden* illumination, of *effortless* insight, is emphasized; together with an insistence on the interplay of the contraries which is Hermetic and Keatsian. The Cave of Quietude is one of those "havens of intenseness" mentioned in the Haydon letter of April 1818; and so is the chequered lawn of "Indolence." A "consequitive" mind like Dilke's or Taylor's [27] reaches its conclusions by stages; a "complex" mind like Bailey's [28] acquires its wisdom by accumulation; but Keats passes "into a sort of oneness" [29] at moments of great "intensity" which come without warning in a condition of "indolence." Indolence, which Keats sometimes calls "abstraction," is a state of perfect freedom from emotional or intellectual or moral commitments, including a lowering of physical vitality—"my pulse grew less and less"—characteristic of trance. Such states came to Keats most easily in solitude and in natural surroundings. There is some evidence that they came to him most frequently at night.

To sum up: What passes for philosophy in Keats is an intense awareness of empathy, of "oneness" with all life (and even, as such poems as "Ailsa Crag" show, with inanimate objects), which is achieved within the creative moment. It does not exclude the processes of reflection, but it cannot be systematized. It does not even exclude the concept of revelation and tradition, as a crucial passage in *Endymion* (II, 727–53) abundantly proves. It does exclude the conventional and the false. One of his letters (to Bailey, 13 March 1818) categorizes "things" as real, semireal, and nothings. Things real are, for instance, the Sun, Moon, and Stars (and, he says, with a whimsical loyalty which tends to obscure his distinction, passages of Shakespeare). Things semireal are love and clouds —things that form and disform and disappear and "require a greeting of the Spirit to make them wholly exist." No-things "are made Great and dignified by an ardent pursuit"—such as poetry. No one knew better than Keats that "things real" are indeed real—we can't get away from them and if we try to they are always there waiting for us with a club when we come back—as we are bound to do. Poetry is the alchemical act, into which the poet puts the whole of himself, and vanishes as an individual; but when the act is over, and the crucible cools, and the poet-magus rakes under the ashes for whatever minute nugget of gold may be the outcome, "the sense of real things comes doubly strong," and he feels himself an outcast, at home neither in the world of real things nor in the world of the forms. No "philosophy" can help him here, for here art is one with sacrifice; and sacrifice joins religion. I was asked by the editor to write a paper on Keats's philosophy; I see that I have written one on Keats's religion.

Notes

1. *The Consecrated Urn* (London, 1959).
2. Note the collocation, which is peculiarly Keatsian: home and imagination, and imagination is rooted in the home. Critics have not sufficiently explored this side of Keats's admiration of Wordsworth.
3. Very close to the Sanskirt *Samvega* or "aesthetic shock" discussed by Ananda K. Coomaraswamy in his *Collected Essays on the Traditional or "Normal" View of Art*, Second Series (*Figures of Speech and Figures of Thought*, London, 1946).
4. "The Marriage of Heaven and Hell."
5. "The Marriage of Heaven and Hell." Both poets are reacting against the eighteenth century doctrine of the mean; Pope's "ruling passion" is not to be shunned but to be cultivated to the limit.
6. Eschewing contemporary cant about duty and the still sad music of humanity (Wordsworth), social service and the fatal grape (Shelley), misery attendant on the curse of genius (Byron), and kindred hoodwinks and eccentricities.
7. W. *Blake*, London.
8. I have been accused (in *The Times* and *The Times Literary Supplement*) of a "blunder" in continuing to ascribe this poem to Keats; in fact, no evidence for its reassessment exists which has not been known to (and rejected by) good judges for many years past.
9. Sonnet, "Cat! who hast pass'd . . ."; sonnet, "Bright Star . . ."
10. See *The Letters of John Keats*, index, under "claret"; sonnet, "It keeps eternal whisperings . . ."
11. E.g., in the "Bright Star" sonnet and the "I cry your mercy" lines.
12. Cf. the reference to Burton's *Anatomy* in the journal-letter of September 17–27, 1819 to his brother and sister-in-law.
13. *Biographia Literaria*, Ch. 14, on the origin of *Lyrical Ballads*.
14. We can have no doubt, from *Manfred*, III, i, 6–18, that Byron enjoyed at least once the experience of union that Plotinus knew three times; the line "It hath enlarged my thoughts with a new sense" may well be the source of Keats's "genders a novel sense." Act II, ii, 89–93 gives an interesting reference to Iamblichus.
15. See *The Consecrated Urn*, Appendix A.
16. George Herbert, "Man."
17. Edward Davies, *Celtic Researches* (1804).
18. Needless perhaps to say, I am taking no responsibility for these etymologies; what matters is how they appeared to Davies and Keats.
19. The last six lines.
20. Letter of December 21, 1817 to George and Thomas Keats.
21. *The Keats Circle*, I.
22. My italics.

3. See above.

24. Forman (ed.), *The Letters of John Keats*, p. 312.

25. *Ibid.*, 215.

26. *Endymion* IV, 531–42. "Pale" must be read as a noun. The whole passage is difficult, and the student should consult J. Middleton Murry's essay, or pp. 183–85 of my *The Consecrated Urn*.

27. *Letter to George & Georgiana Keats*, September 24, 1819; Letter to Taylor, 30 January 1818.

28. *Letter to Bailey*, November 22, 1817.

29. *Endymion*, I, 796.

Stuart M. Sperry, Jr.

17·The Allegory of *Endymion*

MORE THAN ANY OTHER of Keats's longer narrative poems,
Endymion has in recent years been the subject of intensive
critical revaluation and dispute. One hesitates to summarize
familiar history, but it is necessary to recall that until the
last fifteen years or so the allegorical interpretation given the
poem by Sir Sidney Colvin, Robert Bridges, and Ernest de
Selincourt had stood relatively unchallenged since about the
turn of the century. While differing with respect to minor
points of interpretation, these critics were essentially agreed
that the poem should be read as a parable of the poet's longing
for and eventual union with the spirit of ideal beauty. With
regard to structure, they resolved the action of the poem into
a series of gradually higher stages of human development,
beginning with the love of sensuous beauty, leading in time
to humanitarian service and active sympathy for fellowman,
and ending with the recognition that these, rightly perceived,
are one with the ideal.[1] In recent years, however, the traditional reading of the poem has been increasingly challenged.
It is impossible in short space to do justice to the arguments
of such writers as Newell Ford and E. C. Pettet; their attack
has taken a variety of forms, but it is safe to say they have
questioned the whole validity of allegorical interpretation of
the poem.[2] Where older critics had discerned the more or less
orderly development of a theme of poetic growth toward the
ideal, Ford and Pettet see little more (with the exception of a
few isolated passages) than "a straightforward love poem"[3]

Reprinted from *Studies in Romanticism*, II (1962), 38–53. *Studies in
Romanticism* is published by the Graduate School, Boston University.

chiefly informed by Keats's erotic dreams and desires. As a result, the traditional idea of Endymion's quest as an allegory of the poet's search for higher beauty or truth has been made to appear a mere rationalization evolved by critics unwilling or unable to confront the frank expression of Keats's longing for an "everlasting erotism," [4] or more simply the sexual fantasies of a virile young man.

The disagreement between the two viewpoints raises fundamental questions about the poem's structure, theme, and ultimate meaning. Does the work embody a coherent fable expressing certain convictions as to the nature of beauty, truth, and poetic experience; or is it merely a series of elaborate episodes connected by subconscious associations and the thread of a legend? Is there a fundamental continuity of theme or only the narrative framework of a story? Is the poem best understood as a deliberate affirmation of ideals of beauty and truth, or as the product of largely unconscious drives and fantasies? It is unlikely that such questions can be rapidly settled, for finer distinctions and qualifications quickly suggest themselves and assume importance in interpretation. The major differences, however, remain and bear witness to the range of disagreement regarding the nature and significance of the longest of Keats's narrative poems and to the need for re-examining the problems it still presents. Those problems are best taken up, I believe, by considering *Endymion* as a reflection of Keats's concern with visionary experience.

In order to interpret *Endymion* adequately it is necessary to consider it in the light of Keats's early poetry. More than anything else the concerns and preoccupations that fill the first volume of *Poems* (1817) provided the ferment from which the idea for *Endymion* sprang, and they are likely to afford the surest clues for understanding the later work. Of these, none is more evident than Keats's concern with the nature of poetry and imaginative experience, questions, it seems clear from his letters, with which he was still very much preoccupied when he began *Endymion* in the spring of 1817. The most important of the early poems are nothing so much as enthusiastic celebrations of the power of poetry and the imagination to vitalize nature, to create myth, and to infuse human life with new pleasure and meaning. Yet if we scan

the early poems more carefully in search of a coherent idea
of the imagination and its operation, we find little more than
a number of disparate and frequently conflicting tendencies.
There is, first of all, the inclination toward a vague and sketchy
kind of Platonism that seems almost instinctive with Keats.
His perception of life was from the first securely rooted in the
world of sensory impressions. Yet there are also moments
when earth and its reality seem to dissolve in a sense of almost
mystical ecstasy:

> Fair world, adieu!
> Thy dales, and hills, are fading from my view:
> Swiftly I mount, upon wide spreading pinions,
> Far from the narrow bounds of thy dominions.[5]

These lines, and certain other passages like them, express
Keats's early desire for and absorption in a kind of visionary
experience. Yet it would be wrong to give such utterances
anything like the force of a Platonic or Neoplatonic conviction. For one thing the poet's perception at such moments is
much too nebulous and fanciful to correspond to any clear
intuition of "higher reality"—the vision of some knights "in
playful quarrel," a sudden gleam of light, the music of a
"faint-heard hymning." [6] Moreover, the whole experience
shades very rapidly into a quite different conception of poetry
as frank escapism or wish fulfillment and the idea that the
poet merely tells "the most heart-easing things" to "sooth
the cares, and lift the thoughts of man." [7] At times the visionary trance seems actually to bring the poet "Shapes from the
invisible world, unearthly singing"; [8] at others, it affords only
a pleasing kind of beguilement, as when it

> Charms us at once away from all our troubles:
> So that we feel uplifted from the world,
> Walking upon the white clouds wreath'd and curl'd.[9]

Keats's ambivalence toward imaginative experience, so natural
and untroubled in his early verse, was destined to become a
far more serious concern in his later poetry.

Involved with these confused ideas and perceptions, and
obviously related to them, is Keats's keen awareness of imagination as the psychological process by which poetry is composed.
Nothing is clearer in the 1817 volume than the importance
of sleep and dreams and their kinship with poetry, as the title

of the longest of the early poems, "Sleep and Poetry," suggests. Like many other poets, Keats was from the first aware of his dependence on moods of sudden and unexplained creativity for

> many a verse from so strange influence
> That we must ever wonder how, and whence
> It came.[10]

Does the poet look for inspiration to some far-off visionary kingdom or to the inner world of his own dreams? For Keats the creative process and visionary experience tend to flow together, but he was aware of the important question of their relationship long before he attempted, toward the end of his career, a fundamental distinction between vision and mere dream.

These half-questions and confused notions of imaginative experience culminate in such a way as to reveal for the first time a source of inner conflict in "Sleep and Poetry," Keats's most ambitious work before *Endymion*. The vision of the charioteer and the car moving gracefully between heaven and earth and of the "hurrying glow" with which the driver writes of the beautiful and mysterious shapes that surround him is surely the most significant of Keats's early attempts to harmonize and identify the act of poetic creation with visionary experience of some more permanent kind. The vision explains his own desire for "Wings to find out an immortality" and gives meaning to that "vast idea" holding "The end and aim of Poesy," of which he could write, "'Tis clear / As any thing most true." [11] Nevertheless, the vision fades at length, leaving him once more amid the "muddy stream" of "real things" to struggle against doubt and despondence. Was it of permanent or transitory meaning? Did it outline a quest to "human senses fitted" or one that must end in madness or the fate of an Icarus? [12] The vision and its passing in "Sleep and Poetry" express for the first time Keats's conflicting attitudes toward imaginative experience and begin to define the tension fundamental to the greatest of his later poetry.

It is difficult not to see an important connection between the problems left half-stated in the early poems and the theme and ultimate concern of *Endymion*. The Endymion legend is obviously no ordinary love story. Its involvement with dreams and visions, its contrast between mortality and immortality,

and its culmination in transcendence connect it unmistakably
with the visionary preoccupations of Keats's earlier verse. It is,
in short, impossible to regard the poem, as some critics do, as
a simple love story or romance, ignoring the fact that in the
Endymion myth Keats deliberately chose a legend ideally suited
to developing and exploring metaphorically his deepening
sense of imaginative experience. His choice of the Endymion
legend, a story ending in the transcendence of mortality, suggests that he was struggling, if only uncertainly, toward some
fulfillment of those otherworldly longings and intuitions that
characterize the poet in the early verse. In "I Stood Tip-toe"
he had already partly indentified the poet with Endymion,
his mythical creation, as a hero who had "burst our mortal
bars" (ll. 190 f.); and later, when *Endymion* was nearly completed, he was to refer back to his first book as a demonstration
of his belief in "the truth of Imagination." [13] This is not to
argue that Keats began *Endymion* having resolved his earlier
doubts regarding the nature of imaginative experience or that
he set out to express some clearly conceived idea of higher
reality. It is likely, nevertheless, that *Endymion* took its primary impulse from that vague idealism basic to Keats's nature
which marked his lifelong commitment to poetry and the
imagination, an idealism that, as he realized, could be worked
out and defined only in terms of his poetry.

Endymion, in other words, should be regarded primarily
as an experiment, "a test, a trial," as Keats himself put it, not
merely of his "Powers of Imagination" (1, 169) but of his
deepest instincts and beliefs. As such its deeper significance,
or "allegory," was in all probability nothing clearly fixed in
his mind before he began but something that matured and
developed as he progressed—that worked itself out within the
poem. Undoubtedly there were certain general starting points.
The Endymion myth was, as we have seen, connected from
the first in Keats's mind with the problem of visionary experience, and the fable, by its very nature, demanded that he work
toward some affirmative solution. The "one bare circumstance"
(1, 170) of the legend readily lent itself to development as an
extended narrative quest in which by trials of doubt and disappointment his hero's faith in visionary beauty could be
tested, explored, and ultimately rewarded. It seems obvious that
an idea of progression dominates the major action of the

poem, vaguely corresponding to the hierarchy of values out-lined in Endymion's speech on happiness in book one. Begin-ning with the love of natural objects, a scale of values mounts upward toward the more intense, imaginative pleasures of sympathy and ultimately love.[14] Later in the poem Endymion's sympathy for Alpheus and Arethusa, Glaucus's pity for the drowned lovers, and their joint service in restoring Circe's victims to life are too clearly turning points within the narra-tive to be dismissed as random bits of episode. In his pursuit of visionary beauty Endymion was not to be permitted to neglect the need for service in this world, although whether Keats could adequately reconcile the two realms and their demands upon his hero remained a problem he had yet fully to face.

Allowing the full significance of the quest to evolve as he proceeded, Keats set out to dramatize his hero's struggles and achievement of immortality, and we are reminded of this basic intention at intervals along the way. At the beginning of book two Endymion is informed that, like his namesake in "I Stood Tip-toe," he

> must wander far
> In other regions, past the scanty bar
> To mortal steps.   (ii, 123–25)

Again at the end of book three, after many disappointments, he is mysteriously reassured of his coming reward and of his love's intent to "snatch" him "into endless heaven" (iii, 1026–27). Yet this rudimentary plan was from the outset compli-cated, partly for dramatic purposes but also for deeper reasons, by a strong element of skepticism. Endymion's speech on hap-piness in book one, in which he affirms belief in his visions as a "hope beyond the shadow of a dream," is counterbalanced by his sister Peona's warnings against deceiving fantasies and "the mere nothing that engenders them" (i, 756). Thereafter he is shown the Bower of Adonis, which seems to hold the promise of the earthly transcendence he desires. Yet as En-dymion's dream-journeys toward his immortal love become more ecstatic and intense, the end of the cycle—the fading of the dream, the return to earth, and the sense of loss and despondency—is similarly intensified. In book three he must rescue Glaucus, a feeble and helpless old man who has all but lost his life in a quest that bears certain resemblances to his own. It is in book four, however, that most critics have sensed, in one way or another, a significant change in the direction of Keats's allegory. The appearance of the Indian maiden is sudden and altogether unprepared for. At the very time when he should be struggling upward on the final lap of his journey toward the "chief intensity," Keats's hero is unexpectedly confronted with the choice between two quite different and competing ideas of love—the one transcendent, ecstatic, and immortal, the other warm, earthly, and filled with the passion of the human heart. The dilemma, perhaps, is not irreconcilable; yet the reader senses that the whole scope and significance of Endymion's quest has somehow changed or at least been seriously complicated. As book four progresses, the struggle between the two ideals for possession of the hero's soul becomes more intense and divisive, up until the very ending. It is only with the appearance of the Indian maiden that Endymion comes seriously to doubt the reality and worth of his heavenly desire and even, in a moment of extreme anguish, totally rejects her:

> I have clung
> To nothing, lov'd a nothing, nothing seen
> Or felt but a great dream! . . .
>   . . . Caverns lone, farewell!
> And air of visions, and the monstrous swell
> Of visionary seas! No, never more
> Shall airy voices cheat me to the shore
> Of tangled wonder, breathless and aghast.
>   (iv, 636–38, 651–55)

With such words he has, as it were, come round to agreeing with his sister's judgment, and the whole value and meaning of his pilgrimage are brought into question. His outcry has traditionally been explained as only the last pangs of doubt before the ultimate realization that Cynthia and the Indian maiden are one. But such an explanation ignores the note of deeper conviction that characterizes Endymion's despair, nor is it sufficient to account for the extreme brevity and joylessness of the conclusion, or why Keats must intervene, not far from the end, to apologize for the prolonged turmoil of his hero.

> Ensky'd ere this, but truly that I deem
> Truth the best music in a first-born song.
>   (iv, 772–73)

How is one to account for the remarkable anticlimax which readers generally have felt and which Keats himself was unable to ignore? The "truth" seems to be, as Glen O. Allen has argued,[15] that the emphasis of Keats's allegory had changed significantly in the course of composition and that the "enskying" of his hero had lost for the poet much of its climactic importance. Endymion is not apotheosized in Cynthia's visionary heaven but is destined for a human love within the mortal world. The meaning of the final identification of the goddess with the Indian maiden—that the beauty glimpsed by the imagination and the promptings of the human affections are the same —has been pointed out by the most traditional critics of the poem. Yet the fact remains that the two loves are felt to be quite different and that their reconciliation, in dramatic and emotional terms, is more apparent than real. The truth Keats discovered at the end of his poem emerged only through the process of composition and was too complex to be adequately conveyed within the old design and framework of his fable.

Such a hypothesis can be supported by examining within the poem itself certain shifts of emphasis that suggest a remarkable maturing and development in Keats's aesthetic awareness. Probably the central passage in book one is Endymion's speech on happiness which outlines, like a vast "Pleasure Thermometer," as he was later to refer to it (I, 218), the various degrees of pleasure leading to the "chief intensity" of bliss. In the roundelay of the Indian maiden in book four the perception of sorrow is for the first time admitted as an unavoidable and creative element in the experience of beauty. In his famous letter to Bailey of November 22, 1817, written when he was half way through his final book, Keats cited both book one and "O Sorrow" as demonstrations of his "favorite Speculation" as to the truth of the imagination. Yet he must himself have been aware of important differences between them, and if we give his words a certain emphasis, we can see his concern to bring the two parts of his poem more fully into accord. "I am certain of nothing," he wrote, "but of the holiness of the Heart's affections and the truth of Imagination —What the imagination seizes as Beauty must be truth— whether it existed before or not—for I have the *same* Idea of *all* our Passions *as of Love* they are all in their sublime, crea-

tive of essential Beauty" (I, 184).[16] Keats, in other words, had
already begun to move toward that deeper conception of
beauty springing from intense awareness of the whole of human
life in all its joy and sorrow that was to become the theme of
Hyperion.[17] This is not to say that the "Ode to Sorrow" is
much more than a weak and sentimental approximation to
that ideal, but insofar as it attempts to reconcile sorrow within
a deeper apprehension of beauty, it is a step in that direction.
In any case, it is difficult to ignore the increasing concern
with human unhappiness manifest throughout Keats's letters
in the late fall of 1817, when he was at work on his fourth
book,[18] or to fail to see some reflection of that concern in the
conception and treatment of the Indian maiden as a counterpart to Cynthia. One might say, perhaps, that by the end of
the poem the pleasure principle expounded in Endymion's
speech on happiness in book one had at least been modified
by a recognition of the need for a broader and deeper participation in the whole of human experience. In the same way
the earlier idea of Endymion's quest as a search for "oneness"
or ecstatic self-annihilation in sympathetic feeling has in the
end become partly resolved (through the working out of
Keats's fable) in an awareness much closer to the simultaneous
perception of joy and sorrow, mortality and immortality, desire
and human limitation that gives to Keats's later verse its
essential character. Critics have for long seen a clear development in Endymion's growth from selfish isolation to humanitarian sympathy and action. But the structure of the poem
seems to reveal deeper changes in Keats's aesthetic and emotional awareness. By the end of the poem Cynthia and the
promise of immortality were, as ideals, no longer adequate
to express the truth of Keats's new perceptions. Yet it was too
late to alter radically the direction and meaning of the quest
or to reconcile Cynthia in any satisfying way with new and
different values.

    Endymion, then, is a work whose scope and meaning to
a large extent evolved during the months Keats worked on it
and which is, therefore, as an allegory not fully coherent for
the reason that it embodies new truths and insights Keats
discovered only in the course of composition which could not
be perfectly expressed within its old design. This is not to say
the poem is any less an allegory or to agree with those who

read it as a simple love story best explained by Keats's erotic desires, although such oversimplification of the poem has become so current that it must be considered in greater detail.

It is significant, first of all, that for critics of the erotic school the early books have always contained the key to the poem, and their arguments repeatedly return to Endymion's long love encounters with his moon goddess. Yet if the earlier assumptions in this paper are correct, Keats was from the first attracted to the Endymion myth not as a mere love story but as an analogue to visionary experience and by his desire to treat the character and validity of that experience in an extended way. There is little point in denying that the poem contains a strong element of eroticism, which is hardly surprising, considering its romantic interest and Keats's sensuous nature. Yet time and again critics have failed to see that Keats's erotic imagery frequently suggests instincts and feelings that, while associated with the sensual impulse, run deeper. At the height of his rapture with Cynthia in book two, for example, Endymion exclaims:

> "O known Unknown! from whom my being sips
> Such darling essence, wherefore may I not
> Be ever in these arms?"
>
> (ii, 739–41)

She is a "second self," his "breath of life," who promises him that

> "I will tell thee stories of the sky,
> And breathe thee whispers of its minstrelsy.
> My happy love will overwing all bounds!
> O let me melt into thee; let the sounds
> Of our close voices marry at their birth;
> Let us entwine hoveringly—O dearth
> Of human words! roughness of mortal speech!
> Lispings empyrean will I sometime teach
> Thine honied tongue—lute-breathings, which I gasp
> To have thee understand, now while I clasp
> Thee thus."
>
> (ii, 812–22)

To read such a passage as mere sexual description is to fail to see that something more than sensual passion is involved. The images of mouth and lips, of kissing, sipping, speech seem to possess a more than physical significance. Endymion draws emotional vitality and life from the unknown form whom

he embraces and who seems, mysteriously, almost part of himself, the source of feelings that cannot be expressed in words.
The imagery, that is to say, frequently suggests not so much
the physical passion of real lovers as the communion of the
poet with the vital springs of his imaginative life. The larger
context of the love embrace suggests an ecstasy of imaginative
fulfillment conveyed metaphorically through the details of
bodily passion.

To interpret the love theme in *Endymion* as a part of
Keats's broader visionary concern is not to explain away the
erotic elements in the poem but to restore them to their proper
perspective. As readers our attention is not drawn to the love
interludes for their own sake but for their part in the whole
cycle of Endymion's visionary experience, of which the union
with Cynthia is the culminating moment, but nevertheless
only a part. As in the earlier poetry the process begins with
inner withdrawal, symbolized by Endymion's retreat through
mossy caves and bowers until, feeling "endued / With power
to dream deliciously" (ii, 707–08), he falls asleep. Following
the exclusion of the outer world, the dream begins through
which is conveyed a state of intense imaginative awareness
that underlies, at some far deeper level, the rational, conceptual
functions of the mind:

> . . . it was but a dream: yet such a dream
> That never tongue, although it overteem
> With mellow utterance, like a cavern spring,
> Could figure out and to conception bring
> All I beheld and felt.
>
> (i, 574–78)

The dream is not characterized merely by images of sensual
gratification but by synesthesia and effortless movement, by
warmth and the sudden flowering of foliage, and by the vital,
flowing quality that we associate with certain states of intense
imaginative experience. But such pleasures and sensations cannot be long enjoyed. At or near their climax a counter-move-
ment toward earth begins, the fabric of the dream collapses, and
Endymion is left in mere slumber, in "stupid sleep" (i, 678).
Moreover, the intensity of the dream destroys, by force of contrast, all the natural beauty of the Latmian glades and mead-
ows, leaving Endymion in depression and despair. The love
dream in *Endymion* is, in other words, largely an extended

metaphor conveying through its various phases that visionary experience that Keats first clearly articulated in "Sleep and Poetry" and which was to develop, with various shades of nuance, as a major theme throughout much of his later poetry.

Only by means of such an analogue as the love dream could a poet of Keats's nature effectively dramatize the psychological and emotional reality of visionary experience within the terms of poetry. Cynthia is his principal metaphor to describe such heightened awareness, a symbol of its "chief intensity," and thus essential as a means of translating the stages of a mere progression into action that is vital, fluid, and emotionally meaningful. Moreover, only through the dramatic working out of such a principle was Keats able to realize and to define his own deeper instincts and attitudes. The progression boldly set forth in book one was necessary to him as a starting point, but to fail to see that it undergoes important qualifications during the course of the poem is to miss much of the dramatic subtlety and conflict implicit in Keats's narrative. Although Endymion longs for the ultimate transcendence he seeks, he is never able to escape the alternating cycles that (as in Keats's later poetry) seem inseparable parts of the dream experience. As his unions with Cynthia become more ecstatic and intense, they are followed by periods of deeper despondency and disillusionment. Even those moments when he seems most happy in the possession of his love are not free of ominous overtones. Beyond the warmth and security of the love embrace there extends a phantasmagoric world of meteors and falling stars, of chilling airs and awesome dens and caverns; and the "dizzy sky," the hints of madness, and the threat of a precipitous fall (ii, 185 f.) reintroduce the theme of the Daedalian overreacher. The uncertainty, in short, that characterizes Keats's attitude toward visionary experience in the early poems is even more apparent throughout *Endymion*.

Keats may have sought, as some critics have argued, to suggest in the Bower of Adonis the kind of apotheosis he intended for his hero. With its accumulated store of cream and ripened fruit where the sleeper dreams of his coming joys with Venus, the Bower represents that perfectly self-contained world of sensuous and imaginative experience for which Endymion longs, idealized beyond all threat of interruption. The sleeping Adonis resembles, as much as anything, the infant, in the womb or cradle, whose every need is satisfied. Indeed, Cynthia's love affords at times something of this same gratification to Endymion, who is pictured as having "swoon'd / Drunken from pleasure's nipple" (ii, 868–69). If, however, one accepts the Bower of Adonis as a parallel to Endymion's quest, it seems necessary to ask in what way the story of Glaucus in book three, the only sustained interlude in the poem, is related to the major themes of Keats's narrative. Like Endymion, Glaucus has longed for passionate joys beyond his reach and found apparent satisfaction in an otherworldly love in some ways like Endymion's own:

> "Who could resist? Who in this universe?
> She did so breathe ambrosia; so immerse
> My fine existence in a golden clime.
> She took me like a child of suckling time,
> And cradled me in roses."
>
> (iii, 453–57)

Glaucus, however, has confused Scylla with Circe, the Bower of Adonis with the Bower of Bliss, and one morning he awakes to find his "specious heaven" transformed to "real hell" (iii, 476). Amid bursts of cruel, ironic laughter the enchantress, revealed in her true ugliness, proceeds to parody the whole conception of the love nest:

> "Ha! ha! Sir Dainty! there must be a nurse
> Made of rose leaves and thistledown, express,
> To cradle thee my sweet, and lull thee: yes,
> I am too flinty-hard for thy nice touch:
> My tenderest squeeze is but a giant's clutch.
> So, fairy-thing, it shall have lullabies
> Unheard of yet: and it shall still its cries
> Upon some breast more lily-feminine."
>
> (iii, 570–77)

Glaucus has discovered not Cynthia but La Belle Dame. How is one to interpret this misadventure with regard to Endymion's own pursuit? Does the episode merely serve to heighten Endymion's triumph and superior powers by contrast with Glaucus's failure, which he must help to overcome? Or does it possess a deeper significance? Is it partly an expression of Keats's more mature realization (fully revealed in *Lamia*) that the search for fulfillment in imaginative experience alone may prove destructive and that the imagination can deceive and enslave as well as prove a guide to happiness or truth? Such questions and the complexities they raise, however, are rapidly lost at the end of the book in the joyful deliverance and celebration of the lovers and in Cynthia's renewed promise of "endless heaven" (iii, 1027) for her swooning favorite. Then at the outset of book four Endymion suddenly discovers the Indian maiden and is confronted by a dilemma different from any he has yet faced.

It is difficult not to suspect that the idea for the Indian maiden evolved in Keats's mind as a necessary expedient for allaying certain difficulties and contradictions that had emerged only in the course of his narrative. For philosophic, aesthetic, and emotional reasons it was impossible for him to return wholeheartedly to the old idea of the quest, for he had introduced into his poem complexities that Cynthia, as an unqualified ideal, was inadequate to resolve. The conclusion that his poem now demanded, he realized, was not his hero's elevation to "the chief intensity" but rather some balance between light and shade, desire and restraint, mortality and immortality. Keats needed some ideal of human, earthly beauty to counterbalance the influence and importance of Cynthia. This is not to argue that toward the end of his poem he suddenly lost faith in visionary experience, but rather that, without abandoning his desire for "wings to find out an immortality," he had come to see the equal necessity of "a pair of patient sublunary legs" (II, 128). The Indian maiden is no dazzling enchantress but a warm, human lover, and Endymion's affection for her is, by comparison with his passion for Cynthia, calm and understanding. While, however, Keats may have realized the necessity for a greater reconciliation between visionary experience and the ties of this world, such a conclusion did not readily lend itself to the old climactic design and structure of his narrative. Moreover, such a resolution was one that, for psychological and emotional reasons, he found himself unable to dramatize in any deeply satisfying or "truthful" way. Throughout the fourth book the opposition between Cynthia and the Indian maiden and the worlds they represent becomes steadily more apparent. When Endymion and his new-found love attempt to soar into Cynthia's airy regions, the pale light of the moon dissolves the very flesh of her rival, leaving

Endymion in loneliness and despair. In such ways the conflict between the two ideals becomes dramatically more real and intense at the very time when Keats was most committed to their reconciliation. The simple device of identifying the Indian maid and Cynthia was an intellectual solution, not a felt conviction, as Keats himself and most readers since his day have recognized. Realizing his own inability to deal with the deeper problems that his poem had raised, he resolved to press on to the end resolutely but "in lowliness of heart" (iv, 29), and the brevity and gloom of the conclusion testify to his sense of disappointment. He had revealed and in part expressed the conflict that was to become most central to his later poetry, but he had outrun the limits of his experience.

Immature and uncertain as it is, *Endymion* remains of all Keats's narrative poems in many ways the most central to an understanding of his genius, for it explores the various paths along which he was to develop and contains the germ of much of his later work. Read in one way, the poem is a youthful *Eve of St. Agnes*, a transcendent love dream in which all disharmonies are resolved through a final identification of vision and reality. Read in another way, the poem reveals deeper and growing misgivings as to the validity of visionary experience, doubts which he was never able fully to resolve but which were to develop in time into the open skepticism of "La Belle Dame" and *Lamia*. Yet again, in its steadfast humanitarianism, its increasing concern with human sorrow, and its groping toward a deeper and more meaningful conception of beauty, it looks forward to the greater themes that were to occupy Keats in the most ambitious of his narrative attempts, the two *Hyperions*. To understand *Endymion* adequately it is necessary to read the poem in all these ways—that is allegorically. To do so, however, is not to discover an allegory that is perfectly coherent or consistent with itself, but rather one that changed and developed as Keats wrote, that (to adapt his own phrase) "created itself" (I, 374). Ultimately *Endymion* has most to reveal when seen as an integral part of that larger allegory that was Keats's life and achievement, possessing something of the same incompleteness and contradiction. To read the poem within this larger context is only to observe the poet's own dictum that "A Man's life of any worth is a continual allegory" and that "his works are the comments on it."

Notes

1. Sir Sidney Colvin, *John Keats: His Life and Poetry, His Friends, Critics, and After-Fame* (London, 1920), pp. 171–205; Robert Bridges, *Collected Essays, Papers, &c.*, IV, "A Critical Introduction to Keats" (London, 1929), 85–93; *The Poems of John Keats*, ed. Ernest de Selincourt (London, 1926), pp. xl–xli, 428, 443–45. The groundwork for the interpretation was actually laid, as Colvin acknowledged, by Mrs. F. M. Owen in *John Keats, A Study* (London, 1880). In after years the interpretation was given a specifically neoplatonic bent by Claude L. Finney (*The Evolution of Keats's Poetry*, Cambridge, Mass., 1936, I, 291–319) and integrated more fully within the larger pattern of the poet's intellectual development by Clarence D. Thorpe (*The Mind of John Keats*, New York, 1926, pp. 57–62 *et passim*).

2. Newell F. Ford, "*Endymion*—A Neo-Platonic Allegory?" *English Literary History*, XIV (1947), 64–76; "The Meaning of 'Fellowship with Essense' in *Endymion*," PMLA, LXII (1947), 1061–76; *The Prefigurative Imagination of John Keats* (Stanford, 1951), pp. 39–86; E. C. Pettet, *On the Poetry of Keats* (Cambridge, Eng., 1957), pp. 123–202. Amy Lowell was among the first to attack the allegorical interpretation (*John Keats*, Boston, 1925, I, 318 *et passim*). Some more recent critics have been content to disregard it. See, for example, Bernard Blackstone's lengthy discussion of the poem as "magical, alchemical, occultist" in *The Consecrated Urn* (London, 1959), pp. 116–203; and Robert Harrison's "Symbolism of the Cyclical Myth in *Endymion*," *Texas Studies in Literature and Language*, I (1960), 538–54, a Jungian interpretation. A summary of conflicting views together with a qualified defense of the older position will be found in Jacob D. Wigod, "The Meaning of *Endymion*," PMLA, LXVIII (1953), 779–90.

3. Pettet, p. 153. Cf. Ford, *The Prefigurative Imagination*, pp. 85–86.

4. The phrase is used by Ford ("*Endymion*—A Neo-Platonic Allegory?" p. 69) to describe the central theme of the poem. Although the discussion of *Endymion* in his book-length study is considerably more complex, one may say that it leads, like Pettet's, to an essentially erotic interpretation of the poem.

5. "To My Brother George," ll. 103–106. Citations from Keats's poetry are to *John Keats: Selected Poems and Letters*, ed. Douglas Bush (Cambridge, Mass., 1959). Where possible, references are included in parentheses within the text.

6. "To My Mother George," ll. 25f.; "Sleep and Poetry," ll. 32f.

7. "Sleep and Poetry," ll. 245f., 264f.

8. "I Stood Tip-toe," l. 186.

9. *Ibid.*, ll. 138–40.

10. "Sleep and Poetry," ll. 69–71.

11. *Ibid.*, ll. 84, 290f.

12. *Ibid.*, ll. 79–80, 270f., 301f.

13. *The Letters of John Keats*, ed. Hyder E. Rollins, 2 vols. (Cambridge, Mass., 1958), I, 184. References by volume and page number to this edition are hereafter included in parentheses within the text. To avoid confusion, small capital roman numerals are used to designate volume numbers of the *Letters*, while lower case roman numerals designate references by book number to *Endymion*.

14. Keats's ideal of love here is more than mere sensuous passion, for it is closely linked with friendship and reflects the humanitarian concerns of the early poetry (see Bush, p. 319).

15. "The Fall of Endymion: A Study in Keats's Intellectual Growth," *Keats-Shelley Journal*, VI (1957), 37–57. See also John Middleton Murry's discussion of the poem (*Keats*, London, 1955, p. 166f.) which begins with a consideration of the lines last quoted. I am particularly indebted to Allen's essay and essentially agree with his contention that during the composition of *Endymion* Keats's attitude toward visionary experience underwent a significant change, a change that is both essential to an understanding of his poem and reflected in it. I also follow Allen in reading the poem within the larger pattern of Keats's intellectual development. However, I cannot accept his premise that Keats began *Endymion* having fully accepted the "Neoplatonic view that poetic inspiration carries the poet into higher reality" (p. 41). Nor do I believe there is sufficient evidence for concluding that Keats, either in *Endymion* or his later poetry, altogether repudiated his early faith in imaginative experience, as Allen seems to argue (pp. 39, 50). While in general Keats's attitude toward the poetic imagination became increasingly skeptical, that development was slow and tortuous and found the poet at the end of his career still committed to the imagination and to poetry. *The Fall of Hyperion* was Keats's last and greatest effort to reconcile the poetic imagination with a realistic and humane awareness of existence, but the problem is left unresolved.

16. The italics are mine.

17. The change should be described as a modification of rather than a break with the conceptions earlier expressed in Endymion's speech on happiness. In January 1818, Keats revised that passage for the press, commenting to his publisher Taylor that its argument "will perhaps be of the greatest Service to me of any thing I ever did—It set before me at once the gradations of Happiness even like a kind of Pleasure Thermometer." He went on immediately, however, to speak of it as only a "first Step towards the chief Attempt in the Drama—the playing of different Natures with Joy and Sorrow" (I, 218–19). The qualification is an important one and provides another indication of the direction toward which he was moving.

18. See his remarks to Bailey in late October that "Health and Spirits can only belong unalloyed to the selfish Man—the Man who thinks much of his fellows can never be in Spirits" (I, 175); his comments, again to Bailey, in early November on "Griefs and Cares" (I, 182); and, on November 22, his remarks to Reynolds on "Heart-vexations" (I, 188) and to Bailey on "Worldly Happiness"—"I scarcely remember counting upon any Happiness—I look not for it if it be not in the present hour" (I, 186). Keats's letters up to and including his early work on *Endymion* do not demonstrate a comparable maturity.

18 · Keats's Sylvan Historian:

History Without Footnotes

THERE IS MUCH in the poetry of Keats which suggests that he would have approved of Archibald MacLeish's dictum, "a poem should not mean / But be." There is even some warrant for thinking that the Grecian urn (real or imagined) which inspired the famous ode was, for Keats, just such a poem, "palpable and mute," a poem in stone. Hence it is the more remarkable that the "Ode" itself differs from Keats's other odes by culminating in a statement—a statement even of some sententiousness in which the urn itself is made to say that beauty is truth, and—more sentential still—that this bit of wisdom sums up the whole of mortal knowledge.

This is "to mean" with a vengeance—to violate the doctrine of the objective correlative, not only by stating truths, but by defining the limits of truth. Small wonder that some critics have felt that the unravished bride of quietness protests too much.

T. S. Eliot, for example, says that "this line ["Beauty is truth," etc.] strikes me as a serious blemish on a beautiful poem; and the reason must be either that I fail to understand it, or that it is a statement which is untrue." But even for persons who feel that they do understand it, the line may still constitute a blemish. Middleton Murry, who, after a discussion of Keats's other poems and his letters, feels that he knows what Keats meant by "beauty" and what he meant by "truth," and that Keats used them in senses which allowed them to be

Reprinted from *The Well Wrought Urn*, by Cleanth Brooks by permission of the author and Harcourt, Brace & World, Inc. Copyright 1947 by Cleanth Brooks.

properly bracketed together, still, is forced to conclude: "My own opinion concerning the value of these two lines *in the context of the poem* itself is not very different from Mr. T. S. Eliot's." The troubling assertion is apparently an intrusion upon the poem—does not grow out of it—is not dramatically accommodated to it.

This is essentially Garrod's objection, and the fact that Garrod does object indicates that a distaste for the ending of the "Ode" is by no means limited to critics of notoriously "modern" sympathies.

But the question of real importance is not whether Eliot, Murry, and Garrod are right in thinking that "Beauty is truth, truth beauty" injures the poem. The question of real importance concerns beauty and truth in a much more general way: what is the relation of the beauty (the goodness, the perfection) of a poem to the truth or falsity of what it seems to assert? It is a question which has particularly vexed our own generation—to give it I. A. Richards' phrasing, it is the problem of belief.

The "Ode," by its bold equation of beauty and truth, raises this question in its sharpest form—the more so when it becomes apparent that the poem itself is obviously intended to be a parable on the nature of poetry, and of art in general. The "Ode" has apparently been an enigmatic parable, to be sure: one can emphasize *beauty* is truth and throw Keats into the pure art camp, the usual procedure. But it is only fair to point out that one could stress *truth* is beauty, and argue with the Marxist critics of the thirties for a propaganda art. The very ambiguity of the statement, "Beauty is truth, truth beauty" ought to warn us against insisting very much on the statement in isolation, and to drive us back to a consideration of the context in which the statement is set.

It will not be sufficient, however, if it merely drives us back to a study of Keats's reading, his conversation, his letters. We shall not find our answer there even if scholarship does prefer on principle investigations of Browning's ironic question, "What porridge had John Keats?" For even if we knew just what porridge he had, physical and mental, we should still not be able to settle the problem of the "Ode." The reason should be clear: our specific question is not what did Keats the man perhaps want to assert here about the relation of beauty and truth; it is rather: was Keats the poet able to exemplify that relation in this particular poem? Middleton Murry is right: the relation of the final statement in the poem to the total context is all-important.

Indeed, Eliot, in the very passage in which he attacks the "Ode" has indicated the general line which we are to take in its defense. In that passage, Eliot goes on to contrast the closing lines of the "Ode" with a line from *King Lear*, "Ripeness is all." Keats's lines strike him as false; Shakespeare's, on the other hand, as not clearly false, and as possibly quite true. Shakespeare's generalization, in other words, avoids raising the question of truth. But is it really a question of truth and falsity? One is tempted to account for the difference of effect which Eliot feels in this way: "Ripeness is all" is a statement put in the mouth of a dramatic character and a statement which is governed and qualified by the whole context of the play. It does not directly challenge an examination into its truth because its relevance is pointed up and modified by the dramatic context.

Now, suppose that one could show that Keats's lines, *in quite the same way*, constitute a speech, a consciously riddling paradox, put in the mouth of a particular character, and modified by the total context of the poem. If we could demonstrate that the speech was "in character," was dramatically appropriate, was properly prepared for—then would not the lines have all the justification of "Ripeness is all"? In such case, should we not have waived the question of the scientific or philosophic truth of the lines in favor of the application of a principle curiously like that of dramatic propriety? I suggest that some such principle is the only one legitimately to be invoked in any case. Be this as it may, the "Ode on a Grecian Urn" provides us with as neat an instance as one could wish in order to test the implications of such a maneuver.

It has seemed best to be perfectly frank about procedure: the poem is to be read in order to see whether the last lines of the poem are not, after all, dramatically prepared for. Yet there are some claims to be made upon the reader too, claims which he, for his part, will have to be prepared to honor. He must not be allowed to dismiss the early characterizations of the urn as merely so much vaguely beautiful description. He must not be too much surprised if "mere decoration" turns

out to be meaningful symbolism—or if ironies develop where
he has been taught to expect only sensuous pictures. Most of
all, if the teasing riddle spoken finally by the urn is not to
strike him as a bewildering break in tone, he must not be too
much disturbed to have the element of paradox latent in the
poem emphasized, even in those parts of the poem which
have none of the energetic crackle of wit with which he usually
associates paradox. This is surely not too much to ask of the
reader—namely, to assume that Keats meant what he said and
that he chose his words with care. After all, the poem begins
on a note of paradox, though a mild one: for we ordinarily do
not expect an urn to speak at all; and yet, Keats does more
than this: he begins his poem by emphasizing the apparent
contradiction.

The silence of the urn is stressed—it is a "bride of quietness"; it is a "foster-child of silence," but the urn is a "historian" too. Historians tell the truth, or are at least expected
to tell the truth. What is a "Sylvan historian"? A historian who
is like the forest rustic, a woodlander? Or, a historian who
writes histories of the forest? Presumably, the urn is sylvan
in both senses. True, the latter meaning is uppermost: the
urn can "express / A flowery tale more sweetly than our rhyme,"
and what the urn goes on to express is a 'leaf-fring'd legend"
of "Tempe or the dales of Arcady." But the urn, like the "leaf-
fring'd legend" which it tells, is covered with emblems of the
fields and forests: "Overwrought, / With forest branches and
the trodden weed." When we consider the way in which the
urn utters its history, the fact that it must be sylvan in both
senses is seen as inevitable. Perhaps too the fact that it is a
rural historian, a rustic, a peasant historian, qualifies in our
minds the dignity and the "truth" of the histories which it
recites. Its histories, Keats has already conceded, may be
characterized as "tales"—not formal history at all.

The sylvan historian certainly supplies no names and
dates—"What men or gods are these?" the poet asks. What
it does give is action—of men *or* gods, of godlike men or of
superhuman (though not daemonic) gods—action, which is
not the less intense for all that the urn is cool marble. The
words "mad" and "ecstasy" occur, but it is the quiet rigid urn
which gives the dynamic picture. And the paradox goes further: the scene is one of violent lovemaking, a Bacchanalian

scene, but the urn itself is like a "still unravish'd bride," or like a child, "of silence and slow time." It is not merely like a child, but like a "foster-child." The exactness of the term can be defended. "Silence and slow time," it is suggested, are not the true parents, but foster-parents. They are too old, one feels, to have borne the child themselves. Moreover, they dote upon the "child" as grandparents do. The urn is fresh and unblemished; it is still young, for all its antiquity, and time which destroys so much has "fostered" it.

With stanza ii we move into the world presented by the urn, into an examination, not of the urn as a whole—as an entity with its own form—but of the details which overlay it. But as we enter that world, the paradox of silent speech is carried on, this time in terms of the objects portrayed on the vase.

The first lines of the stanza state a rather bold paradox— even the dulling effect of many readings has hardly blunted it. At least we can easily revive its sharpness. Attended to with care, it is a statement which is preposterous, and yet true—true on the same level on which the original metaphor of the speaking urn is true. The unheard music is sweeter than any audible music. The poet has rather cunningly en- forced his conceit by using the phrase, "ye soft pipes." Actually, we might accept the poet's mataphor without being forced to accept the adjective "soft." The pipes might, although "un- heard," be shrill, just as the action which is frozen in the figures on the urn can be violent and ecstatic as in stanza i and slow and dignified as in stanza iv (the procession to the sacrifice). Yet, by characterizing the pipes as "soft," the poet has provided a sort of realistic basis for his metaphor: the pipes, it is suggested, are playing very softly; if we listen carefully, we can hear them; their music is just below the threshold of normal sound.

This general paradox runs through the stanza: action goes on though the actors are motionless; the song will not cease; the lover cannot leave his song; the maiden, always to be kissed, never actually kissed, will remain changelessly beauti- ful. The maiden is, indeed, like the urn itself, a "still un- ravished bride of quietness"—not even ravished by a kiss; and it is implied, perhaps, that her changeless beauty, like that of the urn, springs from this fact.

The poet is obviously stressing the fresh, unwearied charm of the scene itself which can defy time and is deathless. But, at the same time, the poet is being perfectly fair to the terms of his metaphor. The beauty portrayed is deathless because it is lifeless. And it would be possible to shift the tone easily and ever so slightly by insisting more heavily on some of the phrasings so as to give them a darker implication. Thus, in the case of "thou canst not leave / Thy song," one could interpret: the musician cannot leave the song even if he would: he is fettered to it, a prisoner. In the same way one could enlarge on the hint that the lover is not wholly satisfied and content: "never canst thou kiss, / . . . yet, do not grieve." These items are mentioned here, not because one wishes to maintain that the poet is bitterly ironical, but because it is important for us to see that even here the paradox is being used fairly, particularly in view of the shift in tone which comes in the next stanza.

This third stanza represents, as various critics have pointed out, a recapitulation of earlier motifs. The boughs which cannot shed their leaves, the unwearied melodist, and the ever-ardent lover reappear. Indeed, I am not sure that this stanza can altogether be defended against the charge that it represents a falling-off from the delicate but firm precision of the earlier stanzas. There is a tendency to linger over the scene sentimentally: the repetition of the word "happy" is perhaps symptomatic of what is occurring. Here, if anywhere, in my opinion, is to be found the blemish on the ode—not in the last two lines. Yet, if we are to attempt a defense of the third stanza, we shall come nearest success by emphasizing the paradoxical implications of the repeated items; for whatever development there is in the stanza inheres in the increased stress on the paradoxical element. For example, the boughs cannot "bid the Spring adieu," a phrase which repeats "nor ever can those trees be bare," but the new line strengthens the implications of speaking: the falling leaves are a gesture, a word of farewell to the joy of spring. The melodist of stanza ii played sweeter music because unheard, but here, in the third stanza, it is implied that he does not tire of his song for the same reason that the lover does not tire of his love—neither song nor love is consummated. The songs are "for ever new" because they cannot be completed. The paradox is carried further in the case of the lover whose love is "For ever warm and still to be enjoy'd." We are really dealing with an ambiguity here, for we can take "still to be enjoy'd" as an adjectival phrase on the same level as "warm"—that is, "still virginal and warm." But the tenor of the whole poem suggests that the warmth of the love depends upon the fact that it has not been enjoyed—that is, "warm and still to be enjoy'd" may mean also "warm *because* still to be enjoy'd."

But though the poet has developed and extended his metaphors furthest here in this third stanza, the ironic counterpoise is developed furthest too. The love which a line earlier was "warm" and "panting" becomes suddenly in the next line, "All breathing human passion far above." But if it is *above* all breathing passion, it is, after all, outside the realm of breathing passion, and therefore, not human passion at all.

(If one argues that we are to take "All breathing human passion" as qualified by "That leaves a heart high-sorrowful and cloy'd"—that is, if one argues that Keats is saying that the love depicted on the urn is above only that human passion which leaves one cloyed and not above human passion in general, he misses the point. For Keats in the "Ode" is stressing the ironic fact that all human passion *does* leave one cloyed; hence the superiority of art.)

The purpose in emphasizing the ironic undercurrent in the foregoing lines is not at all to disparage Keats—to point up implications of his poem of which he was himself unaware. Far from it: the poet knows precisely what he is doing. The point is to be made simply in order to make sure that we are completely aware of what he *is* doing. Garrod, sensing this ironic undercurrent, seems to interpret it as an element over which Keats was not able to exercise full control. He says:

> Truth to his main theme [the fixity given by art to forms which in life are impermanent] has taken Keats farther than he meant to go. The pure and ideal art of this "cold Pastoral," this "silent form," has a cold silentness which in some degree saddens him. In the last lines of the fourth stanza, especially

the last three lines . . . every reader is conscious, I should suppose, of an undertone of sadness, of disappointment. The undertone is there, but Keats has not been taken "farther than he meant to go." Keats's attitude, even in the early stanzas, is more complex than Garrod would allow; it is more complex and more ironic, and a recognition of this is important if we are to be able to relate the last stanza to the rest of the "Ode." Keats is perfectly aware that the frozen moment of loveliness is more dynamic than is the fluid world of reality *only* because it is frozen. The love depicted on the urn remains warm and young because it is not human flesh at all but cold, ancient marble.

With stanza iv, we are still within the world depicted by the urn, but the scene presented in this stanza forms a contrast to the earlier scenes. It emphasizes, not individual aspiration and desire, but communal life. It constitutes another chapter in the history that the "Sylvan historian" has to tell. And again, names and dates have been omitted. We are not told to what god's altar the procession moves, nor the occasion of the sacrifice.

Moreover, the little town from which the celebrants come is unknown; and the poet rather goes out of his way to leave us the widest possible option in locating it. It may be a mountain town, or a river town, or a tiny seaport. Yet, of course, there is a sense in which the nature of the town—the essential character of the town—is actually suggested by the figured urn. But it is not given explicitly. The poet is willing to leave much to our imaginations; and yet the stanza in its organization of imagery and rhythm does describe the town clearly enough; it is small, it is quiet, its people are knit together as an organic whole, and on a "pious morn" such as this, its whole population has turned out to take part in the ritual. The stanza has been justly admired. Its magic of effect defies reduction to any formula. Yet, without pretending to "account" for the effect in any mechanical fashion, one can point to some of the elements active in securing the effect: there is the suggestiveness of the word "green" in "green altar"—something natural, spontaneous, living; there is the suggestion that the little town is caught in a curve of the seashore, or nestled in a fold of the mountains—at any rate, is something secluded and something naturally related to its terrain; there is the effect of the phrase "peaceful citadel," a phrase which involves a clash between the ideas of war and peace and resolves it in the sense of stability and independence without imperialistic ambition—the sense of stable repose.

But to return to the larger pattern of the poem: Keats does something in this fourth stanza which is highly interesting in itself and thoroughly relevant to the sense in which the urn is a historian. One of the most moving passages in the poem is that in which the poet speculates on the strange emptiness of the little town which, of course, has not been pictured on the urn at all.

The little town which has been merely implied by the procession portrayed on the urn is endowed with a poignance beyond anything else in the poem. Its streets "for evermore / Will silent be," its desolation forever shrouded in a mystery. No one in the figured procession will ever be able to go back to the town to break the silence there, not even one to tell the stranger there why the town remains desolate.

If one attends closely to what Keats is doing here, he may easily come to feel that the poet is indulging himself in an ingenious fancy, an indulgence, however, which is gratuitous and finally silly; that is, the poet has created in his own imagination the town implied by the procession of worshipers, has given it a special character of desolation and loneliness, and then has gone on to treat it as if it were a real town to which a stranger might actually come and be puzzled by its emptiness. (I can see no other interpretation of the lines, "and not a soul to tell / Why thou are desolate, can e'er return.") But, actually, of course, no one will ever discover the town except by the very same process by which Keats has discovered it: namely, through the figured urn, and then, of course, he will not need to ask why it is empty. One can well imagine what a typical eighteenth-century critic would have made of this flaw in logic.

It will not be too difficult, however, to show that Keats's extension of the fancy is not irrelevant to the poem as a whole. The "reality" of the little town has a very close relation to the urn's character as a historian. If the earlier stanzas have been concerned with such paradoxes as the ability of static carving to convey dynamic action, of the soundless pipes to play music sweeter than that of the heard melody, of the figured lover to have a love more warm and panting than that of breathing flesh and blood, so in the same way the town implied by the urn comes to have a richer and more important history than that of actual cities. Indeed, the imagined town is to the figured procession as the unheard melody is to the carved pipes of the unwearied melodist. And the poet, by pretending to take the town as real —so real that he can imagine the effect of its silent streets upon the stranger who chances to come into it—has suggested in the most powerful way possible its essential reality for him—and for us. It is a case of the doctor's taking his own medicine: the poet is prepared to stand by the illusion of his own making.

With stanza v we move back out of the enchanted world portrayed by the urn to consider the urn itself once more as a whole, as an object. The shift in point of view is marked with the first line of the stanza by the apostrophe, "O Attic shape . . ." It is the urn itself as a formed thing, as an autonomous world, to which the poet addresses these last words. And the rich, almost breathing world which the poet has conjured up for us contracts and hardens into the decorated motifs on the urn itself: "with brede / Of marble men and maidens overwrought." The beings who have a life above life—"All breathing human passion far above"—are marble, after all.

This last is a matter which, of course, the poet has never denied. The recognition that the men and maidens are frozen, fixed, arrested, has, as we have already seen, run through the second, third, and fourth stanzas as an ironic undercurrent. The central paradox of the poem, thus, comes to conclusion in the phrase, "Cold Pastoral." The word "pastoral" suggests warmth, spontaneity, the natural and the informal as well as the idyllic, the simple, and the informally charming. What the urn tells is a "flowery tale," a "leaf-fring'd legend," but the "Sylvan historian" works in terms of marble. The urn itself is cold, and the life beyond life which it expresses is life which has been formed, arranged. The urn itself is a "silent form," and it speaks, not by means of statement, but by "teasing us out of thought." It is as enigmatic as eternity is, for, like eternity, its history is beyond time, outside time, and for this very reason bewilders our time-ridden minds: it teases us.

The marble men and maidens of the urn will not age as flesh-and-blood men and women will: "When old age shall this generation waste." (The word "generation," by the way, is very rich. It means on one level "that which is generated" —that which springs from human loins—Adam's breed; and yet, so intimately is death wedded to men, the word "generation" itself has become, as here, a measure of time.) The marble men and women lie outside time. The urn which they adorn will remain. The "Sylvan historian" will recite its history to other generations.

What will it say to them? Presumably, what it says to the poet now: that "formed experience," imaginative insight, embodies the basic and fundamental perception of man and nature. The urn is beautiful, and yet its beauty is based— what else is the poem concerned with?—on an imaginative perception of essentials. Such a vision is beautiful but it is also true. The sylvan historian presents us with beautiful histories, but they are true histories, and it is a good historian.

Moreover, the "truth" which the sylvan historian gives is the only kind of truth which we are likely to get on this earth, and, furthermore, it is the only kind that we *have* to have. The names, dates, and special circumstances, the wealth of data—these the sylvan historian quietly ignores. But we shall never get all the facts anyway—there is no end to the accumulation of facts. Moreover, mere accumulations of facts —a point our own generation is only beginning to realize— are meaningless. The sylvan historian does better than that: it takes a few details and so orders them that we have not only beauty but insight into essential truth. Its "history," in short, is a history without footnotes. It has the validity of myth—not myth as a pretty but irrelevant make-believe, an idle fancy, but myth as a valid perception into reality.

So much for the "meaning" of the last lines of the "Ode." It is an interpretation which differs little from past interpretations. It is put forward here with no pretension to novelty. What is important is the fact that it can be derived from the context of the "Ode" itself.

And now, what of the objection that the final lines break the tone of the poem with a display of misplaced sententiousness? One can summarize the answer already implied thus: throughout the poem the poet has stressed the paradox of the speaking urn. First, the urn itself can tell a story, can give a history. Then, the various figures depicted upon the urn play music or speak or sing. If we have been alive to these items, we shall not, perhaps, be too much surprised to have the urn speak once more, not in the sense in which it tells a story—a metaphor which is rather easy to accept—but, to have it speak on a higher level, to have it make a commentary on its own nature. If the urn has been properly dramatized, if we have followed the development of the metaphors, if we have been alive to the paradoxes which work throughout the poem, perhaps then, we shall be prepared for the enigmatic, final paradox which the "silent form" utters. But in that case, we shall not feel that the generalization, unqualified and to be taken literally, is meant to march out of its context to compete with the scientific and philosophical generalizations which dominate our world.

"Beauty is truth, truth beauty" has precisely the same status, and the same justification as Shakespeare's "Ripeness is all." It is a speech "in character" and supported by a dramatic context.

To conclude thus may seem to weight the principle of dramatic propriety with more than it can bear. This would not be fair to the complexity of the problem of truth in art nor fair to Keats's little parable. Granted; and yet the principle of dramatic propriety may take us further than would first appear. Respect for it may at least insure our dealing with the problem of truth at the level on which it is really relevant to literature. If we can see that the assertions made in a poem are to be taken as part of an organic context, if we can resist the temptation to deal with them in isolation, then we may be willing to go on to deal with the world view, or "philosophy," or "truth" of the *poem as a whole* in terms of its dramatic wholeness: that is, we shall not neglect the maturity of attitude, the dramatic tension, the emotional *and* intellectual coherence in favor of some statement of theme abstracted from it by paraphrase. Perhaps, best of all, we might learn to distrust our ability to represent any poem adequately by paraphrase. Such a distrust is healthy, Keats's sylvan historian, who is not above "teasing" us, exhibits such a distrust, and perhaps the point of what the sylvan historian "says" is to confirm us in our distrust.

Shiv K. Kumar

19 · The Meaning of *Hyperion*: A Reassessment

"THERE IS probably no fragment in our literature which we would rather see completed than *Hyperion*," [1] observes De Selincourt; and, one may add, any conjecture as to how Keats might have worked out this poem to a satisfactory conclusion must inevitably be linked up with its essential import. No wonder, critics from Sidney Colvin down to Walter Jackson Bate have expounded diverse theories as to the most intriguing question of all—why did Keats abandon *Hyperion*? Why was he not able to complete a poem that was to explore "all forms and substances / Straight homeward to their symbol-essences"? [2] Scholarly investigation into this problem has often shied away from focusing itself on *l'éssence fondamentale* of this fragment. The main contention of this essay will be to show how it was Keats's failure to sustain his imaginative hold on the central concept of *l'évolution créatrice* that was primarily responsible for his abandoning *Hyperion*.

Although the facts regarding the genesis and growth of *Hyperion* have been repeated often enough, it has seldom been conclusively inferred that this poem epitomizes the entire span of Keats's poetic career. We should remember, for instance, that Keats alluded to this poem for the first time in his letter to Haydon (September 23, 1817) as " . . . a new Romance which I have in my eye for next Summer." [3] It may also be safely conjectured that "Oceanus the old" in *Endymion*, musing "for ever" in his "quiet cave" (Bk. III, 994–97), is essentially of the same mould as Oceanus, "Sophist and sage,"

Written especially for this book.

cogitating "in his watery shades" on the evolutionary process
(*Hyperion*, Bk. II, 163–243). And even after giving up *Hyperion* on September 21, 1819,[4] at the zenith of his poetic
development, it is not idle to speculate that Keats might have
brooded over the possibilities of completing a poem that had
remained a tantalizing fragment. Why did he, then, leave
his *magnum opus* incomplete which, from its earliest conception to partial execution and final abandonment, had witnessed
some of the most soul-making phases of his life—the Scottish
tour with Charles Brown, the death of Tom, the emotional
involvement with Fanny Brawne and the progressive aggravation of his fatal illness?

We may here pause to add that the same question may
be raised in respect of *The Fall of Hyperion* which, however,
has been rightly assessed as a much weaker poem; in length
something less than a fragment, in vision and design somewhat
warped and blurred. *The Fall*, this "very abstract poem"[5] (to
quote Keats's own comment), presents the central concept
on the dialectical plane through Moneta, the Roman counterpart of Greek Mnemosyne. The former, as her name suggests,
admonishes and catechizes in terms of "consequitive reasoning" (to use Keats's own expression), whereas Mnemosyne
emerges as a symbol of intuitive knowledge, who strives to
awaken the soul of man to a realization of spiritual beauty.
There is, besides, "a certain ambiguity in Moneta's position,
for she had been the priestess of Saturn and also the foster-parent of Apollo."[6] "The ferment in Keats's mind," observes
David Perkins, "produced as much confusion as complexity"[7]
in *The Fall*. Nor does the second version achieve any significant dimension in dramatically projecting, through incisively
contrasted characters, the central tragic situation. If one were
to apply to this poem the criterion that Keats expounds in
his letter to John Hamilton Reynolds ("in my dramatic capacity I enter fully into the feeling"[8]), it is evident that in *The
Fall* he seems to operate only on the periphery, failing to
wedge his way deep into the heart of the experience.

In any case, this essay will restrict the scope of its inquiry
to the first *Hyperion* and investigate into the reasons that led
to the final abandoning of the poem. But before we proceed to examine this problem, it may be useful here to give a
résumé of the various interpretations that have been advanced
so far to explain the incomplete nature of the poem.

Miltonic inversions, avowedly declared by Keats as one of the reasons for his abandoning *Hyperion*, offer only a partial explanation of this problem. "I have given up *Hyperion*—there were too many Miltonic inversions in it." [9] But it is not difficult to see that this explanation refers merely to technical procedures, whereas, as we shall see later, Keats's fundamental dilemma lay much deeper.

Sidney Colvin's statement that Keats's failure to complete *Hyperion* was due to "something not wholly congenial to his powers in the task itself," [10] only gives an edge to the real problem, instead of offering an adequate interpretation. Equally vague and inconclusive is Garrod's observation that "if Keats himself stopped because he did not know how to go on, it would be nothing out of nature, and perhaps, indeed, out of nature if it were otherwise." [11] And Douglas Bush proceeds from a premise of doubtful validity when he remarks that "Keats perceived his poem to be mainly façade . . . the architecture was so much out of proportion that Keats did not see his way to a satisfactory ending or recasting." [12] Bush then adds that Keats might have given up this poem because of "his revulsions against a too high and hard conception of poetry." [13] This view cuts right across the lofty ideals that Keats placed before poetry. In his letter to John Hamilton Reynolds (February 3, 1818), he declares that "poetry should be great and unobtrusive, a thing which enters into one's soul, and does not startle it or amaze it with itself, but with its subject." [14] A poet who had advised Shelley to "load every rift of [his] subject with ore" [15] would not have retreated from any "high and hard conception of poetry."

It has also been suggested that Tom's death was mainly responsible for his abruptly giving up *Hyperion*,[16] but we know that even after this tragic event, Keats continued to create great poetry. No single occurrence, however disconcertingly agonizing, could have dried up the creative impulse in a poet who had made complete disinterestedness the ideal of his life.

W. J. Bate argues that "the first *Hyperion* had come to a close partly because too much had been given the Titans: whatever happened afterwards had to be presented under the threat of anti-climax." [17] This interpretation does not take cognizance of the fact that it is only through investing the Titans with a certain measure of noble grandeur that Keats succeeds in raising the tragic complex of this poem. Equally

untenable is Bate's view that after Oceanus' speech, the poem
had lost its momentum, and no effort or determination could
make it proceed any further. "Obviously this is the heart of
the poem. This was what he wanted to say; and having said
it, his poem was substantially finished." [18] This is only begging
the whole question of the intention of the poet and hardly
offers a plausible explanation.

"How was the poem to proceed?" asks De Selincourt.

> Woodhouse, who evidently knew Keats's original design, as-
> serts that "the poem if completed would have treated of the
> dethronement of Hyperion, the former god of the Sun, by
> Apollo—and incidentally of those of Oceanus by Neptune,
> of Saturn by Jupiter, etc., and of the war of the Giants for
> Saturn's re-establishment—with other events, of which we have
> but very dark hints in the mythological poets of Greece and
> Rome. In fact, the incidents would have been pure creations
> of the poet's brain." [19]

Whereas Keats never reached as far as the war of the Giants,
which would have been undoubtedly "an inartistic anti-climax,"
it is not difficult to see how he had already alchemized whatever elements he might have borrowed from Greek mythology,
introducing significantly the "notion of a world-evolution"
which, according to Bosanquet, "was wholly alien to the
Greeks." [20]

Middleton Murry presents a rather provocative, and somewhat ingenious, interpretation of Apollo as a symbol of "poetic
nature" to infer that *Hyperion* is a complete poem and no
fragment at all. "When he had finished it he had told all he
knew of that nature, which was his own; he could tell no
more. . . . He gave up sometime about the beginning of
April, yet he did not give up, for the poem, as I have said,
was finished." [21]

It is evident that none of these theories carries any appre-
ciable measure of plausibility as to why Keats abandoned
Hyperion. These interpretations either pertain to mere technical procedures or lay too much emphasis on the so-called
"original design" of the poem, not realizing that poetic genius
works out its own destiny and explores unforeseeable avenues
in the process of creation itself.

It may, however, be admitted that in spite of minor shifts
of emphasis there is a certain measure of broad agreement

among critics in regard to the basic theme of *Hyperion*. There
is hardly any critic who has not interpreted this poem, directly
or by implication, as "a poem of progress," [22] although the
terms of reference employed vary with each critic. "Here is
evolution, upward evolution," [23] observes Thorpe, but the
precise nature of this evolutionary process is not fully elabo-
rated. To Paul Elmer More "the old dynasty of formless
powers" is "driven into oblivion by new creators of form and
order," [24] while Garrod describes *Hyperion* cryptically as "the
epic of the Revolutionary Idea . . . in history, as in mythology, the Revolutionary Idea begins when children refuse any
longer to be eaten by their parents." [25] Sidney Colvin also
draws attention to the evolutionary process when he remarks
that *Hyperion* symbolizes "the dethronement of an older and
ruder worship by one more advanced and humane, in which
ideas of ethics and of arts [hold] a larger place besides ideas of
nature and her brute powers." [26] But he fails to explore the
larger implications of his approach. James Ralston Caldwell
endorses the same theme; although he overemphasizes the
"passionate" nature of Apollo as against the "placidity" of the
Titans: "It is in the passionate existence, the 'burning and
the strife,' that Apollo differs from the placid Titans; it is in
this one aspect that he is first in beauty and first in might." [27]
This seems to ignore Apollo's ceaseless search for nonidentity,
the continual surrender of his ego to something larger than
himself.

Strangely enough, even those critics who accept evolutionary change as the governing concept of *Hyperion* look for
convenient points of rest, as if unable to cope with the prospect
of eternal progression. They soon lapse into the inevitable
fallacy of visualizing the ultimate destination of the evolutionary process as a point of definitive perfection. Douglas
Bush, for instance, considers "the changelessness of eternity" [28]
as the final goal of this process, and to Robert Bridges *Hyperion*
symbolizes "a self-destructive progress towards good . . . light
and song passing into union and perfection out of elemental
crudeness." [29] It is obvious that Bridges' notion of "union and
perfection" is static, barring all possibilities of further evolution. The entire dilemma of these perfection-oriented minds
is forcefully summed up by Henri Bergson in his famous lecture
on "The Perception of Change":

They are accustomed to *terra firma*. . . . They must
have "fixed" points to which they can attach thought and
existence. . . . Change, if they consent to look directly at it
without an interposed veil, will very quickly appear to be the
most substantial and durable thing possible. Its solidity is
infinitely superior to that of a fixity which is only an
ephemeral arrangement between mobilities.[30]

This ceaselessly dynamic process of *l'évolution créatrice*,
not recognizing any fixities, is, to my mind, the central concept
in *Hyperion*; and, indeed, several passages in the poem could
be adduced in support of this view. To quote Oceanus for
instance:

> And first, as thou wast not the first of powers,
> So art thou not the last; it cannot be:
> Thou art not the beginning nor the end.
>
> (Bk. II, 188–90)

And a little later Oceanus adds, as if to make qualitative
progression explicit beyond any possibility of ambiguity:

> . . . Mark Well!
> As Heaven and Earth are fairer, fairer far
> Than Chaos and blank Darkness, though once chiefs;
> And as we show beyond that Heaven and Earth
> In form and shape compact and beautiful,
> In will, in action free, companionship,
> And thousand other signs of purer life;
> So on our heels a fresh perfection treads,
> A power more strong in beauty, born of us
> And fated to excel us, as we pass
> In glory that old Darkness: nor are we
> Thereby more conquer'd, than by us the rule
> Of shapeless Chaos . . .
> Yea, by that law, another race may drive
> Our conquerors to mourn as we do now.
>
> (Bk. II, 205–31)

This passage, central to any assessment of *Hyperion*, has
not been adequately understood and analyzed. In its emphasis
on free will, perpetual novelty, and change, it seems to anticipate Bergson's concept of creative evolution, although Keats
appears to relate this process to a ceaseless unfolding of beauty
in its more spiritual, "more comely" and more "wondrous"
aspects.

Let us now consider this passage in some detail, and
understand its various implications. First, Oceanus seems to

suggest that each successive wave of evolution should be understood, not as simple replacement or substitution of brute force by beauty, but as a progressive attainment of higher and still higher levels of perfection. If, for instance, Heaven and Earth "are fairer, fairer far / Than Chaos and Blank Darkness," the Titans, although "in form and shape compact and beautiful," are still superseded by "a power more strong in beauty." Yet this does not preclude the Olympians themselves from being vanquished, in their turn, by yet "another race."

Secondly, it may be noticed that Oceanus lays distinct emphasis on free will as against predetermination, since the Titans are declared "in will, in action free," and invested with a "thousand other forms of purer life." It should now be obvious that if the Titans find themselves paralyzed, it is because they are unable to create any new forms of imaginative experience. It is significant that Saturn is depicted as impotently whipping himself into an artificial state of creative fervor when, in fact, he knows fully that he can no longer create anything new:

> . . . and there shall be
> Beautiful things made new, for the surprise
> Of the sky-children; I will give command . . .
>
> (Bk. I, 131–33)

He repeats a little later:

> But cannot I create?
> Cannot I form: Cannot I fashion forth
> Another world, another universe,
> To overbear and crumble this to nought?
> Where is another chaos? Where?
>
> (Bk. I, 141–45)

To Saturn's impotent cry "Where is another chaos? Where?" one might answer that it lies dormant in the mind, perpetually awaiting transformation into novel forms. It is obvious that although Saturn is trying hard to regain his old creative vigor, the impulse has dried up, and he feels the pressure of blank futility weighing heavily on his mind: in his own words, he feels "smother'd up." Surely, the creative urge does not look around for convenient opportunities, since any situation should have potentialities for a fresh endeavor. In marked contrast Apollo's music symbolizes creative amazement, his fingers strike "new tuneful wonder" from his golden lyre:

"Yes," said the supreme shape,
"Thou hast dream'd of me; and awaking up
Didst find a lyre all golden by thy side,
Whose strings touch'd by thy fingers, all the vast
Unwearied ear of the whole universe
Listen'd in pain and pleasure at the birth
Of such tuneful wonder.
                                      (Bk. III, 61–67)

The creation of the universe was itself a manifestation of
the urge to seek new forms:

From chaos and parental darkness came
Light, the first fruits of that intestine broil
That sullen ferment, which for wondrous ends
Was ripening in itself. The ripe hour came,
And with it light, and light, engendering
Upon its producer, forthwith touch'd
The whole enormous matter into life.
                                      (Bk. II, 191–97)

This description of the creation of life out of matter
corresponds with Bergson's theory of the origin of life, and
particularly with his use of the famous metaphor of *élan vital*
(here "light") injecting itself into matter and creating living
forms of existence, which will evolve into novel and unforeseeable dimensions along a process of ceaseless progression.

This notion of creation, growth, and evolution is further
buttressed by the use of suggestive organic imagery which is
one of the subtle manipulations of Keats's poetic genius in
Hyperion. This is how Oceanus expounds his concept of "ripe
progress" in terms of vegetation:

Say, doth the dull soil
Quarrel with the proud forests it hath fed,
And feedeth still, more comely than itself?
Can it deny the chiefdom of green groves?
Or shall the tree be envious of the dove
Because it cooeth, and hath snowy wings
To wander wherewithal and find its joys?
We are such forest-trees, and our fair boughs
Have bred forth, not pale solitary doves,
But eagles golden-feather'd, who do tower
Above us in their beauty, and must reign
In right thereof . . .
                                      (Bk. II, 217–28)

A close scrutiny of *Hyperion* will reveal how Keats has
tried to depict the Titans as spatial entities, angular and en-

cased in their narrow selves in order to justify their supersession
by the Olympians. Saturn sits "gray-hair'd . . . quiet as a
stone / Still as the silence about the lair" (Bk. I, 4–5), together
with other Titans "fierce, *self-hid* or prison-bound" (Bk. I,
161), while Hyperion "his ample palate took / Savour of poi-
sonous *brass and metal* sick" (Bk. I, 188–89). These Titans,
"instead of thrones, *hard flint* they sat upon, / Couches of
rugged stone, and slaty ridge / Stubborn'd with iron" (Bk. II,
15–17)—all "Dungeon'd in *opaque element*," with "all their
limbs / Lock'd up like veins of metal, crampt and screw'd; /
Without a motion." [31] Creus lies beside "his ponderous iron
mace . . . and a shatter'd rib of rock" (Bk. II, 41–42), while
Cottus "prone he lay . . . for still upon the flint / He ground
severe his skull" (Bk. II, 49–51), and Asia leans "upon a tusk"
under "a crag's uneasy shelve." Oceanus himself wears a face
"*astonied*" with a "severe content."

Into this world of paralytic inertia, hemmed in by iron,
tusk and hard flint, bursts forth the new Olympian order. No
wonder Saturn is perplexed, unable to account for the might
of the Olympians:

> Who had power
> To make me desolate? whence came the strength?
> How was it nurtur'd to such bursting forth . . .
> (Bk. I, 102–104)

Book III introduces Apollo, charged with boundless creative energy, wandering "forth / Beside the osiers of a rivulet"
(Bk. III, 33–34), listening to "the thrush . . . calm-throated,"
and "the murmurous noise of waves," and weeping "out of
pain and pleasure." "The liegeless air yields to [his] step aspi-
rant," as young Apollo strives forth in search of spiritual enlightenment. He is associated

> With that new blissful golden melody,
> A living death was in each gush of sounds,
> Each family of rapturous hurried notes,
> That fell one after one, yet all at once,
> Like pearl beads dropping sudden from their string:
> And then another, then another strain,
> Each like a dove leaving its olive perch,
> With music wing'd instead of silent plumes . . .
> (Bk. II, 280–87)

Through the metaphor of ceaseless qualitative interpenetration
of musical notes, or of the dove's flight into space, "with music

wing'd instead of silent plumes," Keats has tried to invest
Apollo with a creative dynamism, which stands in sharp contrast to the despondency and stasis of the Titans. If the Titans
symbolize inert matter, "the dull soil," Apollo, through repeated association with "light" symbolizes creative energy,
élan vital itself.

In terms of Keats's concept of negative capability, it should
be possible to understand how the Titans fail to transcend the
limitations of their narrow personal identities. Each Titan
bewails the loss of his realm, overwhelmed by wrath, grief, and
envy. This is how Saturn expresses poignantly his sense of loss
to Thea:

> Look up, and tell me if this feeble shape
> Is Saturn's; tell me, if thou hear'st the voice
> of Saturn; tell me, if this wrinkling brow,
> Naked and bare of its great diadem,
> Peers like the front of Saturn . . .
>
> (Bk. I, 98–102)

As contrasted with the despondent and self-absorbed Saturn,
Apollo is depicted as striving for nonidentity in his quest for
universal experience. This explains why Apollo is singularly
free from such soul-debasing emotions as wrath, envy, and
despair. He has no personal grief of his own: "I strive to search
wherefore I am sad" (Bk. III, 87). Apollo symbolizes the true
"poetical character" which "has no self . . . is everything and
nothing . . . has no character . . . enjoys light and shade." [32]
Significantly he beseeches the Goddess Mnemosyne:

> Point me out the way
> To any one particular beauteous star,
> And I will flit into it with my lyre,
> And make its silvery splendour pant with bliss . . .
>
> (Bk. III, 99–102)

This should recall to one's mind a similar observation made
by Keats in his letter to Benjamin Bailey (November 22,
1817): ". . . if a sparrow come before my Window I take
part in its existence and pick about the Gravel." [33] Evolutionary process, in fact, constitutes this progressive surrender
of selfhood in a continuous struggle towards self-transcendence.

What is the symbolical significance of Mnemosyne in this
process of evolutionary change? Interpreted in terms of Berg-
sonian metaphysics, she symbolizes *mémoire par excellence*,

the totality of historic consciousness, which "stores up the past by the mere necessity of its own nature": [34]

> Names, deeds, gray legends, dire events, rebellions
> Majesties, sovran voices, agonies,
> Creations and destroyings . . .
>
> (Bk. III, 114–16)

It is these elements constituting the totality of knowledge that "pour into the wide hollows of [Apollo's] brain," and make a God of him. It should, however, be clearly understood that the coalescence of these elements will take place only in moments of heightened intuitive perception, so aptly described by Wordsworth as "spots of time." This process is never the result of "consequitive reasoning," or the kind of catechistic dialogue that takes place between the poet and Moneta in *The Fall of Hyperion*. It is significant, in this context, that Mnemosyne, the "ancient power," with "an antique mien" and eyes "with their eternal calm," does not communicate in terms of logic; she remains, during Apollo's importunate questioning, "mute" and inarticulate. "There is one reality," observes Bergson, "which we all seize from within, by intuition and not by simple analysis." [35] It is this reality that dawns within Apollo's consciousness in the presence of the "lonely Goddess," Mnemosyne, who is the symbol of intuitive knowledge which is none other than pure memory. It is clear that in his quest for knowledge, Apollo relies upon his own intuitive faculties, for reason here is a futile instrument. It is true that at first he does resort to direct questioning:

> Where is power?
> Whose hand, whose essence, what divinity
> Makes this alarum in the elements,
> While I here idle listen on the shores
> In fearless yet in aching ignorance?
> O tell me, lonely Goddess, by thy harp,
> That waileth every morn and eventide
> Tell me why thus I rave, about these groves!
>
> (Bk. III, 103–10)

But soon he realizes that the answers must come ultimately from within his own soul, independent of all external aids. Then, quite suddenly, in a moment of epiphanic revelation, he sees "into the life of things":

Mute thou remainest—Mute! Yet I can read
A wondrous lesson in thy silent face:
Knowledge enormous makes a God of me.
Names, deeds, gray legends, dire events, rebellions,
Majesties, sovran voices, agonies,
Creations and destroyings all at once
Pour into the wide hollows of my brain,
And deify me, as if some blithe wine
Or bright elixir peerless I had drunk,
And so become immortal.
                                                    (Bk. III, 111–20)

The accompanying "wild commotions," culminating in
Apollo's shriek, cannot be dismissed as merely symbolizing the
dramatic and unexpected nature of all such revelations, for
they surely betray a somewhat disturbing loss of control on
the poet's part over his central concept. For Apollo's frenzy
("his golden tresses famed / Kept undulations round his eager
neck") suggests the Dionysian, and since the Dionysian is at
the opposite pole from the Apollonian, the new sun-god's
shriek acquires a significance hitherto unnoticed. This state of
consciousness (into which Keats's Apollo enters after his deification) has been characterized by Nietzsche in *The Birth
of Tragedy* as "all of Nature's excess in joy, sorrow and knowledge become audible, even in piercing shrieks." [36] The shriek,
therefore, comes as a bewildering finale to the "knowledge
enormous" that has made a God of Apollo, and appears to
represent the *total* perfection of Apollo, since now he is invested with every conceivable kind of perfection. Apollo can
develop no further.

We should now be in a position to answer the crucial
question that we posed at the beginning of this essay—why
did Keats abandon *Hyperion?* Keats, as we have so far tried to
show, had set out to project in a mythological context the concept of *l'évolution créatrice.* In his letter to Haydon, he had
remarked that in *Hyperion* "the march of passion and en-
deavour will be undeviating," [37] and he reiterates in his letter
to John Hamilton Reynolds that "there is really a grand march
of intellect" [38] ("intellect," it may be noted, is here used in a
nonratiocinative sense, being synonymous with consciousness).
Each stage in this "grand march," however seemingly perfect,
is to be succeeded by "a fresh perfection," so that this process
may continue endlessly, without reaching any state of finality.

But it is manifest that when Keats conceived Apollo's deification, he poured "into the wide hollows of his brain" not only all the elements of "knowledge enormous," but even added an altogether petrifying Dionysian dimension. Since Apollo is a metaphor for the creative process, his perfection would imply the cessation of the evolutionary process itself. If Keats had retained imaginative hold on his concept of perpetual renewal and progression, he would have portrayed Apollo as a god of partial perfection (though superior in moral and imaginative excellence to the Titans), since even the Olympian order was only a stage in the undeviating "march" of the evolutionary process. It was, therefore, not the Miltonic inversions, nor again any deviation from the "original design" of the poem but the aesthetic dilemma of presenting a continually evolving Apollo that rendered all further progress impossible.

It is interesting to note how many critics, unable to fathom the underlying concept in *Hyperion*, read into this fragment indeterminacy, "misgiving," ambiguity, and perplexity—elements which have dominated critical assessments of this poem so far. According to Garrod, for instance, Keats "was held by that death-shriek, or birth-shriek, of his own Apollo; that he was startled into misgiving; that some disquiet of the creating imagination assailed him; that he felt himself brought up sharply against the need of defining, the need of clarifying his own conception." [39]

The real problem, as this essay has attempted to show, is not Keats's failure to define or clarify his central concept (this had been done with great success by Oceanus); nor was he "held" by Apollo's shriek. The only satisfactory explanation seems to be that his "creating imagination," which had been so adequate to the task of portraying the inertness and dull despondency of the Titans, began to fail him when confronted with the task of portraying a ceaselessly evolving Apollo. Lapsing into "fixities and definites," the poet had, in conceiving the deification of his sun-god, allowed him to be smothered under the weight of a faultless perfection. *Hyperion* could proceed no further.

Notes

1. *The Poems: John Keats*, ed. E. de Selincourt (London, 1951), p. 486. All references to the text are from this edition.

2. *Ibid.*, p. 113 (*Endymion*, Bk. III, 699–700).

3. *The Letters of John Keats*, ed. M. B. Forman (Oxford, 1952), p. 50. All subsequent references to this book will be mentioned as *Letters*.

4. *Letters*, p. 384.

5. Quoted by W. J. Bate in *John Keats* (Cambridge, Mass., 1963), p. 563.

6. *John Keats: A Reassessment*, ed. Kenneth Muir (Liverpool, 1958), p. 111.

7. David Perkins, *The Quest for Permanence: The Symbolism of Wordsworth, Shelley and Keats* (Cambridge, Mass., 1959), p. 277.

8. *Letters*, p. 391.

9. *Ibid.*, p. 384.

10. Sidney Colvin, *Keats* (London, 1929), p. 157.

11. H. W. Garrod, *Keats* (Oxford, 1957), p. 67.

12. Douglas Bush, *Mythology and the Romantic Tradition in English Poetry* (New York, 1963), p. 119.

13. *Ibid.*, p. 126.

14. *Letters*, p. 95.

15. *Ibid.*, pp. 507–508.

16. W. J. Bate, *op. cit.*, p. 403.

17. *Ibid.*, p. 602.

18. *Ibid.*, p. 394.

19. *The Poems: John Keats*, ed. E. de Selincourt, p. 486.

20. Bernard Bosanquet, *A History of Aesthetic* (New York, 1961), p. 325.

21. J. Middleton Murry, *Keats and Shakespeare* (London, 1925), pp. 79ff.

22. *The John Keats Memorial Volume*, ed. E. de Selincourt (London, 1921); essay by W. P. Ker, "Note on Hyperion."

23. C. D. Thorpe, *The Mind of John Keats* (New York, 1926), p. 139.

24. Paul Elmer More, *Shelbourne Essays* (New York, 1907), p. 124.

25. H. W. Garrod, *Keats*, p. 66.

26. Sidney Colvin, *John Keats: His Life and Poetry: His Friends, Critics and After-Fame* (New York, 1917), p. 427.

27. J. R. Caldwell, "The Meaning of Hyperion," *PMLA*, LI, No. 4 (1936), 1096.

28. Douglas Bush, *op. cit.*, p. 121.

29. Robert Bridges, *Collected Essays* (Oxford, 1929), p. 115.

30. Henri Bergson, *The Creative Mind*, trans. M. L. Andison (New York, 1946), p. 177.

31. *Hyperion*, Bk. II, 24–26 (italics mine).

32. *Letters*, p. 226 (Letter to Richard Woodhouse, October 27, 1818).

33. *Ibid.*, p. 68.

34. Bergson, *Matter and Memory*, trans. N. M. Paul and W. S. Palmer (London, 1913), p. 92.

35. Bergson, *An Introduction to Metaphysics*, trans. T. E. Hulme (London, 1913), p. 8.

36. *The Philosophy of Nietzsche* (New York, 1927), p. 967.

37. *Letters*, p. 82 (Letter dated January 23, 1818).

38. *Ibid.*, p. 143 (Letter dated May 3, 1818).

39. H. W. Garrod, *Keats*, p. 70.

SUGGESTIONS FOR FURTHER READING

ROMANTICISM

Books
Lascelles Abercrombie, *Romanticism* (London, 1926).
M. H. Abrams, *The Mirror and the Lamp* (Oxford, 1953).
W. J. Bate, *From Classic to Romantic* (New York, 1961).
Northrop Frye (ed.), *Romanticism Reconsidered* (New York, 1963).
Robert F. Gleckner and Gerald E. Enscoe (eds.), *Romanticism: Points of View* (Englewood Cliffs, N.J., 1963).
D. G. James, *The Romantic Comedy* (Oxford, 1948).
Arthur O. Lovejoy, *The Great Chain of Being* (Cambridge, Mass., 1957).

Articles and Essays
Cleanth Brooks, "Notes for a Revised History of English Poetry," *Modern Poetry and the Tradition* (London, 1948), pp. 214–36.
E. B. Burgum, "Romanticism," *The Kenyon Review*, III (1941), 479–90.
Christopher Caudwell, "The Bourgeois Illusion and English Romantic Poetry," *Illusion and Reality* (New York, 1947).
Alex Comfort, "Art and Social Responsibility: The Ideology of Romanticism," *Art and Social Responsibility: Lectures in the Ideology of Romanticism* (London, 1946).
H. N. Fairchild, "Definition of Romanticism," *The Romantic Quest* (New York, 1931).

319

Albert Guérard, "On the Logic of Romanticism," *Essays in Criticism*, VII (1957), 262–73.

D. W. Harding, "The Character of Literature from Blake to Byron," *From Blake to Byron* (London, 1957), pp. 33–64.

T. E. Hulme, "Romanticism and Classicism," *Speculations* (London, 1960), pp. 111–40.

Arthur O. Lovejoy, "On the Discrimination of Romanticisms," *PMLA*, XXXIX (1924), 229–53.

Herbert Read, "Surrealism and the Romantic Principle," *Introduction to Surrealism* by André Breton and others (London, 1936).

Stephen Spender, "The Romantic Imagination," *The Struggle of the Modern* (London, 1963), pp. 3–23.

Philip Wheelwright, "Four Ways of Imagination," *The Burning Fountain* (Bloomington, Ind., 1959), pp. 76–100.

A. N. Whitehead, "The Romantic Reaction," *Science and the Modern World* (Cambridge, Eng., 1943), pp. 93–118.

WORDSWORTH

Books

F. W. Bateson, *Wordsworth: A Re-Interpretation* (London, 1954).

Colin C. Clarke, *Romantic Paradox: An Essay on the Poetry of Wordsworth* (London, 1962).

Helen Darbishire, *The Poet Wordsworth* (Oxford, 1950).

H. W. Garrod, *Wordsworth: Essays and Lectures* (Oxford, 1923).

H. D. Havens, *The Mind of a Poet* (Baltimore, 1941).

David Perkins, *Wordsworth and the Poetry of Sincerity* (Cambridge, Mass., 1964).

A. F. Potts, *Wordsworth's Prelude: A Study of Its Literary Form* (Ithaca, 1953).

Herbert Read, *Wordsworth* (London, 1930).

J. C. Smith, *A Study of Wordsworth* (London, 1944).

Newton P. Stallknecht, *Strange Seas of Thought* (Bloomington, Ind., 1958).

Articles and Essays

A. C. Bradley, "Wordsworth," *Oxford Lectures on Poetry* (London, 1909), pp. 99–150.

Cleanth Brooks, "Wordsworth and the Paradox of the Imagination," *The Well Wrought Urn* (New York, 1947), pp. 124–50.
Patrick Crutwell, "Wordsworth, the Public and the People," *Sewanee Review*, LXIV (1956), 71–80.
William Empson, "Sense in *The Prelude*," *The Structure of Complex Words* (London, 1952), pp. 289–305.
Janette Harrington, "Wordsworth's *Descriptive Sketches* and *The Prelude* Book VI," *PMLA*, XLIV (1929), 1144–58.
Herbert Hartman, "The Intimations of Wordsworth's Ode," *The Review of English Studies*, VI (1930), 129–48.
F. R. Leavis, "Wordsworth," *Revaluation* (London, 1956), pp. 154–202.
Lionel Trilling, "The Immortality Ode," *The Liberal Imagination* (New York, 1942), pp. 129–53.

COLERIDGE

Books
J. B. Beer, *Coleridge the Visionary* (New York, 1962).
Edmund Blunden and E. L. Griggs (eds.), *Coleridge: Studies by Several Hands* (London, 1934).
J. F. Danby, *S. T. C. Anima Naturaliter Christina* (London, 1951).
Humphry House, *Coleridge* (London, 1953).
J. L. Lowes, *The Road to Xanadu* (London, 1930).
I. A. Richards, *Coleridge on Imagination* (London, 1934).
Max F. Schulz, *The Poetic Voices of Coleridge* (Detroit, 1964).

Articles and Essays
Maud Bodkin, "A Study of the *Ancient Mariner* and the Rebirth Archetype," *Archetypal Patterns in Poetry: Psychological Studies of Imagination* (Oxford, 1934), pp. 26–89.
R. L. Brett, "Coleridge's *The Rime of the Ancient Mariner*," *Reason and Imagination* (Oxford, 1960), pp. 78–107.
Kenneth Burke, *The Philosophy of Literary Form* (New York, 1947), pp. 78–83 (An interpretation of *The Ancient Mariner*).
Douglas Bush, "Coleridge," *Mythology and the Romantic Tradition in English Poetry* (Cambridge, Mass., 1937), pp. 51–55.

G. W. Knight, "Coleridge's Divine Comedy," *The Starlit Dome* (London, 1941), pp. 83–97.

A. H. Nethercot, "Christabel," *The Road to Tryermaine* (Chicago, 1935).

Elder Olson, "A Symbolic Reading of 'The Ancient Mariner'," *Visions and Revisions in Modern American Literary Criticism*, ed. Bernard S. Oldsey and Arthur O. Lewis, Jr. (New York, 1962), pp. 240–49.

Fred Manning Smith, "The Relation of Coleridge's *Ode on Dejection* to Wordsworth's *Ode on Intimations of Immortality*," PMLA, L (1935), 224–34.

Robert Penn Warren, *The Rime of the Ancient Mariner: An Essay* (New York, 1946).

Carl R. Woodring, "Coleridge and the *Khan*," *Essays in Criticism*, IX (1959), pp. 361–68.

BYRON

Books

W. J. Calvert, *Byron: Romantic Paradox* (Chapel Hill, N. C., 1935).

M. K. Joseph, *Byron the Poet* (London, 1964).

G. W. Knight, *Lord Byron: Christian Virtues* (London, 1952).

E. J. Lovell, *Byron: The Record of a Quest: Studies in a Poet's Concept and Treatment of Nature* (Austin, Texas, 1949).

W. H. Marshall, *The Structure of Byron's Major Poems* (Philadelphia, 1963).

P. L. Thorslev, *The Byronic Hero: Types and Prototypes* (Minneapolis, 1962).

P. G. Trueblood, *The Flowering of Byron's Genius* (Stanford, 1945).

Articles and Essays

W. H. Auden, "Don Juan," *The New Yorker*, XXXIV (April 26, 1958), 133–50.

Marius Bewley, "The Colloquial Mode of Byron," *Scrutiny*, XVI (1949), 8–22.

T. S. Eliot, "Byron," *On Poetry and Poets* (London, 1957), pp. 193–206.

Oliver Elton, "The Present Value of Byron," *The Review of English Studies*, I (1925), 24–39.

F. R. Leavis, "Byron's Satire," *Revaluation* (London, 1956), pp. 148–53.

Bertrand Russell, "Byron," *History of Western Philosophy* (London, 1961), pp. 716–21.

Paul West, "Byron and the World of Things: An Ingenious Disregard," *The Keats-Shelley Memorial Association Bulletin,* No. XI (Rome, 1960), 21–32.

SHELLEY

Books

Carlos Baker, *Shelley's Major Poetry: The Fabric of a Vision* (Princeton, 1948).

Harold Bloom, *Shelley's Mythmaking* (New Haven, 1959).

A. Clutton-Brock, *Shelley: The Man and the Poet* (London, 1909).

Rose Greig Woodman, *The Apocalyptic Vision in the Poetry of Shelley* (Toronto, 1964).

F. A. Lea, *Shelley and the Romantic Revolution* (London, 1945).

Sylva Norman, *Flight of the Skylark: The Development of Shelley's Reputation* (Norman, Okla., 1964).

N. I. White, *The Unextinguished Hearth: Shelley and his Contemporary Critics* (Durham, N. C., 1938).

Articles and Essays

Douglas Bush, "Shelley," *Mythology and the Romantic Tradition in English Poetry* (Cambridge, Mass., 1937), pp. 129–68.

Donald Davie, "Shelley's Urbanity," *Purity of Diction in English Verse* (London, 1953), pp. 133–59.

Graham Hough, "Shelley," *The Romantic Poets* (London, 1953), pp. 122–50.

Ian Jack, "Shelley," *The Oxford History of English Literature 1815–1832* (Oxford, 1963), pp. 77–104.

F. R. Leavis, "Shelley," *Revaluation: Tradition and Development in English Poetry* (London, 1949), pp. 203–32.

C. S. Lewis, "Shelley, Dryden and Mr. Eliot," *Rehabilitations any other Essays* (London, 1939), pp. 3–34.

Frederick A. Pottle, "The Case of Shelley," *PMLA*, LXVII (1952), 589–608.

Bennett Weaver, "Prometheus Bound and Prometheus Unbound," *PMLA*, LXIV (1949), 115–33.

Stewart C. Wilcox, "Imagery, Ideas and Design in Shelley's 'Ode to the West Wind,' " *Studies in Philology*, XLVII (1950), 634–49.

KEATS

Books

W. J. Bate, *John Keats* (Cambridge, Mass., 1963).

Bernard Blackstone, *The Consecrated Urn* (London, 1959).

J. M. Murry, *Keats and Shakespeare* (London, 1926).

E. R. Wasserman, *The Finer Tone: Keats' Major Poems* (Baltimore, 1953).

Katherine M. Wilson, *The Nightingale and the Hawk, A Psychological Study of Keats's Ode* (London, 1964).

C. D. Thorpe, *The Mind of John Keats* (Oxford, 1926).

Articles and Essays

Kenneth Burke, "Symbolic Action in a Poem by Keats," *Grammar of Motives and a Rhetoric of Motives* (New York, 1962), pp. 447–63.

Douglas Bush, "Keats and his Ideas," *The Major English Romantic Poets: A Symposium in Reappraisal*, ed. C. D. Thorpe, Carlos Baker, and Bennett Weaver (Carbondale, Ill., 1957), pp. 231–45.

J. R. Caldwell, "The Meaning of Hyperion," *PMLA*, LI (1936), 1080–97.

R. H. Fogle, "Synaesthetic Imagery in Keats," *Keats: A Collection of Critical Essays*, ed. W. J. Bate (Englewood Cliffs, N.J., 1964), pp. 41–50.

H. N. Fairchild, "Keats and the Struggle-for-Existence Tradition," *PMLA*, LXIV (1949), 98–114.

Clarisse Godfrey, "Endymion," *John Keats: A Reassessment*, ed. Kenneth Muir (Liverpool, 1958), pp. 2–38.

Ian Jack, "Keats," *Oxford History of English Literature 1815–1832* (Oxford, 1963), pp. 105–29.

D. G. James, "The Two Hyperions," *Keats: A Collection of Critical Essays*, ed. W. J. Bate (Englewood Cliffs, N.J., 1964), pp. 161–70.

Kenneth Muir, "The Meaning of *Hyperion*," *John Keats: A Reassessment*, ed. Kenneth Muir (Liverpool, 1958), pp. 102–22.

E. de Selincourt, "Keats," *Oxford Lectures on Poetry* (Oxford, 1934), pp. 180–206.

Jacob D. Wigod, "The Meaning of *Endymion*," *PMLA*, LXVIII (1953), 779–90.

Morse Peckham is Professor of English at the University of Pennsylvania. His publications include *Beyond the Tragic Vision* (1962) and *Man's Rage for Chaos* (1965).

R. A. Foakes is Senior Lecturer in English at the University of Durham. He is the Arden editor of *King Henry VIII* (1957), and the author of *The Romantic Assertion* (1958).

Douglas Bush has been Gurney Professor at Harvard since 1957. His publications include *Mythology and the Romantic Tradition in English Poetry* (1937), *Paradise Lost in Our Time* (1945), *English Literature in the Earlier Seventeenth Century* (1945), and *Milton* (1964).

Thomas M. Raysor is Professor Emeritus of English at the University of Nebraska. An eminent Coleridgean scholar, his publications include *Coleridge's Shakespearean Criticism* (2 vols., 1930), and *Coleridge's Miscellaneous Criticism* (1936).

Edwin Morgan has been Lecturer in English at the University of Glasgow since 1950. His published works include *The Vision of Cathkin Braes* and *Beowulf: A Verse Translation*.

Newton P. Stallknecht is Professor of Philosophy at Indiana University. He is the author of *Studies in the Philosophy of Creation* (1934) and *Strange Seas of Thought* (1945).

L. G. Salingar is Lecturer in English, Cambridge University.

Elmer Edgar Stoll was Professor of English at the University of Minnesota from 1915 to 1942. His publications include

Othello (1915), *Hamlet* (1919), *Art and Artifice in Shakespeare* (1933), and *From Shakespeare to Joyce* (1944).

Humphry House was a Fellow of Wadham College, Oxford. His publications include *The Dickens World* (1941), *Coleridge* (1953), and *Aristotle's Poetics* (1956). He died in 1955.

Wilfred S. Dowden is Chairman of the Department of English, Rice University. He has edited *The Letters of Thomas Moore* (1964).

Andrew Rutherford is Lecturer in English at the University of Edinburgh. He has published *Byron: A Critical Study* (1962) and has edited *Kipling's Mind and Art* (1964).

C. M. Bowra was Professor of Poetry, Oxford from 1946 to 1951. He is the author of *The Heritage of Symbolism* (1943), *The Creative Experiment* (1949), *The Romantic Imagination* (1950), and *Primitive Sons* (1962).

Richard Harter Fogle has been head of the Department of English at the University of Tulane since 1954. He is the author of *The Imagery of Keats and Shelley* (1949), *Hawthorne's Fiction* (1952), and *The Idea of Coleridge's Criticism* (1962).

Carlos Baker is Woodrow Wilson Professor of Literature at Princeton University. His publications include *Shelley's Major Poetry* (1948) and *Hemingway: The Writer And Artist* (1952).

Stewart C. Wilcox is Professor of English at the University of Oklahoma, and is a frequent contributor to scholarly journals.

Bernard Blackstone was Byron Professor of English Literature at the University of Athens, 1951–1961. His publications include *William Blake* (1948), *Virginia Woolf* (1948), *The Consecrated Urn* (1959), and *The Lost Travellers* (1962).

Stewart M. Sperry, Jr., is Associate Professor of English at Indiana University. He has contributed several articles on Keats to *PMLA* and other learned periodicals.

Cleanth Brooks has been Professor of English at Yale since 1947. His publications include *Modern Poetry and the Tradition* (1939), *The Well Wrought Urn* (1947), and (with W. K. Wimsatt) *Literary Criticism: A Short History* (1957).